EARLY HUMAN OCCUPATION IN BRITISH COLUMBIA

EARLY HUMAN OCCUPATION IN BRITISH COLUMBIA

Edited by Roy L. Carlson and Luke Dalla Bona

Printed in Canada on acid-free paper ∞

ISBN 0-7748-0536-6 (hardcover)
ISBN 0-7748-0535-8 (paperback)

Canadian Cataloguing in Publication Data

Early human occupation in British Columbia

      Includes bibliographical references and index.
      ISBN 0-7748-0536-6 (bound)
      ISBN 0-7748-0535-8 (pbk.)
      1. Paleo-Indians — British Columbia. 2. Tools, Prehistoric — British Columbia. 3. British Columbia — Antiquities. I. Carlson, Roy L., 1930- II. Dalla Bona, Luke R. (Luke Robert), 1964-

E78.B9E27 1995   971.1'01   C95-910800-9

Financially assisted by the Province of British Columbia through the British Columbia Heritage Trust.

UBC gratefully ackowledges the ongoing support to its publishing program from the Canada Council, the Province of British Columbia Cultural Services Branch, and the Department of Communications of the Government of Canada.

UBC Press
University of British Columbia Press
6344 Memorial Rd
Vancouver, BC V6T 1Z2
(604) 822-3259
Fax: 1-800-668-0821
E-mail: orders@ubcpress.ubc.ca

CONTENTS

PREFACE

This volume has been long in the making but we think the result is worth the long wait. It originated from a symposium organized by Roy Carlson at the Canadian Archaeological Association meeting held at Whistler in the Spring of 1988. The presenters felt that the papers given would make a useful volume, and following the meeting everyone rushed home to finalize, re-write, or reorganize his paper. Luke Dalla Bona joined the team for the specific purpose of designing the volume and formatting the papers. In December of 1988 five of the completed chapters and the table of contents were submitted to UBC Press. Their reply was that they had positive feedback on the volume, but their Press Committee only considered completed manuscripts. It was three years before the editors received the last of the revised papers from their authors. During this period each paper was reviewed by two anonymous referees, papers were returned to the authors with comments, and authors returned copy with their revisions. In 1993 a draft of the entire volume was submitted to UBC Press in response to their request for volumes for their new Northwest Native Studies series. Jean Wilson, senior editor for UBC Press, sent the volume out to two anonymous assessors for comment and review, and submitted it to the SSHRC funded Aid to Publications program. The latter returned it with the comments that it wasn't designed for a professional audience of other archaeologists (!!!) and that it wasn't integrated enough to suit them. This rejection should be taken as a compliment since the mandate of that strange program is to assist in publication of manuscripts that are otherwise unpublishable. The last of the two anonymous asssessors' comments was finally received by UBC Press in May of 1994. Both external assessors strongly recommended publication of the monograph as well as some reorganization and strengthening of particular chapters. In the interim, the Canadian Archaeological Association had again met, this time in Edmonton, and two papers with exciting new data on Haida Gwaii (Queen Charlotte Islands) were presented by Daryl Fedje and Martin Magne. These authors were invited to submit their papers for publication in this volume, which they did, and their contributions greatly strengthen the section on the Microblade Tradition.

This final volume contains all of the papers given in the original symposium, and all have been up-dated and expanded beyond their original scope. Chapters 13, 14, and 16 are in addition to the original papers. The authors of these chapters were invited to submit their papers in order to achieve as complete a coverage as possible. The opinions and conclusions of each author are his own and it is interesting to discover where the differences lie. The introductory and concluding chapters were written to provide a broader context for the descriptive chapters in the body of the work. We wish to thank Archaeology Press, Simon Fraser University, for permission to use many of the illustrations in Chapter 20. We would also like to thank the ARPP program (University of Manitoba) and Lakehead University without whose laserprinters, this book could never have been proofed

Although it has been a long time between inception and completion, the final result in the opinion of the editors is a much better publication than it would have been if published earlier. It is up to date and contains data available nowhere else.

THE EDITORS

Roy L. Carlson, Simon Fraser University, Burnaby
Luke Dalla Bona, Ontario Ministry of Natural Resources, Thunder Bay

EARLY HUMAN OCCUPATION
IN BRITISH COLUMBIA

1 INTRODUCTION TO EARLY HUMAN OCCUPATION IN BRITISH COLUMBIA

Roy L. Carlson

This volume is about the archaeological evidence for the very earliest British Columbians, evidence that dates to between 10,500 and 5000 C-14 years BP (before the present). Each chapter has been written by archaeologists specializing in the particular region covered. Since no written records existed anywhere in the world at that time, human history must of necessity be worked out from analyses of artifacts and other remains found in archaeological sites, and from examination of the environment as it existed in the past. The natural environment of the province has not always been as it is today. Until about 14,500 years ago British Columbia was covered with glacial ice, and no one could have lived here.

By the time of the earliest dated habitations in the province, Charlie Lake Cave just east of the Rockies at 10,500 BP (Chapters 2, 3) and on the central coast at 9700 BP (Chapters 9, 10, 16), the glaciers had waned and British Columbia had become accessible to migrating peoples in possession of the technical skills necessary for survival in the newly deglaciated landscape. People were present in Alaska and the Yukon in regions north of the glaciers where there was insufficient precipitation for glaciers to form by 12,000 years ago or earlier (Cinq-Mars 1979), and are found south of the glaciated regions at the East Wenatchee site on the Columbia River in eastern Washington by 11,200 years ago (Mehringer and Foit 1990). Environmental changes at the end of the Ice Age and their effects on settlement and on the archaeological record are discussed in four chapters (Chapters 6, 12, 13, 17).

THE BERINGIAN CONNECTION

The ancestors of the earliest peoples in British Columbia came from Beringia, the unglaciated region of Siberia and Alaska on both sides of the Bering Strait including the now inundated Bering platform. The genetic similarities between native peoples of North and South America and those of northeast Asia are indications that these peoples share a common biological ancestry (Szathmary 1981, 1994). The most detailed genetic similarities determined to date are those involving the attributes of teeth (Turner 1992, 1994). Because of acidic soils in British Columbia bones of any sort are rarely preserved in sites pre-dating 5000 BP. The earliest human osteological remains discovered to date consist solely of the crowns of teeth (Figure 1) from Namu dating between 9000 and 6500 BP which exhibit the Sinodont type of dentition common to northeast Asia and the New World, and a headless skeleton from Gore Creek near Kamloops dating to 8250 BP (Chapter 17). In addition to the biological similarities there are similarities in the artifact complexes of the late Paleolithic in Siberia and the Early Period in British Columbia.

Artifact complexes at any given point in time are products of traditional ways of making and doing things, of adaptation to particular environmental or cultural circumstances, and of accessibility to the flow of new information and inventions which spread around the world in ancient as well as modern times. The common classes of artifacts of eastern Siberia which make up these late Paleolithic complexes are bifacial foliate (leaf-shaped) projectile points and knives, microblades and cores, pebble tools, and composite bone and antler tools used in hunting and fishing (Derevianko 1990, Mochanov and Fedoseeva 1984). The common artifact classes of British Columbia during the pre-5000 BP period are the same as those of the late Paleolithic of eastern Siberia, although there are differences in frequencies and in types and styles. These classes are typical of northern North America as a whole, but not of the rest of the Americas. The similarities in artifacts indicate interaction through migration, diffusion, and/or trade between peoples of these regions. Since these artifact classes occur earlier in Siberia it is quite clear that the direction of flow of people and culture was at least initially from Siberia to Alaska and not the reverse. Although there is a high degree of overall cultural similarity within this northeast Asian/northwest American cultural interaction sphere, there are also variations which permit the recognition of localized cultures and cultural traditions both in Siberia and North America.

Cultures and cultural traditions are defined on the basis of both the way of life of ancient peoples as indicated by the environment and subsistence remains found in archaeological sites, and by the uniqueness of accompanying types and styles of artifacts. Assemblages that contain the same or similar types of artifacts are considered to belong to the same cultural tradition providing they are found in a continuous distribution in time and

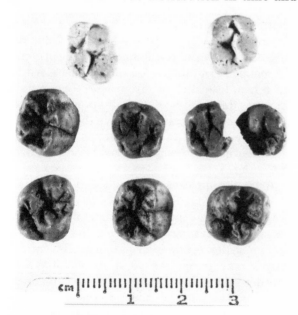

Figure 1. Crowns of teeth from Namu showing Sinodont attributes. Top row ca. 6500 BP. Lower rows ca. 8000-9000 BP.

space and other aspects of the assemblages are not radically different. The greater the similarity in forms and fabrication techniques of the artifacts and the closer the propinquity of the artifact assemblages in time and space, the greater the probability of ethnic congruity of the people who occupied the sites and made the tools. Cultures are localized and temporally shorter expressions of more widespread and longer lived cultural traditions, although there is considerable overlap in the use of these two concepts. The Siberian cultural tradition which shows the greatest similarity to the early cultural traditions of Alaska and British Columbia is the widespread Diuktai (Mochanov and Fedoseeva 1984) of northeast Asia.

The Beringian portion of Alaska is geographically intermediate between Siberia and British Columbia, and in the late Ice Age up to about 10,000 years ago was connected by dry land to Siberia. There are four cultures of Beringian Alaska within the 12,000 to 9000 BP period which share some similarities with both Siberian and British Columbian traditions: the Nenana Complex (Hoffecker, Powers, and Goebel 1993, Yesner 1994); the Denali or Paleoarctic Tradition (Anderson 1970, Dixon 1993, West 1981); a regional variant of the Fluted Point Tradition sometimes called Northern Paleoindian (Dixon 1993); and a number of assemblages found both in the Brooks Range of northern Alaska (Kunz and Reanier 1994) and in the Kuskokwim region of southwest Alaska (Ackerman 1994) which resemble the Agate Basin variant of the Plano Tradition. The early cultures of the Alaska Panhandle are the same as those of the northern coast of British Columbia (Chapter 12).

EARLY CULTURAL TRADITIONS OF BRITISH COLUMBIA

Archaeological remains – those things archaeologists dig for – do not speak for themselves. Their "meanings" in respect to the goals of reconstructing, understanding, and explaining the past must be inferred through the process of comparison with remains from many sites and the determination of significant similarities and differences. In order that such comparisons can be made, archaeological reports contain a great many facts about what was found where, what it was found with, and where it fits chronologically. The transformation of archaeological facts into an historical record requires not only presentation of the facts and use of the comparative method, but the integration of such facts into a cultural-historical model based on general principles about culture and human na-

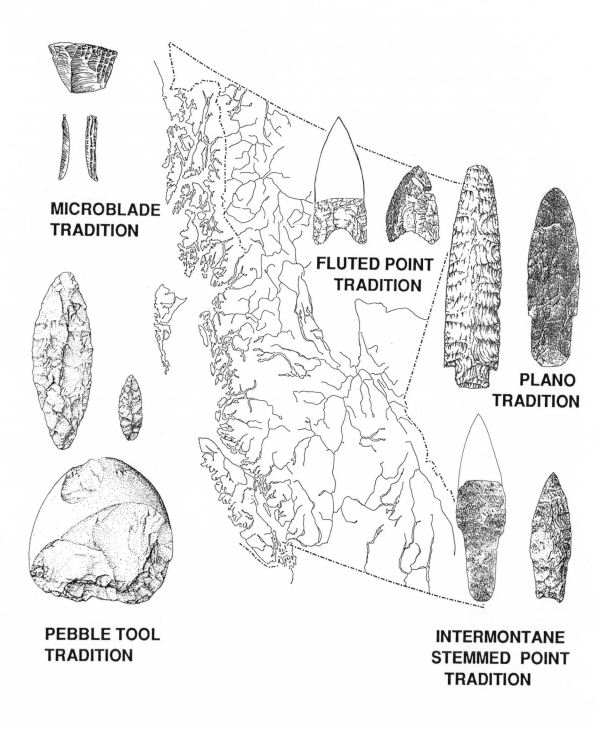

MICROBLADE TRADITION

FLUTED POINT TRADITION

PLANO TRADITION

PEBBLE TOOL TRADITION

INTERMONTANE STEMMED POINT TRADITION

Figure 2. Diagnostic artifact complexes used to define the early cultural traditions in northwestern North America.

ture (Carlson 1983c). Archaeology is a dynamic field of research and new facts are constantly being discovered, so evaluation of integrative schemes is an on-going process. This volume contains basic descriptive archaeological facts loosely organized into a model of five early cultural traditions.

Using the principles outlined above and projectile point form and microblade technology as the diagnostic artifactual remains, it is possible to group the archaeological remains from the early part of the pre-5000 BP period in British Columbia into the following cultural traditions: the Fluted Point Tradition, the Plano Tradition, the Intermontane Stemmed Point Tradition, the Pebble Tool Tradition, and the Microblade Tradition. Peoples bearing these cultural traditions were responsible for the earliest settlement in different regions of the province. The artifact names used to label most of these traditions do not imply that their content is limited to these artifacts. Each cultural tradition is conceptualized as possessing both a distinctive way of life and similar types and styles of tools which indicate a close historical relationship among the local and regional components. The diagnostic artifacts relevant to this model are shown in Figure 2. The chapters in this volume are organized accordingly.

Cultural traditions must be envisioned as constantly changing even though the rate of change in the far distant past was not as rapid as in our modern industrialized society. As such, the final section entitled Transitional Cultures contains archaeological data from the later part of the pre-5000 BP period that indicate considerable cultural change. The archaeological remains described in this section are conceptualized as interfaces between the early cultural traditions in which processes of cultural change resulted in considerably changed artifact assemblages. The concluding chapter is a short summary of the later cultures of British Columbia, those that post-date 5000 BP.

The preceding model of cultural traditions is not without precedent. I first developed it in 1978 (Carlson 1979) and it has been evolving ever since. Some changes have been made although the essential features have remained much the same. Since the focus of interest was the Northwest Coast and the interior Columbia-Fraser Plateau, the Plano Tradition was not included in the initial version. Also in that iteration the Intermontane Stemmed Point Tradition was called the Lind Coulee Tradition after the site in eastern Washington (Daugherty 1956) where it was first discovered. In 1980 I had the opportunity to study collections of relevant artifacts from other sites in Washington, Oregon, Nevada, and California and it became apparent that Lind Coulee was a regional variant of a much more widespread cultural tradition throughout the West between the Rocky Mountains and the Coast-Cascade-Cordilleran range, so I renamed it the Stemmed Point Tradition which also had the effect of making the name consistent with the artifact names used for the other traditions. I used this name in a paper presented at the Society for American Archaeology meetings in San Diego in 1981 which was later published (Carlson 1983a). I was unaware that Alan Bryan (1980) had opted for the same term, but was using it as the name for a technological tradition, which included the stemmed points of the Plano Tradition of the Plains as well as those of the intermontane west, rather than for a cultural tradition. This usage has since necessitated adding the term "Intermontane" to Stemmed Point Tradition to differentiate it from the Plano Tradition with its somewhat different projectile points which centres east of the Rocky Mountains. In 1983 I still entertained the possibility that the Stemmed Point Tradition was coeval in time with the Fluted Point Tradition. It is now quite certain that it post-dates the Fluted Point Tradition except possibly in marginal areas where fluted points continued into younger periods.

A reader unversed in the nuances of archaeological terminology will probably become confused by the varied use of some of the same terms by different contributors to this volume. "Pebble tools" and "cobble tools" are slightly different terms for the same thing, whereas "technological tradition" and "cultural tradition" are similar terms for things that are somewhat different. A technological tradition refers to the distribution of a single technology, e.g., pebble tools, in time and space, whereas a cultural tradition, for example the Pebble Tool Tradition, refers to not only the pebble tools and their distribution, but also the associated economy, subsistence, other artifacts, belief systems, social relationships, etc. for which there may or may not be direct evidence. Technological traditions are obviously part of cultural traditions and may indeed form the basis for the recognition of particular cultural traditions, but technological traditions may be shared by diverse peoples whereas cultural traditions frequently presume ethnic homogeneity of their bearers. Two other terms which warrant mention are cultural "phase" and cultural "complex." A phase is a recognized unit of culture content, e.g., Marpole phase, which is found within a limited local area such as an island group or a river valley, and occupies a short time period. The artifact assemblages diagnostic of a particular phase differ partly in style and composition from those of preceding and succeeding phases in the same locality. "Complex" is an enigmatic term and is sometimes used to refer to a purely technological expression and sometimes in much the same way as a phase. Definitions and discussion of these terms and others can be found in Willey and Phillips (1958).

The organization of this volume is not without its problems. Some regions contain cultural components that cross the 5000 BP cut-off date such as the "Middle Period" in the Mid-Fraser Thompson River region (Chapter 17). Also, the Namu obsidian industry (Chapter 16) centres in Period 2 of the Namu sequence, but does continue into later periods. The editors considered such deviations and decided to include those that complement rather than detract from the other data. Another problem is that there is new and better data on several of these traditions from adjacent regions than there is from British Columbia itself. As such it was decided to include some data from the Alaska Panhandle (Chapter 12) and from the Banff locality in Alberta (Chapter 5) in the interest of better understanding the archaeology of British Columbia. The political borders of the past were different from those of today.

The Fluted Point and Plano Traditions

The Fluted Point Tradition is the most widespread early cultural tradition in the entire New World. Its hallmark is a large bifacially flaked stone spear point with a distinctive attribute: both faces of the point have been thinned by removal of long channel flakes from the basal end which produces concave flake scars called flutes. The purpose of fluting was to thin the point and thus facilitate its hafting to the end of the spear shaft. The Fluted Point Tradition ranges in age from at least 11,200 to 10,000 years BP and is made up of a number of regional and temporal variants. Since fluted points have not been found in Siberia the fluting technique was probably invented in the New World (See Carlson 1991c).

The earliest widespread expression of the Fluted Point Tradition is a culture called Clovis (See Bonnichsen and Turnmire 1991) with dates concentrated between 11,200 and 10,900 years ago (Haynes 1991) at sites in the Plains and Southwest regions of the United States. The Clovis site clos-

est to British Columbia is the East Wenatchee site in Washington on the Columbia River east of the Cascade Mountains (Mehringer 1988). Several Clovis sites are "kill sites" where fluted points were found in direct association with the bones of the ice age elephant, the mammoth. Many more Clovis sites are finds of single points. Chapters 2, 3, and 4 describe assemblages from the northeast corner of British Columbia which belong to the latter part of the Fluted Point Tradition, and Chapter 17 provides a hint as to its presence in the Thompson River region. The rather late date of the Charlie Lake assemblage in northeast BC and the attributes of the fluted points from that region indicate that they originated from a culture dating toward the end of the Fluted Point Tradition as glaciers were shrinking and climatic conditions began to approach those of the present day. The ancestors of this fluted-point-using people at Charlie Lake must have once headed south following this same route, whereas at this time some of their descendants were moving north, possibly trying to continue a way of life doomed by changing climatic conditions and the extinction of Ice Age animals.

Sometime after 10,500 years ago fluted spear points were replaced in northeast British Columbia by types of large spear points belonging to the Plano Tradition. Scottsbluff, Agate Basin, and probably Alberta points belong to this tradition and have a main area of distribution in the grasslands east of the Rocky Mountains between 10,000 and 7000 years ago (Jennings 1983). They are lanceolate and not fluted and some of the types are prepared for hafting by indenting the edges of the proximal end to form a stem. All of the finds in British Columbia are isolated undated surface finds (Chapters 4, 17). The peoples using these types of spear points in regions where they have been found in good archaeological context were bison hunters, and were probably at least in part descendants of the earlier peoples of the Fluted Point Tradition. It is also possible that Plano point types such as Agate Basin represent the arrival of new peoples from the Arctic where very similar points have recently been found in early archaeological contexts (Kunz and Reanier 1994). It is probable that an evolution from fluted points to some of the various Plano point types took place on the Plains. No Plano point types from BC have been found in a datable archaeological context. A change from fluted to stemmed point forms also took place in the Great Basin resulting in the Intermontane Stemmed Point Tradition.

The Intermontane Stemmed Point Tradition

Large stemmed, non-fluted spear points different in style from those of the Plano Tradition of the Plains are typical of the intermontane region between the Rocky Mountains and the Coast-Cascade-Cordilleran range between approximately 10,500 and 8000 years ago (Carlson 1983a:73-86). There are no dated occurrences of this tradition in British Columbia, but there are a number of isolated surface finds in the interior (Chapters 6, 17). The closest dated point is from Crowsnest Pass in Alberta where big horn sheep and bison remains associated with a large stemmed point were dated at 8550 years ago (Driver 1982). Other remains dated about 1500 years earlier are described by Fedje (Chapter 5) from sites near Banff. The peoples bearing this tradition clearly relied on hunting, and in some sites in eastern Washington small bone hooks which are parts of spear throwing devices have been found (Rice 1972). The earliest assemblages are found in eastern Oregon, Idaho, and Nevada, and it is probable that the hafting technique of stemming evolved in that region from fluting, and then spread among related peoples northward throughout the Columbia River drainage and into the Rocky Mountains. Stemming is a more efficient method of hafting than is fluting (Musil 1988) and various styles of this hafting configuration eventually replaced fluting throughout North America. A unique type of chipped stone crescent which is typical of the Intermontane Stemmed Point Tradition in regions to the south has not yet been found in British Columbia.

The Pebble Tool Tradition

Whereas the three cultural traditions summarized so far centre in the continental interior and are only marginally represented in British Columbia, the Pebble Tool Tradition (Carlson 1979, 1983a, 1990b) centres on the Northwest Coast. The typical stone points (some may be knives) are simple leaf-shaped (foliate) forms without flutes or stems. Also found are numerous choppers and scrapers made from large pebbles (cobbles in the geological sense) which give this tradition its name. It might have been better to name it the "Foliate Biface Tradition" in order to achieve more uniformity with the labels for the other traditions. Pebble tools are not absent from sites of the other cultural traditions, but do not occur with such regularity and frequency. At one time it was thought that the earliest part of this tradition lacked bifacial projectile points and possibly predated the last glacia-

tion. Haley (Chapter 7) demonstrates that this is not the case, that there is no *early* Pebble Tool Tradition without bifacial projectile points, only a *later* one. The Pebble Tool Tradition is found from the Queen Charlotte Islands south through the Strait of Georgia and lower Fraser across the international boundary into Puget Sound and on to the lower Columbia and Oregon coast. The sites are in locations which indicate that fishing and sea mammal hunting rather than land hunting were the most important subsistence activities. Assemblages belonging to the Pebble Tool Tradition are described in Chapters 7 to 11, and later derivatives modified by influences from adjacent cultures in Chapters 18 and 19. Pebble tools occur as isolated finds in many coastal locations. Not all pebble tools are early; they continued in use on some parts of the coast as expedient tools until at least 2000 years ago. The coastal distribution of this tradition indicates that its bearers must have had efficient watercraft and the technical knowledge for taking fish and sea mammals.

There is a difference of interpretation among archaeologists as to the origin and spread of this tradition. Several archaeologists (Chapters 11, 17) use the term "Old Cordilleran Culture" for assemblages of the Pebble Tool Tradition. This usage is derived from the idea that the bearers of this culture or tradition were interior hunters who spread out of the mountains and gradually adapted to coastal life as they moved northward along the coast (Butler 1961). The opposite view is that these were coastally adapted peoples who spread down the coast from the north 10,000 years ago or earlier and then spread up the river valleys into the interior as salmon became the principle resource (Carlson 1983a:90). Matson (Chapter 11) argues the first position on the basis of the earliest Glenrose assemblage with its abundant remains of land fauna whereas Carlson (Chapter 9) presents data which indicate that the artifact assemblage which typifies the Pebble Tool or Old Cordilleran is earliest on the coast in the north and is later in time to the south and in the interior where it succeeds the Fluted Point and Intermontane Stemmed Point Traditions. Butler's (1961) original model was based on the assumption that this artifact complex with its leaf-shaped points and simple flaked stone tools was earliest in the interior. Subsequent research (Cressman 1977:134, Layton 1972, Mehringer 1988, Rice 1972:164) has shown this assumption to be incorrect.

Part of the problem of Pebble Tool Tradition origins is related to the changed sea levels of the late glacial and early post-glacial periods. Current reconstructions of coastal environmental conditions between 13,200 and 10,000 BP (Barrie et al. 1994) suggest that toward the beginning of this period the region between the Queen Charlotte Islands and northern Vancouver Island and the mainland consisted mainly of an ice-free, unforested coastal plain with fresh water lakes and streams. Although the BC coast was deglaciated before the interior, people could not have reached the BC coast until such time as deglaciation had progressed to the point that either a coastal plain along the western edge of Alaska or passages from the ice free areas in the Yukon had opened. There is a date on the bones of grizzly bear from northern Prince of Wales Island of 12,295 ±120 BP (Baichtal 1994). If bears could reach the coastal islands by that time, why not humans?

If the early Pebble Tool Tradition peoples were primarily hunters, the overall significance of the biotic zone on the northern and central BC coast with its shift from a treeless coastal plain at 13,200 BP to a region of islands and protected waterways by 10,000 BP, is that it is the best candidate for the time and place of the beginnings of a shift from tundra hunting and fishing strategies to those coastal marine adaptations which became increasingly important and provided the subsistence base for the cultural elaboration present in younger periods. Namu (Chapters 9, 10), with its beginning date of 9700 BP, provides the earliest dated evidence of the Pebble Tool Tradition. Undated lithic scatters on beaches which were first recorded on the central coast in 1970 (Apland 1982, Carlson 1972) and later in the Queen Charlottes (Hobler 1978, Fedje 1993), and interpreted as remnants of early sites washed out as sea levels rose (Chapter 13), could have beginning dates even earlier than Namu. The assemblage of pebble tools and flakes from the ancient raised beach at Skoglunds Landing in the Queen Charlotte Islands (Fladmark 1990) is undated by C-14, but could be the oldest so far discovered on the BC coast.

The Nenana Complex of central Alaska (Hoffecker, Powers, and Goebel 1993; Yesner 1994) with beginning dates of 11,820 to 11,010 BP both predates the earliest remains so far discovered on the BC coast and exhibits a complex of simple artifact types similar to those of the Pebble Tool Tradition. These artifacts are foliate bifaces and pebble tools used as core scrapers or planes. As with the earliest Pebble Tool Tradition assemblages, neither a microblade industry nor burins are in evidence. Salmon remains are found in some sites but are not nearly as frequent as bird and land mammal remains (Yesner 1994). The Nenana Complex of central Alaska is at present the best candidate for the ancestor of the Pebble Tool Tradition of coastal British Columbia.

The Microblade Tradition

The Microblade Tradition appears earliest in the northern part of the province. The sites of this tradition are characterized by assemblages containing small, parallel-sided, stone flakes called microblades and the nodules (cores) of stone from which these small blades were detached. In Siberia it is known from actual examples that microblades were inset into the sides of slotted bone or antler points to form the cutting edges, and such slotted bone points have been found in early sites in Alaska (Ackerman 1994). The use of multiple small stone insets is a radically different way of making stone projectile heads and knives from that found in the other early traditions in which a single piece of stone was shaped and flaked on both faces to make a piercing or cutting tool. In sites with components of the Microblade Tradition bifacial points are not completely absent, but are outnumbered by products of microblade technology. Except for this custom of making stone tools differently, the way of life of the peoples of this tradition was probably little different from that of peoples of the Pebble Tool Tradition. Sites of the Microblade Tradition are frequently associated with sea levels that are different from those today, either higher or lower.

Is the Microblade Tradition a separate cultural tradition or does it only mark the introduction of a new technology? Different ways of making microblades are indicated by the different types of microblade cores recovered (Chapters 14, 16). To what extent are these differences the result of the size and flaking properties of the stone used, and to what extent are they the result of different traditions of tool manufacture? As a distinct cultural tradition the Microblade Tradition is best represented in the Alaska Panhandle (Chapter 12), the Queen Charlotte Islands (Chapters 13, 14), and the Skeena (Chapter 15). At sites of the Pebble Tool Tradition such as Namu (Chapters 9, 16) and the Fraser Canyon sites (Chapters 7, 8) microblade technology is absent in the earliest assemblages, but does appear later. The situation parallels that of central Alaska where in the Nenana complex microblade technology is unknown, but then becomes common in the succeeding Denali complex (Hoffecker et al. 1993). The typical "campus" or "Gobi" type of microblade core made by the peoples of both the Diuktai culture of Siberia and the Denali of Alaska is a wedge-shaped microblade core made by sectioning a biface. The early cores in the Queen Charlotte Islands and Namu are different; they are part of a stone flaking industry that includes bifaces, but biface production is only rarely part of the sequence of making microblade cores. The significance of both the presence and absence of microblade technology in early assemblages, and of the varied techniques of making microblades, is still under debate by archaeologists.

Transitional Cultures

Archaeological remains that date between 10,500 and 7000 years ago can be grouped reasonably well into the five cultural traditions just described, whereas younger remains that date about 7000 to 5000 years ago are less easily categorized. This later period should be considered a time of acculturation during which the characteristic technologies of the earliest peoples remained neither stagnant nor separate, but changed and spread among neighbouring peoples. Fluting disappeared entirely by about 10,000 years ago and was replaced by stemming. On the southern coast assemblages which contain microblades as well as pebble tools and leaf-shaped points became common. In the Fraser-Thompson region (Chapter 15) the varied assemblages indicate impinging cultural influences from all directions. At Kettle Falls on the upper Columbia in the Shonitkwu Period (Chance and Chance 1985), assemblages containing elements of many of the early technologies are found all together in deposits predating the volcanic ash spread by the Mazama eruption of 6700 years ago. The undated assemblages from Coquitlam Lake (Chapter 18) and the Somass River (Chapter 19) resemble those from Kettle Falls and probably date to the same time.

Archaeological research is on-going in British Columbia. As I write this, I am looking at a fax I received this morning from Philip Hobler. He and his crew have just discovered a projectile point of pure quartz from excavations at the site of Tsinni

Tsinni on a geologically ancient terrace high above the Bella Coola valley. All of the pieces of the archaeological puzzle of early human occupation in British Columbia have not yet been discovered.

The much fuller archaeological record of the younger periods in the Pacific Northwest as a whole indicates that the sharing of new technology and ideas among adjacent peoples continued throughout the prehistoric period. Initial populations must have been kept small by the scarcity of food in the early post-glacial environment, but by 7000 years ago animal and fish populations had undoubtedly grown, and with them human populations. Thus both adaptation to the more abundant resources of the post-glacial and the borrowing of ideas and technology changed the appearance of the archaeological record and reduced some of the differences in technology evident at the beginning of the Early Period. Significant growth in the complexity of culture is not evident, however, until after 5000 BP. This later growth is summarized in Chapter 20.

NOTES ON RADIOCARBON (C-14) DATES

The dates used in this volume are radiocarbon (C-14) dates uncorrected by reference to tree-ring correction curves. Recent work (Stuiver et al. 1986, Stuiver and Becker 1993) has demonstrated that radiocarbon dates older than about 2300 years ago give a date that is younger than the actual calendar date, and that this discrepancy increases with age. Corrections are not available for the entire time span covered by this volume, 10,500 to 5000 C-14 years ago, so it was decided to give all dates in the text as uncorrected C-14 dates. Table 1 in Chapter 9 lists both corrected and uncorrected dates for the site of Namu and provides an idea of the magnitude of the difference. It should be remembered that this difference is not very great, that the calibrated date would only be slightly older than the C-14 dates given in the text, and that the relative chronology of sites dating to the period covered in this volume remains the same.

2

THE PREHISTORY OF CHARLIE LAKE CAVE

Knut R. Fladmark

Surface finds of Paleoindian styles of projectile points, particularly Plano/Scottsbluff-like forms, have been made by farmers, amateur surface collectors, and archaeologists in several interior areas of British Columbia (e.g., Fladmark 1981). However, until 1983 none had been recovered from an excavated, dated context. Given the strategic location of this province, astride crucial portions of both proposed interior and coastal routes for early human populations moving south from Beringia (e.g., Fladmark 1983), the complete absence of any firmly dated Paleoindian occupations in British Columbia represented a troublesome gap in knowledge pertaining to the initial colonization of this continent. This situation began to change in 1983 with the excavation of the Charlie Lake Cave site in northeastern British Columbia, which yielded a small fluted point component at the base of a deep sedimentary and cultural sequence spanning about the last 10,500 years.

Charlie Lake Cave first came to my attention in the summer of 1974 in the course of directing initial heritage impact surveys of the Peace River Valley, and in 1983 I obtained Social Sciences and Humanities Research Council funding for a single short season of excavation at the site, assisted by Jon Driver and Diana Alexander as principle co-investigators. Further excavations took place at Charlie Lake Cave in 1990 and 1991. Analysis of this material is still in progress. Although more artifacts were recovered, the outline of the cultural sequence presented here has been modified in only one significant way. A microblade core was recovered from a context securely dated at about 9500 BP. The core is made on a roughly rectangular piece of tabular chert. It has a unifa-

cially flaked keel and a poorly prepared striking platform. At least six microblades had been detached from one end of the core, but none was associated with this isolated find. The core bears a superficial resemblance to some early Holocene cores from Alaska. More details and comparisons will be provided in a later paper. Charlie Lake Cave is located about 9 km northwest of the modern city of Fort St. John in the Peace River district of northeastern British Columbia. The site is barely visible today to travellers on the Alaska Highway as a small south-facing sandstone abutment near the crest of a low wooded ridge forming the southeastern margin of Charlie Lake, about 6 km north of the Peace River itself. The ridge area is currently developed as a low-density residential subdivision and the site is on private property (Figures 1 and 2).

Charlie Lake Cave itself technically meets the requirements of a true small endogenic cave, rather than rockshelter, consisting of a single main chamber penetrating about 6 m into the hill, by a maximum of about 4.5 m wide. The one entrance to the cave is so low and narrow that an adult must stoop almost to hands-and-knees to enter (Figure 3), although near the back of the inner room even a relatively tall adult can safely stand upright (Figure 4). Two bedrock-floored secondary chambers also open off the back of the main room, but are too small to have ever been appropriate for human use. The cave is developed in a vertical sandstone escarpment which outcrops discontinuously along the northeast shore of Charlie Lake, belonging to the "Dunvegan Sandstone Formation" of Cretaceous age. Because Dunvegan Sandstone is known to occasionally contain "coal deposits," we were cautious about using unidentified carbonaceous materials from the excavations for radiocarbon dates. Consequently, all of the early dates on the site, as well as two of the later dates, were obtained on bison bone collagen.

Although the presence of the cave is a prominent local physical characteristic and the feature which first attracted my attention to this location, the cave itself turned out to be relatively sterile of aboriginal cultural deposits. Instead, the site accumulated and preserved its long stratigraphic sequence because of a unique alignment of bedrock features located outside the cave mouth which has retained thousands of years of archaeosedimentary aggradation.

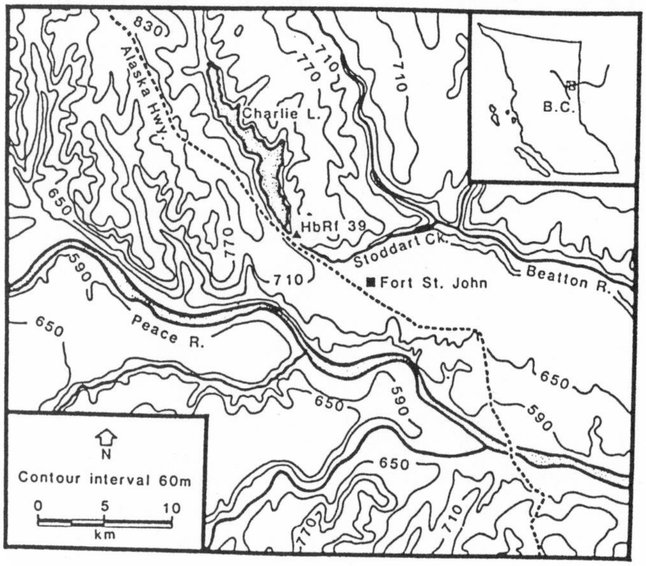

The "parapet" is the name that we applied to a large independent block of sandstone which parallels the main escarpment in front of the cave, and which has acted as a natural abutment to entrap and retain sedimentary accumulations derived from the mouth of the cave and the overlying hillside (Figure 5). The parapet and other similar sandstone outcrops seen along the hillside are large blocks detached and tilted slightly away from the main bedrock escarpment, possibly as a result of Pleistocene glacial plucking or large scale cryoclastism. The inclination of the sandstone bedding planes in the parapet generally parallel those of the main escarpment, which rules out any significant angular displacement of the parapet block, such as from the collapse of an originally much larger rockshelter-style roof overhang (Figure 6).

Figure 1. Location of HbRf 39.

Figure 2. Aerial view of site location, indicated by the arrow, looking northwest over the Alaska Highway and Charlie Lake.

Figure 3. View of main escarpment and cave mouth before excavation.

Figure 4. View into the main room of the cave. Small secondary chambers open to the right and left of Richard Gilbert.

Most of the deep bedrock crevice formed by the detachment of the parapet was probably rapidly infilled by mass-wastage and cryoclastic rubble, resulting in the coarse, resistant, and organically sterile sediments encountered in the lowest stratigraphic zone in our excavations. More than 10,000 years of gradual sedimentary accumulation in the crevice between the parapet block and the main bedrock escarpment containing the cave, created the important "platform" area, where our excavations were concentrated (Figures 5 and 6). In total, eight complete 1 by 1 m units and four partial units were excavated in the platform in 1983 to a maximum safely manageable depth, usually averaging 3 to 4 m below surface. We also placed two excavation units in the cave itself, but those proved shallow and unproductive, reaching consolidated bedrock within only 30 to 40 cm. Excavation was by trowelling, with all matrix dry-screened through 3 mm mesh.

The sedimentary sequence encountered in excavations in the platform area includes five main stratigraphic zones, labeled I to V from bottom to top, which were traceable across the entire excavation area with considerable confidence. Zone I, the basal stratigraphic unit, consists of a very resistant sandy sandstone rubble, ranging in particle-size from large boulders to clay, with a very low proportion of allochthonous or non-local rocks. It was penetrated to a maximum depth of only 40 cm in one unit in 1983 due to the difficulty of excavation, but appeared generally sterile of both faunal remains and any definite micro or macro cultural indicators. Zone I is currently interpreted as mainly coarse mass-wastage deposited during or shortly after the initial detachment

of the parapet from the main bedrock escarpment. The 1990 and 1991 project at this site penetrated through Zone I sediments reaching consolidated bedrock about 1 to 1.5 m below the bottom of the 1983 excavations, encountering no lower cultural materials. In Figure 8, which is a view of the west wall of excavation unit 5, Richard Gilbert is sitting on Zone I sediments, while pointing to the lowest cultural component in overlying Zone IIa.

Zone II lay deeper than about 2.5 m below the surface in all excavation units, and consisted of a silty-sand, with numerous sandstone bedrock fragments. Near its base was a stratigraphic sub-unit designated Zone IIa, primarily consisting of apparently reworked tills and glaciolacustrine sediments probably originally deposited on the hillside above the cave and washed into the crevice, beginning about 11,000 BP (Figure 9). A few hundred years later the first humans utilized the crevice area for butchering bison, and perhaps other short-term functions. At this time it is conceivable that a late stage of Glacial Lake Peace still occupied the adjacent plateau surface (Mathews 1978, 1980). If that was the case, then what is now the Stoddart Creek valley in front of the cave site might have been an arm of that large pondage, and speculatively a strategic animal and human crossing and meeting point.

The lowest cultural level at Charlie Lake Cave was located in stratigraphic Zone IIa, which relatively clay and rubble-rich, proved highly resistant to trowelling and had to be broken up by short-handled picks; consequently most of the early cultural materials were found in the screen. The 1983 Component 1 assemblage consists of only four stone tools and five flakes, all found near

Figure 5. General view of platform area before excavation, looking northwest – the cave entrance is just to the right of Oslynn Benjamin holding the stadia rod, and the "parapet" is to the left.

the base of Zone IIa, close to the contact with Zone I. The most diagnostic artifact is a stubby, lanceolate, extensively resharpened point of black chert, weighing 6.67g and measuring 39.3 mm in length (Figure 10a). Its maximum width of 28.4 mm occurs approximately three-quarters of the distance back from the tip, while its maximum thickness of 5.6 mm is reached at the mid-point of the central axis. Hafting modification consists of a 6 mm deep V-shaped basal notch and multiple shallow basal thinning scars which terminate in hinge fractures 19 mm from the basal notch and 14 mm short of the tip on one face. Second and third generation thinning flakes overlap the first series, but carry only about 15 mm onto the point. Lateral edge-grinding of the point is slight, extending only about 13 mm up from the base on one side and 20 mm on the other, while the basal edge itself does not appear to have been ground. Overall, the point has a slightly asymmetrical form, caused by one relatively straight and one curved lateral edge, which suggests that it may have been ultimately

modified or reworked to function as a knife in its last phase of use. Preserved blood residues of an unidentified animal, were located on the point by T. Loy, then of the British Columbia Provincial Museum.

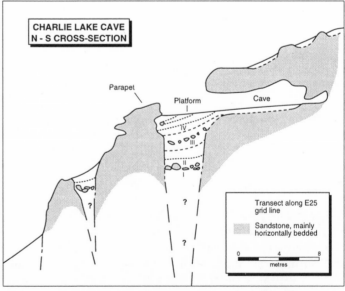

Figure 6. Generalized cross-section through Charlie Lake Cave and excavated "platform" sediments, Zones I to IV.

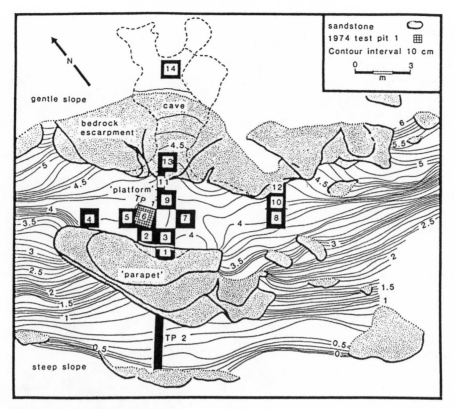

Figure 7. Local topography and location of 1983 excavation units at Charlie Lake Cave. Earlier test pit locations are indicated by "TP1."

The side-scraper or retouched flake was found in the same excavation unit and level as the point, and is a dark gray chert flake, roughly triangular in plan form, measuring 39.9 by 29.7 by 7.1 mm (Figure 10c). Both sides are formed by steep fracture edges, while the base of the triangle is retouched into a relatively straight unifacial bit with an edge-angle of about 50°. All secondary flake scars are fresh and unworn, although there is some microfracturing evident along one of the steep lateral edges.

The third flaked tool from Component 1, found approximately 2 m west of the point and scraper in the same stratigraphic zone, is a large "boat-shaped" core-tool of light yellow medium-grained quartzite, measuring 148.5 by 57.8 by 47.2 mm, and weighing 465.1 g (Figure 11). Its elongate ovate upper surface consists of a single unretouched flat flake scar, which served as the striking platform for the removal of a large series of secondary flakes around the entire rim, resulting in a streamlined, symmetrically rounded longitudinal plan and a sharply converging triangular "keeled" form in transverse cross-section.

One end of the core-tool is carefully unifacially retouched into an acute chisel-like bit, with a general edge-angle of 30° and a bit-angle of 50 to 60°, while the opposite extremity is blunted by a series of hinge fractures. This artifact has a well-worn feel, with most flake scar ridges and the ventral "keel" being smoothed and rounded, and it may have functioned as some kind of heavy duty adze-like chopping tool for butchering game or working bone and wood. No detritus or other specimens of yellow quartzite were found at the site and this piece must have been curated and brought in from some other place of origin. The core-tool is an unusual specimen, with few good parallels in other dated and published Paleoindian assemblages, to my knowledge. Four examples of similar quartzite core-tools were found in the later seasons of excavation.

The fourth artifact from Component 1 in 1983 was the most unexpected find. From the same excavation unit and level as the point and the scraper, came a single small, delicate, biconically perforated bead of soft, shiny gray-green schist (Figure 10b). Approximately pentagonal in shape, measuring 13.5 by 11.6 by 1.7 mm, the bead is basically just a thin unmodified schist pebble with a roughly conical hole drilled in each face, meeting more or less on centre. Although the faces of the bead are smooth, except for some tiny protuberant crystalline inclusions, they have not obvi-

15

ously been ground or polished, nor have the edges. However, the perforation is definitely artificial, and must have been drilled in from both sides and not punched or gouged. Such drilling need not have required any specialized technology in this relatively soft stone; indeed the fluted projectile point tip itself has proportions matching the taper of the bead's perforations. To my knowledge this is the first perforated stone bead positively associated with an excavated, dated, fluted point assemblage in North America, although bone beads have been reported from several Paleoindian sites. It is difficult to reconstruct the cultural activities which might readily account for an assemblage consisting of only one point, one scraper, five large core-tools, and one tiny bead, all unbroken, associated with butchered bison bones; particularly when two of those artifact types are rare or nonexistent in other published Paleoindian assemblages.

Besides the retouched stone tools and bead, the Zone IIa deposits also yielded several small black chert flakes, possibly reflecting small-scale bifacial thinning or retouching activities, in excavation units 1 to 3 m east of the fluted point and bead, plus a faunal assemblage dominated by bison bones.

Component 1 is directly associated with four radiocarbon dates on bone collagen, produced by both accelerator mass spectometry and normal analytical methods, of 10,100 ±210 (RIDDL 392); 10,380 ±160 (SFU 378); 10,450 ±150 (SFU 300), and 10,770 ±120 BP (SFU 454), or an average age of about 10,425 BP. Two of the dated bison bones exhibit scratches which could be interpreted as deliberate cut-marks and were from the same excavation unit and level as the point, scraper, and bead, while another dated bone was in close association with the quartzite core-tool (Figure 12). Two additional radiocarbon dates of 9990 ±150 (RIDDL 393) and 9760 ±160 (SFU 355) were also obtained from just above the stratigraphic interface between Zones IIa and IIb.

Figure 8. View into excavation Unit 5, complete. Gilbert points to the location of the lowest cultural component. The rod is 4 m long. This is also the same N.21-22, E.22 section drawn in Figure 13.

Zone IIb, overlying the earliest occupation, was characterized by continuous active weathering of the sandstone and deposition of its sedimentary products in the crevice. Unfortunately, Zone IIb itself yielded no modified artifacts and its associated Component 2 consists of only eighty-one black chert detrital flakes. Artifact descriptions for Components 2 to 11 are based on the 1983 excavations only.

In stratigraphic Zone III, which began deposition about 8500-9000 BP, organic matter began to become a visually significant component in the crevice fill, with thin richly humic beds interca-

Figure 9. Close-up of Zone IIa and IIb sediments at the base of the N.21-22, E.22 section shown in Figures 8 and 13.

Figure 10. Photograph of three of the Component 1 artifacts: (a) fluted point, (b) bead, and (c) retouched flake.

17

Figure 11. Photographs of three views of the large quartzite core-tool from Component 1.

lating with mineral strata at the toes of fans against the north side of the parapet. A major fall of large sandstone slabs near the base of Zone III associated with dates of 8400 ±240 (SFU 357) and 7800 ±800 (SFU 370) correlates with a hiatus in cultural occupation. A fragmentary human mandible, probably of an elderly female, and a small collection of detritus comprises Component 3, found immediately above the rock-fall and associated with an accelerator date of 7400 ±300 (RID-DL 10). That mandible was the only human physical remains found at the site.

Zone III is a complex stratigraphic unit consisting of multiple, thin, intricately interbedded alternating mineral and organic bands, grouped into stratigraphic subzones labeled a to e from bottom to top (Figure 13). The upper levels of Zone III are marked by distinctive reddish silty sands, and despite events such as the rock-fall, overall Zone III is characterized by a much finer mean particle size range than the levels underlying or overlying it. These sedimentary parameters probably reflect a relatively passive physical environment and increased rates of chemical weathering at this time. Indeed, deposition of Zone III between about 8500 and 4500 BP (±200 years), correlates well with the classic Hypsithermal climatic period.

In the upper parts of Zone III were found the small cultural assemblages of Components 3, 4, 5, and 6 including three medium-sized projectile points of generalized side-notched or corner-notched forms: one definite chert microblade fragment (the only microblade from the site), and two generalized leaf-shaped bifaces. A total of 159 flakes were also associated with these components.

Zone IV is a highly organic, dark pebbly sand, characteristic of the upper 1.0 to 1.3 m of sediments across the entire platform excavation area. Despite its obvious organic accumulation, which suggests that biotic factors had by this time overtaken rates of mineral sedimentation, Zone IV is characterized by a relatively coarse mean particle size, matched only by the much earlier Zone II sediments. Associated radiocarbon dates indicate that Zone IV was probably deposited between about 4200 and 1400 BP.

Component 7 in the lower part of Zone IV yielded two relatively large corner-notched points and twenty-seven flakes, followed in the middle part of that zone by two small stemmed points, one larger "Oxbow-like" point and 164 flakes in Component 8. Component 9 in the upper part of Zone IV yielded one relatively large expanding stem point and another 182 flakes.

Figure 12. Close-up view of presumed butchering marks on a bison long-bone fragment from stratigraphic Zone IIa. The longest cut-mark is about 1.5 cm.

Zone V at the top of the stratigraphic section consists of a thin buried pedogenic Ah horizon traceable across most of the platform excavation area, capped by about 30 to 40 cm of dark organic silty sand, containing both prehistoric and historic cultural materials. Artifacts found in Components 10 and 11 in this zone include three small side-notched points, the base of another small expanding stem point, sixty-eight flakes, and assorted recent historic materials. No radiocarbon dates are associated with this zone.

In total, ten later cultural components were found stratigraphically in sequence above Zone IIa and the earliest occupation, supported by a further twelve radiocarbon dates (Figure 13). These components generally consist of small assemblages of flaked stone tools, including occasional projectile points and retouched flakes, all roughly similar in overall content and degree of diversity to the earliest occupation.

The repeated pattern through time of relatively meagre anthropogenic sedimentary inputs, despite a small, constricted and focused area for human occupation and cultural imprinting, suggests that this site was never seriously utilized as a general purpose habitation area. It is probable that throughout its entire ca. 10,500 years of use by aboriginal people it mainly periodically functioned as a short-term campsite and work area, associated with local resource exploitation activities such as bison hunting.

As noted previously (Fladmark, Driver, and Alexander 1988:383), direct cultural relationships for the small Paleoindian assemblage from Charlie Lake Cave are difficult to pin down with certainty. The few other excavated fluted-point sites so far known in Canada date to the same 10,000 – 10,500 BP time period (e.g., Gryba 1983, MacDonald 1969). Like Charlie Lake Cave, their points tend to be relatively small, multiple, basally-thinned forms, unlike the extensively fluted points of the contemporary Folsom complex, or the larger styles of the 11,000 – 11,500 BP "classic" Clovis complex, both best defined in the central and western United States. Given the well-established age of the American Clovis complex, the Charlie Lake Cave Paleoindian assemblage is clearly 500 to 1000 years too late to have been left by any early "proto-Clovis pioneers" penetrating southwards from Beringia via the ice-free corridor. Of course, this picture could quickly change with the future dating of new fluted point sites in this area. However, on the basis of present information, the early assemblage from Charlie Lake Cave seems best interpreted as a late variation in a "fluted point continuum" with its earliest manifestations located south of the Wisconsinan glacial limits in what is now the United States. Thus, the oldest cultural component at Charlie Lake Cave site was probably left by Paleoindians filtering *northwards* into west-central Canada after the retreat of the Laurentide ice-front and the development of a productive environmental regime about 10,000 to 11,000 years ago. After that earliest occupation, the site seems to have continued to be used in much the same way, as a periodic hunting and processing camp for small groups of people, up until the historic period.

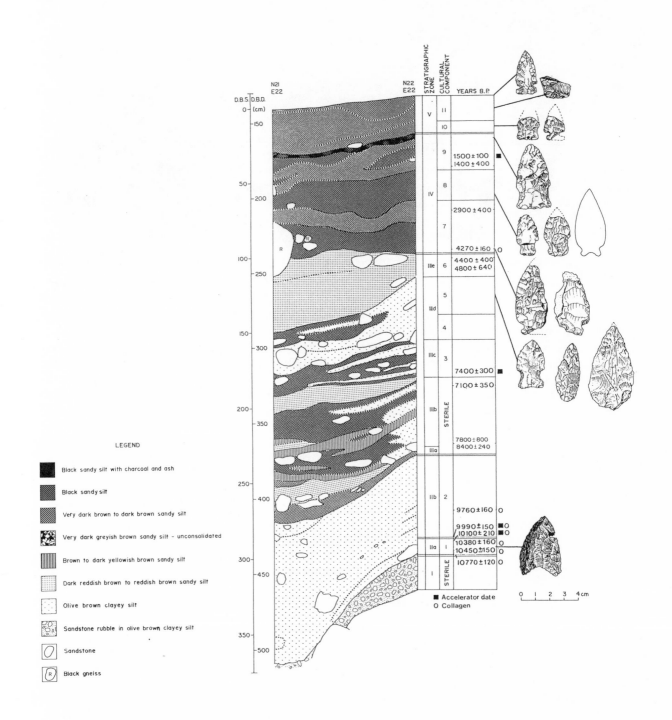

Figure 13. A typical vertical section north-south through the platform excavation area (N. 21-22, E. 22) showing the stratigraphic association of radiocarbon dates and projectile points from the 1983 excavations.

3

THE SIGNIFICANCE OF THE FAUNA FROM THE CHARLIE LAKE CAVE SITE

Jonathan C. Driver

The Charlie Lake Cave site, Peace River District, northeastern British Columbia, is the only excavated, dated site in Canada in which an association of fauna and a fluted point assemblage occurs. There are two major reasons for a detailed analysis of the fauna. First, because the fauna includes a variety of small vertebrates, it provides us with important information concerning animal populations in a newly deglaciated landscape. Second, it provides a glimpse of the subsistence activities of Paleoindians in the Peace River area. As this region was close to the retreating ice sheets, the fauna reflects subsistence strategies employed by Paleoindians as they colonized newly available land. These topics are discussed in more detail in this chapter than has been possible in previous, more descriptive, studies (Driver 1988, Fladmark, Driver, and Alexander 1988).

THE SITE

The Charlie Lake Cave site is located on the south-facing slope of a low sandstone escarpment which forms the north side of the Stoddart Creek valley, a few hundred metres downstream from Charlie Lake, British Columbia. Detailed description of the site is unnecessary in view of previous publications (Fladmark, this volume, Fladmark, Alexander and Driver 1984, Fladmark, Driver, and Alexander 1988). The faunal remains discussed in this chapter were recovered from a deep gully between a small sandstone cliff in the bedrock escarpment and a large block of sandstone (referred to as the "parapet") downslope from the cliff face. Charlie Lake Cave is located in the bedrock cliff, but contains shallow deposits with little time depth. Excavations penetrated the gully deposits to a depth of about 3.5 metres. Cultural and faunal material were found in all major strata except the lowest zone (Zone I), which consisted of large sandstone boulders in a silt/clay matrix.

Radiocarbon dates show that the earliest fauna was deposited between 10,700 BP and ca. 9000 BP in a silty clay with larger sandstone clasts. This depositional unit, Zone II, is divided into two subzones. Subzone IIa dates 10,700 to 10,000 BP, and contains the fluted point assemblage described elsewhere (Fladmark, this volume, Fladmark, Driver, and Alexander 1988). Subzone IIb dates 10,000 to 9000 BP and contains flakes but no other diagnostic cultural remains. The two subzones are separated on the basis of slight changes in sediments, but both were probably the result of re-deposition of glaciolacustrine sediments mixed with weathered bedrock and larger bedrock clasts.

At the time of the deposition of Zone II sediments, the gully would have been accessible from east and west ends. One should not think of fauna being deposited in a closed sediment trap, but rather that the downslope "parapet" allowed sediments moving down the hillside to accumulate behind it. Bones may have been incorporated in the sediments either by moving downslope and becoming trapped behind the rock or by being added to the accumulating pile of sediments by natural or cultural agencies which introduced bones from any direction.

THE FAUNA

The fauna from subzone IIa is fairly sparse when compared with the thousands of specimens recovered from later zones at the site (Driver 1988).

Identified specimens are recorded in Table 1. The mammal fauna is dominated numerically by ground squirrels (*Spermophilus* sp.), which do not occur in the area today, and which disappear completely from the faunal record shortly after the end of Zone II (ca. 9000 BP). It is not possible to identify the species of ground squirrel represented, but either Columbian (*S. columbianus*) or Richardson's ground squirrel (*S. richardsonii*) are present; other species can be excluded on the basis of size or dental morphology. Other important species include snowshoe hare (*Lepus americanus*), bison or large artiodactyl (all assumed to be *Bison* sp.), and a large lagomorph (*Lepus* sp.) which may be either arctic hare (*Lepus arcticus*) or a jackrabbit (e.g., *L. townsendii*). Neither of these large lagomorphs occurs in the region today and either species would be expected in an open, unforested environment. The single specimen of muskrat (*Ondatra zibethicus*) in this subzone is a tooth. The specimen is stained a much darker brown than other rodent teeth from these deposits, and is identical in colour to specimens from the upper part of the site. It is interpreted as a specimen which fell from the section during excavation, and should not be considered as part of the fauna. The avian fauna is dominated by cliff swallow (*Hirundo pyrrhonota*), and many of the unidentified passerine bones are probably also from this species. This early occurrence suggests that swallows readily extended their northern summer migration to follow the retreating ice sheets. A few fish bones were also found in the upper part of this subzone. None were identified, but specimens from subzone IIb have been identified as sucker (*Catostomus* sp.).

A more diverse fauna occurs in subzone IIb. This diversity need not result completely from a more diverse biota; it may be partly the result of an increased sample size. The mammalian fauna is dominated by snowshoe hare, setting the trend for the entire Holocene assemblage in which this species is consistently the most numerous (Driver 1988). Ground squirrels are a minor component of the fauna, and occur mainly in the lower part of the subzone. Microtines are better represented, and include *Microtus xanthognathus* (chestnut-cheeked vole), a relatively rare species, although still present in the region today. Small *Microtus* could not be identified to species because diagnostic teeth were missing, but either meadow vole (*M. pennsylvanicus*) or long-tailed vole (*M. longicaudus*) were present. Gapper's red-backed vole (*Clethrionomys gapperi*) was present and bison also occurs. In the avian fauna, cliff swallow

no longer dominates. Aquatic birds are well represented, including grebes (*Aechmophorus* sp. and *Podiceps auritus*), a small number of surface feeding ducks, ruddy duck (*Oxyura jamaicensis*), coot (*Fulica americana*), and a rail. Upland birds include the *Tetraoninae* (grouse or ptarmigan) and a set of phalanges from short-eared owl (*Asio flammeus*).

ORIGIN OF THE FAUNA

The taphonomic history of the entire fauna is difficult to establish, mainly because many species are present in small numbers. Furthermore, the fauna as a whole consists predominantly of small mammals and birds, and recent taphonomic studies have concentrated much more on the larger mammals. Nevertheless, it is important to try to understand the origin of the fauna in view of the association with artifacts. If one were to propose that the entire faunal assemblage was the result of human hunting, then this site would provide a view of Paleoindian subsistence very different to the widely held hypothesis that the early occupants of North America were subsisting largely on big game.

Specimens which owe their presence at the site to human activity cannot be identified unequivocally. The most convincing case can be made for bison. A number of bison and unidentified large artiodactyl bones (assumed to be bison) display cut marks (Fladmark, Driver, and Alexander 1988) in locations consistent with human butchery (Table 2). Binford (1981) has noted that similarities in artiodactyl anatomy from species to species result in similar patterns of butchery in cultures separated widely in time and space. The location of cut marks on the specimens described in Table 2 can be reproduced in ethnographic and archaeological examples (e.g., Binford 1981, Frison 1973). Many bison and large artiodactyl bones display spiral fractures, some with a well-defined point of impact, which has also been cited as good evidence for smashing of bones by humans (Binford 1981).

However, one cannot be completely certain that the bison and large artiodactyl bones arrived at their ultimate location as a result of human activity. A number of specimens demonstrate good evidence for carnivore chewing (Table 2). Unfortunately, on no specimens do the carnivore marks and cut marks overlap, and one cannot determine positively whether humans or carnivores modified the bison bones first. However, if one assumes that the carnivores chewed the bones after they had

Table 1. Identified fauna, Zone II, Charlie Lake Cave, 1983 season.

Taxon	Subzone IIa	Subzone IIb
Pisces (fish)	4	14
Amphibia (frogs)		2
Aechmophorus sp. (large grebe)		2
Podiceps auritus (horned grebe)		15
Medium sized grebe		4
Anatini (surface feeding ducks)	1	2
Anas crecca (green-winged teal)		1
Anas platyrhynchos (mallard)		1
Oxyura jamaicensis (ruddy duck)		1
Tetraoninae (grouse or ptarmigan)		13
Rallidae (small rail)		2
Fulica americana (American coot)		10
Charadriiformes (small wader)	2	
Asio flammeus (short-eared owl)		8
Passeriformes	1	11
Hirundo pyrrhonota (cliff swallow)	16	3
Lepus americanus (snowshoe hare)	18	145
Lepus sp. (large hare/jackrabbit)	4	
Marmota sp.		1
Spermophilus sp. (ground squirrel)	122	24
Peromyscus sp. (deer mouse)	6	2
Clethrionomys gapperi (Gapper's red-backed vole)		2
Ondatra zibethicus (muskrat)	1	
Microtus sp. (vole)	2	3
Microtus xanthognathus (chestnut-cheeked vole)		2
Microtine	2	19
Canis sp. (wolf/dog)		1
Mustela nivalis (least weasel)		2
Mustelidae (weasel family)		1
Bison sp. (bison)	8	11
Large artiodactyl	3	6

been discarded by humans, then the sample of bones may be biased by either selective transportation of bones to the site by carnivores or selective destruction and removal of bones from the site by carnivores. One should certainly not assume that the large ungulate and bison bones are lying where they were discarded by hunters. Thus, although the evidence strongly favours the hunting of bison by Paleoindians, the assemblage is not simply the refuse left after a successful hunt. In this regard, it is interesting to note that a minimum of three bison are represented by only twenty-eight fragments. This suggests that either humans or carnivores were very selective in their choice of bones.

While analysis of surface damage to the bones of large mammals may provide evidence of their taphonomic history, this method reveals much less about the origin of smaller vertebrates. For example, a complete undamaged phalanx of a snowshoe hare could be the result of *in situ* death, discard by a human or animal predator, or downslope movement of bones originally deposited upslope by either of the first two processes. Broken bones may also result from human or animal predation or from mechanical effects during and after deposition, and no keys have been developed to distinguish such breakage patterns. Furthermore, modes of damage caused by particular predators vary widely. For example, humans may cook small vertebrates whole, strip the meat and cause minimal bone damage, or may pound bones into small fragments. In a review of the actions of great horned owls (*Bubo virginianus*), Kusmer (1986) noted that bones of prey such as duck or snowshoe hare might be discarded as picked skeletons or might be broken during consumption. It would be extremely difficult to distinguish these processes from those produced by humans. At the microscopic level, erosion of bones due to digestive processes may be detectable (e.g., Kusmer 1986), but insufficient studies have been undertaken to distinguish the effects of various predators, and the effect of human digestive processes on small bones is also unknown. As humans, mammalian carnivores, and owls may all discard bones before consumption of prey, absence of digestive erosion cannot be used to rule out any of these predators.

Element frequency is not very useful in analyzing even the most common small vertebrates at the site. Bones were recovered from 3 mm mesh during excavation, and it is likely that some specimens were missed as a result of this recovery procedure. For example, ground squirrel metapodials are infrequent, whereas those of snowshoe hare are common; this may well result from the smaller ground squirrel bones passing through the screen. For snowshoe hare one finds that the frequency of phalanges is correlated with size. Thus, first phalanges are more common than second phalanges and third phalanges are missing. Analysis of relative abundances of limb bones of ground squirrel (Table 3) demonstrates that frequency of elements deviates strongly from the pattern expected for complete skeletons, but the reasons for the over-abundance of forelimbs is difficult to determine. On the other hand, snowshoe hare conforms reasonably closely to the expected pattern (Table 4).

Observations during excavation suggest that some portions of small vertebrates were deposited as articulating units. For example, I observed articulated limbs or feet of ground squirrels and *Tetraoninae*. The articulating set of short-eared owl phalanges from Zone IIb were presumably deposited as a single unit. Such patterns may suggest rapid burial and relatively undisturbed sediments, but they do not identify the mode of death nor the means of transportation to the site. Overall, the small vertebrate fauna from Zone II suggests transportation to the site by either owls or raptors, rather than by mammalian carnivores. Carnivores would be expected to reduce bone to small fragments by chewing and ingestion; many

of the bones of snowshoe hare and ground squirrel are either complete or more than half complete (Tables 4 and 5).

Unfortunately, one cannot completely rule out the possibility that some of the small vertebrates may have been brought to the site by humans. Analysis of damage to small vertebrate skeletons by humans has received little attention in the archaeological literature, and, as noted above, treatment of small vertebrates is likely to be variable. One feature that is missing from all small vertebrate specimens at Charlie Lake is a distinctive burning pattern which often characterizes small mammals eaten by humans (Dansie 1984, Vigne and Marinval-Vigne 1983). There was no evidence of any burning of small vertebrate bones in Zone II.

In order to attempt to resolve the problem of human use of small vertebrates, analysis of bone distribution was undertaken. The distribution of bones is plotted in Figure 1 in which data from both subzones is combined. It is notable that two units (units 3 and 9) frequently contain the greatest percentage of specimens of particular taxonomic categories. Thus, unit 3 contains the highest frequencies of ground squirrel, snowshoe hare, grebes, ducks and coot, and cliff swallow; unit 9 contains the highest frequencies of microtines and grouse. This cannot be accounted for by the depth of sediment. For example, the volume of Zone II deposits in unit 4 is 0.89 m^3 while in unit 3 Zone II deposits occupy 0.79 m^3. Yet unit 3 contains a much greater concentration of bones than unit 4. Similarly, the volume of Zone II sediments in unit 5 (where relatively little fauna was recovered) is 1.2 m^3, while unit 9 contains a relatively large number of bones in 0.43 m^3.

Although one could wish for a larger excavation area, it appears that most taxonomic groups occur most densely in the two units furthest from the east and west end of the gully and closest to the gully margins. I suggest that this is because most species were being deposited at the site by owls or raptors which roosted in or on the rocks bordering the gully. It is notable that the only specimens which were definitely hunted by humans (bison and large artiodactyl) have a somewhat different distribution. This taxonomic group is the only group which does not appear with the highest frequency in either unit 3 or unit 9; it is also the only group whose highest frequencies are in the three western units – 4, 5, and 6. These western units also produced the four artifacts from the fluted point assemblage of subzone IIa. The

Table 2. Bison and large artiodactyl bones, Zone II, Charlie Lake Cave, 1983 season.

Element	Portion	Carnivore damage	Cutmarks
Cranium	3 fragments		
Tooth	Premolar		
Vertebra	Fragment		
Sacrum	Anterior	Right side	
Pelvis	Fragment		
Rib	Midsection	Both ends	Medial side
Humerus	Distal + shaft	Proximal end	
Humerus	Distal	Epicondyles	Epicondyles
Humerus	Shaft fragment	One end	Epicondyles
Radius	Distal +shaft		
Radius	Shaft		
Ulna	Proximal	Proximal end	Olecranon
Carpal	Whole		
Metacarpus V	Proximal		
Metacarpus	Proximal		
Tibia	Proximal + shaft		
Tibia	Distal + shaft	Both ends	
Tibia	Shaft		
Metapodial	Shaft		
Phalanx 1	Whole		
Phalanx 2	Whole		
Phalanx 2	Whole		
Phalanx 2	Proximal		
Sesamoid	Whole		
Sesamoid	Whole		

projectile point, scraper, and bead were excavated from unit 5, and the core/scraper from unit 4. Unit 5 produced over 90 per cent of the flakes from the cultural assemblage of subzone IIb. Thus, there is clear evidence that human activities were associated with the western end of the gully, while the major deposition of smaller vertebrates occurred at the eastern end, notably at the gully margins, and without associated artifacts. This associational data strengthens the case that only bison and large artiodactyl bones were deposited as a result of human activity.

PALEOENVIRONMENTS

At the time of the initial deposition of subzone IIa sediments extensive glacial lakes may have filled many valleys in the region (Mathews 1978, 1980). The chronology of proglacial events is not particularly well dated, but by 10,200 BP at the latest the Clayhurst stage of Glacial Lake Peace, with shorelines at the elevation of the Charlie Lake Cave site, had drained. For much, if not all, of Zone II times the environments in this region would have been characterized by immature river systems, probably carrying much greater loads than modern rivers. Slopes would have been unstable as a result of glacial lake drainage.

The paleoenvironmental implications of the Zone II fauna have been discussed elsewhere (Driver 1988). One can argue convincingly that the change from subzone IIa to subzone IIb marks the transition from a largely open landscape to one in which coniferous forest was predominant. In IIa the presence of bison, a large lagomorph, ground squirrels, and cliff swallows are indicative of open conditions, while snowshoe hare indicate the presence of some forest. The virtual absence of waterfowl from subzone IIa seems to indicate that drainage regimes were not sufficiently stable to allow colonization by the plants and animals upon which waterfowl depend. In IIb there is a notable decline in ground squirrels and cliff swallow, and the large lagomorphs are absent. The increased frequency of snowshoe hare, together with the presence of chestnut-cheeked vole and Gapper's red-backed vole suggest that boreal forest dominated the environment. The increase in waterfowl demonstrates that a variety of productive aquatic habitats were established and that migratory species had extended their northern range.

Sediments from Zone II cannot be correlated across excavation units, except in so far as one can distinguish the two subzones. Lack of microstratigraphy, coupled with the sloping nature of the deposits means that subdivisions of subzones based on arbitrary excavation levels only have meaning within an individual excavation unit. Only excavation unit 3 contains sufficient fauna to warrant analysis of changing frequencies of species within subzones. Figure 2 plots the relative frequency of waterfowl, cliff swallow, snowshoe hare, and ground squirrel for ten arbitrary levels in layer 15 in unit 3. A date of 10,100 ±210 BP (RIDDL 393) was obtained on ground squirrel bone from 15-10. A date of 9990 ±150 BP (RIDDL 392) was obtained on bison bone from 15-6. The IIa/IIb boundary is between 15-6 and 15-7. 15-1 probably dates to about 9500 BP.

The most striking aspect of these data is the rapidity of the change in the fauna. This is particularly notable in the switch from ground squirrel as the most abundant small mammal in subzone IIa to snowshoe hare in IIb. Waterfowl also appear suddenly in the upper part of IIb. The suddenness of the change is also reflected in palynological studies from the region. MacDonald (1987) has analyzed lake bed cores from sites about 120 km northeast of Charlie Lake. At the base of the cores there is a zone dating 11,000 to 10,000 BP with high relative frequencies of sedges, grasses, and

herbs, together with deciduous trees such as birch and aspen. At about 10,000 BP there is a rapid increase in conifer pollen (mainly spruce), which MacDonald interprets as the establishment of boreal forest.

Palynological and faunal evidence suggests that the open environment which followed deglaciation lasted no more than 1000 years. Paleoindian occupation took place within that interval. The establishment of boreal forest occurred quite rapidly, possibly over a period of a few hundred years. The new vegetation drastically altered the nature of the faunal community.

SUBSISTENCE

As discussed above, one can only make a convincing case for Paleoindian predation on bison at Charlie Lake Cave. In spite of the variety of other fauna, only bison is consistently associated with artifacts and only bison displays definite evidence of human procurement and processing. At Charlie Lake Cave we are seeing an isolated incident in Paleoindian life; perhaps a couple of days is represented. Whether or not this subsistence pattern represents a common event in the seasonal round cannot be determined. It has been argued that the big-game hunting aspect of Paleoindian subsistence has been over-emphasized and that in some areas of North America a wider range of smaller species was utilized (see, for example, Frison 1977, Johnson 1987). At Charlie Lake there is good evidence for large mammal hunting and the interpretation of Paleoindians as big-game hunters should not be overthrown, at least for this area of

Table 3. Ground squirrel limb bones, Zone II, Charlie Lake Cave, 1983 season.

Element	Complete element	>50% present	<50% present
Humerus	7		
Proximal humerus			1
Distal humerus		10	9
Radius	3		
Proximal radius		1	2
Distal radius		7	1
Ulna	2		
Proximal ulna		5	5
Distal ulna			2
Metacarpus	2		
Proximal femur		4	2
Tibia	2		
Proximal tibia		3	1
Distal tibia			2
Metatarsus	8		

Table 4. Snowshoe hare limb elements, Zone II, Charlie Lake Cave, 1983 season.

Element	Complete element	>50% present	<50% present
Proximal humerus			2
Distal humerus			3
Radius	1		
Distal ulna			1
Metacarpus	10		
Proximal metacarpus		1	3
Distal metacarpus		2	1
Proximal femur		1	
Distal femur			1
Proximal tibia			1
Distal tibia		1	3
Metatarsus	19		
Proximal metatarsus		4	4
Distal metatarsus		4	3
Phalanx 1	15		
Proximal phalanx 1		2	6
Distal phalanx 1			4
Phalanx 2	9		
Proximal phalanx 2			1

North America.

As discussed above, both faunal and palynological data are best interpreted as a grassland with scattered patches of woodland or forest during the 11,000 to 10,000 BP period. Evidence from Charlie Lake and from paleontological sites in other areas of the Peace River (Burns 1986, Churcher and Wilson 1979) suggests that the fauna available to hunters was dominated by large mammals, specifically bison. There is no evidence that either fish or waterfowl were available in sufficient abundance to constitute a major alternative resource.

Open landscapes dominated by large mammals and containing few vegetable resources suitable for human consumption are mainly confined to temperate and arctic areas of the northern hemisphere. Ethnographic data on hunter-gatherers in such environments show a strong reliance on large mammals, which were often hunted by communal techniques; in fact communal hunting of large mammals as a major subsistence strategy is largely confined to such conditions (Driver 1990). Recent examples of such strategies include bison hunters of the northern Plains, caribou hunters of the Canadian arctic, and caribou hunters of eastern Asia. Archaeological evidence from equivalent landscapes in the Late Pleistocene suggests similar adaptations (e.g., Klein 1973). It is entirely predictable, given what can be reconstructed of paleoenvironments in the Peace River area, that hunter-gatherers in such an environment would concentrate their efforts on big game, specifically on species which aggregated as herds for at least part of the year.

The Paleoindians at Charlie Lake were a northern extension of populations of bison-hunters who occupied the grasslands east of the Rockies during the Late Pleistocene and early Holocene. In much of that zone bison hunting remained the major subsistence method up to the ethnographic period. However, the rapid encroachment of boreal forest in the Peace River area after 10,000 BP must have necessitated a swift and complex readaptation to new resources with new distributions. By 9000 BP at the latest, and perhaps as early as 10,000 BP, grazing areas for bison had become substantially curtailed, and it seems very likely that bison populations would have declined drastically. Additionally, bison social organization may have changed in response to fragmentation of feeding areas and a reduction in the quality of forage.

While bison populations declined, other resources became more abundant. The increase in waterfowl has already been discussed. Other animals which become more common later in the Charlie Lake sequence include fish, beaver, muskrat, and snowshoe hare (Driver 1988), all typical species of the boreal forest today. The boreal for-

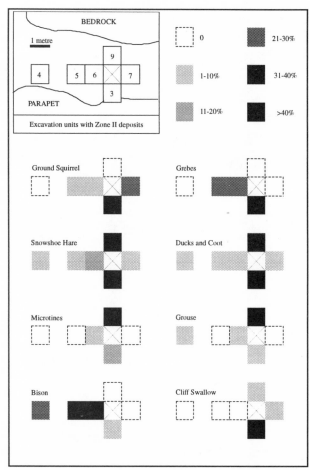

Figure 1. Distribution of selected taxonomic categories by excavation unit, Zone II, Charlie Lake Cave, 1983 season (shading indicates the percentage of specimens of a particular taxon that occur in each unit).

est adaptation of the ethnographically known Athabascan groups probably developed as early as 9000 BP in the Peace River region of British Columbia.

Acknowledgments

I am grateful to Knut Fladmark for the opportunity to study the fauna from this site, and for the provision of so much information on artifacts and stratigraphy. The many people who assisted in the identification of the fauna reported here have been acknowledged in previous publications. I thank Roy Carlson for the opportunity to participate in the symposium on early British Columbia. This research was funded by SSHRC grants to Knut Fladmark and the author. Further excavations were undertaken at Charlie Lake Cave in 1990 and 1991. The stratigraphy of Zone II has been revised to include more subzones, but the stratigraphic break described here as the IIa/IIb boundary is still unrecognised, and is still dated to about 10,000 BP. The beginning of Zone II probably dates about 10,500 BP. The end of Zone II now appears to date at about 9500 BP. More fauna were recovered in these excavations. Bison is still the only large mammal identified. Some species have been added to the microfauna and these will be reported elsewhere. The environmental reconstruction proposed here is still supported.

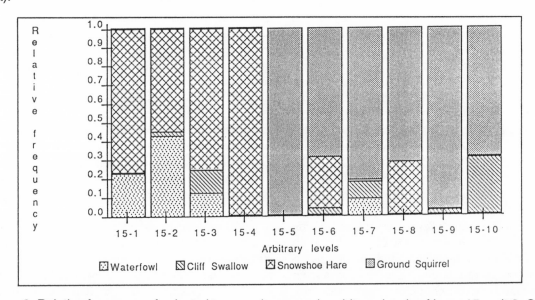

Figure 2. Relative frequency of selected taxonomic groups in arbitrary levels of layer 15, unit 3, Charlie Lake Cave, 1983 season.

4

PALEOINDIAN SITES IN THE VICINITY OF PINK MOUNTAIN

Ian R. Wilson

During a 1986 archaeological inventory of a proposed pipeline in northeastern BC, a site containing evidence of early occupations was discovered (Wilson 1986a). Subsequent investigations involving minor test excavations and monitoring of construction revealed several stone tools associated with Paleoindian complexes (Wilson 1986b, 1989). The results of this work led the author and Roy Carlson to follow up with a brief reconnaissance program (Wilson and Carlson 1987). Since the region around Pink Mountain is virtually unexplored archaeologically and has a limited road network, and because funding was minimal, the inventory was exploratory and wide ranging. The survey concentrated on surface exposures near convenient access points and on identification of private collections of artifacts. This chapter focuses on Paleoindian sites identified during the two brief programs.

The study area is within the eastern foothills of the Rocky Mountains in northeastern BC, west of the small community of Pink Mountain, which is situated on the Alaska Highway between Fort St. John and Fort Nelson (Figure 1). The region is characterized by broad, flat valleys and high rugged hills with occasional low mountain peaks. Several major rivers including the Beatton, Halfway, Cameron, and Sikanni Chief have their headwaters in the region. The eastern flanks of the Rocky Mountains are within the hypothesized ice-free corridor (see, for example Carlson 1991c, Reeves 1971). Though there are differing opinions regarding the suitability of the corridor for movement and/or occupation, and even of the presence of such an ice-free zone, it is clear that the eastern foothills represent one of the earliest habitable areas in the province.

The Pink Mountain site, HhRr 1, is situated on a long, relatively narrow, high ridge (Figure 2) overlooking the Moose Lick Creek Valley to the west and the north. The site is 1160 m above sea level and approximately 200 m above and 1 km distant from Moose Lick Creek. The ridge offers excellent viewpoints of the surrounding countryside.

Artifacts at the Pink Mountain site were found thinly distributed over an area more than 1 km in length and 150 m in width (Figure 3). Two and possibly three areas of artifact concentration were noted, with the main concentration occurring at the crest of the ridge. Only 150 artifacts, including debitage, were recovered from the site. Artifacts were first noted in a road cut and testing showed that the buried cultural level is 5 to 10 cm below the present surface and is 2 to 6 cm thick. No stratigraphic separation of artifacts is apparent and no organics or charcoal have been found. A number of tools were recovered, most of which are made of a locally available black chert. Several macroblades were recovered but no unity of function was apparent as they evince unifacial and bifacial work of varying types.

Although no microblades were found, a microblade core was recovered (Figure 4d). The core is roughly cube-shaped with a battered and irregular striking platform. Ten microblade scars are present around the sides of the core. When the Pink Mountain site was briefly revisited in 1987, an additional microblade core fragment was noted. This small fragment of the distal end of a conical or prismatic core showed four blade removals. Microblade technology has a long time span in northern assemblages, with sites such as Bluefish Cave in Yukon (Cinq-Mars 1979) and Healy Lake in Alaska (Cook 1969) yielding very old dates. As well, microblades

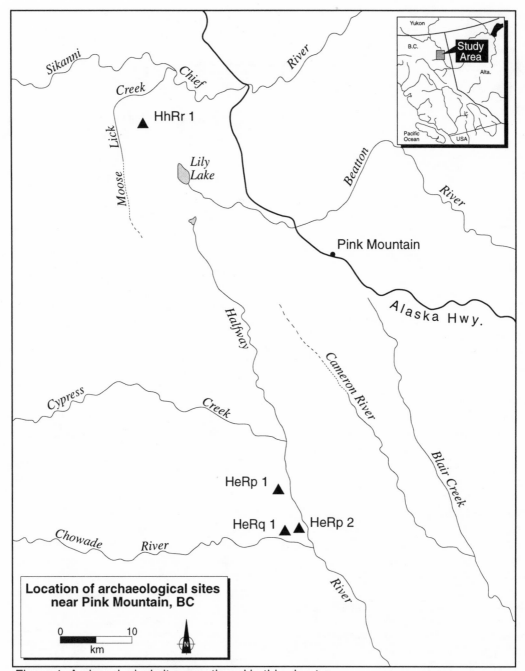

Figure 1. Archaeological sites mentioned in this chapter.

and fluted points are found at several sites in Alaska (Ackerman, this volume, Alexander 1974, Dumond 1980) and on the Northwest Coast.

Black chert scrapers are relatively common at HhRr 1 and include side and end scrapers and combinations of the two. Several generic bifaces are also present in the assemblage.

A number of spear points were recovered (Figure 4). These include a side-notched point very tentatively compared with Salmon River side-notched forms; a basally thinned base of a large spear with straight edges suggestive of the Plainview complex; a leaf-shaped point, probably bipointed, identified as a Lerma/Plano variant; a large well-crafted, stemmed Scottsbluff point; and two basal fragments of fluted points. The latter both evince deeply concave thinned and ground bases, pronounced ears, and channel flakes. It is evident that the Pink Mountain site has artifacts from several cultural occupations including, at least a variant of Clovis (the Fluted Point Tradition), and Scottsbluff.

Figure 2. *Upper:* HrRr 1 from the east. The crest of the hill where the Scottsbluff point was found is the highest point of land at the site which extends from there several hundred feet downslope toward the viewer. *Lower:* Test trench near the site datum. The dark layer in the profile is the original surface and is covered by overburden from access road construction. Artifacts originated from the thin white layer immediately below the dark layer.

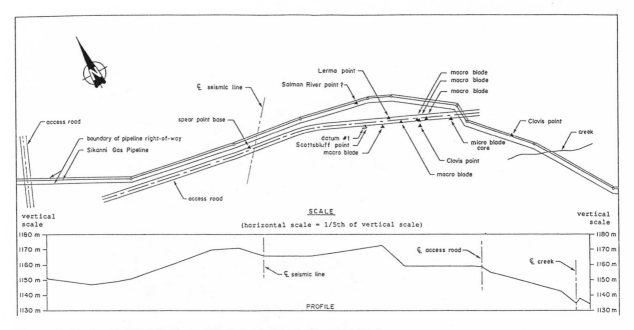

Figure 3. Horizontal distribution of tools and site profile at HrRr 1.

The Lerma/Plano point is thought to be associated with the Northern Cordilleran tradition generally found in or west of the Rocky Mountains which is perhaps coincident with the similar Plano tradition, derived from the Plains. Northern Cordilleran components, dated elsewhere to 6000 to 10,000 BP, lack a microblade industry but do contain blade-like flakes (Clark and Morlan 1982). However, leaf-shaped points are generally not a good time marker in the north.

The Scottsbluff point is the first of its kind found in an archaeological site in BC, though similar materials are known from private collections elsewhere in the province. Scottsbluff is part of the Cody complex, typically associated with the Southern Plains. Cody complex materials are poorly known in Canada but are found as far east as the Great Lakes region in Ontario (Storck 1982) and as far north as the Peace River area in BC, where surface materials are found in private collections (Fladmark 1981). In the Northern Plains, Pettipas (1980) identifies the Little Gem complex based on Scottsbluff points, lower numbers of Eden and Alberta points, with other types similar to Milnesand, Agate Basin, Lerma, and Plainview. A microblade and microcore were also identified as part of the complex. Northern Cody complex sites tend to reveal more recent dates than from the Southern Plains, perhaps indicating a later expansion of Scottsbluff hunters, usually associated with bison kill sites.

Fluted points are known in BC largely through surface collections including material from the Peace River region (Fladmark 1981). Elsewhere in the Canadian west, surface Clovis materials have been found in southern Alberta (Wormington and Forbis 1965), west central Alberta (Doll and Kidd 1978), and the Peace River region of Alberta (Ives 1980). In the north, fluted points are reported in the Northwest Territories (MacNeish 1955), northwest Yukon (Irving and Cinq-Mars 1974), and Alaska (Alexander 1974, Dixon 1976, Dumond 1980). Recent excavations have yielded Clovis-like materials from the foothills of southern Alberta (Gryba 1983) and from Charlie Lake Cave in the BC Peace River region (Fladmark, this volume). The Pink Mountain fluted points bear close resemblance to the point from Charlie Lake Cave, which in turn is similar to Gryba's material from the Alberta foothills. These tools may well form a regional variant of the classic Clovis type associated with the northern Rocky Mountains. Though few dates from northern fluted point assemblages are available, limited evidence suggests a south to north spread of the fluted point tradition. More recent studies have yielded a number of points similar to the Charlie Lake Cave and Pink Mountain specimens, in private collections around the former shoreline of Glacial Lake Peace (Gryba 1988).

In terms of the 1987 inventory, ten new sites were identified with half of these tentatively assigned to Archaic or Paleoindian occupations. Three sites evince unequivocally early point types (Figure 5). HeRp 1 is situated on a high hill overlooking a narrow creek valley about 2 km west of the Halfway River. Several black chert tools are scattered over the surface of the site which has been disturbed by

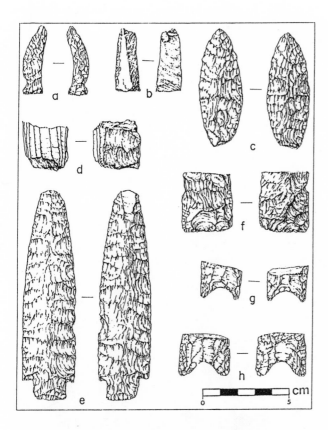

Figure 4. Artifacts from HrRr 1 – (a) side-notched "Salmon River" point fragment; (b) laterally retouched macroblade; (c) leaf-shaped "Lerma" point; (d) microblade core; (e) Scottsbluff point; (f) spear point base; (g, h) fluted "Clovis" points.

cattle ranching. Two spear points were collected from road exposures. One (Figure 5e) is a large point possibly related to an early notched point technology. The second point (Figure 5d) represents a classic Alberta point, known in northeastern BC from private collections (Ball 1978, Spurling 1980). In the northern plains of the United States these points are dated between 9000 and 10,000 BP. Alberta points are also found in Alberta and Saskatchewan. HeRq 1 is located on a small rise near the confluence of the Chowade and Halfway rivers. A small intermittent creek is adjacent to the rise. A number of artifacts of black chert were noted in a roadcut, and local collectors have a large lanceolate point from the site. The point (Figure 5a) is long, narrow, and exhibits parallel flaking, and its base is missing. It is very similar to Agate Basin forms (cf., Frison and Stanford 1982). HeRp 2 was recorded on the basis of a large private collection gathered primarily from cultivated fields and road cuts near the confluence of the Chowade and Halfway rivers. It is obvious that several different sites are represented but the collectors were secretive and the provenance of different tools was not determined. Several artifacts suggest Paleoindian occupations, including one asymmetrical stemmed point resembling those of the poorly reported Nakah phase from Fisherman Lake. This phase is seen to relate to the Northern Plano Tradition dated between 6000 and 9000 years ago (Millar 1968). A large, thin, well-made side-notched spear point (Figure 5c) may also relate to this period. Finally, a base of a fluted point is also present in the collection.

Conclusions are necessarily tentative due to the small amount of data. Early sites are associated with high elevations and with small tributary creeks rather than major water bodies. Elevated ridges or large knolls seem to have been preferred locales, and were possibly dry areas in an otherwise wet postglacial environment.

It is clear that the region has great potential for early material although the nature of the sites is frustrating. Typically, sites tend to be areally large with thinly disbursed material. Soil deposition is minimal and deposits tend to be shallow with little likelihood of vertical separation of components. No organics have yet been recovered from sites in the region and direct dating of deposits is problematic. Compounding these problems are difficulty of access and lack of exposure. Regardless, further work in the region is likely to shed light on early populations.

Figure 5. Early bifaces in local collections examined during the 1987 survey. (a) Agate Basin point from HeRq 1; (b) preform from HeRq 1; (c) notched, concave base point from HeRp 2; (d) Alberta point from HeRp 1; (e) notched point from HeRp 1.

34

5 EARLY HUMAN PRESENCE IN BANFF NATIONAL PARK

Daryl Fedje

Over the past few years excavations at several archaeological sites in Banff National Park have produced significant new data allowing an increased level of interpretation for the Paleoindian period. These sites include Vermilion Lakes and Eclipse, both of which are well dated and among the earliest in Western Canada exhibiting good stratigraphic context. The following will provide brief descriptions of these sites and then focus on the Early Prehistoric or Paleoindian portion of the material record.

The study area lies in the northern Rocky Mountains some 10 km east of the Alberta–BC border (Figure 1). Paleoenvironmental studies conducted by White (1987) indicate the Bow Valley in the environs of the Vermilion Lakes was ice free and available for occupation well before 12,000 BP. The recovery of spear points diagnostic of the Clovis-Goshen and Folsom-Midland horizons from unstratified context at the Minnewanka site (349R/ EhPu 1) suggests that prehistoric people were present in the Banff area by ca. 11,000 BP (Christensen 1971, Fedje 1983, Reeves 1976).

The Vermilion Lakes site (153R/EhPv 8; Figure 2) is situated at the toe of a debris-flow fan on the north side of the Bow River Valley a few kilometers west of the town of Banff. The Paleoindian record at this deeply stratified site includes a minimum of six occupations dating between ca. 10,700 BP and 9600 BP (Fedje and White 1988; Figure 3). Data recovered from investigations conducted between 1983 and 1985 suggest a series of relatively short-term activities; however, excavations were limited in extent and the activity areas encountered likely comprise only a small portion of the record for the site.

The Eclipse site (62R/EhPv 14; Figure 4) is situated on an aeolian capped bedrock bench overlooking the Cascade River a few kilometers east of Banff Townsite. The site is stratified and contains a Late Prehistoric and a Paleoindian component (Fedje 1988a).

The early component is consistently associated with a weak regosol which underlies, in turn, a strongly developed brunisol and a thick layer of Mazama tephra (Figure 5). Organic preservation in this component was poor although sufficient charcoal and charred fat was recovered from a small surface hearth feature to run four radiocarbon (AMS) assays. Following Long and Rippeteau (1974), the mean age for these samples is 9675 BP with a standard error of ca. 75 years.

CULTURAL CONSTRUCTS

The Banff prehistoric record is incompletely known but there are sufficient data to begin construction of a paleocultural framework for this area. Accordingly, tentative construct designations have been developed on the basis of dated components from the Bow and Red Deer valleys (Fedje 1988b). For the earliest part of the record (Figure 6) five phases are proposed based on dates and diagnostic evidence obtained from the aforementioned Vermilion Lakes and Eclipse sites. These constructs in turn have been grouped into trial complexes, Banff I and Banff II, predicated on lithic technology.

Banff I

The earliest phases proposed are Christensen and Minnewanka. These are based on the recovery, from the surface at the Minnewanka site (Figure

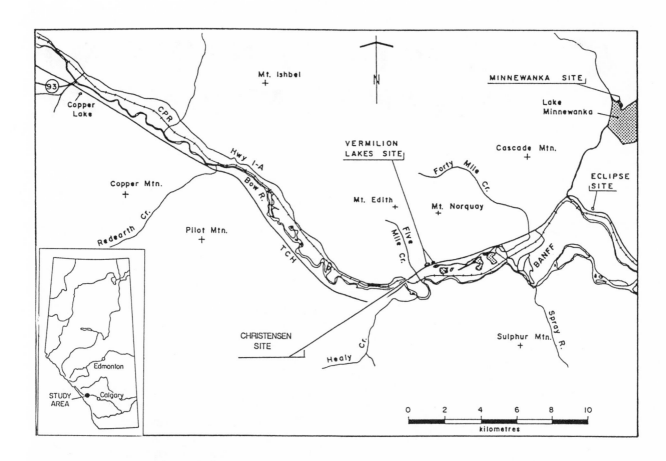

Figure 1. Banff National Park (central portion).

Figure 2. Vermilion Lakes site location.

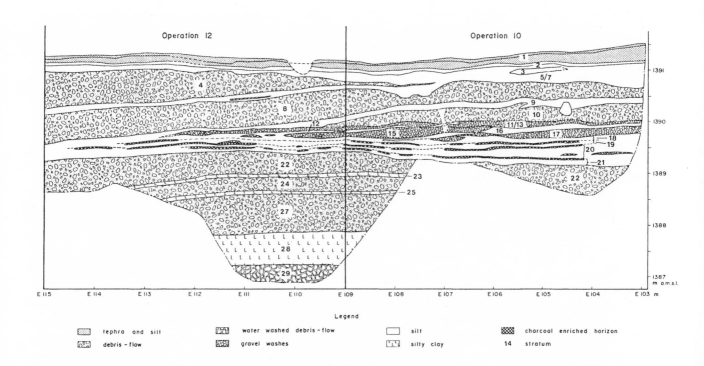

Figure 3. Vermilion Lakes site operation 153R10 south wall profile.

Figure 4. Eclipse site location.

1), of a small collection of basally thinned projectile points (Figure 7a-e) which compare closely to those diagnostic of the Fluted Point Tradition (Frison 1978). The Christensen and Minnewanka phases are suggested to date from ca. 11,000 to 10,600 BP and ca. 10,600 to 10,200 BP respectively from assumed correlation with Clovis (e.g., Figure 7a-c, e) and Folsom (e.g., Figure 7d) complexes described for the northern Plains (Frison 1978). The earliest occupation levels at the Vermilion Lakes site date from 10,700 to 10,300 BP (Fedje and White 1988). These are tentatively assigned to the Minnewanka phase. While no projectile points were recovered from these levels, the dating and lithic assemblages from this site suggest association with the later part of the Fluted Point Tradition.

These phases, then, are grouped to the Banff I complex dating from ca. 11,000 BP to 10,200 BP which is characterized by the use of large basally thinned projectile points apparently hafted onto split or beveled spear shafts or foreshafts. The assemblage of debitage from the Vermilion Lakes site assigned to this complex includes flakes with high platform angles struck from small tabular cores. Debitage includes a significant proportion of lamellar (blade-like) flakes, but large biface thinning flakes and large bifacial cores, common in subsequent subphases, are absent. Bifaces and biface fragments exhibit opportunistic flake scars with relatively deep bulbs of percussion. Biface edges are generally unground during the preform manufacture stage as evident from recovered specimens and from the assemblage of biface thinning flakes.

Lithic material use is strongly dominated by local materials, including more than 99 per cent of the sample of ca. 5000 artifacts. A strong preference for chert is apparent with one material type, black chert from the lower Livingstone and upper Banff formations, constituting more than 95 per cent of the assemblage. Non-local lithic material includes only one specimen of a type sourced to the Western Slopes of the southern Canadian Rocky Mountains (Top of the World).

Although limited, the associated faunal assemblages from the Vermilion Lakes site suggest a focus on exploitation of sheep and a lesser emphasis on bison. Habitation structures or windbreaks are inferred from features at this site. These include a circular (3.5 m diameter) above-ground structure likely constructed with poles and a hide or vegetal covering. Associated hearths were small and neither lined nor excavated. These early occupations at the Vermilion Lakes site support a general hunting and gathering adaptation by peoples already familiar with local resources.

Banff II

The subsequent phases are Vermilion at ca. 10,200 BP to ca. 9800 BP and Eclipse at ca. 9800 BP to ca. 9600 BP. These are better known with several occupation layers at the Vermilion Lakes site (Fedje and White 1988) assigned to the former and one each from the Vermilion Lakes and Eclipse sites (Fedje 1988a) assigned to the latter. Both phases are characterized by stemmed projectile points, large bifacial cores, and large stone tools. There is an increased use of microcrystalline siltstones and quartzites, for stone tool manufacture.

These phases are differentiated solely on the basis of age and associated diagnostic projectile points. The points are leaf-shaped (Vermilion) and shouldered (Eclipse) respectively (Figure 7f, g-i), and both types appear designed for setting into a socket-type haft as described by Bryan (1980) for the Stemmed Point Tradition.

The assemblage of large bifacial cores, massive thinning flakes, and large stone tools recovered from the aforementioned Vermilion/Eclipse components is also consistent with those of early Stemmed Point assemblages of the Columbia Plateau (Choquette 1987b) and Great Basin (Bryan 1988). This is in contrast to the stronger focus on small- to medium-size flake tools and greater emphasis on production of blade-like flakes observed in the earliest levels at the Vermilion Lakes site and in Fluted Point age site assemblages from the Plains in the northern United States (Frison 1978, Frison and Stanford 1982).

Although sample sizes are not large, material use between the Vermilion/Eclipse phase components and the earliest levels at the Vermilion Lakes site (pre-10,200 BP) is quite different (Figure 8). Siltstone and quartzites account for 64 per cent of the Vermilion assemblages and 67 per cent of the Eclipse assemblages with cherts accounting for the remainder (about 35 per cent for each). This is opposed to the aforementioned pre–10,200 BP assemblages, where siltstones and quartzites account for 4 per cent of the total and cherts 96 per cent. Non-local lithic materials account for about 1 per cent in each of the phases. Most of this is a siliceous sandstone with the nearest known outcrops being in the Kananaskis area, 60 to 80 km southeast of the Vermilion Lakes.

The Banff II complex dating from ca. 10,200 to 9600 BP combines these (Vermilion and Eclipse) phases (and very tentatively the Norquay phase as well) and is characterized by the use of stemmed pro-

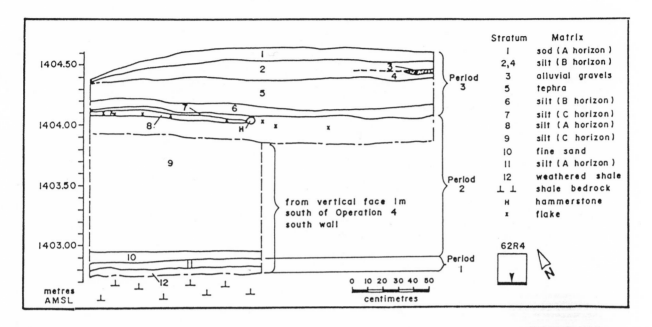

Figure 5. Eclipse site, south wall profile, operation 4.

jectile points (Figure 7) apparently used on socketed spear shafts or foreshafts. Large stone tools are also diagnostic of this construct. These include massive domed endscrapers, slab and cobble choppers (Figures 9, 10), and various tools produced from very large biface thinning flakes (Figure 11). Blade-like flakes are rare. Lithic material use is dominated by microcrystalline sedimentary rock (more than 60 per cent) including primarily local weakly siliceous siltstones and secondarily local quartzites.

Lithic technology was very efficient employing low angle reduction of bifacial (discoidal) cores (Figure 12). Bifaces exhibit broad shallow bulbar scars. Biface preform edges were heavily ground as is evident from recovered fragments and from biface thinning flakes, a large proportion of which exhibit heavy grinding on (low angle) striking platform remnants. Large flake blanks produced in this process were used as simple tools and subsequently discarded or marginally retouched, or were worked into unifacial formed tools such as perforators and side scrapers. Large bifaces were the end product of bifacial core reduction with these "exhausted cores" worked into spear points or bifacial knives.

Non-local materials account for about 1 per cent of total lithics with most of this being siliceous sandstone from sources in the foothills and Front Ranges of the Rocky Mountains immediately south and east of the Banff area. Cherts are still strongly dominated by local black chert from the Banff and Livingstone formations. Soapstone, recovered from one occupation, derives from the Cathedral formation with the closest known source in the alpine just west of the Continental Divide. Utilization of all parts of this mountain valley area is indicated.

Faunal assemblages from this period are better known than for Banff I. Sheep are by far the most abundant species utilized although deer, bison, and small mammals such as beaver and hare were also exploited.

Habitation structures were apparently small with maximum dimensions of less than 4 m; but evidence in this regard is scanty and therefore equivocal. Hearths were unlined and include both surface and shallow basin (excavated) types. Sandstone slabs associated with some hearths were apparently used as roasting surfaces.

As with Banff I, these people were well adapted to this mountain valley environment and familiar with a wide range of resources. There is more evidence for association with other mountain valley groups to the south than for the former construct but, it must be reiterated that sample sizes are small for both constructs and all interpretations must be considered tentative at this time.

Yrs BP	Complex	Phase	Diagnostic	Complex	Phase	Diagnostic
0		Piegan/Stoney/Kutenay Kutenay Echo Creek* Spray River*	Musketball cf., Kootenay s.n. cf., Prairie s.n.		Shuswap Red Deer III*	Kamloops Horizon[1] types
1000		Sawback*	Avonlea s.n., tri.			
2000	Banff IV	Fortymile*	Besant s.n.	Red Deer	Red Deer II*	Plateau Horizon[1] types
3000		Second Lake*	cf., Pelican Lake			
		Beaverdam	cf., Hanna s.n.		Red Deer I*	Shuswap Horizon[1] types
		Muleshoe	McKean			
4000						
5000		Bow River II*	Early side notched	s.n. side notched tri. triangular ~ stratified context underlying Mazama tephra * stratified context, C-14 dated		
6000	Banff III					
7000		Bow River I*	Early corner notched	**Note** Cultural construct boundaries are approximate.		
8000		Timberline	cf., Lusk	The relationship and timing (sequent and/or contemporary occupations) of some Banff IV (Kootenay and/or Blackfoot) and Red Deer (Salishan) complex sites is not certain. The ethnographic and archaeological records reveal major shifts in the territories or ranges of these groups and ethnicity can only be assigned with confidence to a small number of sites in the park.		
	?	Cascade River~	cf., Scottsbluff			
9000		Norquay~	Norquay stemmed			
10,000	Banff II	Eclipse* Vermilion*	Eclipse stemmed Vermilion stemmed	[1]Richards and Rousseau 1987		
		Minnewanka*	cf., Folsom, Midland			
11,000	Banff I	Christensen	cf., Clovis, Goshen			

Figure 6. A provisional paleocultural sequence for the Banff region (from Fedje 1988b).

Figure 7. Projectile points from Banff National Park. (a-c, e) Christensen phase (cf., Clovis complex) basally thinned points from the Minnewanka site; (d) Minnewanka phase (cf., Folsom complex) basally thinned point from the Minnewanka site; (f) Vermilion phase leaf-shaped stemmed point from the Vermilion Lakes site; (g) Eclipse phase shouldered stemmed points from the Vermilion Lakes and (h, i) Eclipse sites; (j) Norquay stemmed point from the Norquay site.

41

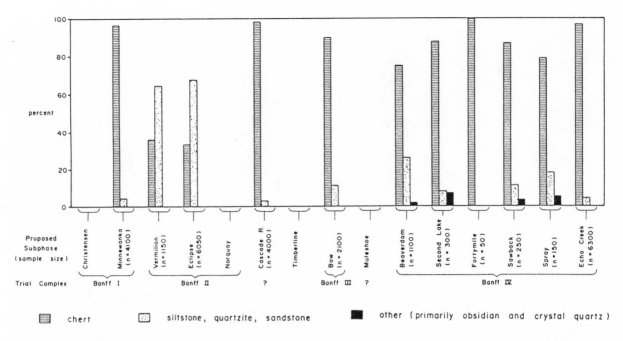

Figure 8. Material type percentages in Banff assemblages.

DISCUSSION

Data appear adequate to make a case for significant change between Banff I and Banff II. The evidence is primarily technological and includes a significant difference in approach to lithic reduction and in choice of stone employed.

Banff I reduction technology could employ relatively small chert nodules or thinly bedded cherts most of which are quite brecciated in this area. Although over 4000 artifacts are assigned to this complex, this number includes less than 0.5 per cent formed tools. These are dominated by small bifaces, sidescrapers, and gravers. No large stone tools were recovered from Banff I levels.

Banff II (Stemmed Point Tradition) technology was dependent upon use of large non-brecciated cobbles or blocks available locally only from relatively massive sedimentary sources such as quartzites, siltstones, and fine sandstones. Lithic production was primarily by low angle reduction of large biface cores in contrast to the focus on high angle reduction of tabular cores evident in Banff I assemblages. The Banff II tool kit is quite extensive and, in addition to the diagnostic stemmed points, is characterized by large unifacial stone tools including massive domed scrapers, choppers, and flake tools.

This complex compares favourably with elements of the Stemmed Point Tradition (Bryan 1980, 1988, Carlson 1983a) which is proposed by Bryan (1988) to have originated in the Intermontane West

(Columbia-Great Basin) area of what is now northwestern United States) before 11,000 BP. Bryan hypothesizes that this tradition replaced the Fluted Point Tradition in the Eastern Slopes of Wyoming through to southern Alberta by about 10,500 BP. Just west of the Divide, Choquette (1982, 1987a, this volume) documents a complex of traits with strong similarities to that of the proposed Banff II complex for the Kootenay area of southern BC, northern Idaho, and northwestern Montana. These traits include a "preference for fine-grained siliceous sedimentary stone ... a lithic technology oriented primarily to production of large expanding flakes with low angle striking platforms from large bifacial cores ... a tool kit dominated by large bifaces, large discoidal unifaces, and large unifacial flake tools" (Choquette 1982:3). This Goatfell complex apparently dates from ca. 11,000 BP to ca. 8000 BP and is assigned to the early Stemmed Point Tradition.

The Banff I and II assemblages are sufficiently different to suggest the introduction of a distinct technology into the Banff area shortly before 10,000 years ago. Both the Plains and the Intermontane West are possible sources for this change, although the strong similarities between Banff II and the Goatfell complex point more directly to the latter.

SUMMARY

The Banff I and Banff II complexes both appear to support a strongly local mountain valley hunter-gatherer adaptation by people already familiar with the area and its resources. Evidence of movement or contact beyond the area of the local seasonal round is limited, although the introduction of fine siliceous sandstone from the eastern slopes just south of the Banff area suggests consistent contact with other mountain valley adapted groups to the south during Banff II complex times. The introduction of Stemmed Point Tradition technol-

ogy may well have been from the south via such eastern slopes groups.

These interpretations must be considered tentative at this time as both site type and component assemblage samples are relatively small and may not be truly representative. However, they do provide direction and potential avenues for further research.

Figure 9. Large domed scrapers from Banff II complex occupation levels at the Eclipse (a) and Vermilion Lakes (b,c) sites.

Figure 10. Choppers from Banff II occupation levels at the Eclipse (a) and Vermilion Lakes (b,c) sites.

Figure 11. Flake tools from Banff II occupation levels at the Vermilion Lakes (a-f) and the Eclipse (g) sites.

Figure 13. Cores (a, b) and bifaces (c, d) from Banff I occupation levels at the Vermilion Lakes site.

Figure 12. Discoidal cores (a, b) and refit biface (c) from the Eclipse site.

44

6

EARLY POST-GLACIAL HABITATION OF THE UPPER COLUMBIA REGION

Wayne Choquette

This chapter discusses some aspects of the early post-glacial archaeological record of the upper Columbia River basin, which consists of the land drained by the main stem of the Columbia River and its tributaries above the mouth of the Spokane River (Figure 1). A discussion of the paleoenvironment considers geological, climatological, and palynological data resulting from a number of independent studies. This is followed by summary descriptions of two archaeological complexes, the Goatfell complex and the Shonitkwu Period microblade complex. The chapter concludes with a synthesis and an assessment of the significance of these data. The archaeological record derives from a variety of survey and excavation projects directed by the author, from an excavation directed by Diana French, and from the sequence developed for the Kettle Falls locality by David Chance of the University of Idaho.

PALEOENVIRONMENTAL CONSIDERATIONS

The efforts of paleoenvironmental researchers during the past twenty years have rewarded us with a much clearer picture of the timing and events associated with the deglaciation and vegetal colonization of Western Canada, though admittedly much work remains to be done refining the sequence. It is apparent that Prest's 1969 ice cover map with its huge ice sheets and isochrons suspiciously paralleling the international boundary is not an accurate depiction of the latest Pleistocene glaciation. The serrated crests of the southern Canadian Rocky Mountains are ample evidence that there never was a coalescent ice mass covering the entirety of southern Canada. Glaciation was extensive at times during the Pleistocene, to be sure, and all but the highest

peaks to the west of the Rockies were apparently overridden by ice at least once. However, it must always be born in mind that the ultimate source of glacial ice is the ocean and we are considering mountainous terrain of extremely varied composition. As archaeologists, we must scrutinize our biases regarding early human inhabitation that are influenced by geological extrapolations into poorly known terrain. Many of them do not take climate and physiography sufficiently into account, and furthermore, can suffer from data discontinuities produced by the international boundary.

The evidence now at hand does not support the conception that the southern half of British Columbia was beneath one coalescent mass of ice in the last 20,000 years. Instead, the large valley glaciers which occupied the Flathead Valley and the Rocky Mountain Trench evidently headed in discrete ice caps and were nourished by many tributary glaciers originating in individual cirques. Further research will likely confirm an apparent non-synchroneity between the documented advances and retreats in the Cascade and Coast ranges and those events at the eastern edge of the Cordillera. Out-of-phase glacial activity resulting from differences in elevation and relationships to water source and prevailing winds has been documented in the mountains at the BC-Alaska boundary (Miller and Anderson 1974). This may be analogous, on a smaller scale, to the terminal Pleistocene situation in the Cordillera as a whole. At that time, the growth and decay of the smaller ice caps that debouched into the valleys now drained by the Columbia River and its tributaries could have been responses to their own mass balances which would in turn have been strongly influenced by local conditions.

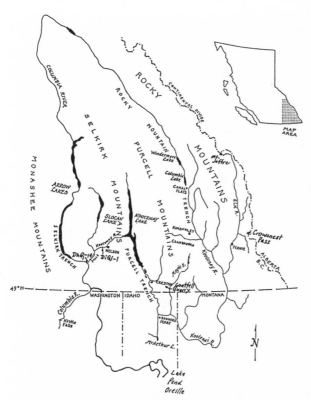

Figure 1. The upper Columbia River drainage.

The study area is as far from the ultimate source of the glacial ice (the oceans) as geography permits, so an assertion that it was not as extensively glaciated as areas further west should come as no surprise. Furthermore, it was apparently deglaciated sooner. The widespread occurrence throughout the upper Columbia drainage of varved lacustrine sediments and abandoned valley-wall deltas and beaches indicates that there was probably as much water as ice in the region in latest Pleistocene times (Figure 2). Geological studies have not yet provided an absolute chronology for all of the lakes, but several dates provide a useful elevational sequence. Glacial Lake Missoula was a particularly large pro-glacial lake which came close to spilling over the Crowsnest Pass at its highest stand, 1358 m above sea level (a.s.l.) when it also extended well up the Rocky Mountain Trench. Glacial Lake Missoula drained catastrophically prior to 13,000 years ago (Mullineaux et al. 1978). Glacial Lake Elk in the Elk Valley was impounded by an independent ice lobe originating on the flanks of the Lizard Range; it spilled over the Crowsnest Pass until it emptied, probably catastrophically, before 12,000 BP (Harrison 1976). Glacial Lake Kootenai in the lower Kootenay River basin had been at a 762 m a.s.l. stand for some time before both Mount St. Helens J and Glacier Peak G

tephras were deposited in it (Mierendorf 1984). Mount St. Helens layer J dates to about 11,800 BP (Mullineaux et al. 1975), while Glacier Peak layer G is no younger than about 11,200 BP (Mehringer, Sheppard, and Foit Jr. 1984). Further west, on the other hand, "the absence of layer G from a substantial area of northern Washington ... indicates that the margin of the ice sheet in most areas was south of the International Boundary" (Clague 1981:17) when this tephra was ejected. A lower or limiting age estimate for the abandonment of the 762 m outlet in the southern Purcell Mountains and the establishment of the Kootenay River regime above 700 m is provided by a date of 11,730 ±410 BP (Beta-5228) on charred plant remains collected from the earliest burned floodplain surface found in the middle Kootenay Valley (Mierendorf 1984:120). Glacial Lake Columbia subsequently occupied the Glacial Lake Kootenai basin. Its extent is indicated by a prominent terrace at 595 m that extends up the Columbia River from the Richmond, Fryxell, Neff, and Weis (1965) "Great Terrace" at the Grand Coulee to north of Revelstoke, BC and up the Kootenay River to east of Libby, Montana. An upper limiting age assessment for this large lake is provided by dates of 10,000 ±150 (GSC 1012) and 9990 ±150 (GSC 1059) on the 488 m above sea level shoreline of a much smaller lake in the Selkirk Trench (Fulton 1971).

As with the geological dates, this relatively understudied part of northwestern North America does not have precise chronological control on early postglacial biotic representation. However, palynologists unanimously infer an open vegetation in which sage, grasses, birch, spruce, and fir are prominent 12,000 or more years ago (cf. Ferguson and Hills, 1985, Mack et al. 1978a and 1978b, Mack, Rutter, and Valastro 1978, Hebda 1981). The charred plant remains on the earliest burned floodplain in the Middle Kootenay Valley mentioned above indicate that fire was already part of the regional ecology by 11,730 ±410 years ago.

Acidic soils have thus far frustrated attempts to obtain a faunal record from early contexts west of the continental divide. The potentially earliest remains are at present only unconfirmed word-of-mouth reports of "large bones" from deeper than 8 m in a gravel pit near the Crowsnest Pass and two proboscidean teeth from the west side of Kootenay Lake near Kaslo, BC. Abundant fauna have been reported from the adjacent eastern slope. The presence of landlocked salmon in Kootenay Lake may be taken to indicate that anadromous salmon once ran at least that far. In historic times, Pacific salmon could not ascend the falls on the Kootenay River below Kootenay Lake. The 10,000 BP dates on the 488 m lake in the Selkirk Trench cited above provide an upper limiting age for the present 532 m a.s.l. level of Kootenay Lake that is controlled by these falls. The conclusion that salmon could have been ascending into the study area before 10,000 years ago is entirely within expectations: one must bear in mind that the mouth of the Columbia and many of its tributaries are well to the south of the Pleistocene ice front and salmon runs were undoubtedly established in that drainage long before any of British Columbia's other rivers could support them. We should also be aware of the possibility that other fish, such as steelhead and charr, could have also been present in significant quantities.

Two important paleoclimatic factors must be considered with regard to the deglaciation of the upper Columbia drainage and its colonization by plants, animals, and humans at an early time level. The first is physiographic configuration: the Columbia Plateau in present-day Washington consists of a large level expanse rimmed by mountains. The south end of the Monashee and Selkirk mountains of the Columbia Mountain system meet with the Purcell-Cabinet-Bitterroot chain to form a great arc bounding this enclosed basin on the north and east. This arc forms a huge southwest-facing "solar-bowl" with a large thermal mass. From a northwestern North American perspective, this would create a favourable "microclimate" with respect to surrounding regions.

The second paleoclimatic factor is the influence of the Pleistocene glaciers themselves on atmospheric circulation. The presence of a great expanse of ice to the northeast contributed to a predominantly meridional circulation (Vance 1987). In combination with the katabatic flow of dense frigid air and divergence from a high pressure centre over the Laurentide ice mass, this would have resulted in a southwestward air flow toward the study area for a significantly greater proportion of the year than is characteristic of modern times. The study area would be in the sheltered leeward of mountains, favouring the creation of adiabatic or "chinook-like" conditions on the western flanks of the Rocky, Purcell, and Selkirk mountains. The upper Columbia region, especially the western part, could thus have been influenced by a dry northeasterly airflow in late Pleistocene times. The well-defined "steppe tundra" of sage, grass, and scattered spruce and fir that characterizes the pre-10,000 BP pollen spectra of the great southwest-facing arc in northeastern Washington, northern Idaho, southeastern-most BC, and northwestern Montana seems to be a community

adapted to cold, dry conditions. This can be contrasted with the tundra communities dominated by herbs and birch that inhabited areas to the northeast. The distribution of these early plant communities is consistent with the circulation regime postulated above.

Summarizing this section, it can be concluded that glaciation in the upper Columbia drainage during the latest Pleistocene was not as extensive as in areas further west or north. The area was ice-free sooner, and the landscape during the period between at least 13,000 years ago and 10,500 BP was dominated by large branching lakes and an open vegetal cover dominated by sage, grasses, and scattered conifers.

THE ARCHAEOLOGICAL RECORD
The Goatfell Complex

The earliest cultural components known at present in the upper Columbia have been found on terraces, beaches, dunes, and glaciofluvial bars at or above the 595 m level of Glacial Lake Columbia. This archaeological manifestation, named the Goatfell complex, has been described in detail elsewhere (cf., Choquette 1982a, 1982b, 1984a-c, 1985, 1987a, 1987b) and will be summarized only briefly here.

The lithic technology of the Goatfell complex people was characterized by the production of large expanding flake blanks by percussion from large bifacial cores after platform abrasion. A marked preference for microcrystalline stone, primarily tourmalinite and quartzite, is evident. Also characteristic are large sidescrapers, discoidal unifaces, and flake tools. Most of the projectile points from above 595 m a.s.l. are stemmed, weakly shouldered forms, many exceeding 10 cm in length (Figure 3). Some of them are percussion flaked.

The Goatfell complex is well represented in a linear series of workshops extending from Goatfell Quarry in the southwestern Purcell Mountains southward and westward to the shores of Glacial Lake Columbia. This settlement pattern likely represents seasonal transhumance between valley bottom lakeside winter camps and summer hunting and quarrying terrain in the mountains.

Direct radiocarbon dating of the Goatfell complex has yet to be accomplished. However, Goatfell complex cultural deposits were found in the earliest fluvial sediments deposited on the highest post-glacial terrace in the Moyie River valley (Choquette 1983) and more than a metre below a pre-Mazama unconformity in the Purcell Trench (Gough 1984). The geomorphological associations and the presence of a viable environment at least 12,000 years ago both support a postulated antiquity of 11,000 or

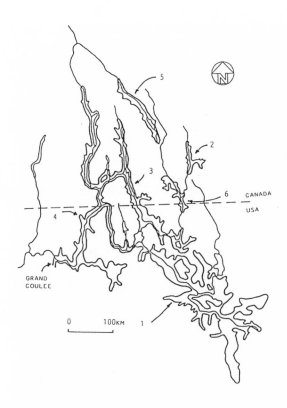

Figure 2. Major pro-glacial lakes in the Upper Columbia Drainage (after Alden 1953, Kelley and Sprout 1956, Kelley and Holland 1961, and Richmond et al. 1965). (1) Glacial Lake Missoula; (2) Glacial Lake Elk; (3) Glacial Lake Kootenai; (4) Glacial Lake Columbia; (5) Glacial Lake Windermere; (6) Unnamed. (NB These lakes were not all contemporaneous; thus the eastern part of Glacial Lake Columbia was within the pre-existing Glacial Lake Kootenai basin and both Glacial Lake Elk and the unnamed glacial lake in the Rocky Mountain Trench may have been within the maximum extent of Glacial Lake Missoula. The actual northward extent of the latter has yet to be determined.)

more years BP for the inception of the Goatfell complex land and resource use pattern. Cultural deposits of the related Windust Phase found in the gravels of the Clearwater River, Idaho only some 200 km south of the present study area have been dated at 10,800 BP (Ames et al. 1981).

The Shonitkwu Period

Kettle Falls on the Columbia River 40 km south of the international boundary was the second most important aboriginal fishery on that river in late prehistoric/early historic time. Now within the Roosevelt Reservoir impounded by the Grand Coulee Dam, the vicinity of the falls was the subject of intensive archaeological salvage investigations during the 1970s (cf., Chance and Chance 1977a, 1977b, 1979, 1982, 1985, Chance, Chance, and Fagan 1977).

Artifacts characteristic of the earliest cultural period defined for the locality, the Shonitkwu, include leaf-shaped and lanceolate projectile points, large flake tools, cobble sinkers with double ground notches, a substantial bone industry, and a well-developed microblade industry that includes at least one keeled microcore. The predominant lithic materials are locally available quartzite from which a range of heavy tools was made, plus brown, black, and maroon argillite from the adjacent mountains. There are no radiocarbon dates for the Shonitkwu Period, but the deposits occur in cobble gravels well below Mazama ash.

Further up the Columbia, the early prehistory is not well documented at present, since most of the archaeology has been focused on cultural depressions. However, two possible candidates for Shonitkwu Period occupation have been identified. One is DiQi 1, a stratified site at the uppermost falls on the Kootenay River below Kootenay Lake, where the stratigraphically earliest component identified by French (1973) occurred below a component characterized by large side-notched points. The earliest assemblage contains five bifaces, six retouched flakes, a graver, and four microblades, three of which were of local Kootenay argillite. This component was also distinguished by the local occurrence of a banded rhyolite not present in later deposits. The second site, DhQj 14, is situated on a high terrace more than 120 m above the present confluence of the Kootenay and Columbia rivers. This site is being severely eroded at the present time, revealing a number of well-developed buried soil horizons. Several varieties of volcanic and low grade metamorphic stone including rhyolite, maroon and black argillite, and Kootenay argillite are represented in the surface collected sample from this site. There is one unused keeled or wedge-shaped microblade core (Figure 4), plus several core rejuvenation flakes from wedge-shaped, conical, and tabular microblade cores. Larger lamellar flakes of coarser argillites are also present, as are biface thinning flakes. Four projectile points have been surface collected from this site, two leaf-shaped, one lanceolate, and one large side-notched.

The lithic material represented in this assemblage is strikingly dissimilar to that of the Goatfell complex, a sparse representation of Kootenay argillite being the only common characteristic. The maroon, black, and brown argillites represent links with Kettle Falls, but the volcanics suggest a northwest orientation as well. The technology is also dissimilar to that of the Goatfell complex. The function of the microblades is of course conjectural, but a riverine orientation of the Shonitkwu Period culture is obvious when one considers that fishing was carried out at Kettle Falls and some type of watercraft must have been used to reach Hayes Island at the falls where the major occupation sites are situated (Chance, Chance, and Fagan 1977).

DISCUSSION

There are obvious similarities between the large stemmed points of the Goatfell complex and those found associated with Pleistocene levels of pluvial lakes in the Great Basin. Several writers (eg., Bryan 1980, Carlson 1983a) include Windust/Lind Coulee stemmed points within a generalized stemmed point tradition that dominates the early assemblages of intermontane western North America. The Goatfell complex can be added to this tradition. The lithic technology of sites associated with the pluvial lakes is not consistently reported upon in the literature, but as a sample, the following statements by Davis (1968:46) regarding the Panamint Basin in southern California are representative: "A biface series characterizes these and related industries … Primary flakes and trimming flakes were frequently massive and sidestruck." That an identical lithic technology characterized the Goatfell complex and the widespread early archaeological remains from the now-desert basin and range province is an even stronger indication of a cultural relationship than the close similarities in projectile point morphology.

Warren and Ranere (1968:12) noted that there is no evidence of an adaptation to an arid environment in the earliest cultural layers in the Great Basin. Indeed, it is apparent that the late Pleistocene paleoenvironment of the Great Basin was quite similar to that of the study area in immediate post-glacial time.

A mosaic of subalpine conifers and shrub communities covered much of the Great Basin region during the Late Wisconsin … Sagebrush steppe, shrub communities, meadows, and pockets of conifers would have formed a Late Wisconsin continent of cool summer habitat from the Wasatch Front across the Great Basin to the Sierra Nevada … Much of the northern Great Basin was covered by cold-dry steppe during the Late Wisconsin (Thompson and Mead 1982:44, 50).

It is known that extensive portions of the Great Basin were occupied by large pluvial lakes during the Late Pleistocene. As understanding of the chronology of the pluvial lake system grows, it becomes apparent that the paleoclimatic dynamics were complex. For example, two of the larger lakes, Lahontan and Bonneville, were apparently out of phase during the Late Wisconsin, the former having two high stands between 25,000 and 22,000 BP and 13,500 and 11,000 BP (Benson 1978). The latter reached its highest stand about 16,000 BP, drained catastrophically to a stand about 100 m lower, then began a slow recession before 13,000 BP (Scott, McCoy, Shroba, and Rubin 1983). This east-west variability in lake cycles in the northern Great Basin is likely related to the east-west variability in the chronology of deglaciation further north. By 11,000 BP, fluctuations of what was left of Lake Bonneville were no more than 12 m above the present Great Salt Lake and most of the rest of the pluvial lakes had likewise drained by 11,000 BP.

The picture that emerges is one of a Late Pleistocene environment in the Great Basin that was characterized by extensive lakes in the valley bottoms, sage, grass, and shrub communities on the lower slopes, and islands of subalpine conifers in sheltered places at higher elevation. This environment persisted until 10,500 to 11,000 years ago and is basically the same type of environment that is represented in the pollen assemblages from the study area that date in the 13,000 to 10,500 BP range.

Evidence of human inhabitation of the Great Basin in the late Pleistocene is not abundant, but it is clear that people were also part of at least the latest stages of the pluvial lake environment. The northward time slope for the ages of these early remains compared to the ages of the Windust Phase and the Goatfell complex parallels the time slope for the development of post-glacial vegetation in the upper Columbia. When this is combined with the cultural relationships demonstrated by the lithic artifact assemblages, an obvious conclusion is that humans moved northward out of the Great Basin as the pluvial lakes dried out in terminal Pleistocene times. They entered the study area from the south, following the montane parkland-steppe-lacustrine ecosystem as it expanded into deglaciated terrain.

In contrast, a northern origin for the Shonitkwu Period microblade industry is an inescapable conclusion when one considers the lithic material representation and especially the lithic technology. With regard to wedge-shaped microblade cores, Carlson (1983a:93) has observed that such artifacts are diagnostic of Late Paleolithic industries found

Figure 3. Stemmed bifaces from local collections: (a) biface from the Moyie River Valley, BC, 14.8 cm long; (b) point from Lake Pend Oreille, Idaho, 6 cm long; (c) point from Kootenay Lake, BC, 9.7 cm long.

Figure 4. Microblade core and rejuvenation flake from DhQj 14.

in Siberia and have heretofore only been known in North America from the Arctic and from Mount Edziza in northwestern BC. It would appear that the Shonitkwu Period inhabitation is a representation of the ephemeral presence of early microblade-using people who passed through northwestern North America in early post-glacial time.

SUMMARY AND CONCLUSION

This paper has described two distinctive archaeological manifestations that were present in the area drained by the upper Columbia River in early post-glacial time. The Goatfell complex is apparently the older since its earliest manifestation is found associated with pro-glacial lakes. It displays a focus on the southwestern Purcell Mountains where its bearers quarried black tourmalinite and processed it via a biface core technology into large bifaces and side-struck flake tools. Most of the projectile points are stemmed forms. These technological attributes, plus the apparent initial orientation to a lacustrine setting, link the Goatfell complex with the late Pleistocene archaeological complexes defined for the Great Basin to the south.

The second early post-glacial archaeological manifestation is focused on the falls and confluence of the Columbia and lower Kootenay rivers at the southwestern edge of the study area. It is characterized by a microblade industry and the utilization of an almost entirely different suite of raw materials,

materials, predominantly argillites and rhyolites. These characteristics ally the Shonitkwu Period assemblages with the north from which the people responsible for their deposition must have come.

Carlson (1983a and Chapter 1)) has identified five early basal cultural traditions, each different in content and each adapted to a somewhat different ecological niche. As described in this chapter, two of these, the Intermontane Stemmed Point Tradition and the Microblade Tradition, are represented in the study area. Their expressions here are sufficiently different to warrant the conclusion that these two complexes probably represent the remains of two separate cultural groups. The former arrived in the region from the south where its bearers apparently lived around the large pluvial lakes during the last major Pleistocene stade, whereas the latter was a more recent arrival in North America via the Bering Land Bridge during or at at the end of that stade.

It is clear from the paleoenvironmental record that the upper Columbia drainage had become free of glacial influence earlier than had regions to the west and north. The archaeological record indicates that the evolution of the region's environment had reached a sufficient degree of diversity by terminal Pleistocene/early Holocene time to have supported two divergent human cultural adaptive patterns. While it is true that the study area is in an out-of-the-way part of the country and province, its geographic setting contains a most significant heritage record. We have only scratched the surface of what these sites may have to offer, and it is imperative that efforts be increased to ensure the preservation of this precious heritage.

7 THE PASIKA COMPLEX REVISITED

Shawn Haley

In 1968, Charles Borden published the following hypothesis concerning the cultural assemblage recovered from the South Yale site (Figure 1) in southwestern British Columbia:

> The stone technology of these early groups that camped on the banks of the Fraser River in late glacial times apparently had NOT reached the stage which would have enabled them to manufacture thin, bifacially worked knives and projectile points ... Not only in their stone technology but also in their hunting methods they appear to have persisted in continuing traditions resembling those of a very ancient chopper and chopping-tool culture of eastern Asia (Movius 1949, Chard 1959). (Borden 1968b:12)

Borden contended that the unifacial pebble tool industry that dominated the South Yale assemblage represented an early tradition which he called the Pasika complex and characterized as follows:

1) It consisted predominantly of core tools made on well-rounded river cobbles (Figure 2). They comprised a wide range of specialized types of readily discernible form and pattern.

2) The remainder were spalls or flakes. Some were retouched but none was deliberately retouched to achieve a particular form.

3) All of the artifacts were unifacially flaked by hard hammer percussors with some preliminary reduction being accomplished using a bipolar technique (cf., Haley 1981; 1982).

4) Perhaps the most important characterization was a negative one:

> Pasika materials recovered from undisturbed deposits are not associated with artifacts or other manifestations of any of the dated post-Pleistocene cultures in the Fraser Canyon ... [The Pasika stoneworkers] ... seem to have lacked the techniques required for flattening and thinning stone projectile points and knives of thin bifacial form (Borden 1968a:61, cf., Borden 1968b, 1968c, 1973, 1975)

He placed Pasika at the bottom of the known Fraser Canyon chronological sequence and assigned it a date of 12-11,500 to 9000 years BP (Figure 3). He also suggested that the South Yale material was similar to the ancient chopper/chopping-tool complexes of eastern Asia (Borden 1968b:12, 1968c, 1969). It should be noted that Borden had had a longstanding interest in the peopling of the New World and in Asia-North America aboriginal contact. This interest is illustrated by the number of papers he wrote on that subject (Borden 1954, 1962, 1968c, 1969, 1973, 1975, 1979).

In short order, this late Pleistocene pebble tool industry acquired the status of a cultural tradition and was cited as evidence for early humans in the New World in a number of summary and introductory texts. Unfortunately, the database, a complete South Yale site report, was never presented and it was necessary for scholars to accept or reject the Pasika hypothesis largely on faith. The reactions of other researchers were mixed (Browman and Munsell 1969, MacDonald 1971, Willey 1966), although, as the data available had to be extracted from preliminary or summary papers (Borden 1968a, 1968b, 1968c, 1973, 1975, Mathewes et al. 1972, Mitchell 1965), the majority of researchers adopted a wait-and-see position. That position remained essentially unchanged for almost two decades.

Archaeologists working on the Northwest Coast were forced to deal with the Borden hypothesis whenever cobble tools were recovered from their sites. One of the most effective reactions to the cobble tool problem was developed by R.L. Carlson (1979) using data gathered from the site of Namu on the central coast of British Columbia. He suggested that the cobble tool assemblages could be subdivided into two segments which he called the early and the late Pebble Tool Tradition (Carlson 1979, 1983a). The essential difference between these two segments lies in the character of the assemblages. Both phases contained hammerstones, large flakes, pebble cores, and unifacial pebble tools, but bifaces were present in the late phase and absent from the early phase (Carlson 1979:221-2). The Pasika complex fit into the early Pebble Tool Tradition. Other attempts to determine the what and when of Pasika have all met with limited success. So, after lengthy discussions with Carlson and other Northwest Coast scholars, it was decided that I should re-examine the raw data (artifacts and site records) from the South Yale site in the hope that the problem of the early Pebble Tool Tradition could be resolved one way or the other. The results of this new study (Haley 1987), of which this chapter is a summary, clearly disputes Borden's late Pleistocene pebble tool industry hypothesis. There is no *early* Pebble Tool Tradition, only a *late* Pebble Tool Tradition.

LATE PLEISTOCENE CULTURE
Each major characteristic or line of evidence used to support the concept that the South Yale assemblage represented the remains of a late Pleistocene pebble tool industry were examined. What follows is a summary of that examination.

Chopper Typology
It was suggested that the pebble tools, the choppers, exhibited a wide range of specialized types of readily recognizable form and pattern related directly to function (Borden 1968a:61). This idea, that the Pasika choppers consisted of typologically distinct classes, was a key aspect of the overall hypothesis. The types were tested using a set of sixteen variables (including Borden type) (Table 1) to see if the at-

tributes clustered around the discernible types. The G-statistic test of independence (Sokal and Rohlf 1969) was applied to seventy-eight pairs of variables in a random sample of 200 choppers from the South Yale site. The results did not support the wide range of specialized types readily discernible from any pattern. Instead, the statistical analysis indicated that the chopper attributes were dependent on two characteristics of the original piece of raw material. Borden's (1968a) typology was related to six attributes (Figure 4). However, four of the basic attributes (edge shape, edge placement or location, number of scars, and retouch stage) used to define his types were dependent on the type of stone. Of the remaining two, edge angle was dependent both on

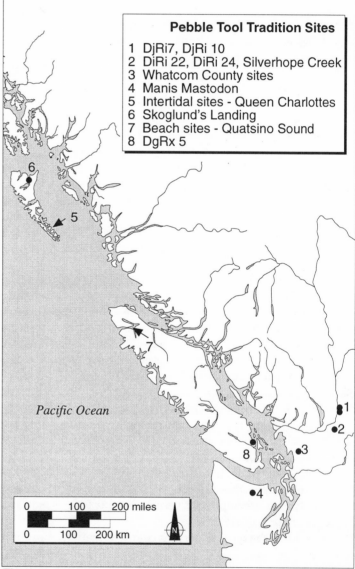

Figure 1. Location of Pebble Tool Tradition sites in the Pacific Northwest.

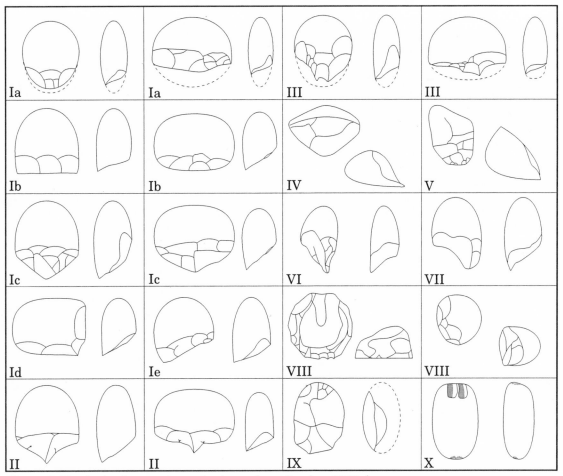

Figure 2. Borden's chopper types (redrawn from Borden 1968a).

cobble shape and edge placement. The typology developed was primarily related to two elements – stone type (indirectly) and the original shape of the cobble (directly). Therefore, we can suggest that the typology has no significance and cannot effectively be used as a classification system since only two attributes, both of which are inherent in the unmodified raw material, were used to generate the types.

It is possible, indeed likely, that the makers of the tools were selecting cobbles of particular shape and stone type with which to manufacture tools with predetermined attributes. It is also possible that these predetermined attributes were related to intended function. However, this would suggest that the cobble tools were the main goal of the manufacturer and all other artifacts produced were either byproducts or discards. As the following discussion shows, this is not the

Table 1. Chopper attributes used in tests of statistical independence.

Variable number	South Yale/Crescent Beach samples	Kersting sample (Valley 1979)
1	Borden type	Minerology
2	Stone type	Weight
3	Weight	Length
4	Length	Width
5	Width	Thickness
6	Thickness	L/W Ratio
7	Cobble shape (original)	Degree of peripheral
8	Flaking arc	flaking
9	Edge shape	
10	Edge angle	Edge angle
11	Edge placement/location	
12	Number of flake scars	Number of flakes removed
13	Flake scar width (mean)	
14	Flake scar length (mean)	
15	Scar termination type	
16	Stage of retouch	
-		Wear
-		Number of projections

Years BP	Climatic phases	Cultural phases	South Yale radiocarbon dates
		Esilao	
1000	Late post-glacial	Emery	
2000		Skamel	
3000		Baldwin	
			3130 ± 500
4000			4200 ± 380
5000	Hypsithermal	Eayem	5240 ± 100
6000			5900 ± 130
7000			
8000		Mazama	
9000	Early post-glacial	Milliken	
10,000	Sumas		
11,000		Pasika	
12,000	Everson interstadial		
13,000			
14,000	Terminal Vashon		

Figure 3. Geoarchaeological chronology for the Fraser Canyon area and radiocarbon dates from the South Yale site.

ments, coins, buttons, glass, and bottle caps) contained in the South Yale material in small quantities. The site assemblage is then not without the more sophisticated artifacts and technologies.

A Pure Component

It could be argued that the presence of bifacial material at the site does not preclude the unifacial nature of the Pasika component if those bifacial materials can be shown as contextually separate from the complex. According to the site records, the site can be divided into three possible components (Figure 6) with a degree of temporal significance: (a) the pit house feature on Terrace I; (b) the rock shelters on terrace II in the South Yale Ridge/Old River Channel area (the only area with clearly defined stratigraphic profiles); and (c) the deposits scattered across the terraces (I to IV), an area of extensive instability. Because of the stratigraphic integrity of the rock shelter area, that portion of the site was concentrated upon in terms of a pure case. The cobble tools are only part of a complex, sophisticated, and well thought out technological system.

Unifacial or Bifacial

Key to placement of Pasika into an early context was the apparent lack of bifacially manufactured artifacts and therefore, by extension, the lack of knowledge/ability to produce such tools. An examination of the total artifact inventory from South Yale demonstrated that although a great many of the artifacts were indeed unifacial, there was also a large number of other artifacts found there, including bifacially flaked projectile points (Figure 5), microblades and microblade cores, ground stone knives, mauls, and decorative objects. The inventory does not reflect a site that is exclusively unifacial in nature. In addition, the percentages of the bifacial artifacts to the total assemblage are not at all out of line with other prehistoric sites (cf., Archer 1980, Fladmark 1970a, LeClair 1976, von Krogh 1975).

There were also historic artifacts (metal frag-

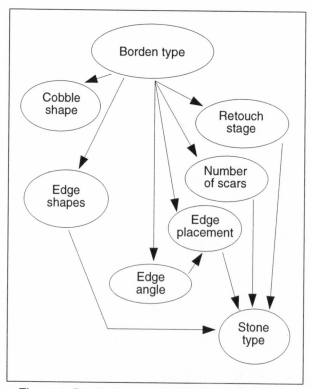

Figure 4. Borden type and related attributes (arrows indicate statistical relationships).

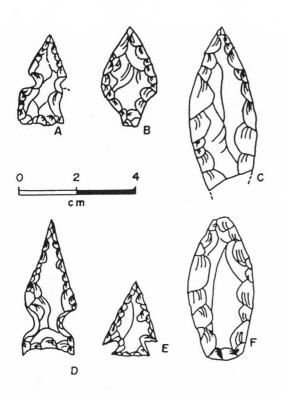

Figure 5. Typical bifaces from South Yale (DjRi 7). (A) DjRi 7-4774, Terrace I N6-12, E18-24; (B) 2128, Terrace I surface; (C) 4717, Terrace I N22-28, E18-24; (D) 4808, Terrace II hub 164 S3-N3, W8-14DBS 1.3'; (E) 718, Terrace I Test Pit 9 DBS 2-8"; (F) 2193, Terrace I surface.

component. The materials found in several excavation units were plotted by level and by whether or not they were assignable to the Pasika complex. (Materials not belonging to Pasika included bifacial material, microblades and microblade cores, and ground stone.) Summary graphs (Figure 7) and a profile of one such unit (Figure 8) demonstrate that the vertical distributions of both Pasika and non-Pasika materials in these units came close to matching one another. Both types were spread throughout the deposit, with only one Pasika artifact in each unit being located (in isolation) in the lowest cultural unit. In other words, the two distributions in each unit seem to fit together as contemporaneous, inseparable by visual means, but two artifacts out of a total count of over 12,000 do not qualify as a pure component.

Sediments and Contexts

Everything apparently hinges on the geological interpretation of the site, including the origin and age of the terraces and other features, and the identification of their surface sediments as aeolian or fluvi-

al. If the terraces are of fluvial or glaciofluvial origin; if the artifacts were *in situ* in such sediments; and if, as Borden (1975) notes, many of them are water worn, then an early age estimate may be justified, since such terraces were possible formed during a period of significantly higher sea level – therefore before 9,000 BP (Fladmark 1982:104-5).

One of the lines of evidence used to support the hypothesis that the site was occupied at or about the time the terraces were formed deals with the kind of sediment in which the artifacts were recovered. If the sediment is fluvial in origin, as Borden (1968c) argues, then the water levels had to be such that periodic flooding of the terraces was possible at the time of terrace formation. If on the other hand, the sediments are not fluvial in origin, the context of the cultural material can be called into question at least as far as the presumed dates are concerned.

Much of Borden's argument hinges on a geological study done on the terraces of the South Yale site (Swonnell 1971). According to that study, the three lower terraces were at least in part formed by glacial or glaciofluvial action near the end of the Pleistocene. As I read that geological report, I was struck by a curious phraseology. Each time sediments laid down by meltwater were mentioned, they were referred to as gravels of various forms. In fact Swonnel's (1971) report is littered with phrases like "these sands and gravels are overlain by silts" and "silts overlying a cobble pavement." The sand and silt deposits at South Yale were considered not to be involved with or included in the geological evaluation of the South Yale locality. The geological and glaciological processes and their interpretations all pertain to the gravels and not to the silts that contain 100 per cent of the cultural material. In that case, the geological formation of the terraces is irrelevant to our study unless the silt deposits can be demonstrated to have been laid down during the formation period. In order to do that, and thereby establish the late Pleistocene dating for the Pasika materials, the sediment (the sands and silts, not the gravels) must be shown to have been fluvial in origin.

Since Borden had relied on the geoglacial report and not run tests on the sediments, I decided to do so. Available samples were limited but level bags provided enough material for mechanical tests and they were augmented by several small core samples taken by myself in 1982. Tests to determine particle size, surface appearance of the grains, and mineral content of the soils were conducted using methods refined at Trent University (Watson 1976a, 1976b). These tests were selected as they best dif-

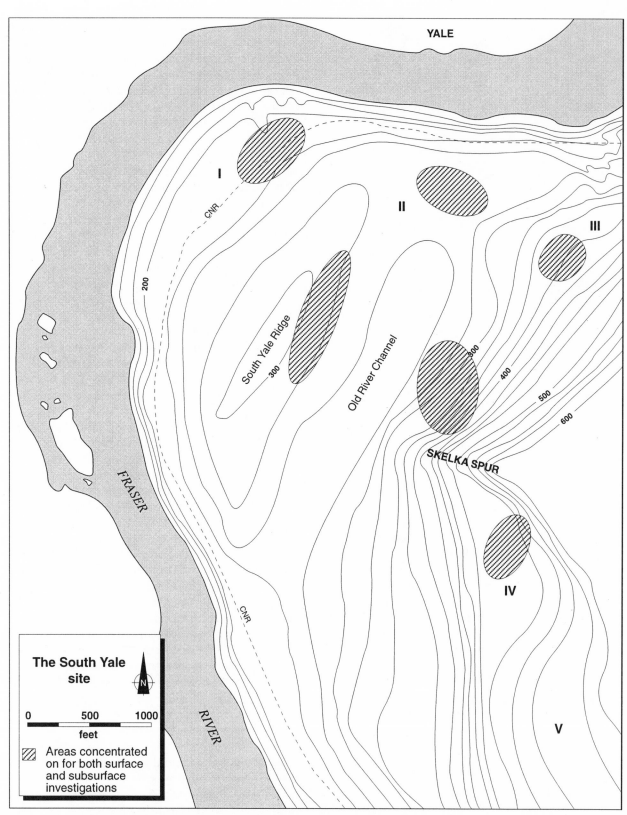

Figure 6. The South Yale site (revised from Borden 1968a). Roman numerals indicate terrace numbers. The majority of excavated units are contained within the areas of line-shading.

56

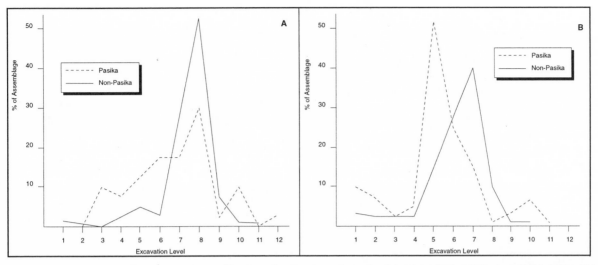

Figure 7. Summary of Pasika and non-Pasika distributions in units (a) #164 NO-6,EO-6 and (b) #164 N4-S4, E13-19.

ferentiated between wind and water deposited sediments. In all cases (particle size, surficial rounding of grains, surface finish, heavy mineral content, mineral hardness, laminations, calcium carbonate, colour, and porosity), the findings indicated that the sands and silts of the South Yale locality, those deposits that lay above the glacial gravels and which contained the cultural materials, were aeolian in origin and not fluvial. The general nature of the matrix does not support a fluvial or glaciofluvial origin for those sediments. There is no link between the surficial deposits and the genesis of the terraces at the South Yale site.

Combined with the evidence for aeolian genesis, several observations suggest, although not conclusively, that the deposits may have been disturbed, making the cultural deposits secondary to some extent. Certain areas, most noticeably the rock shelter sediment traps, were clearly undisturbed but the following comments on the site matrix as a whole cast doubt on the integrity of the majority of cultural deposits at the site: (1) organic materials, wood and bark, which should not have survived in the deposits were recovered at the interface of the silts and basal gravels; (2) historic artifacts were recorded in direct association with Pasika materials where no such relationship should have existed; (3) no clear stratigraphy or strong *in situ* formation was observed in most areas; (4) temporally diagnostic artifacts (hand mauls, projectile points) lay in reversed stratigraphic position; and (5) artifacts that could be refitted together were found considerable distances, both vertically and horizontally, apart. In some cases refitted materials were recovered on different terraces suggesting localized downslope movement.

Patination

The presumed contemporaneity of the Pasika complex occupations with periods of terrace formation is suggested by the following:

> The patina acquired by the Pasika material suggests that they weathered *in situ* along with the soil zones ... Each of the three [lower] terraces has yielded strongly water-worn sediments. This condition of water-wear could have developed only through prolonged exposure to the abrasive action of water and sand at times when the river at flood stage still rose above the surface of the terrace (Borden 1968a:68).

Patination and water-wear were also used to argue for Pasika contemporaneity with terrace formation times. Research into patination has demonstrated that its use as a dating method is extremely complex. Causal identification of the presence or absence of patination is insufficient to suggest antiquity. Without detailed chemical and petrographic studies of both the artifacts and the matrix, it is impossible to separate older from more recent artifacts of the same composition. There is no foundation whatsoever for suggesting that if the artifacts were patinated then they were contemporaneous with the terrace formation, particularly when artifacts from the upper, non-glacial terraces were also patinated.

Similar arguments can be used in terms of the "water-worn" specimens. Artifacts of this type are rare but found on all terraces. Their surfaces, including the modified edges, have been altered by an abrasive action. Borden (1968a) suggests that water and

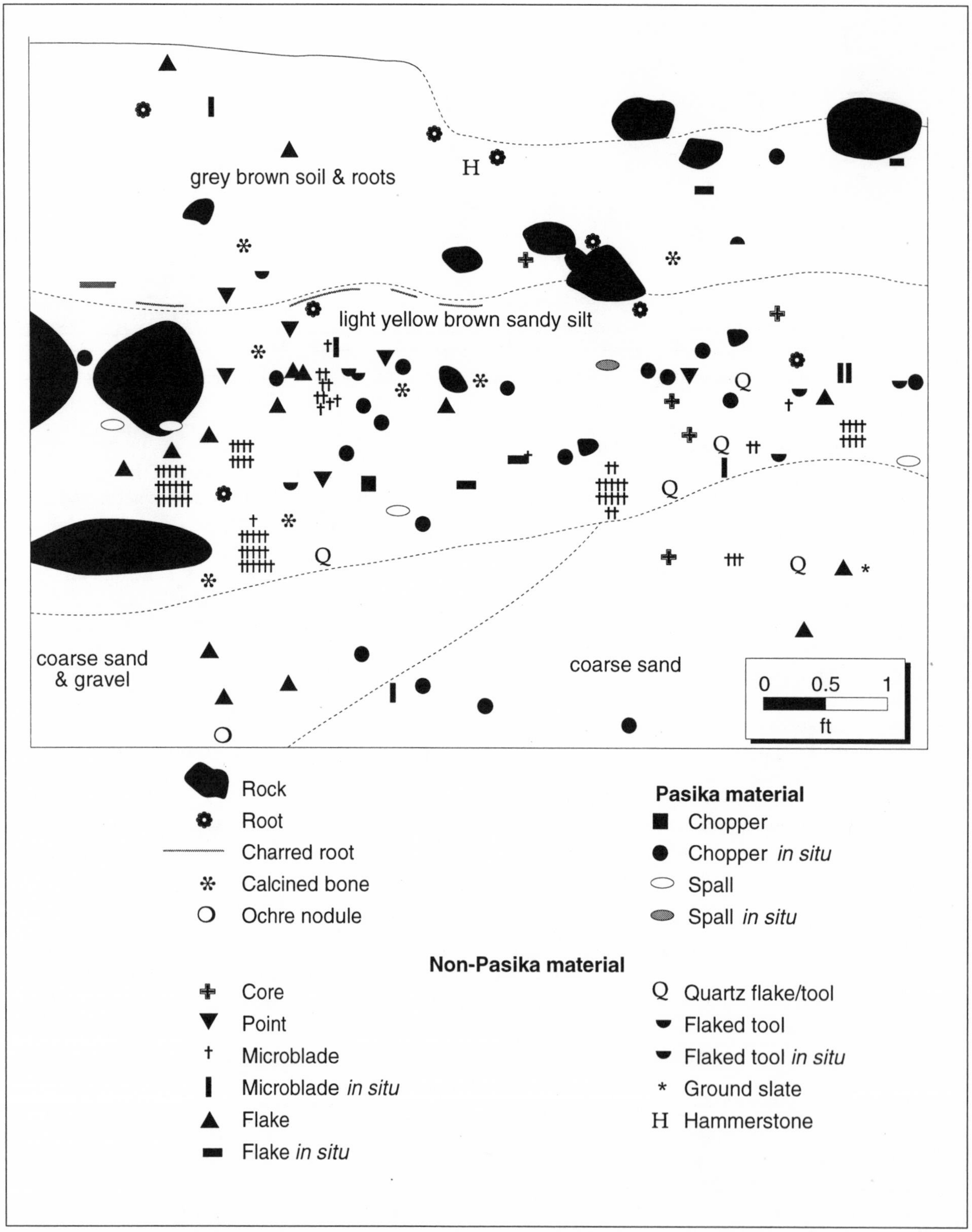

grey brown soil & roots
H
light yellow brown sandy silt
Q
coarse sand & gravel
coarse sand
0 0.5 1
ft
Rock
Root
Charred root
Calcined bone
Ochre nodule
Pasika material
Chopper
Chopper in situ
Spall
Spall in situ
Non-Pasika material
Core
Point
Microblade
Microblade in situ
Flake
Flake in situ
Q Quartz flake/tool
Flaked tool
Flaked tool in situ
* Ground slate
H Hammerstone

Figure 8. East wall profile of unit 164 N4-S3, E13-19 with *in situ* artifact distribution.

sand combined to create that abrasion. However, Cressy (1928) and others note that an aeolian environment is considerably more abrasive than an aqueous one, and given that the sediments appear to be wind-deposited, sand and wind could just as easily have been the abrasive. Patination and water-wear, then, cannot be used as evidence for contemporaneity of Pasika and terrace formation.

LATE PLEISTOCENE DATING

Borden (1965, 1968c, 1975) simultaneously pursued several lines of evidence to arrive at his 12,000 to 9000 years BP temporal placement for Pasika. One line of evidence he began but abandoned was radiocarbon dating of charcoal samples from the South Yale site. He submitted one sample for testing. In his, and in my, estimation, it was the best sample available to him at the time. In his site notes, Borden (1970) indicates his rationale for having the sample processed. "It seems likely that the date on this sample (#31) will indicate the time of formation of Terrace III and the approximate age of the pebble tool industry from the orange-brown loam overlying the coarse grey sand … Estimated age 11,000 ± BP."

The sample was a single piece of charcoal recovered at or near the base of the cultural deposit. When a radiocarbon estimate of 5240 ±100 years BP was returned, Borden rejected the date as coming from an intrusive burned root (Borden 1975).

I realized that one date was insufficient and I selected other samples from those collected by Borden using the following characteristics: (1) charcoal found in a single piece or from a clearly restricted area; (2) charcoal found as part of a cultural feature, such as a hearth; and (3) charcoal found in clear association with Pasika material, or lacking clear association, the charcoal must be stratigraphically below Pasika materials. According to that criteria, Borden's sample #31, with the date of 5240 ±100, was indeed the best. I examined forty-seven other charcoal samples and selected three: (1) sample #32 from Terrace I in clear association with Pasika materials and near the bottom of the cultural deposit; (2) sample #44, Terrace II, came from a hearth at a depth of 4.5 feet (1.3 to 1.5 m) below the surface and

near Pasika materials; and (3) sample #26, Terrace III, was found 2.8 feet (0.8 to 0.9 m) below the surface and in a hearth stratigraphically below the Pasika deposit. The samples were processed by the Radiocarbon Lab at Simon Fraser University and the radiocarbon estimates returned (Table 2) certainly did not support the 12,000 to 9000 years BP placement of Pasika. Instead, they ranged from 2630 to 6030 years BP. Using the one standard deviation, the dates span only 400 years, a remarkably short time considering the diversity of sample locations and depths below the surface. Compared to the Fraser Canyon archaeological chronology (Figure 3), we find that all of the radiocarbon dates fall within the Charles (Eayem) and Baldwin Phases. Given the total artifact inventory at South Yale, including microblades, contracting stem and other point types, these dates and the Charles-Baldwin temporal placement for Pasika is not at all surprising.

As an interesting aside, stratigraphically above charcoal sample #44, which yielded a date of 5900 ±130 years BP, fragmentary fish vertebrae, identified by Borden as salmon, were recovered. Fladmark (1975:207-8) comments that

> it is difficult to conceive of any salmon … attaining full productivity prior to the stabilization of stream gradients about 5000 BP. Some sockeye may have been passing the Fraser Canyon as early as 7500 BP, but they could not have achieved a quantitative development equivalent to that of the historical period until 2500 years later.

Salmon remains dating around 5000 years BP, at the earliest, were then recovered stratigraphically above (but close to) the charcoal that yielded a radiocarbon estimate of 5770 to 6030 years BP.

Four radiocarbon dates available for South Yale, all within a 3500 year span (2600 to 6000 years BP), negate the extensive body of evidence cited by Borden for his 12,000 to 9000 BP placement of Pasika. All of his evidence, although much of it probably accurately dates the formation of the terraces at South Yale and the initial occupation of vegetation in the area, is secondary and does not date the cul-

Table 2. Radiocarbon dates from DjRi 7.

Sample	Terrace	Date	Reference	Source
32	I	3130 ±500	SFU248	Haley 1983b
26	III	4200 ±380	SFU225	Haley 1983b
31	III	5240 ±100	18208	Borden 1975
44	II	5900 ±130	SFU228	Haley 1983a

tural material proper. At least, the radiocarbon estimates are more closely related to that cultural material.

TECHNOLOGICAL ADAPTATION

At each step, the evidence has failed to support the hypothesis that Pasika represented the remains of a late Pleistocene cultural tradition. It is not a discrete cultural complex. It is not demonstrably older than the known cultural traditions. However, there can be no doubt that Pasika was a real phenomenon distinguishable in form, if not in context, from the rest of the South Yale assemblage. In stone type and raw form, degree of care taken in tool preparation, and other less tangible elements, the cobble based artifacts can be seen as quite distinctive. If it is not a late Pleistocene cultural tradition or even a cultural tradition of unknown temporal loci, without independent temporal or spatial significance, then what does it represent? I would suggest that it is the remains of a technological system developed and designed to maximize the utilization of cobbles as a raw material source and that it was operated simultaneously with other "more sophisticated" lithic technologies.

Pasika Technological Process

The model (Haley 1987) is in need of further refinement but I will attempt to summarize it now as far as it is understood. Keep in mind that (a) no cobbles follow identical pathways through the model, (b) all defined tool types are artificial constructs around morphological attribute modes, and (c) this is a static description of a once dynamic and reactive lithic reduction system. (It was reactive in the sense that the process was constantly adjusted and altered depending on how the raw material responded to the earlier steps.)

1. *Initial Selection and Treatment*: Cobbles of a certain size, shape, and raw material were selected during or prior to the initial step. Flat, discoidal cobbles were reduced using direct hand-held or block-on-block percussion. Other shapes, notably oval and round cobbles, were split using a bipolar technique (Haley 1981). Initial treatment had a possible output of up to nineteen different artifact forms including by- and waste-products (Figure 9). From here, pathways diverge and cobbles were treated differently depending on the desired outcome and the perceived potential of the particular parent body.

2. *Chopper Edge Creation/Initial Sharpening* (Figure 10): Once the initial treatment was completed, the edge of the cobble was concentrated upon.

Using characteristics such as location of flaking and the platform face, up to nine different tool categories could be defined as coming from this stage in the process.

3. *Successive Chopper Resharpening*: The next series of steps, used to sharpen or shape an edge or to resharpen and reshape an edge after it had been dulled, involved the repeated removal of flakes. The chopper morphology was radically altered by increased edge involvement, increased edge angle, and by the introduction of variations in the edge shape depending on the degree of modification and the location of that modification. It is a complex sharpening and use cycle that could have been and was repeated a number of times. The frequency of recycling was limited only by the thickness of the central mass of each particular cobble.

4. *Chopper Edge Rejuvenation*: Once the edge became too battered or thick to resharpen, it could be rejuvenated by the removal of a large flake that included the entire edge area (Figure 11). The core or chopper could then be recycled back into the previous step. The core rejuvenation flake was sometimes used as a core from which tiny flakes, roughly the size of a thumbnail, were struck (Haley 1982).

5. *"Exhausted Chopper" Production* (Figure 12): From here, the choppers were retouched in a variety of ways until it was no longer possible or profitable to modify the edge properly. Even ignoring the intermediate stages (and resultant tool types), seventeen artifact types were defined for this stage including a possible eleven chopper types.

6. *Flake/Spall Tool Production*: So far, I have concentrated on the "parent body" aspect of the procedure, but the flake/spall tool production was of at least equal importance. They represent a large category of expedient tools which were used until dulled or until the job was finished, then they were discarded. Retouched flakes, regardless of shape and size, were treated in a limited number of ways. However, even without considering the variations in flake size and shape (Figure 13), there are numerous flake tool types possible.

THE TOTAL SYSTEM

Initially, Borden (1968b) identified thirty artifact (chopper and spall tool) categories at South Yale. Those types accounted for a small percentage (approximately 30 per cent) of the total. The proposed reduction system, summarized above, identified seventy-seven types (Figure 14) but accounted for 100 per cent of the Pasika assemblage. It is, as far as I can determine, the best fit explanation for the diversity of artifacts made from cobble material.

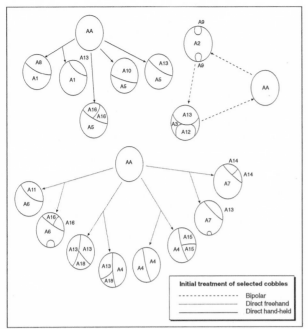

Figure 9. Initial treatment of selected cobbles. Arrows indicated a specific blow from a hammerstone beginning with an unmodified cobble (AA). The letter A indicates the initial treatment stage of manufacture and the letter/number combinations each signify an identifiable artifact. High numbers are flakes or spalls and low numbers are cobble core artifacts.

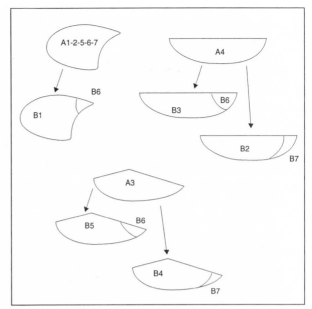

Figure 10. Split cobble chopper edge creation and initial edge sharpening. Arrows indicate specific blows from the hammerstone. The letter B indicates the split cobble stage of manufacture and the letter/number combinations signify identifiable artifacts produced at this stage.

Once the model had been completed, I tested it against the raw data from the South Yale site and from the Union Bar site (Haley 1987) just as I had the late Pleistocene culture hypothesis. The technological adaptation process hypothesis was provisionally accepted.

OTHER SITES

As a final check, I broadened my study to include the sites on the Northwest Coast assignable to the early Pebble Tool Tradition (Carlson 1979, 1983a, Fladmark 1982, Grabert 1979). I dealt with these sites (Figure 1) using available published and unpublished reports as my database. The wide variance in report content and approach made it impossible for me to conduct extensive detailed testing. It did, however, allow me to make some general statements about the sites. Of the ten relevant sites or groups of sites, less than half had been excavated. Six of the sites or groups of sites, were surface collected only and almost all of those were from disturbed contexts (bulldozed areas, ploughed fields, or beaches), while, in all cases where early Pebble Tool Tradition sites had been excavated, either the context of the Pasika-like artifacts was poor or the number of artifacts very small. In one case, the entire early Pebble Tool

Tradition component consisted of only two artifacts (Mitchell, Murray, and Carlson 1981:40, Murray 1982:145). Nowhere in the Pacific Northwest is there a known site that supports the early Pebble Tool Tradition hypothesis.

SUMMARY

That the Pasika technology did represent a very specific and specialized aspect of the cultures of the Pacific Northwest cannot be doubted. It appears to have been based on a concerted effort to obtain necessary and varied tools from a very restricted raw material form – the cobble – with a minimum of energy expenditure. That the basic tool forms remained essentially unchanged for millenia can be taken as evidence for the efficiency of the tool forms and of the tool manufacturing process. It is my opinion that the Pasika complex can best be understood as a method or technological procedure for making the best possible use of an extremely common raw material to provide most of the day-to-day tool needs of the people. The high percentage of these tools in the various assemblages may reflect the fact that not only was the method of tool manufacture efficient and easy, it was simple enough to allow for the creation of a disposable toolkit.

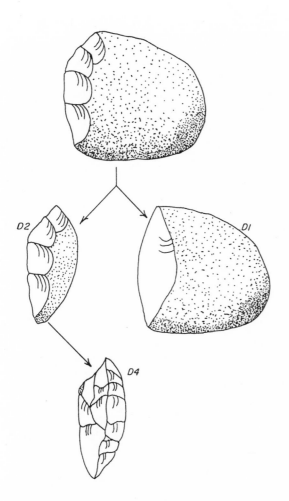

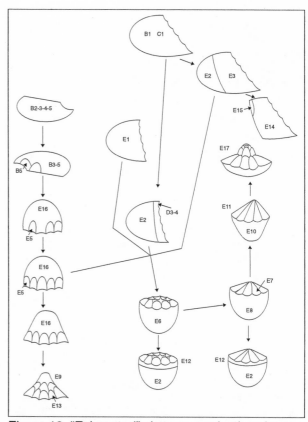

Figure 12. "Exhausted" chopper production. Arrows indicate the specific blows from the hammer-stone. The letter E indicates the exhausted chopper stage of manufacture and the letter/number combinations signify identifiable artifacts produced at this stage.

Figure 11. Chopper edge rejuvenation. Arrows indicate specific blows from a hammerstone. The letter D indicates the edge rejuvenation stage and the letter/number combinations signify indentifiable artifacts produced at this stage.

The Pasika complex does not exist at South Yale as the remains of a complete culturally diagnostic lithic-complex dating from the late Pleistocene. Four radiocarbon dates fall within a 3500 year span with the earliest date being approximately 6000 years BP. The presence of microblades and microblade cores and a variety of formed bifacial tools in clear association with the Pasika materials at the site suggest that the various industries, including Pasika, formed parts of a larger and much fuller lithic techno-complex. Given that no other sites on the Northwest Coast can provide a sufficient database to support the existence of an early Pebble Tool Tradition, we must look elsewhere for the earliest evidence of human entry into the New World. The *early* Pebble Tool Tradition simply did not and does not exist based on our current knowledge of the prehistory of western North America.

Figure 13. Flake and spall tool production. Beginning with unmodified flakes or spalls, minimal edge retouch can create any of the seventeen, edge modified flakes/spalls represented here.

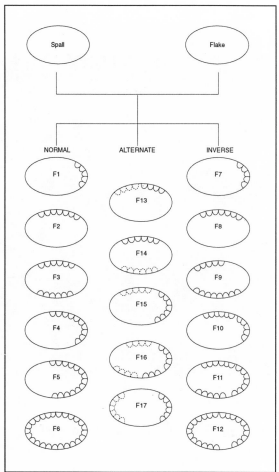

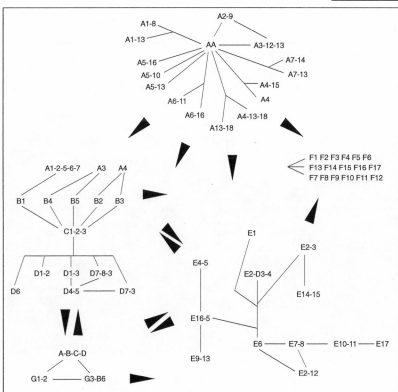

Figure 14. Artifacts produced during the Pasika cobble reduction sequence. All of the possible artifacts cluster into five reduction stages. Relationships are illustrated by fine lines. Triangles demonstrate the connections between clusters (or reduction stages).

Figure 15. Some of the thousands of pebble tools from the South Yale site.

Figure 16. The South Yale site viewed from the north looking south across the Fraser River from the town of Yale. The site covers the entire point of land in the centre of the photograph (see Figure 1).

8 EARLY PERIOD COMPONENTS AT THE MILLIKEN SITE

Donald Mitchell and David L. Pokotylo

Between 1956 and 1960, our view of Pacific Northwest prehistory was substantially altered by three announced associations of excavated assemblages and early radiocarbon age estimates. The Lind Coulee site in eastern Washington, the Five Mile Rapids site at the Dalles on the lower Columbia River in Oregon, and the Milliken site (DjRi 3) in British Columbia's lower Fraser River Canyon pushed back the earliest evidence of human occupation by several millennia, to the period from 9000 to 7000 BP.

Comprehensive reports on the Lind Coulee and Five Mile Rapids sites have long been available (Cressman 1960, Daugherty 1956) but apart from two brief preliminary papers (Borden 1960, 1961) and material in two reconstructions of regional prehistory (Borden 1968b, 1975), no data have been published for the third of those early sites. In fact, thirty-three years after discovery and excavation of the sites and eleven years after Carl Borden's death, materials collected by his Fraser Canyon Project remained unanalyzed.

In this chapter, we present results of the initial stage of that long postponed analysis by providing summary data on the two earliest site components (Borden's Milliken and Mazama phase occupations) and a third previously unreported component, and by examining their similarities and differences. Preparation of full reports of DjRi 3 (the Milliken site) and the adjacent and related DjRi 5 (Esilao site) are currently under way.

DESCRIPTION OF SITE

DjRi 3 is located on the east bank of the Fraser River, at the mouth of a narrows still appreciated by native fishermen as an excellent place to take salmon (see Figures 1 and 2). The lowest deposits of the site are now approximately 18 m above high water, but, as mentioned below and discussed later, there is good evidence that when first occupied, the site was subject to seasonal flooding.

Mathews (in Borden 1960:106) describes the site as occupying

> a rock-rimmed embayment low on the east wall of the Fraser Canyon. The recess, though now partly concealed by the growth of talus and alluvial fans, is clearly cut off on the north by rock, and could not have been created by any through-going reach of the Fraser River; instead it seems to have been excavated by glacial action and merely occupied by a back eddy at a high-water stage of the river.

The embayment has been filled, over the centuries, by deposits from the river, from a seasonal stream, and from human occupation until eventually it formed a more-or-less level bench, high above the present Fraser (see Figure 3).

Dimensions of the site were not determined in the field. Given the presence of the "rock-rimmed embayment," it cannot have exceeded 45 m between the ridge along the river's edge and the canyon wall. Its length, paralleling the river, is more difficult to estimate. A rock outcrop lies at the northern end, but stream and human deposits to the south probably merge with those of the separately-recorded DjRi 5, whose limits are also undetermined. A maximum length including what is likely the furthest extent of the southerly site would be almost 350 m. Excluding what might reasonably be considered site DjRi 5, about 180 m can be identified with DjRi 3.

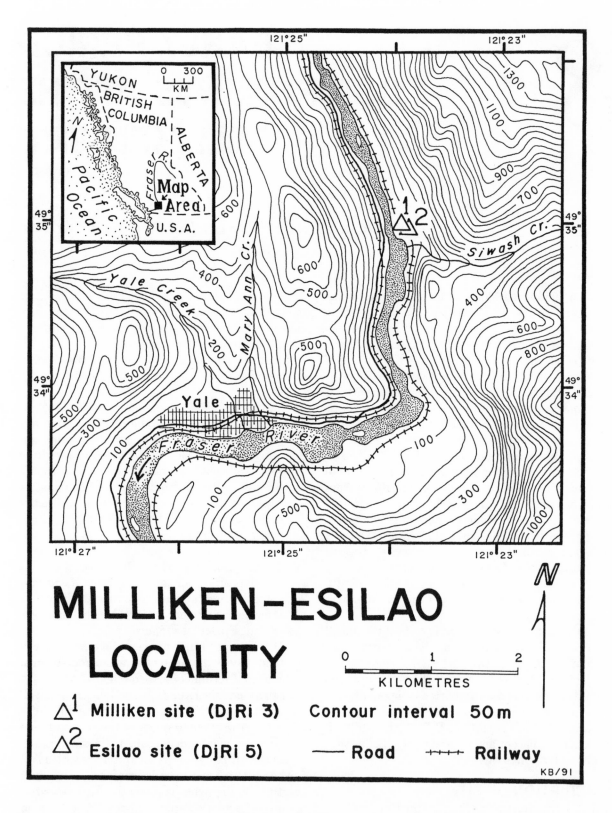

Figure 1. Map of Milliken site location in the lower Fraser Canyon and southwestern British Columbia.

Figure 2. Photo of Milliken site setting, looking down river to the southwest.

The deep stratification of the site first became obvious when a portion of the outer rock ridge gave way in the early 1950s, spilling sand and gravel across the Canadian National Railway tracks. This slide exposed a deep succession of variously coloured sand and gravel layers held in place by remaining segments of the original rock ridge.

HISTORY OF INVESTIGATION

Carl Borden first visited site DjRi 3 with its discoverer, August Milliken, in the summer of 1956. A small collection of artifacts was made from the exposed face of what was obviously a deeply-buried cultural horizon. Some associated charcoal was also collected for dating (Borden 1960). By 1959, crew and finances were assembled for the start of the Fraser Canyon Project and the first work began on the site. That season, a 10 by 50 foot trench was excavated in the upper stratigraphic zones (A to C) and a 10 by 30 foot segment of this carried down some 25 feet (7.6 m) to below the bottom layer (Zone G), for which an 8150 BP age estimate had by then been obtained. A small exploratory trench further disclosed that five feet beneath the "early" horizon, was another occupation level.

The 1960 excavations expanded work to the northeast of the 1959 trench and, of course, carried several squares down to the occupation zone (I) discovered the previous summer. During 1961, the fi-

nal season of work, further excavation was carried out in all known occupation levels and a shaft sunk to watertable to test underlying deposits. Part of this season's effort, however, was budgeted for the start of the work at nearby DjRi 5, and for the next two years that site held the attention of the Fraser Canyon Project.

STRATIGRAPHY

One of the fortunate characteristics of the Milliken site is the nature of its stratigraphy. Although there is difficulty determining significant breaks in the uppermost 2.5 m of the site, strata are clearly delineated in the remaining 12 m or so of deposit. More important, culture-bearing stratigraphic zones are separated from each other by substantial deposits of near sterile sands and gravel.

Of the twelve major zones identified by the excavators, we need be concerned with only the middle seven, D to J, as these contain or in part isolate the earliest cultural horizons. Zones A to C are associated with occupations post-dating about 2800 BP. Zones K and L, along with the lower third of J, consist of at least 6 m of silt, sand, and gravel layers underlying the earliest cultural material. A detailed analysis of sediments in Zones A to J is in Swanson (1964). A schematic representation of the major zones appears as Figure 4.

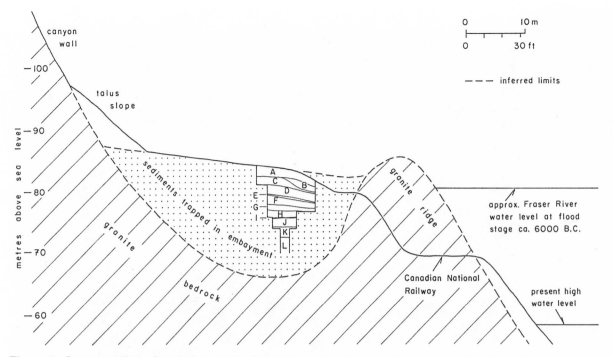

Figure 3. Cross-section of rock-rimmed embayment and major stratigraphic zones at the Milliken site.

Zone D

This easily-distinguishable unit consists of from 1.2 to 1.7 m of angular pebbles, cobbles, and larger rocks – sometimes open and loosely packed, sometimes bedded in coarse sand and partly cemented. The general appearance of the profiles is of a series of alternating bands of gravel and sand with up to five pairs being distinguishable. A charcoal-stained layer at 45 to 60 cm below the surface of D is visible in the northern part of the site, and a second layer at about mid-depth in the deposit. These internal layers and the surface of the zone all slope downward toward the north-west – from the canyon wall side of the excavation toward the river and from the down-river toward the up-river side.

A "brown gravel" deposit that is not internally stratified overlies what Borden called the "D" gravel deposits in the southern parts of the excavation. During excavation, it was initially considered part of Zone D, but by the last year it was separately distinguished and interpreted as waterlaid, redeposited "D" gravels originating in the unexcavated eastern part of the site. However, the deposit seems too rich in artifacts to have originated from the nearly sterile gravels of D. As the matrix is similar to D, we have called this zone D1, and we identify Borden's original zone as D2. In our presentation, D1 also includes a deposit capping the original D at the southern limit of the

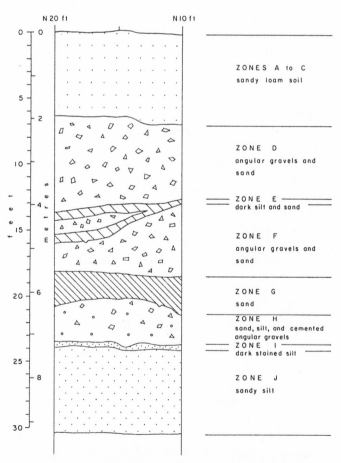

Figure 4. Schematic profile of major soil zones excavated at the Milliken site.

68

excavation trench, identified on the excavation pro-files as "coarse gravel of the type containing cobble impements."

Zone D2 contained very few artifacts and little other cultural material. These deposits have been interpreted as fan gravels – the product of a small, now intermittent stream that presently empties into the Fraser River near the mouth of Siwash Creek to the southeast of the site (Borden 1961:6, 1965:168).

Zone E

Ranging from 5 to 65 cm in thickness, the zone consists basically of two sets of strata (approximate-ly five in the lower and three in the upper set) separated in part of the site by up to 30 cm of sterile gravel and merging elsewhere into a single set of layers. The sediments are dark (described by the excavators as "black") and silty with occasional spreads of dark-stained coarse sand and pea-gravel. Zone E contains the bulk of the "Mazama" compo-nent assemblage.

Zone F

From 75 to 170 cm of rough, angular gravels and sands separate culture-bearing Zones E and G. Although in appearance very much like Zone D, the material in this unit differs in that only a single gravel/sand pair of bands is evident, and in that some of the gravel and the lowermost sandy layer are cemented, by an as yet undetermined agent or process, into a distinctive 15 cm thick deposit. As with D, the Zone F sands and gravels are interpreted as relict alluvial fan deposits resulting from action of the small seasonal stream behind the site.

Zone G

Mainly consisting of various grades of sand, this easily distinguishable layer ranges from 60 to 90 cm in thickness. The upper portions of the sand are stained dark, with the darkness resolving as two distinct bands of about 7 cm thickness each separat-ed by a lighter layer of some 8 cm. Toward the eastern part of the excavation, layers of gravel up to 40 cm thick divide the sands into two and then three bands. At the base of the zone in this part of the site is a deposit of sandy silt.

Zone G deposits, which contain most of the "Mil-liken" component assemblage, were laid down by the Fraser River during high-water stages (Borden 1960:106, 1961:6, 1965:168). The site was then in a rock-walled seasonal embayment of the river (Swan-son 1964, Figure 1). Gravels separating the various layers of G are thought to have a similar origin to the gravels of Zones D and F.

Zone H

This unit is more complex than any so far described. It consists of cemented coarse angular gravels, loose sand and gravel, loose sand, and silty material. The deposit is from 75 to 90 cm in thickness and contains from three to six dark-stained sand and silty sand layers, sometimes separated from one another by other material, sometimes adjoining, and some-times merged. The gravels of this zone, too, were possibly brought to the site by the nearby stream (Borden 1965:165-8). The dark-stained layers con-tain a few isolated artifacts we consider part of the "Milliken" component assemblage.

Zone I

This zone is comprised of from one to three dark grey or reddish-brown stained silts that range from 8 to 14 cm in thickness. The silts have the same origin as those of Zone J (see below) and the stains result from human action.

Zone J

In the northern part of the excavation, this zone, which immediately underlies the first signs of hu-man activity at the site, is built up of layers of sand and silt of varying thickness and various pale shades of brown. Zone I is of the same material, distinguish-able only by the dark staining. In the southern part of the excavation, the upper part of the zone included some rock in sizes ranging from pebbles to boulders. Zone J is about 1.9 m thick, but, as indicated above, the lower third of it, along with zones K and L, form at least 6 m of sterile basal silt, sand, and gravel. Excavations at the site stopped at the watertable, not at the bottom of deposits. All of these lower deposits were laid down by the Fraser River (Borden 1965:165, Swanson 1964:44).

CULTURAL ASSEMBLAGES

Cultural material was found in each of the above described zones although evidence of human occu-pation was predominantly situated in Zones D1, E, and G. A very few items came from the lower part of Zone D, the upper part of Zone F, and from Zones H, I, and J. For purposes of this study, and in part after Borden (1965, 1967, 1975), we have grouped Zones G, H, I, and J as the "Milliken" component. The "Mazama" component is restricted to material from Zone E, although Borden (1975:68) had included items from zones D and F as well. Given problems in dating the gravel strata, and quite different depositional processes involved, we treat all material from Zones D1, D2, and F as a distinctive "Gravel" component. We later assess the validity of this separation of the early occupations of DjRi 3 into three components. In our discussion of the "Milliken" component we also describe each of the Zone H, I, and J subassemblages.

The main lithic raw material used in tool manufacture throughout all of the components was andesite/basalt – readily available in the area as river pebbles and cobbles. Specific raw material identification is complicated by the degree of weathering present on many specimens which has altered the surface relative to the interior matrix. Thin section analysis of weathered specimens indicates that the matrix is best described as a fine-grained volcanic sandstone (K. Russell and B. Barnes, personal communication 1988) that ranges greatly in colour and texture. The high proportion of flakes exhibiting a water worn pebble cortex suggests extensive use of local materials derived from gravel bars adjacent to the site. Nevertheless, a wide range of "exotic" lithic types (micro and cryptocrystallines, and obsidian) are also present, but low in frequency. Borden (1975:66-7) noted that the obsidian was derived from Oregon; however, only one piece of obsidian, a small biface thinning flake, was recovered. X-ray fluorescence analysis indicates the item's element composition is most similar to fingerprints for Oregon sources, but a new source in the Cascade Mountains in Washington is also a likely source (R. Carlson, personal communication 1987).

The Milliken Component

Artifacts

Types, numbers, and percentages of artifacts are presented in Table 1. Many of the categories bear self-explanatory labels, but some comments follow on the characteristics of classifications that may be less obvious. In all cases where the distinction is made, acute edge angles are 45 degrees or less, steep edge angles are more than 45 degrees. We refer to "flaking" as purposeful retouch, and "chipping" as flake detachment resulting unintentionally or from use.

The single *large leaf-shaped point* (Figure 5a) is 172 mm long. *Medium leaf-shaped points* (e.g., Figure 5b-e) range from 49 to 116 mm in length. *Large leaf-shaped point bases* are distinguished from other leaf-shaped forms by their width and thickness which are more like measurements of comparable portions of the large point than of the medium

points. *Formed bifaces* have been bifacially worked over their entire surface, but in contrast to the categories just discussed, they lack a pointed end. *Formed unifaces* (e.g., Figure 5f, g) are so substantially reworked that the original form of the flake or blade is not readily apparent.

Flakes with bifacial or unifacial retouch (e.g., Figure 5o, p, q) show purposeful, regular retouch to shape and sharpen the working edge of the tool, but unlike the "formed" categories, the original flake outline has been little altered. *Denticulate flakes* have one or more working edges so altered as to form regularly-spaced projections or teeth. *Pebble flakes* (e.g., Figure 5s) are generally large artifacts bearing substantial amounts of original pebble cortex, and have a flake morphology based on the original pebble outline form rather than systematic flaking from a core. These are distinguished from the commonly identified boulder spall tools (of which there are none in the early components at this site) by the presence of a distinct, cortical striking platform set off at a marked angle from the other pebble surface.

Pièces esquillées (e.g., Figure 5r) have one or two pairs of generally straight opposing edges that have been shaped by bipolar flaking. Both paired edges are crushed and battered. The *proximal end fragments of macroblades* (e.g., Figure 5h, i) or *microblades* (Figure 5k) display a striking platform or remnant indicating removal from a prepared core.

Utilized flakes and *utilized pebble flakes* show irregular chipping, abrasion, or polish along one or more working edges but no signs of retouch. *Utilized linear flakes* (Figure 5j) are long, parallel-sided and narrow, but lack evidence of a prepared core blade technology. *Flaked slate and schist objects* are crudely worked from thin slabs of split rock. The edges are usually bifacially modified.

The *pebble graver* (Figure 5n) is a very small tool. Flaking at one end of a small pebble has formed a short projection and this feature shows considerable wear polish. *Pebble core tools* (e.g., Figure 5t) are based on much larger river stones. The pebbles have been altered, usually but not exclusively, by crude unifacial retouch which is generally confined to one end. *Small flat modified pebbles* are proportionately thinner than pebble core tools and, in addition, are based on small, sub-angular water-worn rocks. Several flakes have been detached, usually unifacially, from sometimes isolated portions of the perimeter. *Slab/tabular material* refers to a few heavy, crudely retouched implements that may be analogous to pebble core tools, but are based on angular rocks rather than oval river pebbles.

Two of the *ground/polished stone* artifacts (Fig-

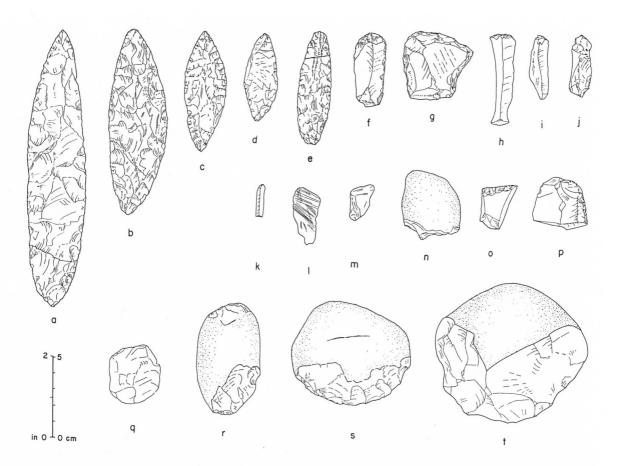

Figure 5. Milliken component artifacts: (a) large leaf-shaped point (No. 7277); (b, c, d) medium leaf-shaped points (Nos. 337, 7391, 7350); (e) medium leaf-shaped point, Zone "I" (No. 9204); (f, g) formed unifaces (Nos. 1908, 7170); (h, i) macroblade proximal end fragments (Nos. 7230, 7320); (j) utilized linear flake (No. 7363); (k) microblade proximal end fragment (No.1913); (l, m) ground/polished stone (Nos. 7260, 7160); (n) pebble graver (No. 7083); (o, p, q) retouched flakes (Nos. 1916, 7335, 1912); (r) pièce esquillée (No. 1829); (s) pebble flake (No. 7216); (t) pebble core tool (No. 7092).

ure 5 l, m) are of considerable interest as they are well made and resemble fragments from the bit and body of a celt. They are made of a distinctive yellow-green heat-altered steatite, came from virtually the same depth, and were found *in situ* about 3 m apart. One has a gently-curved and polished face, the other a similar polished surface, but also a small remnant of an adjacent polished area that forms a sharp, asymmetrically bifacial edge. A third specimen is a thick, heavily-patinated basalt flake with a very small polished facet. In addition, a small flat modified basalt pebble has a small amount of grinding and polishing forming indistinct facets on one surface.

Features

As the excavators kept no separate record of features, we have had to reconstruct lists and descrip-

tions from field notes, floor plans, and profiles. The clearest features are five hearths (defined by ash spreads and concentrations of charcoal), ninety-nine stake or post molds, and one rock alignment described in the field notes as a wall. Other more dubious features include a rock cluster, a spread of red-stained sand, and a shallow, oval depression filled with light-coloured sand.

Three hearths, all of pit form, come from Zone G, and there is one each in Zones H and I. One example from Zone G is about 43 cm in diameter, 13 cm deep, and composed of dark-stained sand in a saucer-shaped basin. A second, of similar profile and composition, measures 10 to 20 cm in thickness and 60 cm in diameter. The third extended into an unexcavated part of the site. It formed a 23 to 30 cm deep basin, if circular, was likely about 45 cm in diameter, and was filled with dark-stained sand and gravel. The Zone H and I hearths were less distinctly defined. Each consisted of charcoal and ash concentrations but form and dimensions of the hearths were not recorded.

Metric dimensions are available for seventy-seven of the ninety-nine stake and post molds recorded in Zones G, H, and I. These range from 3 to 33 cm in diameter, with a median of 8 cm. The interquartile range of diameter values is 5 to 10 cm, although a boxplot (see Hartwig and Dearing 1979) of diameters shows that six molds have "outside" values, exceeding 15 cm (see Figure 6). The features show no pronounced tendency to cluster although a curving, 4.5 m long band of them, of various diameters, may be discerned in three successive 15 cm levels of Zone G. Another association of two substantial post molds (33 cm maximum diameter), an intervening hearth, and a nearby deposit of charred cherry pits may indicate a temporary pole structure.

A 1.2 m long wall of rocks, from two to four tiers high, had its base at or just below the surface of Zone G deposits. Its purpose could not be determined. Similar structures in the upper levels of the site seem to have served as retaining walls.

Floral and Faunal Material

Deposits at site DjRi 3 offer very poor conditions for the preservation of organic material. In the earliest levels, only charred plant remains and calcined bone have survived. At least thirty carbonized choke cherry pits (*Prunus demissa*) were recovered from or reported for the Zone I cultural layer, and for Zone G, they were reported as "numerous." Other, as yet unidentified, seeds of at least two additional species were also collected from the latter zone. Zone G yielded one calcined but unidentifiable fragment of mammal bone.

Chronology

On stratigraphic grounds, the materials in Zones J, I, H, and G are of decreasing age and all are clearly older than the separated and overlying Zone E ("Mazama" component) assemblage. Available radiocarbon age estimates for the zones support this arrangement of the sequence. The Zone E estimate (see below) is the youngest in the series and of the two for the "Milliken" component, the earliest, from Zone I, is 9000 ±150 radiocarbon years (S-113) or 7050 BC (Borden 1961:4), and the other, from Zone G, is 8150 ±310 radiocarbon years (S-47) or 6200 BC (Borden 1960:107). Stuiver and Reimer's (1993) calibration program and data set provide a value of 9980 solar years BP (8030 BC) for S-113, and two

values, 9080 and 9000 solar years BP (7130 and 7050 BC), for S-47.

Subassemblages

For cultural unit comparisons we have grouped all data from Zones H, I, and J in the same analytical unit as the more numerous Zone G material. However, because they are stratigraphically distinct and as one is associated with the earliest age estimate from the site, we separately describe the subassemblages from these lowest zones. Given the small amount of cultural material recovered from these basal layers, both lithic tools and debris are described.

Zone H contained but three tools: two utilized flakes (one with an acute- and one with a steep-angled edge) and a utilized pebble flake. Two cores, one small bifacial thinning flake, two flakes with river pebble cortex platforms, and a single piece of flake shatter were also recovered. One core is made from a high quality grey chert, and has been extensively bifacially flaked over its surface. The other core is of a lightly weathered grey volcanic sandstone that retains its pebble cortex along one margin opposite a bifacial flake removal area. None of the flakes or shatter, appears to have been derived from these two cores.

Features include one probable hearth (described above) and seven stake molds. These last all extend into Zone I from the surface of that zone and may be associated with either a terminal Zone I, or initial Zone H occupation.

Zone I had a somewhat more substantial tool assemblage: one medium-sized leaf-shaped point (Figure 5e), one point tip from what appears also to have been a medium-sized point, four pieces of utilized or retouched slab/tabular material, and five utilized flakes with acute-angled working edges. Most of the uncatalogued material in level bags from this zone has equivocal status as artifacts. Nine water-worn pebbles and a pebble of poor quality chert with some shattered surface area were collected, but show no evidence of intentional alteration. One piece of weathered vein quartz and a small slate flake are also water-worn. Ten pieces of angular shatter derived from bedding planes are present. Only five pieces of debris exhibit striking platforms indicative of systematic flaking; three have pebble cortex platforms. Three pieces of flake shatter likely produced from intentional flaking are also present.

Features include one possible hearth (see description above) and all or some of the seven stake molds that could equally well be attributed to Zones H or I. Over ten of the charred cherry pit samples

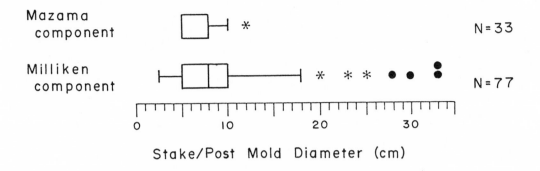

Figure 6. Boxplot of stake and post mold features from Milliken and Mazama phase components.

come from this layer.

Field notes for Zone J excavations report two lithic artifacts, however, only one item is recorded in the artifact catalogue – a flake with acute-angled bifacial retouch along one straight edge (see Figure 5r). This earliest tool from the site is based on an angular hornfels pebble and was recovered from white sands some 135 cm beneath the surface of the Zone J deposits. Except for flecks of charcoal, no other possible cultural materials were in association or in the soil between this find and the Zone I subassemblage. The lightly water-worn artifact was probably redeposited. The missing artifact was observed in the top of the layer.

The Mazama Component

Artifacts

The list of artifacts attributed to this second component is included in Table 1 and representative artifacts are illustrated in Figure 7. Notes on the categories offered in the discussion of the earlier component also apply to this assemblage with three additional explanatory comments. The *asymmetrical wide-notched point* (Figure 7a) is fairly crudely made, of "medium" size (67 mm long), and has a rounded tip. The *decorated pebble* is a pear-shaped, water-worn rock each surface of which bears indistinct markings that may be decoration or may relate to material that was in some way attached to the object. The most definite "design" is on one edge near the narrow end where 12 evenly-spaced lines are visible. The *pounding stone* (Figure 7k) is a broken pebble with the end margin pulverized flat.

Features

Features extracted from notes, profiles, and floor plans include three hearths and thirty-three stake molds. Stake molds exhibit a more limited distribution of diameters relative to those of the Milliken component. Diameters range from 5 to 13 cm, with the median being 8 cm. The interquartile range is 5 to 8 cm, and only two molds have diameters that are "outside" values, exceeding 11 cm (see Figure 6). Although the stake mold data for Milliken and Mazama components have similar median diameters, a Mann-Whitney test indicates a significant difference at the 0.05 level of probability. The stake molds are not randomly distributed, however, it is difficult to make much of the apparent patterns. Five of the larger molds form a 2.1 m long line, and this is paralleled by a less evenly positioned row of four molds that are 75 cm away. Others form arcs or seem to define irregularly-shaped enclosures.

One of the two hearths (they are about 1.68 m apart) is well removed from all but a single stake mold and the other bears no obvious alignment to nearby molds. The first, which was truncated when the central portion of the site slid over the railway tracks, is now a semicircle measuring 132 by 61 by 28 cm. If originally a full circle, it apparently had a 58 by 30 by 10 cm rock at its centre, but as the hearth is composed of three distinct charcoal strata, the rock relates only to the most recent layer. The other hearth is also semicircular in plan with a lens of charcoal partially surrounded by orange ash. The overall dimensions of this feature are 163 by 81 cm. No thickness was recorded.

Floral and Faunal Material

The only item in this category recovered from the site is a single charred choke cherry pit. It was found in hearth ash.

Chronology

The stratigraphic position of Zone E makes the associated assemblage younger than material from or related to Zone G, from which it is separated by the largely sterile deposits of Zone F. The radiocarbon age estimate also places this horizon at a later date than the lower assemblage. That date (S-61) is 7350 ±150 radiocarbon years or 5400 BC (Borden 1961:4). The Stuiver and Reimer (1993) age calibration program yields a solar year equivalent of 8120 BP (6170 BC).

As reported below, an age estimate from the approximate mid-point of the overlying Zone D2 is 7190 ±150 radiocarbon years. In addition, although not present in the excavated part of the site, an ash layer identified with the eruption of Mount Mazama (ca. 6700 BP or 7550 calibrated years ago) is visible in Zone D2 gravels on the face left after the early 1950s slide. The Zone E "Mazama" component, then, should at least be older than these Zone D age estimates.

The Gravel Component

Artifacts

Artifacts from this component are listed in Table 1 and some are illustrated in Figure 8. Although this assemblage has been redeposited, the majority of material is in good condition with relatively few tool edges rounded from tumbling. Large, heavy pebble-based tools predominate, but small items are also present. The majority of artifacts can be assigned to the types previously identified for the Milliken and Mazama components. New artifact types include a *corner-notched contracting stem point* (Figure 8a), *abrasive slab* (Figure 8j), and *pebble with bifacial peripheral flaking*. The *pebble core tool with battering* is a pre-existing type modified to reflect the battered condition of the artifact. A single *disc bead* occurs at the interface of the gravel and overlying Zone C, but has been assigned to the upper stratigraphic unit. The original artifact catalogue also records a quartz crystal tool derived from the gravels, but this item was not found in the collection.

Features

Three features, identified on profiles, can be attributed to this component. A rock "wall", approximately 46 cm high and 10 to 15 cm thick extends for 60 cm along the interface of Zones D and C. A large, shallow pit measuring 1.5 m wide by 25 cm deep, and a smaller one 25 cm wide by 15 cm deep, extend from the Zone D brown gravels into the D2 gravels. No stake molds were reported.

Chronology

A small carbon layer situated slightly above mid-depth in Zone D2 yielded a date of 7190 ±150 BP (GSC 459) (Borden 1975:67, Wilmeth 1978:74-5). The Stuiver and Reimer (1993) calibration program produces a solar year equivalent of 7930 BP (5980 BC). Borden used the mid-zonal position and similarity of Zone E and D age estimates to argue for rapid deposition of the entire zone D2 gravels. Extrapolating the approximately 200 year difference between the Zone E and mid-Zone D2 radiocarbon estimates, Borden (1967) suggested that deposition of the upper half of the D2 gravel was complete 200 years later. However, close inspection of the excavation profiles indicates a series of distinct gravel and charcoal layers that likely post-date the Zone D2 sample and suggest a number of depositional episodes. Also, although ash from the eruption of Mount Mazama was not found in the excavations, it is clearly visible as a thin stratum in what are interpreted as the D2 gravels of an exposed face to the north. As the currently accepted date for this prominent ash fall is about 6700 BP (ca. 7550 calibrated years ago), this too suggests a rather long deposition period for the zone. The termination date for the brown gravel deposit is uncertain but the oldest radiocarbon estimate from the overlying sandy loam deposits is 2800 ±130 (M-1513; 2870 calibrated years BP). One final clue to the age of the Gravel component is provided by the artifact assemblage. The single corner-notched contracting stem point and the abrasive slab present in the Gravel assemblage are characteristic of the Eayem phase component found at the adjacent Esilao site (Borden 1975:72-3) from ca. 5500-3100 BP (calibrated at 6290-3340 BP).

Comparison of Components

In his most detailed discussion of the Early Period data from the Milliken site, Borden (1975:64-9) considered differences among select artifact types sufficient to define two phases. Here we evaluate these interpretations by examining variability among the lithic artifact types identified in our study.

Borden (1975:63-4) originally noted that the Milliken phase cultural assemblage "includes a wide range of about 600 artifacts." This is considerably more than the 450 items tabulated in our analysis. Some of the discrepancy is due to our practice of excluding artifacts from uncertain contexts (such as wall slough), and the twenty-eight catalogued entries missing from the extant collection. However, examination of uncatalogued material from level bags added a number of tools to both the Milliken and Mazama assemblage samples. Borden's description of the Mazama phase assemblage was based on approximately 100 items (1975:67). Our inventory of 136 artifacts excludes specimens from Zone F and the surface of Zone D that Borden had lumped with the Mazama assemblage, and five now missing catalogue items.

In his comparison of the two phases, Borden (1975:69) noted "the persistence in the Mazama phase of major artifact classes that had been present in the preceding phase. While certain differences between the assemblages may reflect true culture change others may be simply due to insufficient sampling."

The Milliken component is 3.3 times larger than

Mazama (450 items vs. 136 items), and 7.9 times larger than the Gravel component (58 items). Looking at the distribution of tool forms among the assemblages, thirty-one types occur in the Milliken assemblage, twenty-five are present in Mazama, and twenty in the Gravel sample. Assemblage diversity, as measured by the variety of artifact types present, is only 1.25 times greater in Milliken, relative to Mazama. Thus, the sample is sufficiently large that assemblage size has no major effect on artifact diversity.

General measurements of diversity, however, mask some important differences evident in the distribution of specific types in each assemblage. Of the forty-two tool types identified, thirteen (31 per cent) are present in all three assemblages, ten (24 per cent) occur only in the Milliken component, five (12 per cent) are unique to each of the Mazama and Gravel components. Six types (14 per cent) are present in both Mazama and Milliken, while the Gravel strata have only one type common to Mazama and to Milliken each. Types specific to only the Milliken assemblage include large leaf-shaped points, formed unifaces, microblade technology, retouched and utilized slabs, ground and sawn stone artifacts, and pebble gravers. Asymmetrical wide-notched points, formed bifaces, unifacial retouched linear flakes, decorated pebbles and pounding stones are present only in the Mazama component but are

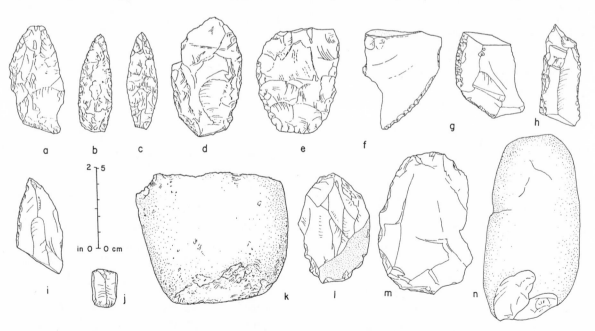

Figure 7. Mazama component artifacts: (a) asymmetrical wide-notched point (No. 1518); (b) point tip (No. 1798); (c) medium leaf-shaped point (No. 1510); (d, e) formed bifaces (Nos. 327, 7073); (f, g) unifacially retouched flakes (Nos. 322, 1706); (h) retouched macroblade (No. 7005); (i) retouched linear flake (Nos. 7024, 7026); (j) pièce esquillée (No. 305); (k) pounding stone fragment (No. 340); (l) retouched pebble flake (No. 1704); (m) flakes slate/schist (No. 302); (n) small flat modified pebble (No. 303); (o) pebble with unifacial peripheral flaking (No. 22470).

Table 1. Artifact tabluations for Milliken, Mazama, and Gravel components.

Artifact class	Component					
	Gravel		Mazama		Milliken	
Asymmetrical wide-notched point	0	.0%	1	0.7%	0	.0%
Contracting stem corner-notched point	1	1.7%	0	.0%	0	.0%
Large leaf-shaped point	0	.0%	0	.0%	1	.2%
Medium leaf-shaped point	0	.0%	2	1.5%	9	2.0%
Leaf-shaped point, tip missing	0	.0%	0	.0%	5	1.1%
Leaf-shaped point base	0	.0%	8	5.9%	17	3.8%
Medial fragment of point	1	1.7%	1	.7%	3	.7%
Point tip	0	.0%	3	2.2%	6	1.3%
Formed biface with acute angle edges	0	.0%	3	2.2%	0	.0%
Formed biface fragment with acute angle edges	0	.0%	5	3.7%	6	1.3%
Formed uniface with acute angle edges	0	.0%	0	.0%	9	2.0%
Formed uniface with steep angle edges	0	.0%	0	.0%	12	2.7%
Flake with acute angle bifacial retouch	3	5.2%	5	3.7%	6	1.3%
Flake with steep angle bifacial retouch	2	3.4%	0	.0%	0	.0%
Flake with acute angle unifacial retouch	6	10.3%	6	4.4%	88	19.6%
Flake with steep angle unifacial retouch	3	5.2%	6	4.4%	35	7.8%
Retouched macroblade	0	.0%	1	.7%	3	.7%
Linear flake with acute angle unifacial retouch	0	.0%	2	1.5%	0	.0%
Macroblade	0	.0%	0	.0%	3	.7%
Macroblade proximal end fragment	0	.0%	0	.0%	7	1.6%
Microblade proximal end fragment	0	.0%	0	.0%	1	.2%
Denticulate flake	2	3.4%	0	.0%	2	.4%
Retouched pebble flake	5	8.6%	7	5.1%	13	2.9%
Pièce esquillée	1	1.7%	8	5.9%	5	1.1%
Utilized linear flake with acute angle edges	0	.0%	1	.7%	2	.4%
Utilized flake with acute angle edges	9	15.5%	36	26.5%	147	32.7%
Utilized flake with steep angle edges	5	8.6%	6	4.4%	8	1.8%
Utilized pebble flake	5	8.6%	5	3.7%	12	2.7%
Pebble flake graver	0	.0%	0	.0%	1	.2%
Pebble core tool	7	12.1%	12	8.8%	19	4.2%
Battered pebble core tool	1	1.7%	0	.0%	0	.0%
Pebble with bifacial peripheral flaking	1	1.7%	0	.0%	0	.0%
Pebble with unifacial peripheral flaking	1	1.7%	1	.7%	0	.0%
Small flat modified pebble	1	1.7%	1	.7%	6	1.3%
Steep angle retouched/utilized slab	0	.0%	0	.0%	4	.9%
Flaked slate and schist objects	2	3.4%	10	7.4%	7	1.6%
Miscellaneous ground and sawn stone	0	.0%	0	.0%	3	.7%
Abrasive stone	1	1.7%	0	.0%	0	.0%
Hammerstone	1	1.7%	4	2.9%	10	2.2%
Pounding stone	0	.0%	1	.7%	0	.0%
Decorated pebble	0	.0%	1	.7%	0	.0%
Total	58	100.0%	136	100.0%	450	100.0%

very low in frequency. Thus, for all three components, common types constitute the majority of the lithic tool assemblages.

With respect to the distribution of particular artifact types in the Milliken phase assemblage, we observed a diversity of retouched flakes and formed unifaces that coincides with the range of "scraper" types described by Borden. Borden (1975:66, Figure 6, No. 1) described an "angle burin made on a stout flake," but this item was missing from the collection. Borden (1975:66) also noted large blade-like flakes that we have classified as macroblades, but states that "true blades are rare, and no blade cores were found. *Microcores and microblades are absent*" (original emphasis). We report one proximal end microblade fragment for the component, but recent experimental evidence suggests this specimen could be a product of biface flaking (Kelly 1984). Additional evidence of prepared cores, or core rejuvenation flakes is needed to confirm the presence of microblade technology during the Milliken phase.

Borden (1975:70) reported that blade technology was lacking in the Mazama phase, however, we identified a single retouched macroblade fragment in the sample. Other artifacts noted as missing from Mazama are "unformed, delicately edge-retouched

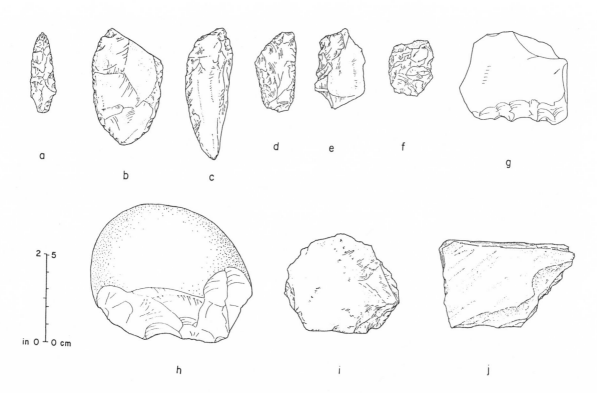

Figure 8. Gravel component artifacts: (a) stemmed point (No. 8796); (b) formed uniface (No. 8781); (c) retouched flake (No. 8803); (d) denticulate flake (No. 8550); (e) pebble core tool (No. 6320); (f, g) retouched flakes (Nos. 8820, 8463); (h) pièce esquillée (No.8790); (i) flaked slate/schist (No. 8428); (j) abrasive slab (No. 8783).

scrapers on very thin flakes" (Borden 1975:70). Although we did not identify this specific artifact type in our analysis, an indirect test of the earlier observations was performed on the thickness of acute and steep angle unifacial retouched flakes. Mann-Whitney tests (see below) indicate no significant differences in thickness for both types between Milliken and Mazama phases. With the exception of pièces esquillées, which are present in the Milliken assemblage, the majority of additions to the Mazama phase noted by Borden (1975:68) are corroborated in our study. We were unable, however, to identify the "dihedral burin made on one end of a narrow straight-edged side scraper" in the sample.

Further phase differences are evident when the relative proportions of artifact types in each assemblage are plotted on a cumulative percentage graph (see Figure 9). The types unique to each assemblage have relatively little effect on the curve; the major shifts are found in types common to both assemblages. In particular, ten types show pronounced differences in frequency distributions among assemblages:
• Flakes with steep and acute angle bifacial retouch have highest proportions in the Gravel component (8.6 per cent vs. 3.7 per cent in Mazama and 1.3 per cent in Milliken).
• Flakes with steep and acute angle unifacial retouch constitute a more substantial proportion of the Milliken assemblage, relative to Mazama and Gravel components (27.4 per cent vs. 8.8 per cent and 15.8 per cent, respectively).
• Pièces esquillées, and flaked slate and schist have a higher proportion in the Mazama assemblage, relative to Milliken and Gravel components (pièces esquillées: 5.9 per cent vs. 1.1 per cent and 1.7 per cent; flaked slate and schist: 7.4 per cent vs. 1.6 per cent and 3.4 per cent, respectively).
• Retouched pebbles (Gravel=8.6 per cent vs. Mazama=5.1 per cent vs. Milliken=2.9 per cent), pebble core tools (12.1 per cent vs. 8.8 per cent vs. 4.2 per cent), and utilized pebble flakes (8.6 per cent vs. 3.7 per cent vs. 2.7 per cent) attain their highest proportions in the Gravel stratum.

We also examined assemblage differences from the perspective of technological organization. Each flaked stone tool was assigned to one of four categories reflecting general tool manufacturing strategies: bifacial formed tools, unifacial formed tools, retouched or utilized flake tools, and pebble-based tools (i.e., all flake and core tools derived from river pebbles and cobbles) (see Table 2). Bifacial formed tools are minimal (3.7 per cent) in the Gravel assemblage. The proportion of bifacial formed tools in the Mazama assemblage (19.2 per cent) is almost twice that of Milliken (10.9 per cent). Both the Gravel and Mazama assemblages lack unifacial formed tools, and this group accounts for only 4.9 per cent of the Milliken sample. Marginally retouched and utilized flakes have quite similar proportions in both the Gravel and Mazama components (57.4 per cent and 59.2 per cent respectively), but comprise 72.3 per cent of the Milliken assemblage. The Milliken component has the lowest proportion of pebble-based tools, whereas the value for the Mazama assemblage is almost twice as large (21.7 per cent). The Gravel component has the highest relative percentage (38.9 per cent). Thus, substantial assemblage differences are evident in the relative emphasis on formed artifacts and pebble-based tools.

While redeposition is likely a contributing factor in formation of the Gravel component assemblage, some of the differences between bifacial, flake, and pebble tool proportions in the Milliken and Mazama components may be due to changes in technological organization. Kelly (1988) suggests that the organizational role of bifaces varies in relation to hunter-gatherer mobility strategies. Borden (1975:66) noted faceted and lipped platforms on flakes and blades in the Milliken assemblage, which are characteristic attributes of soft hammer bifacial thinning activities. Examination of the technological origin of retouched and utilized flake tools indicates differential use of bifaces between the two components. All flake tools were classified according to the kind of flake blank they were manufactured from (see Table 3). In the Mazama component, 10.4 per cent of the flake tools are based on bifacial thinning flakes, while the proportion in the Milliken component is over twice as much (23.1 per cent).

A higher emphasis on using bifaces as cores rather than tools in the Milliken component may account for the twofold proportional increase in use of bifacial thinning flakes for flake tools relative to the Mazama component, and the low percentage of bifacial formed tools noted above. Kelly (1988:719-20) proposes that the use of bifaces as cores and tools should occur under conditions of high residential mobility and limited access to raw material. The differences noted here may, therefore, represent changes in the degree of mobility of the site occupants during the two phases.

Morphological attributes (length, width, thickness) of artifact types occurring in two or more components were tested for significant statistical differences among assemblages. Mann-Whitney tests of the nineteen types common to Milliken and Mazama components, show that only three have significant morphological differences. Thickness of medium leaf-shaped points, length of flakes with steep angle unifacial retouch, and thickness of utilized flakes with acute angle edges are significant at the 0.05 level of probability. Comparisons among all three components were limited to thirteen types. Kruskal-Wallis tests reveal only one additional type attribute, pebble core tool width, significant at the 0.05 level. These results indicate that the artifact types from the three components are quite similar in overall morphology.

DISCUSSION AND CONCLUSIONS

Owing largely to the nature of the archaeological sample, it is possible to reconstruct only selected aspects of the culture and limited kinds of events at DjRi 3. Restrictions are placed by the effects of differential preservation (only stone items and a few carbonized plant remains have survived from the early deposits that are the subject of this report) and of excavation strategy (the judgmentally-placed block excavation does not permit confident generalizations about the entire site). However, with the data available, we offer observations about site formation, season of occupation, site use, lithic technology, and cultural components.

Site Formation

The site was formed during several thousand years of post-glacial time by a combination of environmental and human actions, some of which may be inferred from the distinctive character of the strata described earlier. The sequence of events and, where possible to estimate, their approximate place in time are as follows.

At a time when its canyon was much younger and the Fraser River some 75 or 80 m above its present location, water flowed over a deep, partly-rimmed depression in the river bed. The turbulent stream began to fill this granite hollow with coarse sands and pebbles but before the process was completed, the river had cut its course more deeply to the west. What had once been part of the main river floor became at first a high water river bed and then, as the channel cut deeper and the partial rim of the depression rose above the highest river levels, a seasonally-flooded embayment.

The 5 m of deposits designated as Zones G to K represent this period of transition as the river gradually drew away from the site. Evidence of human presence begins with a single stratigraphically early, but otherwise undated, bifacially-retouched and water-worn flake in the fine silty sands of Zone J. More substantial signs of occupation begin in the dark-stained silts of Zone I (9000 radiocarbon years BP) and continue through Zones H and G, being most evident in the latter, dated at about 8000 radiocarbon years BP (possibly 9000 solar years BP).

The angular gravels of Zone H are not from the river. They likely derive from a creek that seems periodically to have spread substantial deposits of coarse, unsorted rock and sand onto the site, as an alluvial fan. Silt layers, evidence of occasional flooding by the Fraser, bear the few artifacts recovered from this zone. Zone G sands are also fluvial, but because of their uniform size and thickness, they are thought to represent a prolonged period of seasonal flooding of the embayment. Human occupation of the site would have been confined to periods when the Fraser stood at low water.

Several slides, possibly associated with increased activity of the previously-mentioned small creek, built up thick southeast to northwest-sloping layers of coarse angular gravels (Zones F and D) that raised the site surface well above the highest river levels. During this stage of development, there was again a period of human occupation, evident as the dark-stained silt and fine gravels of Zone E (about 8100 BP). Above the thick Zone D gravels are some 2 m of aeolian sand and silt, rich in charcoal, artifacts, and other signs of human activity, but in time (post 3000 BP), these are beyond the scope of this chapter.

Season of Occupation

The Fraser River's periodic flooding provides the minimum pattern for site occupancy. Until 8000 BP, and possibly as late as 7000 BP, the portion of the site investigated was simply not habitable during high water in the late spring and early summer. Of course, people could then have been at the adjacent Esilao site, but excavations there, although deep and still yielding cultural material, were terminated in post Mazama deposits.

The presence of charred cherry pits has been used as a seasonal indicator (Borden 1960:116-17, 1975:63, 69). As choke cherry fruit matures in late summer (i.e., August and September), this does suggest occupancy at least in this season – a period that coincides with low water and re-emergence of the site. However, such evidence only tells us when humans were at the site. It does not mean that would be the *only* time they were there. In brief, we know that until 8000 to 7000 BP, the portion of the site excavated was not occupied in the late spring or

early summer, was inhabited in the late summer, and may or may not have been occupied during all or part of the remainder of the year.

Site Use

Apart from the perhaps incidental use of DjRi 3 as a base for gathering choke cherries, we have little direct evidence of site use. Faunal remains are available in negligible quantities and those few specimens recovered were virtually unidentifiable beyond categorization as land mammal – suggesting, at least, that the occupants also hunted or trapped.

Tool kits of all three early components are what one would associate with hunting, but it must be remembered that only stone implements have survived the centuries and specialized fishing equipment is typically made of bone, antler, wood, and fibre. The assemblages, then, reinforce and strengthen the impression that hunting was one site-based activity, but they do not preclude the existence of others.

Borden (1960) reasoned seasonal evidence provided by the charred cherry pits put people at the site at the same time as a major annual run of spawning salmon and he argued the occupants must have been there for that resource. The events do coincide, and the small, narrowed channel below the site does produce one of the best spearing or netting locations along the river. But, as noted earlier, there is no direct evidence for fishing. We should also recall that stable carbon isotope analysis by Chisholm and Nelson (1983) disclosed an individual at Gore Creek, about 260 km further upstream on the tributary Thompson River and dating from about 6300 BC, was apparently ingesting relatively little (i.e., 9 per cent) marine-origin protein. They conclude that salmon was much less important in the diet then than in later times.

Lithic Technology

Our study of assemblage variability and artifact type morphology indicates continuity among the three Early Period components at DjRi 3, and supports many of the observations originally made by Borden. The salient differences among the assemblages concern more subtle patterning in technological organization, particularly the changing emphasis on pebble-based and formed bifacial tools, and the use of bifacial artifacts, that may reflect differences in the larger adaptive system. We are currently analyzing the debitage from the components to investigate these changes further.

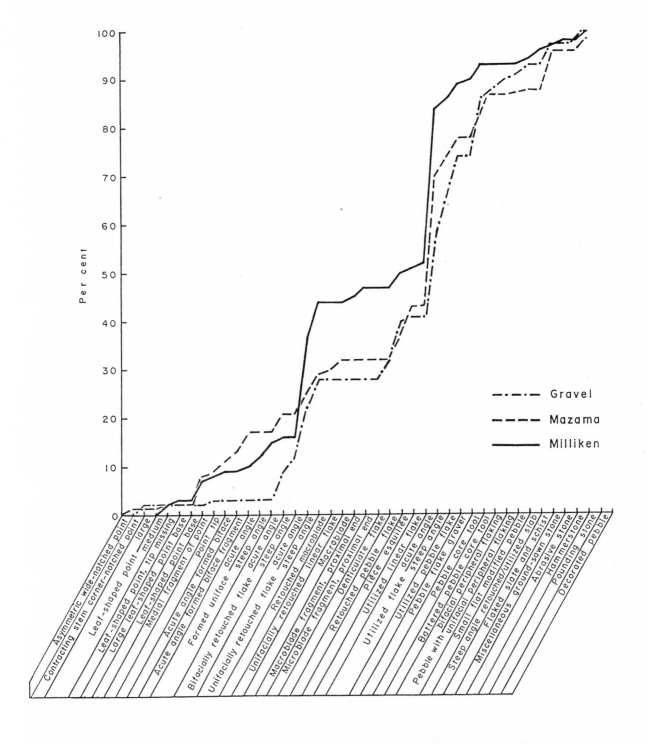

Figure 9. Cumulative percentage graph of Milliken, Mazama, and Gravel component assemblages.

Cultural Components

We have noted that the Milliken, Mazama, and Gravel assemblages display much similarity when all artifact categories are considered. Yet there are also significant differences in the proportions represented by some of these categories. Whether these subdivisions represent units equivalent in degree of separation to other early Pacific Northwest components can only be determined by objective and wide-ranging comparison – a study that is the subject of a forthcoming paper. For the present, we can say that at some level of comparison there is basis for identifying distinct Milliken and Mazama components as had Borden but the later Gravel component must be distinguished from both.

Acknowledgments

Cataloguing of Milliken artifact materials was supported by summer student grants from the British Columbia Heritage Trust. Terry Seidel, Jacqui Metz, and Anne Underhill assisted in the artifact coding. UBC Museum of Anthropology Archaeology Committee Volunteer Associates also helped in cataloguing and curating the collection for study. The UBC Social Sciences and Humanities research grant program provided additional support for the project.

Table 2. Distribution of major technological groups by component.

Component	Bifacial formed tools	Unifacial formed tools	Retouched/utilized flake tools	Pebble-based tools	Totals
Gravel	2 (3.7%)	-	31 (57.4%)	21 (38.9%)	54
Mazama	23 (19.2%)	-	71 (59.2%)	26 (21.7%)	120
Milliken	47 (10.9%)	21 (4.9%)	311 (72.3%)	51 (11.9%)	430
Total	72	21	413	98	604

Table 3. Distribution of technological origins of retouched and utilized flake tools.

Component	Flake technological type					Total
	Flake	Biface thinning flake	Flake shatter	Angular shatter	Pebble	
Gravel	13 (56.5%)	-	9 (39.7%)	1 (4.4%)	-	23
Mazama	28 (41.8%)	7 (10.4%)	30 (44.8%)	2 (3.0%)	-	67
Milliken	80 (26.0%)	71 (23.1%)	155 (50.3%)	1 (0.3%)	1 (0.3%)	308
Total	121	78	194	4	1	398

Figure 10. Excavating the Milliken site. The field crew is resting on the river sands (Zone G) containing the 9000 year old Milliken phase component. Above them rise layers of light-coloured gravels (Zones F to D) in which a few artifacts were found. The thick, dark layer (Zones C to A) capping the stratigraphic profile contains cultural remains of the Middle and Late Periods (See Figure 3).

9

EARLY NAMU

Roy L. Carlson

Namu is a seasonally occupied fishing resort situated near the junction of Burke Channel and Fitzhugh Sound on the central coast of British Columbia. Two names of aboriginal settlements – Ma'was and Na'wamu – are associated with the aboriginal settlement of Namu according to ethnographic records in the Heiltsuk Cultural Education Center at Waglisla. A large prehistoric archaeological site (ElSx 1) is present at Namu. Initial excavation in 1969 and 1970 (Hester and Nelson 1978) uncovered a prehistoric occupational sequence spanning the 9000 years before contact. Further excavation in 1977 and 1978 (Carlson 1979, 1991b, Cannon 1991) refined this sequence and extended the chronology backward in time to 9700 years BP. Further excavation in the summer of 1994 uncovered additional data. The purpose of the following chapter is to present a summary of the artifactual remains that predate 5000 years BP from the 1977, 1978, and 1994 excavations. The entire Namu chronology (Carlson 1991b) has been divided into six periods (Table 1) which incorporate both uncorrected and tree ring corrected C-14 dates; however, all dates given in the text refer to *uncorrected* C-14 dates in keeping with the other chapters in this volume. Cannon (Chapter 10) presents the analysis of faunal remains from Namu, and Hutchings (Chapter 16) a detailed study of the obsidian industry.

THE EXCAVATIONS

The locations of all excavations and relevant site features are shown in Figure 1, and the stratigraphic profiles in Figures 2 and 3. The goal of the excavations was to learn more about the culture of the earliest period so no further work was done in the beachward section of the deposits where the previ-

ous investigators found only assemblages belonging to younger periods. The 1977 field work proceeded through the following steps: re-establishment of the 2 m grid and datum point used previously and mapping of the site; removal of the backfill from the Main Trench (Figure 1) directly behind the bunkhouse, and exposure of the stratigraphic face; excavation parallel to and at right angles to the Main Trench excavation; determination of the limits of the shell midden deposits by probing; and excavation of test pits in areas not previously tested. The main effort was expended on the Main Trench. Excavation units 2 m by 2 m horizontally by 10 cm vertically were the primary excavation units in this and all subsequent excavations; shovels and trowels were used as required. The exact find spots of all artifacts found *in situ* were recorded, and all artifacts found in the screen were recorded by square, level, and stratigraphic unit. All deposits of the pre-5000 BP period were water screened using 1/8th inch mesh screen; a hose attached to a fire hydrant provided the water power necessary to wash the buckets of deposit taken to the screens.

In 1978 further test pitting (Figure 1) resulted in the discovery and excavation of the deep deposits at the river mouth. Initially five test pits behind the rock outcrop at the back of the Main Trench, and three test pits near the river mouth were started. Once it became apparent that very deep deposits were present near the river mouth, two of these squares (Figure 1) were backfilled after being partially excavated to a depth of 30 to 50 cm, so that efforts could be expended on a single 2 m by 2 m unit which was then excavated to its full depth. Profile drawings were made on all four sides of this unit, and the adjoining squares to the east and west were

Table 1. Radiocarbon dates from the site of Namu (ElSx 1).*

Period	C-14 date BP	Tree ring calibrated date BP	Material	Lab. no.
contact				
	480 ±80	(521)	Charcoal	Gak 3121
	680 ±90	(668)	Charcoal	Gak 3122
	980 ±100	(927)	Charcoal	Gak 3123
6	1405 ±120	(1308)	Charcoal	WSU 1942
	1470 ±80	(1361)	Charcoal	Gak 3125
	1840 ±80	(1769)	Charcoal	Gak 3124
	1880 ±90	(1850)	Shell	Gak 3118a
2000 (2000) BP				
	2185 ±85	(2226)	Charcoal	WSU 1939
	2440 ±l00	(2527)	Charcoal	Gak 3119
	2530 ±160	(2650)	Bone	SFU 341
	2540 ±80	(2672)	Charcoal	WSU 1938
	2720 ±80	(2818)	Charcoal	SFU 10
5	2810 ±100	(2922)	Charcoal	Gak 2714
	2880 ±100	(3013)	Charcoal	Gak 2713
	3280 ±100	(3516)	Charcoal	SFU 17
	3330 ±90	(3608)	Charcoal	WSU 1944
	3400 ±100	(3660)	Charcoal	Gak 2715
	3500 ±100	(3774)	Charcoal	SFU 19
3500 (4000) BP				
	3825 ±105	(4218)	Charcoal	SFU 1
4	4290 ±120	(4862)	Charcoal	Gak 2717
	4300 ±125	(4864)	Bone	S2327
	4390 ±160	(4928)	Bone	SFU 343
4500 (5000) BP				
	4540 ±140	(5200)	Charcoal	Gak 2716
	4680 ±160	(5381)	Bone	SFU 342
3	4700 ±125	(5380)	Bone	S2328
	4775 ±130	(5525)	Bone	S2326
5000 (6000) BP				
	5170 ±90	(5940)	Charcoal	WAT 451
	5240 ±90	(5969)	Charcoal	WSU 1943
	5590 ±90	(6375)	Charcoal	WSU 1947
	5590 ±100	(6375)	Bone	SFU 344
2	5700 ±360	(6480)	Charcoal	WAT 456
	5740 ±100	(6506)	Charcoal	WSU 1940
	6060 ±100	(6921)	Charcoal	WSU 1941
6000 (7000) BP				
	6310 ±80	(7210)	Charcoal	Beta 75340
	6550 ±90	(7431)	Charcoal	WAT 517
	7620 ±80	(8502)	Charcoal	Beta 75341
	7800 ±200	(8660)	Charcoal	Gak 3120
1	8570 ±90	(9468)	Charcoal	WAT 516
	9000 ±140	(9920)	Charcoal	WAT 519
	9140 ±200	(10067)	Charcoal	Gak 3244
	9720 ±140	(10676)	Charcoal	WAT 452
10,000 (11,000) BP				

*Calibrated dates BP are given in parentheses. Calibrated dates are based on the computer program provided by the Quaternary Isotope Laboratory at the University of Washington (Stuiver and Reimer 1987). In those instances where this computer program gave several possible calibrated dates, these dates have been averaged to give the single calibrated date shown above. Since this program does not extend beyond the 7800 ±200 BP C-14 date, the six oldest dates (7620 ±80 through 9720 ±140) have

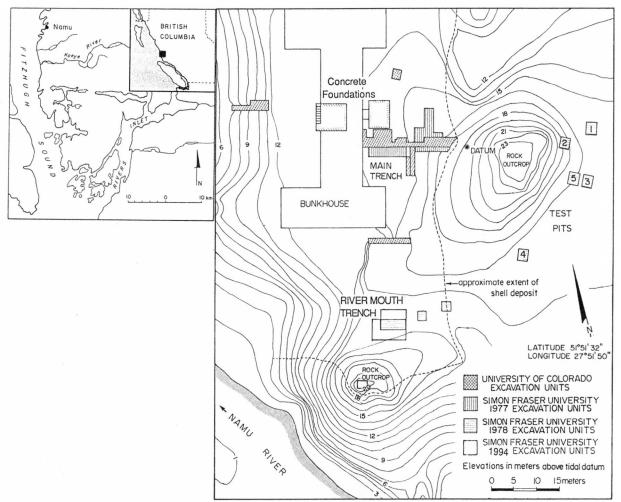

Figure 1. The site of Namu.

then excavated thus forming a single trench 2 m wide by 6 m long from 3.70 to 4.0 m in depth referred to as the Rivermouth Trench. Different strata on the same level were excavated and screened separately, and separate level bags for faunal remains were kept for each stratum by square and level. This deep stratified deposit (Figure 2) provides the main basis for periodization (Table 1) of the pre-2000 BP sequence.

In 1994 the backfill was removed from the Rivermouth Trench and a 2 m by 6 m extension was made to the north. Excavation proceeded in the same manner as previously although it became much

more difficult to follow natural strata because the strata dipped sharply to the northwest, particularly in the square at the northwest corner of the excavation. Water seepage into the lowermost 50 cm of deposit also contributed to excavation problems. Whereas in 1978 there was a reasonable match between levels and natural strata throughout the 2 m by 6 m excavation, such was not the case in 1994, and more levels with strata belonging to different time periods were encountered.

The five test pits excavated in the forested area east of the shell midden deposits in 1977-8 all yielded artifactual remains. Stratification was the same

been calibrated using the following calibration formula: calibrated BP age = the C-14 BP age x 1.05 + 470 years (Stuiver et al. 1986: 969-79). Calibration of the oldest date (9720 ±140 BP) using uranium-thorium calibrations (Bard et al. 1990, Table 1) would actually make this date even older than the 10,676 BP date using the formula, and place it about 11,090 cal years BP. More detailed coverage of the Namu C-14 chronology is given in Carlson (1991b). A date of 2940 ±160 (Beta 75339), which should have dated to the beginning of Period 4, has not been included in this chronology. The small sample size (<1 gm of carbon, once pretreated) probably accounts for this inaccuracy.

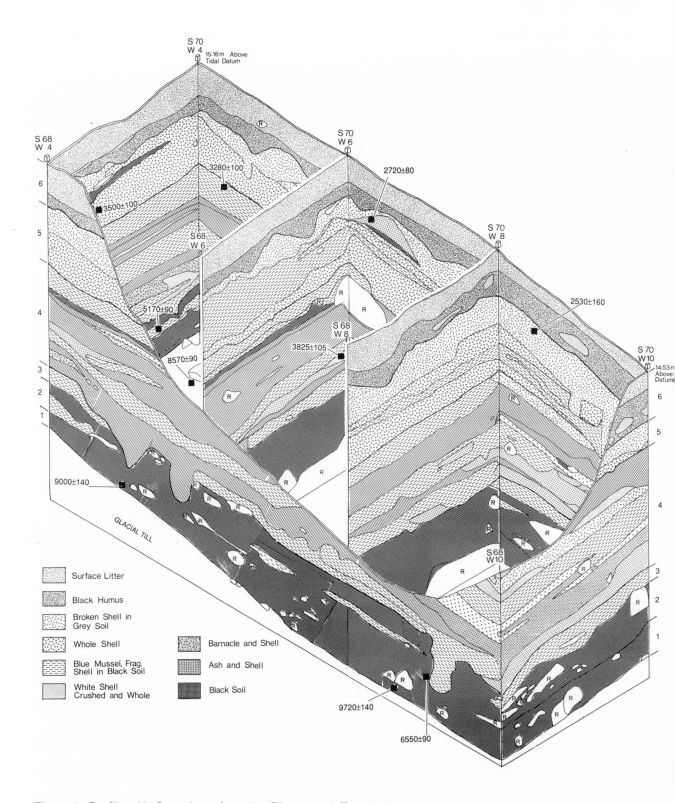

S 70
W 4
15.16m Above
Tidal Datum

S 68
W 4

6

3280±100

3500±100

5

S 68
W 6

2720±80

S 70
W 6

4

5170±90

8570±90

S 70
W 8

3

2

1

3825±105

S 68
W 8

2530±160

S 70
W 10
14.53 m
Above
Datum

6

9000±140

GLACIAL TILL

5

S 68
W 10

4

3

2

1

9720±140

6550±90

Surface Litter

Black Humus

Broken Shell in
Grey Soil

Whole Shell

Blue Mussel, Frag.
Shell in Black Soil

White Shell
Crushed and Whole

Barnacle and Shell

Ash and Shell

Black Soil

Figure 2. Profile with C-14 dates from the Rivermouth Trench. Numbers 1 to 6 refer to the time periods to which the various strata have been assigned on the basis of associated C-14 dates and superposition. The lowermost part of the cultural deposit rests on sterile glacial till about 6 m above present highest high tide. Revised from Carlson (1991b).

86

in all test pits – a dense black shell-free soil up to 70 cm in thickness underlying a 10 to 20 cm thick culturally sterile layer of root mat and humus. Sterile yellow/brown till was found below this cultural deposit. A C-14 date of 5700 ±360 BP (WSU 456) obtained on charcoal from the bottom of the cultural layer in Test Pit 2 marks the beginning of deposition in this part of the site. The types and frequencies of artifacts are consistent with this date and with the artifact assemblages from Period 2 (6000–5000 BP) deposits in the Main Trench and Rivermouth excavations, and as a result, have been assigned to that period.

STRATIFICATION AND PERIODIZATION
The base of the cultural deposit at the Rivermouth Trench is 10.5 m above "0" tide, but only 4.3 m above present high tide. Two stratigraphic units (SU) are observable in the pre-5000 BP sequence, and the uppermost of these is divisible into two sub units, SU 2A and SU 2B. SU 1 is culturally sterile yellow/brown glacial till on which rests SU 2, a brown/black soil with fire-cracked rock, disintegrated sandstone slabs, artifacts and considerable flaking detritus. At the time of deposition of the earliest cultural stratum (SU 2A) this location may have been more of a riverside than a river mouth location. SU 2A, the lowermost culture bearing unit, varies from 0 to 60 cm in thickness and is thickest and oldest at the southwest end of the Rivermouth Trench; it is differentiated from the succeeding SU 2B by the absence of faunal remains. SU 2B is differentiated from 2A by the presence of discontinuous lenses of very fragmentary to pulverized fish and shellfish remains within a black matrix like that of SU 2A. The shellfish lenses were easily differentiatiable from the brown/black matrix in which they were found, and it is clear that they represent depositional events and are not residues of more extensive shellfish remains which have disappeared through chemical decomposition. The earliest faunal remains (Ch. 10) discovered were directly associated with charcoal from SU 2B dated at 6310 ±80 BP. Several pits from the overlying SU 3 and 4 intruded into SU 2 and it is possible that there was some aboriginal mixing of content at the interfaces of the strata. In the northwest corner of the excavation SU 2A is not present and SU 2B rests directly on the glacial till at a depth of 420 cm below the surface.

A subdivision of the cultural content of SU 2 into the following four sub-periods was made on the basis of stratification, surface depth, superposition, and associated C-14 dates, and the artifactual remains (Table 2) have been so grouped: Period 1A, 10,000 to 9000 BP; Period 1B, 9000 to 8000 BP; Period 1C, 8000 to 6000 BP; Period 2, 6000 to 5000 BP. The materials in Period 1A and 1B are from SU 2A. The materials from Period 1C are from the upper part of 2A and the lower part of 2B. The materials from Period 2 are from SU 2B.

The overlying stratigraphic units (SU 3, 4, and 5) in the Rivermouth Trench are composed mostly of molluscan remains, contain many fewer artifacts, post-date 5000 BP, and are not covered in this report.

The Main Trench excavations (Figure 3) revealed the same stratigraphic sequence as that previously described (Hester and Nelson 1978) except that a stratigraphic break was detected in the "black matrix," the lowermost implementiferous stratum, which made it possible to divide it into two units which correspond to SU 2A and 2B of the Rivermouth Trench. SU 2A is found only at the extreme eastern end of the Main Trench (Figure 3) where it rests against a bedrock outcrop and extends westward for only 1 m; its maximum thickness is 60 cm. The two C-14 dates, 9140 ±100 BP and 7800 ±200 BP, previously obtained by the Bella Bella Project date only 2A and not the entire content of the "black matrix" as assumed in the report on the 1969-70 excavations (Hester and Nelson 1978). All of the faunal remains and 90 per cent or more of the artifacts from the 1969-70 excavations in the black matrix belong to SU 2B and date within Period 2 between 6000 and 5000 BP rather than spanning both Periods 1 and 2 from 9000 to 5000 BP.

Only nineteen artifacts were recovered from SU 2A in the 1977 excavations in the Main Trench: obsidian flakes (three); quartz flakes and chunks (nine); andesite flakes (six); and andesite cores (one). These artifacts belong to Periods 1B and 1C between 9000 and 6000 BP.

SU 2B overlies 2A at the eastern extremity of the Main Trench excavation, and extends westward approximately 14 m and laterally to the edges of the excavation (Figure 3). It rests on SU 1, glacial till, except at the far eastern end of the Main Trench where it is superimposed over SU 2A. In appearance it is closely similar to 2A, but is less dense and contains a mussel shell lense at 25 S, 2 E and scattered fragmented shell in squares 4 to 6 W and 6 to 8 W. It incorporates a streak of iron rich sediment at the rear of the deposit which probably represents a chemical alteration of existing deposits. SU 2B reaches 40 cm at its maximum thickness. Two burials (1.11B.1, 1.13D.1) from the previous excavations (Hester and Nelson 1978) belong to stratum 2B. Both are fragmentary, incomplete elderly adults

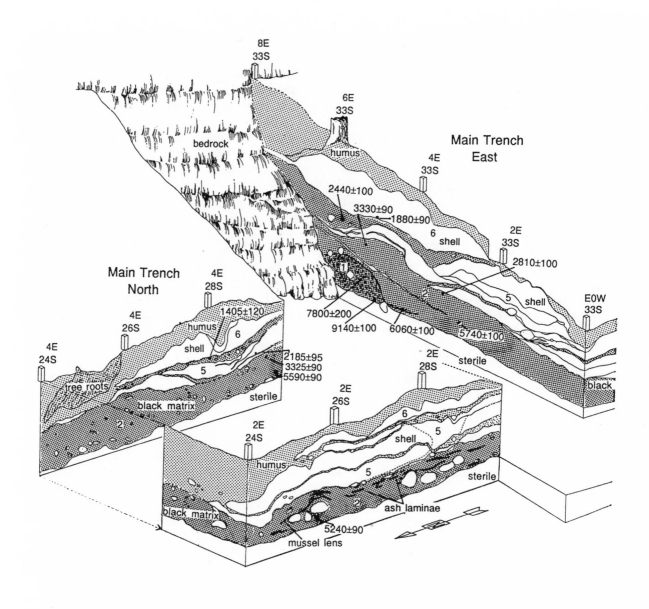

Figure 3. Stratigraphy and C-14 dates in the Main Trench. Numbers 1 to 6 refer to the time periods to which the various strata have been assigned on the basis of associated C-14 dates and superposition. The sterile layer below the cultural deposit is glacial till. Adapted from Carlson (1991b).

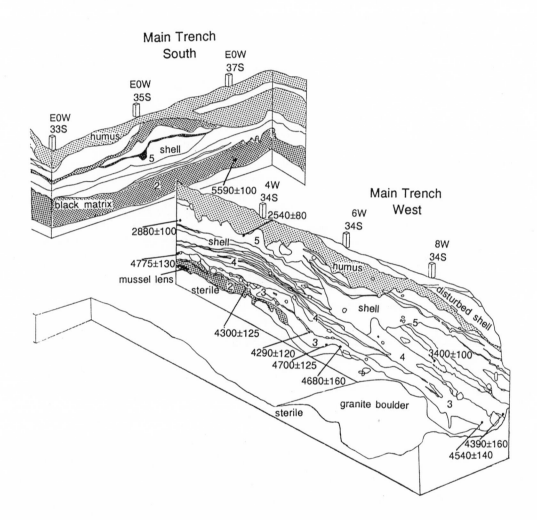

Figure 3 (continued).

lacking grave goods and clear evidence of orientation other than for rocks piled above and below one of them (Curtin 1984). A C-14 date of 5590 ±100 (SFU 344) was obtained on burial 1.11B.1; the other burial was deeper within the same excavation unit. Charcoal, fire-cracked rock, mammal and fish bone, and bone artifacts all occur in this layer. As in the Rivermouth Trench, SU 2B is overlain by massive shell midden deposits which begin between 5000 and 4000 BP, and belong to younger periods.

ARTIFACTUAL REMAINS
Types and frequencies of artifacts are given in Tables 2, 3, and 4. Stone artifacts from the Rivermouth Trench and from the Test Pits are listed in Table 2 by temporal period. Frequencies of bone artifacts are given in Table 4.

Chipped Stone Artifacts
Both local and imported stone were employed for tools. Both macrolithic and microlithic industries are present. The macrolithic industry is based on reduction of river cobbles of andesite, trachyte, basalt, slate, quartzite, and occasionally limestone and granite in descending order of frequency to produce pebble tools, bifaces, scrapers, and other tools. There are a few microliths in some of these materials and in milky quartz and quartz crystal, but the microlithic industry is based mostly on obsidian (Chapter 16) imported from the Rainbow Mountains at the head of the Bella Coola valley to the east, and in some of the younger periods from as far away as Oregon (Carlson 1994). A red and white mottled chalcedony was used for only one artifact, a small point, and could have been either imported or a chance find in till or stream bed deposits. A few flakes and two artifacts of black chert were also recovered.

Debitage
By actual count over 38,000 pieces of debitage including cores (Figure 4 b-g), core fragments, and various types of flakes were recovered from Period 1 and 2 deposits of which most came from the Rivermouth Trench. The macrolithic industry is primarily a core and flake industry. Blades and blade cores (Figure 4d) are very rare. Cores range from cobbles or pebbles from which a single flake was struck to multi-platform remnants from which numerous usable flakes were removed. Several are similar to the tortoise or Levallois type core prepared for the removal of a large single flake; they are part of a logical process of cobble reduction and are not necessarily related to Old World Levallois industries. Flakes show either wide or narrow platforms and are present

in many shapes and sizes including "Levalloisoid" flakes (Figure 5) with wide and sometimes faceted platforms. Most such flakes could have served as tools as struck; a few (Figure 6) have been retouched. A detailed study of all the Namu debitage is currently underway.

Pebble Tools
Two types of pebble tools – core scrapers and unifacial choppers – dominate the assemblage of large tools from the Rivermouth Trench (Table 2) but along with all other artifacts of chipped stone are uncommon in the Main Trench (Table 3). Edge shape on the pebble choppers (Figure 7b-f) is variable; most exhibit evidence of use in the form of small flake scars on the cutting edge. Like the choppers the core scrapers (Figure 7g-j) are unifacial tools made from cobbles, but exhibit a steep scraping edge smoothed from wear, rather than a cutting edge. Rasps (Figure 7k) are pebble ends with centrepetal flake scars and striations indicating their use for grinding or rasping. All three types are probably wood working tools, although it could be argued that several of the choppers are actually cores.

Denticulate Scrapers and Retouched and Utilized Flakes
Denticulate scrapers (Figure 6a, b, d) exhibit steep, jagged marginal retouch on a thick flake or core fragment; in some instances retouch extends around the entire edge of the flake and in other cases it is more limited in extent and is either opposite the bulbar end or along the side. Retouched flakes and utilized flakes have thin, straight, or slightly curving edges, and exhibit no consistent pattern in regard to the relative positions of the bulb and retouched or utilized edge. On utilized flakes the minor edge retouch is presumably from use whereas on retouched flakes the edge retouch, while still marginal, is more pronounced.

Notches, Spurs/Gravers, and Drills
Notches (Figure 8e) are flakes or core fragments with a concave notch resulting from either a single or multiple flake removals. Spurs (Figure 8c, d) consist of a narrow point isolated on both sides by unifacial flake removal on either a flake or core fragment. The one graver consists of a narrow irregular projection isolated on a thick core fragment by unifacial flake removal. The one nearly complete drill (Figure 8g) is bifacially flaked on both the body and the bit. It was found in a disturbed context, but is so similar to the two bit fragments from Periods 1A and 1C, that it can be assigned to Period 1. The body of the other

Table 2. Number of stone artifacts by type and period from the Test Pits and River-mouth Trench at Namu. Period 1A: 10,000 to 9000 BP. Period 1B: 9000 to 8000 BP. Period 1C: 8000 to 6000 BP. Period 2: 6000 to 5000 BP.

	Test Pits	Rivermouth Trench				
Period	**2**	**2**	**1C**	**1B**	**1A**	**Totals**
FLAKED STONE						
Pebble tools						
Core scrapers		8	11	25	8	52
Unifacial choppers	4	3*	3	5	1	16
Pebble rasp			1			1
Scrapers						
End scraper			1			1
Denticulate edge	1	6	12	33	1	53
Thin edge retouched flakes	1	5*	4	13	6	29
Utilized flakes	1	4	8	12	6	31
Notches		2*		3	1	6
Spurs/gravers		1	2	3	1	7
Drills		2	1		1	4
Bifaces						
Preforms	1	12*	8	34	3	58
Knives		3	6	24	3	36
Points, foliate		8	15	28	1	52
Points, tear-drop		1		2		3
Points, incipient stem		1	1	3		5
Points, lanceolate		2		2		4
Points, abrupt tip			1	1		2
Limace		1	1			2
Ovoid, stemmed			1			1
Microliths (non-obsidian)**						
Microblade cores		1	5	4		10
Microblades		7*	5	1		13
GROUND AND PECKED STONE						
Hammerstones	1	3*	1	4	2	11
Ground pebbles	1	1		1		3
Grooved sinkers/bolas				1	1	2
Abraders	2			3		5
Edge ground knife				1		1
Edge ground cobbles	3					3
TOTALS	15	71	86	206	32	412

*One specimen could be from either Period 1C or 2.
**For frequencies of obsidian artifacts see Chapter 16.

Table 3. Period 2 (6000–5000 BP) stone artifacts from the Main Trench.

MACROLITHIC INDUSTRY	
Debitage	
Large cores	10
Core fragments	8
Flakes and fragments	118
Levalloisoid flakes	2
Blades	1
Tools	
Pebble choppers	2
Retouched flakes	1
Spurs/gravers	1
Points, foliate	1
Broad, flat knives	1
MICROLITHIC INDUSTRY	
Microcores, andesite	1
Quartz flakes/chunks	58
Quartz crystal flake	1
Obsidian bi-polar cores	7
Obsidian bi-polar flakes	8
Obsidian microcores	5
Obsidian microflakes	43
Obsidian microblades	34
Obsidian microblade core	2
Obsidian burin spalls	2
Utilized obsidian flakes	10
Obsidian shatter	24
GROUND AND PECKED STONE	
Hammerstones	1
Abraders	1
TOTAL	342

Figure 4. Various stone tools: (a) pebble spall knife unifacially ground on one edge; (b-g) cores. All are from Period 1B except (d) the blade core is from Period 2.

partially complete drill (Figure 8b) shows bifacial flaking only on the bit.

Bifaces

The 165 bifaces (Tables 2, 3) in the assemblage vary in completeness and size, but are quite similar in their general foliate morphology. Many bifaces are best classified as preforms. Bifacial preforms (Figure 11) are irregularly flaked and usually fragmentary as if broken and discarded during fabrication. The large number of preforms is consistent with their direct association with the many flakes and cores found in the Period 1 and 2 deposits in the Rivermouth Trench.

The knives (Figure 10) are broad and thin with flake scars covering most of both faces. All are fragmentary, but the fragments do indicate that they were asymmetric and almost semi-lunar in outline.

The projectile points (Figure 9) vary in size and to a certain extent in shape. The only point from Period 1A (Figure 9a) is of quartzite and has been classified as a point rather than a knife because it is dull along the edges on the lower end for about one-fourth of its length which suggests that it was end-hafted. Later artifacts classified as points are mostly smaller and do not show this attribute. The very small points (Figure 9b, c) were possibly end points for harpoons. Four points (Figure 9c, f, k) have slight insets toward the butt end which almost form a stem. In length-width ratios the points vary from lanceolate (Figure 9n, o) to broad tear-drop forms (Figure 9d, f, l). The latter were made by retouching thin flakes; the bulb is still in evidence on the ventral surface. One preform (Figure 9m) for this style of point was found. Two points (Figure 9q, r) have sharp, abrupt tips. Many of the points are tip and butt fragments; if they were well finished they were classified as points rather than as preforms. Attempts at refitting resulted in only three successful fits (Figure 9e, g, l).

The slug-shaped "limace" (Figure 8f) is plano-convex in cross-section and exhibits flake scars on all faces. Its purpose is unknown. It is not a preform for a biface, but is possibly some kind of microflake core.

Table 4. Period 2 (6500 – 5000 BP) bone artifacts.

	Excavation unit		
	River Mouth	**Main Trench**	**Total**
FISHING AND HUNTING			
Harpoon, bilaterally barbed	1		1
Harpoon, unilaterally barbed	3		3
Harpoon valve fragments		3	3
Bone points	1	5	6
Fish hook barbs, plain	10	9	19
Fish hook barbs, flanged and barbed	6	1	7
Fish hook shank fragment	1		1
One-piece curved fish hook fragment	1		1
Atlatl hooks	2		2
Barbed object	1		1
Grooved point fragment		1	1
MANUFACTURING			
Needles	5	1	6
Ulna awl tip	1	2	3
Awls, irregular butt		2	2
Ground rodent incisor		1	1
OTHER ARTIFACTS			
Antler tine with encircling grooves	2		2
Drilled bone fragment	1		1
Worked object fragments	21	7	28
Grooved and snapped antler beam	1		1
Dagger (?) tips		2	2

The stemmed ovoid (Figure 8a) is of black chert and bifacially flaked.

Microliths

The obsidian industry, which is entirely microlithic, is described in Chapter 16. The milky quartz industry has not been analyzed in detail; some bipolar cores and some flakes the shape and size of microblades are present, but most pieces are either microflakes or chunks classifiable as core fragments. Two microblades from Period 1C are of quartz crystal. Andesite was used for some bi-polar cores and flakes, but the collections have not been completely sorted for this type of artifact.

There are two types of microblade cores present. The tiny (1.2 by 1.5 cm) pyramidal core (Figure 12e) exhibits no platform preparation and shows the removal of four small blades. The other type is a tabular core (Figure 12a, b, d) similar to the Kasta type described in Chapter 14. All of the examples are fragmentary and the diagnostic attributes cannot be measured with accuracy. Many of the obsidian cores (Chapter 16) were probably conical of which the largest fragment (Figure 12c) shows multiple blade removal.

Ground and Pecked Stone

Ground and pecked stone artifacts are uncommon, but a few are found in all periods. Hammerstones are rounded or elongate cobbles which exhibit battering on one or both ends. Ground pebbles are small (ca. 4 cm in diameter) and exhibit striations from grinding on a single flat face. Abraders (Figure 13b, c) are irregular pieces of schist or sandstone which exhibit striations or polish. The ground knive (Figure 4a) from Period 1B is a large thin cobble spall which has been ground and polished on the dorsal face of the edge opposite the bulb; the other is a small fragment. The sinker or bolas stone from period 1A (Figure 13b) is a small oval pebble with a groove encircling the long dimension. The sinker from Period 1B (Figure 13d) is much cruder and consists of a pebble

Figure 5. Levalloisoid flakes, not retouched.
Period: 1B (a-g), 1C (k), 2 (h, i), 3 (j).

with a naturally pitted surface and encircling groove which has been artificially notched at both edges; the groove encircles the narrow diameter. Edge-ground cobbles (Figure 13a) are flat cobblestones which show either polishing or both battering and polishing on a single narrow edge, 1.0 to 1.2 cm wide.

Bone and Antler Artifacts

A small sample of bone and antler artifacts (Table 4, Figures 14 to 17) was found in Period 2 deposits. No bone artifacts were found in earlier deposits, although Period 1C levels did yield a few faunal remains (Chapter 10). In view of the continuities into Period 2 of the types of stone artifacts from the earlier deposits of Period I, it seems probable that these types of bone and antler artifacts were also present during the earlier period. In the descriptions which follow all artifacts were made from land mammal bone unless otherwise specified.

Harpoon Heads

The earliest harpoon head both in terms of stratigraphy and maximum surface depth is a small burned fragment of a bilaterally barbed head (Figure 14b) made of sea mammal bone. This fragment is probably the same type as a complete example (Figure 14a) found slightly later in a level containing deposits of both Periods 2 and 3. The same type was also found in the Main Trench excavations (Hester and Nelson 1978, Figure 33k).

Only two (Figure 14c, d) of the three unilaterally barbed harpoon heads are complete enough for description; they are small with tapering oval bases for insertion into the shaft or foreshaft, and a single line shoulder.

The artifacts classified as self-armed harpoon valves (Figure 14d) appear to be unfinished examples. They come from deposits which date to the very end of Period 2 at 5000 BP. Complete examples (Hester and Nelson 1978, Figure 35g-m) are know from younger periods. This type of composite socketed harpoon head is the most long-lived type known from the coast.

Bone Points

All of the bone points (Figure 15d, e) are fragmentary but may have served as arming tips for hunting weapons.

Fish Hooks

Parts of several different types of fish hooks are present in the assemblage. The most common type consists of elongate barbs (Figure 16a-h) made of ground and polished land mammal or bird bone that have ethnographic analogs as barbs for composite fish hooks with wooden shanks. The larger specimens probably served for halibut, and the smaller ones for salmon and other smaller fish. The different shapes of the butt ends – wedge-shaped, conical, squared, pointed with a D-shaped cross-section, and irregular – indicate some were side-hafted and others end-hafted to the shank. Fish hook barbs of this class are found throughout later periods on the Northwest Coast.

The barbed fish hooks with a basal flange (Figure 16j-p) have no Northwest Coast analogs, but do occur in the Siberian Neolithic (collections in Novosibirsk and Irkutsk) and among the Inuit. The Siberian examples are larger and some are still hafted to their shanks. This type of flanged barb has been found only in Periods 2 and 3 at Namu.

One fragment of a bone shank (Figure 17a) for a composite fish hook was recovered. A groove for holding the barb is present on one face. This is the earliest known example of this type of artifact which is known slightly later from the Queen Charlotte

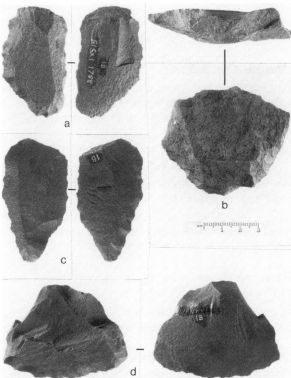

Figure 6. Retouched Levalloisoid flakes: (a, b, d) steep-edged denticulate scrapers; (c) point. Period: 1B (a, c, d), 2 (b).

Islands (Fladmark, Ames, and Sutherland 1990, Figure 7w).

The curved one-piece fish hook (Figure 17b) is fragmentary with both hook and shank ends missing. Complete examples have been found in slightly younger contexts in the Queen Charlotte Islands (Fladmark, Ames, and Sutherland 1990, Figure 17x).

Atlatl Hooks

The two atlatl hooks or spurs (Figure 17c, d) are short pieces of ground bone with an abrupt polished tip, D-shaped cross section, and tapered butt. Their overall morphology suggests that the tapered end was inserted into a socket on the flat upper distal end of the atlatl leaving the abrupt tip exposed for engaging the end of the atlatl dart.

Barbed Object

This artifact (Figure 18a) is an elongate piece of sea mammal bone with barbs along one side and blunt ends. It may be a reworked section of a fixed point or a preform.

Grooved Point Fragment

A pointed fragment of ground and polished sea mammal bone (Figure 18b) with a single opposing groove on each side is possibly part of a point for side

Figure 7. Unifacial pebble tools. (a) pebble end tool; (b-f) pebble choppers; (g, h, i) core scrapers; (k) pebble rasp of sandstone. Period: 1B (a, b, d, e, h), 1C (c, g, j), 2 (e, i), 2 or 3 (f).

Figure 8. Miscellaneous chipped stone artifacts: (a) biface of black chert; (b) drill on unifacial flake; (c, d) spurs; (e) notch; (f) limace; (g-j) drills. Period: 1A (h), 1B (a, d, e), 1C (c, f, i), 2 (j); (g) probably Period 1 or 2.

hafting microblade segments, but is too incomplete for certain identification. This artifact is broken just below the starting point of the grooves.

Needles and Awls
The needles vary from flat oval to circular in cross-section. The three proximal fragments all show an eye which has been sawn (or cut?) rather than drilled from both faces. Only one needle (Figure 19a) is complete.

Awls of deer ulnae are common in all periods of coastal prehistory and probably were multi-purpose tools used to slit herring and other fish and for basketry. The other awls have very sharp points for making perforations, and butt ends unmodified for hafting.

Ground Beaver Incisor
The beaver incisor (Figure 15b) consists of a distal end fragment which has been beveled probably for use as a carving or wood-working tool.

Other Bone and Antler Artifacts
The antler beam (Figure 15a) has been grooved and then snapped, and demonstrates this common method of preparing antler for tool making. The antler tine (Figure 15c) exhibits a series of cut, parallel encircling grooves and may have been intended as

Figure 9. Bifacial projectile points: (a, b) quartzite; (c) pink chalcedony; (h) slate; (d, e, g, i, j, k) andesite; (f) greenstone. Period: 1A (a), 1B (e-i, k, l, p), 1C (b, c, m, n, o, q), 2 (d, j, k).

an ornament. The two artifacts speculatively classified as dagger tips are of highly polished bone and resemble more complete daggers of later periods; they could equally well be parts of knives.

The remaining fragments are pieces of bone or antler which show shaping by grinding and polishing, but are not complete enough to classify. Their presence does attest to the importance of bone and antler as a raw material for artifacts. The many fragments of broken bone which do not show grinding or polishing have been grouped with the faunal remains even though many of them are probably detritus from tool manufacture.

DISCUSSION

Namu contains at 9700 BP the earliest C-14 dated cultural remains on the coast of British Columbia. Geological evidence (Josenhans et al. 1993) indicates that the coastal plain to the north and west of Namu was probably habitable 3000 years earlier, so the earliest assemblage at Namu is not necessarily the earliest that will eventually be found if earlier occupations are not all below present sea level. At that time the coast of British Columbia could not have been an easy place to colonize and make a living.

The early Namu artifacts are for the most part simple forms of generalized piercing, cutting, chop-

Figure 11. Bifacial point (a-c, e, f, h, m) and preform (d, g, i-l) fragments. Period: 1B (b, d, e, h), 1C (a, j, m), 2 (c, e, g, i).

ping, and scraping implements of flaked stone. It is sometimes assumed that flaked stone industries are indicative of land based hunters, particularly if bifaces constitute a large part of the assemblage. On the Northwest Coast such is not the case; large assemblages of flaked stone tools are more indicative of early time placement and archaic technology than of a single primary subsistence pattern. However, in the light of recent geological work it is still quite possible that the earliest inhabitants of the central coast were dependant on land hunting rather than fishing. Between 13,500 and 10,500 years ago sea levels were much lower and a coastal plain with lakes and streams was present to the west of Namu at the Goose Island bank as well as further north (Blaise et al. 1990, Fedje 1993, Josenhans et al. 1993, Luternauer et al. 1989). If this habitat sustained a mammalian land fauna such as caribou or even some of the Pleistocene megafauna, this presence would have been both an incentive for hunting peoples to move into this region and a means for them to make a living. With rising sea levels and submergence of the coastal plain most evidence of such an occupation would now be under water. The earliest cultural component at Namu could be an up-river

Figure 10. Fragmentary broad, bifacial knives from Period 1B.

Figure 13. Ground stone artifacts: (a) edge-ground cobble; (b, c) whetstones; (d) grooved sinker; and (e) bolas stone. Period: 1A (e), 1B, b, c, d), 2 (a).

Figure 12. Microblade cores: (a, b, d) fragments of tabular andesite cores; (c) fragment of conical obsidian core; (e) pyramidal andesite core. Period: 1B (a, b), 1C (e), 2 (c, d).

continuation of such an occupation in the throes of adapting to the salmon based subsistence system in evidence by 6000 years ago.

The earliest assemblage, Period 1A, is dominated by a macrolithic flaked stone industry of just under 1000 pieces. Only thirty-two of these pieces, including preforms are tools. The succeeding assemblages in Periods 1B and 1C are much larger both in terms of tools (Table 2) and the 25,000 to 30,000 pieces of debitage. The most prevalent activity indicated by the composition of the entire Period 1 assemblage is the manufacture of flaked stone tools. The most common tools are large core scrapers, retouched and utilized flakes, foliate bifaces including points, knives, and preforms, and denticulate scrapers. These tools continue as common types throughout Periods 1 and 2. Ground and pecked stone tools are present in small numbers as early as Period 1A and indicate knowledge of this technology. Microblade technology and bone tools are the most notable absences in Period 1A. The latter is a matter of preservation whereas the former is either a matter of the small sample size of this assemblage or of culture history. Microblade technology is also absent in the earliest assemblages from other coastal and up-river sites: Ground Hog Bay (Ackerman et al. 1979); Skoglund's Landing (Fladmark 1990); Bear Cove (C. Carlson 1979); Milliken (Mitchell and Pokotylo, Chapter 8); and Five Mile Rapids (Cressman et al. 1960).

Although the tool assemblage from Period 1B in the Rivermouth Trench is much larger than that of Period 1A, its composition is very much the same except for the appearance of microblades at about the middle of the period. The use of andesite which resulted in the rather crude microblade cores typical of Period 1B is soon succeeded by the use of imported obsidian which resulted in a much more serviceable product (Chapter 18). Foliate points with slight insets at the shoulders also appear at this time. The composition of the assemblage of Period 1C is little different from that of 1B.

Period 2 is the first period for which there is a good representation of artifacts from all three areas of the site – the Main Trench, the Rivermouth Trench, and the Test Pits. In the Rivermouth Trench the assemblage is still dominated by lithic workshop debris which, along with the earlier artifact types (except for obsidian microblades and microflakes), decreases in frequency throughout Period 2. Other than for the much smaller amount of flaked stone debitage and the absence of core scrapers, the assemblages in the Test Pits and Main Trench are very similar to that in the Rivermouth Trench. Edge ground cobbles have only been found in the Test Pits during this period. Microblades (Chapter 18) peak in frequency in Period 2 and the few found after the end of this period are probably either fortuitous or intrusive from earlier deposits.

The unifacial pebble choppers, pebble rasps, and core scrapers are probably the earliest heavy-duty wood-working tools of the Northwest Coast, with the notches, gravers, and drills used for lighter work. The pollen record indicates that cedar was not available in quantity until sometime after 6000 BP (Hebda and Mathewes 1984), so other woods may have been used for frameworks for boats and houses. Large dugout canoes and plank houses were probably not present in the early Namu time period although some kind of watercraft and shelter must have been is use. The denticulate scrapers and retouched flakes could have been used for fleshing and scraping skins for clothing, tents, and watercraft. The large bifaces are spear points and/or knives, and were supplemented by about 8500 BP by small bifaces which were probably the arming tips for harpoons, and by microblades. The microblades were probably inset into projectile heads of bone or antler to form the cutting edges. The spear thrower was presumably used with these projectiles. Evidence for this implement is present in the form of small bone spurs for inserting in the distal end of the spear thrower to engage the end of the spear shaft. The edge-ground cobbles and ground pebbles might be plant processing tools. The small grooved pebbles are usually interpreted as bolas stones, but they could well have been line weights for fishing.

The Namu bone tools, which are first preserved in Period 2 deposits, also provide insights into aspects of early Namu culture. By far the largest number of these artifacts relate to the fishing industry, but sea mammal hunting with harpoons, sewing of skin clothing with bone needles, and wood carving with beaver incisor chisels are also inferable from the remains. Spurs/gravers are present from Period 1A and abraders from Period 1B and indicate that bone was also worked during these earlier periods. The tool industries, the faunal remains (Chapter 10), and the potentialities and limitations of the local habitat indicate that the earliest peoples of Namu hunted sea mammals and fished.

Obsidian does not occur naturally in the near vicinity of Namu; its occurrence there indicates trading relationships or contact with regions where it does occur (Carlson 1994). A single piece of obsidian from Period 1A (10,000 to 9000 BP) has been fingerprinted by X-ray fluoresence and came from the Anahim Peak source in the Rainbow Mountains

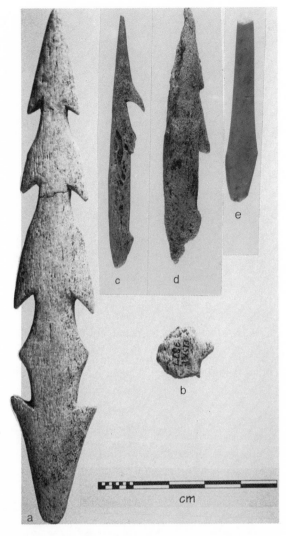

Figure 14. Bone artifacts from Periods 2 and 3: (a, b) bilaterally barbed harpoon head and fragment; (c, d) harpoon heads with line shoulders; (e) valve for self-armed composite harpoon head, tip missing. Period: All are from Period 2 except (a) which could be either Period 2 or 3.

some 200 km to the east. By 8000 years ago obsidian from the Mackenzie Pass source also in the Rainbow Mountains is present, and by 6000 years ago obsidian from a source to the south thought to be in the vicinity of Mount Silverthrone on the mainland opposite the northern end of Vancouver Island. By 4000 years ago a few pieces of obsidian from eastern Oregon reached Namu and other nearby sites.

The artifact types present are also clues to the historical relationships of early Namu culture. Assuming the sample of artifacts is representative, then the forms of these tools and their frequencies are the result not only of the interaction between the tool making tradition, available raw materials, and

Figure 15. Bone artifacts from Period 2: (a) antler beam fragment showing groove and snap technique; (b) beaver incisor chisel fragment; (c) incised antler tine; (d, e) point fragments.

the necessities of life in this particular habitat, but of traditional behaviour patterns of antecedent cultures. The Namu tool assemblages are not isolated manifestations, but are part of a pattern of tool making and use over a wider area. Not surprisingly, the closest comparable assemblages are found at other sites in the coastal environs of British Columbia, Washington, and Oregon. The earliest assemblages are part of a widespread cultural tradition called the Pebble Tool Tradition (Carlson 1983a:86-90, 1990b:60-9) which is identified by the co-occurrence of unifacial pebble tools and leaf-shaped bifaces with other simple flaked stone tools in early sites on the Northwest Coast. The dates on sites of this tradition indicate that between 10,000 and 9000 BP, before the introduction of microblade technology, the Pebble Tool Tradition was moving southward along the coast and spreading up the major river valleys. Slightly later microblade technology originating from cultures to the north was

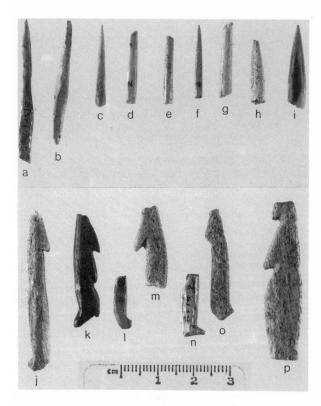

Figure 16. Fish hook barbs and other bone artifacts: (a) possible gorge type fish hook; (b-e) barbs for composite fish hooks; (f) complete barb with squared butt; (g-i) bone point fragments; (j-p) flanged, unilaterally barbed fish hooks. All Period 2 except (k) which is Period 3.

Figure 17. Bone artifacts from Period 2: (a) fragment of a shank for a composite fish hook; (b) fragment of a curved one-piece fish hook; (c, d) atlatl hooks.

adopted by the people of Namu and other Pebble Tool Tradition sites.

At the end of Period 2 at Namu at about 5000 BP the nature of the deposition changed drastically. Massive deposits of clam shell dominate the site and the artifact inventory changes to one dominated by bone tools. The reasons for these changes are not fully understood, but they are probably related in part to changes in sea levels.

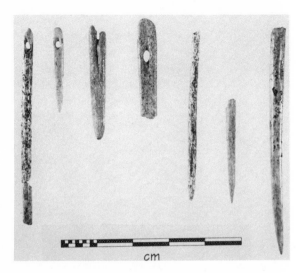

Figure 19. Bone needles from Periods 2 and 3.

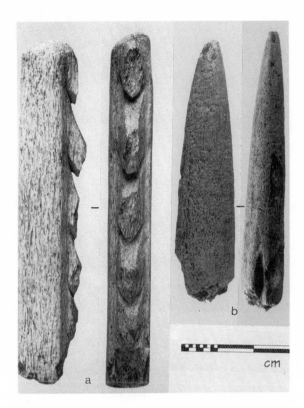

Figure 18. Artifacts of sea mammal bone from Period 2; (a) unilaterally barbed object with blunt ends; (b) point fragment showing traces of bilateral grooves which could have been used for hafting microblade insets.

Figure 20. Excavation of the Rivermouth Trench at Namu in 1994.

Acknowledgments

The 1977-8 excavations were funded by the Archaeological Field School, Department of Archaeology, Simon Fraser University which operated both with permission of BC Packers, the owners of the site at that time, and under a letter of agreement from the Bella Bella Band Council, which included the employment of two band members. A grant from the President's Research Grant Committee paid for the C-14 dates. BC Packers provided considerable logistical support. The 1994 excavation was a joint research project between Simon Fraser University represented by the Department of Archaeology and the Heiltsuk Tribal Council represented by the Heiltsuk Cultural Education Center. Funding was provided by a grant from the British Columbia Heritage Trust to Roy Carlson, and by the Archaeological Field School. The Heiltsuk Cultural Education Center and the Heiltsuk elders provided some food and logistical support including a huge banquet at Waglisla and funding for four high school students as part of their Challenge program. Additional logistical support came from Namu Harbour Resorts Ltd., the current owners of Namu, and from Chris Carlson Guide Service. Maureen Carlson directed the cataloguing of artifacts. Without the support provided by these individuals and agencies and their respective staff, this project would not have been possible. My thanks go to all of these individuals and agencies and particularly to the students enrolled in the Archaeological Field School who in their quest for archaeological knowledge worked long and hard with no financial remuneration.

10

THE EARLY NAMU ARCHAEOFAUNA

Aubrey Cannon

The early Namu archaeofauna indicate the full establishment of a broad-based marine economy as early as 6000 BP. Although there were changes in the emphasis placed on certain classes of fauna in later periods, largely as the result of environmental change in the immediate site vicinity, all elements of the subsistence economy and much of the pattern of later site utilization were already in place during the earliest period for which faunal remains are available.

Studies based on earlier excavations at Namu (Conover 1978) produced a clear picture of changes in the use of shellfish and a limited overview of trends in mammalian fauna. Subsequent excavations by Simon Fraser University in 1977, 1978, and 1994 (R. Carlson 1979, Carlson, Chapter 9) yielded a much greater quantity of vertebrate faunal remains (Cannon 1991), particularly for the period between 6060 and 5170 BP. Although artifacts were recovered from deposits dating to as early as 9720 BP, the earliest fauna are from bulk samples taken in 1994 from strata designated as Period 1C (7620 to 6310 BP). These yielded small quantities of vertebrate fauna, but no remains of shellfish. The majority of faunal remains were recovered from deposits designated as Period 2 (6060 to 5170 BP). Scattered lenses of shell in the Period 2 deposits reduced soil acidity and enhanced the preservation of bone.

DATA

Samples taken from a wall of the 1994 excavations yielded a small amount of faunal material after being washed through a 1/16 inch (1.6 mm) mesh screen. The earliest sample, directly associated with a radiocarbon date of 7620 ±80 years, produced a small number of fish remains, including calcined salmon vertebrae. A sample from a later deposit directly above, which was radiocarbon dated to 6310 ±80 years, produced a larger quantity of bone. Two identified mammal bones, several unidentifiable fragments, and several fish vertebrae were recovered from comparable levels in adjacent excavation units. The recovery and analysis of fauna from the 1977 and 1978 excavations are discussed in greater detail elsewhere (Cannon 1991). The bulk of the matrix was washed through 1/8 inch (3.2 mm) mesh screen. All bone retained in the screens was recovered for later identification. Most of the bone elements were identified to at least the family level. Genera and species identifications were made when they could be established with confidence and the additional information was relevant for understanding the nature of specific economic activities. The frequencies of fauna recovered from the Period 2 deposits are listed in Tables 1 to 3. The minimum number of individuals (MNI) was not estimated because of the well-documented interpretative problems involved (Grayson 1984), but comparison of the basic number of identified specimens (NISP) is more than adequate to appreciate the character of the early Namu subsistence economy.

INTERPRETATION

The small sample of faunal material from Period 1C cannot be considered representative in itself, but it is consistent with the clear maritime orientation evident in later periods. Two identified mammal fragments were from a harbour seal (*Phoca vitulina*) and sea lion (*Eumetopias jubata*). A single unidentified distal tibiotarsus was from a duck-sized bird. The large fish sample included: sixteen salmon

(*Onchorhynchus* sp.) vertebrae; 189 vertebrae and nineteen cranial elements of herring (*Clupea harengus pallasi*); two greenling (*Hexagrammos* sp.) vertebrae; and one vertebrae each from dogfish (*Squalus acanthias*) and cod (Gadidae). This degree of diversity from such a small sample is remarkable, as is the overwhelming focus on marine resources, especially salmon and herring, which is typical of later periods, and the even greater range of vertebrate specimens present in the larger samples from Period 2.

The full pattern of the early Namu subsistence economy is revealed by the much larger quantity of remains recovered during excavations in 1977 and 1978. Information relating to the ethnographic exploitation, species characteristics, and habits of these fauna is presented below under the headings of Fish, Mammals, and Birds. Various lines of evidence relating to the seasons of site occupation are also pulled together under a separate heading, and all of these data, and others relating to shellfish utilization, are used to develop a synthesis of zoo-archaeological insight into the culture, economy, and environment of early Namu.

Fish

The two most important characteristics of the early Namu fishing economy are the variety of fish exploited and the already developed emphasis on salmon as the single most important fish resource (Table 1). The variety of species indicates even earlier development of the skills and technology necessary to exploit fish that exhibit diverse behaviours (e.g., occurring as isolated individuals, schools, or anadromous runs) and inhabit a range of environments (river, shallow foreshore, the bottom of deeper water, etc.). There is little question that a marine fishing-based economy with its requisite knowledge and techniques was in place for some period prior to the time of the earliest preserved fish remains. The only major contrast with later fishing patterns at the site is in the degree of emphasis placed on salmon.

Salmon is predominant among fish remains recovered from Period 2 and later period deposits. Although salmon accounts for 89 per cent of the Period 2 fish remains, this is still significantly below its peak of 97 per cent of the fish recovered from Periods 3 and 4 deposits (4775 to 3825 BP). The Namu fauna seems to support Fladmark's (1975:207-8) suggestion that full productivity of salmon streams may not have been achieved until around 5000 BP, after sea levels (Andrews and Retherford 1978:348) and river-beds had stabilized. Salmon was an important resource well before 5000 BP, but there is a

Table 1. Taxonomic abundance of early period fish (NISP: Number of Identified Specimens).

Taxon	NISP
Rajidae (rays, skates)	1
Squalus acanthias (spiny dogfish)	74
Hydrolagus colliei (ratfish)	59
Clupea harengus pallasi (herring)	28
Oncorhynchus sp. (Pacific salmon)	5720
Gadidae (cods)	81
Sebastes sp. (rockfish)	318
Anoplopoma fimbria (sablefish)	4
Hexagrammidae *Hexagrammos* sp. (greenlings)	76
Ophiodon elongatus	3
Cottidae (sculpins)	3
Pleuronectidae (flatfish)	48

significant increase in later period deposits. The timing and species composition of the early Namu salmon fishery are consistent with later patterns. The major emphasis was on a late fall fishery, primarily for coho (*Oncorhynchus kisutch*) and chum (*O. keta*) and also for some pink salmon (*O. gorbuscha*) (Cannon 1988).

The figures in Table 1 do not reflect the economic importance of herring (*Clupea harengus pallasi*), which is even more abundant than salmon. Much of the herring bone was lost through the 1/8 inch (3.2 mm) mesh screen, but analysis of selected matrix samples (Fawcett 1991) showed herring to be present in very large numbers throughout the fauna-bearing deposits. This observation was also confirmed by analysis of bucket-auger samples recovered in 1994, and by the quantity of herring found in the Period 1C bulk samples. Preliminary analysis of the auger samples shows that herring are up to fifteen times as abundant as salmon. This magnitude of difference is characteristic of all periods, including Period 2. The auger samples have also yielded a very few remains of eulachon (*Thaleichthys pacificus*), including a single specimen from the Period 2 deposits. An isolated find of a dense mass of herring bone on the sterile subsoil surface at the base of the Period 2 deposits within one excavation unit is further indicative that herring was a major resource by at least the 6000 BP date of that deposit. It is ethnographically reported that herring were caught with rakes during the spawning season (February to April) when the fish gather in great numbers in shallow bays. The abundance of herring in the early deposits is a good indication of spring utilization of the site.

Other fish were considerably less important to the subsistence economy, and their exploitation during the early period was roughly consistent with that of later periods. Within the groups of *Sebastes* sp. (rockfish), Gadidae (cods),[1] and Pleuronectidae (flatfish) a variety of different species are represented, though none in economically signficant numbers. Within the family Hexagrammidae, only three elements of the species *Ophiodon elongatus* (ling cod) were identified; the rest were greenling (*Hexagrammos* sp.) species. Halibut (*Hippoglossus stenolepis*) was positively identified within the family Pleuronectidae, but halibut was never a significant resource at Namu; it is very poorly represented in the early period deposits, with just two identified specimens recovered. The subsistence value of skate, sculpin, and ratfish was probably negligible, but their presence in numbers comparable to later periods is another indication of the long-term consistency of the fishing economy.

Spiny dogfish (*Squalus acanthias*) is one species that is slightly more abundant in the early deposits. There may have been a greater cultural emphasis on dogfish in the early period, though it is reported ethnographically that dogfish was disdained as food among Northwest Coast groups. The Kwakiutl normally considered dogfish inedible, though they would resort to eating it during periods of famine or hunger (Rohner 1967:17). Dogfish was an important source of oil, and this may have been its value to the early Namu population. If it was also considered a starvation food, then its abundance might indicate more frequent food shortage. Salmon productivity was still below peak levels, and there is no indication of intensive shellfish utilization prior to 4775 BP. Shellfish supplemented salmon during later periods of Northwest Coast prehistory (Fladmark 1975:88, 250-3), and it is possible that dogfish served a similar role during the early period at Namu.

The significance of the minor fish species is not their subsistence contribution, but their presence in a variety and quantity roughly comparable to later periods. The implication is that there was little change in the later subsistence economy apart from the changes brought about by variations in local salmon productivity.

Mammals

The range of mammals in the earliest fauna-bearing levels (Table 2) is virtually the same as in later periods. The dominant species of later periods, black-tailed deer (*Odocoileus hemionus*) and harbour seal (*Phoca vitulina*), are also most abundant among the early mammalian fauna. Domestic dog (*Canis familiaris*)[2] was another major component of the mammalian assemblage, but none of the dog remains show any signs of human butchering, and dog is not considered here as an element of the subsistence economy.

The importance of deer as a food resource has been questioned (Conover 1978:91, McIlwraith 1948:2), but there is evidence that deer were returned to the site as complete carcasses (Cannon 1991:23-7), which suggests that the meat was at least of some value whatever its overall contribution to the diet. The early emphasis on deer is comparable to that of later periods.

Harbour seal is relatively abundant in the early period, though it occurs in even greater abundance later. The increase in harbour seal in Periods 3 and 4 (4775 to 3825 BP) may reflect a more favourable local environment as the result of slightly lower sea levels, which would expose a greater extent of suitable dry land habitat such as rocky islets and reefs. The increase in salmon may also have made the site vicinity more attractive for seal. Other evidence suggests that greater emphasis was later placed on seal hunting as part of an overall intensification of the subsistence economy to take advantage of the local abundance of resources at strategic seasonal intervals (Cannon 1991:38).

Other sea-mammals, represented by members of the family Delphinidae (dolphins and porpoises) and Otariidae (northern fur-seal and northern sea-lion), were never a major part of the Namu subsistence economy. Delphinidae is slightly more common in the early period deposits, but there is no evidence of the same early emphasis on sea-mammal hunting reported for the site of Bear Cove on northern Vancouver Island (C. Carlson 1979:188).

One interesting aspect of the early mammalian fauna is the relative abundance of a variety of minor fur-bearing species, including smaller species of Mustelidae (mink, marten, etc.), *Castor canadensis* (beaver), *Lutra canadensis* (river otter), and *Ursus americanus* (black bear). The combined total of these species is 17 per cent of the Period 2 mammalian fauna as compared to as little as 6 per cent and no more than 12 per cent in later periods. Ethnographically, all of these species were important as sources of fur, and their early period abundance suggests an early cultural emphasis on the use of fur in clothing. An alternative possibility is that changes in the scale and permanence of site settlement increased the local availability of fur-bearing animals. Each of these species would have been available in the immediate site vicinity, in the littoral zone (mink), on the banks of the Namu River (river otter, and possibly bear during salmon runs), and at the nearby lake (beaver). All may have been more common before intensification of the local subsistence economy brought about an increase in the size and permanence of the settlement. But fur-bearing animals are also less common in later deposits (post 3500 BP) that indicate a smaller scale and less permanent occupation of the site. The implication is that there is probably a cultural basis for the emphasis on fur. It will be interesting to determine whether this pattern is evident at other early sites in the region.

Birds

Birds were never more than a supplementary food resource at Namu, and a variety of different species are represented among the limited number of early bird remains. More specific identifications are listed in Table 3. As with fish and mammals, the character of the early bird assemblage is typical of later periods. Two families, Gavidae (loons) and Anatidae (ducks, geese, etc.), dominate the bird assemblage. Among the Anatidae, all specimens, with the exception of a single goose bone, were identified as either ducks or mergansers, and of the ducks that could be identified to subfamily, all are either Aythyinae (diving ducks) or Merginae (mergansers). The majority of birds are therefore marine waterfowl species that are ethnographically recorded as having been used for food. As with fish and mammals, the bird evidence points to the earlier establishment of a marine-based economy, with the techniques and skills necessary to exploit every available resource.

Among the other minor classes of birds represented are *Haliaeetus leucocephalus* (bald eagle) and Laridae (gulls), which are present in proportions roughly equivalent to later periods. One group that is interesting for its absence is the family Corvidae (ravens, crows, etc.). Crows and ravens are presently common at the site, but they are absent in the early period and extremely rare in later period deposits. If their rarity is a function of proscriptions on eating these species, then there is a long-term continu-

Table 2. Taxonomic abundance of early period mammals (NISP: Number of Identified Specimens).

Taxon	NISP
Castor canadensis (beaver)	11
Erethizon dorsatum (porcupine)	9
Delphinidae (dolphins, porpoises)	20
Canis familiaris (domestic dog)	38
Ursus Americanus (black bear)	6
Mustelidae (mink, marten, etc.)	45
Lutra canadensis (river otter)	10
Enhydra lutris (sea otter)	4
Otariidae (northern fur seal, northern sea lion)	6
Phoca vitulina (harbour seal)	81
Odocoileus hemionus (black-tailed deer)	191

ity in this cultural trait.

Most of the identified and probable species from the early deposits either are available year-round, or typically "winter" on the coast (e.g., most Gavidae, Aythyinae, Merginae), which for many species can extend from early fall to late spring. Birds are not prominent in ethnographic accounts of subsistence practices, but the Haida hunt waterfowl in late fall after the salmon-fishing season (Blackman 1981:15), and contemporary Kwakiutl concentrate on ducks during a part of winter when certain varieties concentrate near shore to feed off rocks (Rohner 1967:61).

SEASONAL INDICATORS

The early Namu vertebrate faunal assemblage provides a number of indicators of seasonal presence at the site. These include the presence of seasonally-limited species of fish and bird and the presence of seasonally-specific neonatal harbour seal. These data provide a seasonal range for particular economic activities at the site.

Among the fish remains, the strongest seasonal indicators are salmon and herring. Based upon the age profile of the recovered salmon remains, the species composition was determined to be almost entirely coho (*Oncorhynchus kisutch*) and/or three-year-old chum (*O. keta*), with smaller numbers of four-year-old chum and pink salmon (*O. gorbuscha*) also present (Cannon 1988). Based upon the timing of the spawning runs of these species, the indication is of a late fall salmon fishery (October to November) that missed the earlier fall runs of most pink and chum salmon. The implication is that the occupants of Namu did not arrive at the site until relatively late in the salmon-fishing season. The absence of chinook (*O. tshawytscha*) and sockeye (*O. nerka*) also indicates the probable absence of a summer salmon fishery. This seasonal pattern of salmon exploitation is maintained throughout later periods.

Herring is also a very specific seasonal indicator. Ethnographically, they were fished at the time of spawning, which is in late winter or early spring (Hart 1973:97). There is no positive seasonal evidence for site occupation during the intervening period between the late November salmon fishery and the early spring herring fishery, but such occupation seems likely given the lack of any specific reason for movement elsewhere.

As mentioned, the bird remains provide little positive seasonal information apart from indicating presence at the site anytime from early fall to late spring, but it is significant that none of the bird remains provide clear evidence of summer site occupation.

The presence of neonatal harbour seal in the early deposits (fifteen of eighty-one total specimens recovered from the site) indicates a site occupation centring around the early June peak in the pupping season (Banfield 1974:370). The lack of harbour seal remains from age categories between neonatal and adult might also be taken to mean that seasonal occupation of the site did not extend much beyond the end of June.

Although some extrapolation from the seasonal evidence is necessary, the positive evidence indicates definite site occupation in mid-October/November, March, and June, and there is every reason to believe that some level of site occupation generally extended from late October to late June, with a strong probability that the site was not occupied from July through early October. The same types of faunal evidence indicate that this pattern of site utilization was maintained throughout later periods. The implication is that Namu was a winter village site from as early as 8000 years ago, and an essentially sedentary pattern of settlement had been established by that time. The further implication is that at least part of the subsistence economy was based on the winter storage of salmon. This pattern

of subsistence and settlement was maintained for a period of some two thousand years before the major accumulation of shell midden deposits began.

SYNTHESIS

The early Namu archaeofauna indicate a strong element of continuity in the overall orientation of the site's subsistence economy. That orientation was overwhelmingly toward the food resources of the sea, which for the early period included fish, sea-mammals, and marine waterfowl. All of the necessary skills and technologies for the exploitation of these resources were in place by 7620 BP. The only component of the later marine economy lacking in the early period was the intensive utilization of shellfish. Given the requisite knowledge of, and orientation toward marine resources in the early period, and given the likely availability of shellfish at this time (Fladmark 1975:210, 248-9), the failure to utilize shellfish at an earlier date must be explained on some other basis. There is no indication that the lack of early evidence for intensive shellfishing is a function of preservation and recovery. If, as suggested by Andrews and Retherford (1978:348), sea levels in the area were slightly higher at this time, then it is unlikely that shell accumulation was confined to some area away from the excavated early period cultural deposits. The excavated deposits also indicate a gradual transition in the extent of shellfishing, from complete absence (Period 1), to periodic gathering, as indicated by scattered lenses of shell (Period 2), to intensive collection, as indicated by the inception of full shell midden formation (after 5170 BP). This evidence strongly suggests that shellfish were much less important in the early period than they were later.

While this chapter has stressed the continuities in the Namu archaeofauna, there are some clear differences in the pre-5000 BP subsistence economy that should also be stressed. The early period exhibits less emphasis on salmon, and almost no utilization of shellfish, and without this stable resource complex in place, it is possible that early occupation of the site was much less intense than in later periods.

Despite changes in the degree of emphasis on salmon and certain classes of mammal, the Namu fauna indicate a stable economic orientation, which is an interesting contrast to the subsistence economies evident at coastal sites further to the south. In a recent synthesis of faunal data from sites in the Queen Charlotte Strait area of British Columbia, Mitchell (1988:281-5) describes a much later (ca. 2000 BP) increase in salmon fishing and sea-mam-

Table 3. Taxonomic abundance of early period birds (NISP: Number of Identified Specimens).

Taxon	NISP
Gavidae (loons)	
small-medium	2
medium	3
large (probably common loon)	2
Podicipedidae (grebes)	
large	1
Phalacrocoracidae (cormorants)	2
Anatidae (ducks, geese, swans)	
Anserinae (geese)	1
Ducks	20
Aythyinae/Merginae (diving ducks/merganzers)	1
Aythyinae (diving ducks)	1
Merginae (merganzers)	2
Haliaeetus leucocephalus (bald eagle)	4
Laridae (gulls)	
small-medium	1
large (probably *glaucous*-winged gull)	2
Tytonidae/Strigidae (owls)	
large	1

mal hunting, which he attributes to cultural replacement by "Wakashan" groups from the central coast region. The Namu fishing-based economy with its early adaptation toward salmon fishing and supplementary sea-mammal hunting saw a dramatic increase in the utilization of these resources some 3000 years earlier, at precisely the ca. 5000 BP date suggested by Fladmark (1975) as the earliest possible date for increased salmon productivity.

If Mitchell's (1988) cultural interpretation for patterns of faunal resource use in the Queen Charlotte Strait region is correct, then the Namu data indicate that although his Wakashan pattern of resource use had developed as far south as Namu prior to 7620 BP, it did not develop much further south until nearly 6000 years later, at which time cultural replacement was relatively rapid and uniform. Clearly such a scenario raises some intriguing questions regarding the nature of cultural relations in the central coast region, and the reasons for their long-standing stability and sudden change. Alternatively, the cultural implications of Mitchell's Queen Charlotte Strait evidence may be much less dramatic than he suggests. Much greater use of relatively marginal resources such as deer and ratfish in the earlier phases at Mitchell's sites suggests that a local deficiency of nutritionally-superior salmon and

seal may be responsible for the subsistence patterns observed there (Cannon 1993).

All elements of the central British Columbia coastal economy were established very early at Namu, and the emphasis on salmon within the marine economy was certainly not a recent phenomenon (cf., Croes 1988). The basic economic pattern at Namu was not even significantly altered by the later increase in salmon productivity. Greater salmon production simply entered a greater quantity of food into an economic system that was already established.

Other researchers have stressed the role of various cultural factors in the long-term development of the ethnographically-recorded Northwest Coast subsistence economy. Several studies have emphasized the need for cultural innovation and technological development to enable the catching, processing, and storage of large quantities of salmon (Burley 1980, Matson 1983, Schalk 1977). In addition, Northwest Coast patterns of subsistence orientation and transition have been attributed to differences in cultural tradition (Borden 1975, Mitchell 1988). At Namu the early dependence on salmon is not associated with any apparent innovation in harvest or storage technology or any gradual development in cultural orientation. The initiation and intensification of salmon fishing follows in accord with resource availability.

The Namu data tend to support Fladmark's (1975) paleoecological model of Northwest Coast prehistory. But despite the correspondence between Fladmark's model and the empirical faunal data from Namu, enhanced productivity of salmon at the time of post-glacial environmental stabilization is insufficient to explain subsequent economic intensification, or the population growth and cultural elaboration that is presumed to have accompanied an increase in economic production. This should have occurred with the inception of an intensive marine economy at least 2000 years earlier. One possibility is that a social and cultural equilibrium established on the basis of earlier conditions was somehow disrupted with the enhanced productivity of an already important salmon resource. Social adjustments predicated on relatively modest increases in salmon production may have provided further incentive for increased production and even population growth as social units sought to compete with one another and establish a new structure and balance in social relations (Cannon 1991:68). What-

Figure 1. Twisting the bucket auger by hand to obtain faunal samples from the midden at Namu.

Figure 2. Removing the sample from the bucket auger for bagging and later analysis.

Figure 3. Stone walled fish trap at the mouth of the Namu River with the tide in.

ever the causes of later increases in subsistence production, the Namu evidence makes it clear that no single technological, environmental, or cultural change was necessary or sufficient to bring about the Northwest Coast pattern of intensive storage-based production and permanent village settlement. The implication is that regardless of the patterns of economic and cultural transition evident at specific site localities, there were no critical thresholds in Northwest Coast economic prehistory. Developments did not lead in linear fashion toward the ethnographically recorded pattern of subsistence and settlement. The basic economic framework was established from a very early date. Subsequent developments in Northwest Coast prehistory will have to be explained in more specific social and historical terms; they cannot be explained with simple reference to technological innovation, cultural migration, or environmental change.

The conclusions presented here are derived from a solid body of empirical evidence, but they are nonetheless limited from having been based on the faunal remains from a single site. Obviously any generalizations from a single site must be limited and somewhat tentative. Only with the recovery of more data, reported in more detail, will it be possible to determine how representative the early Namu economy was of the early regional economy in general. Although the emphasis placed on particular resources should be expected to vary between sites and over time, it is likely that the general character of the central British Columbia coast fishing-based economy was well-established and widespread from a time that considerably predates the earliest Namu faunal remains at 7620 BP. It is unfortunate that to date few other sites have produced the same quality of evidence available for Namu, but it is fortunate that this site gives us at least one clear picture of early subsistence patterns on the Northwest Coast.

Acknowledgments

Bucket-auger sampling at Namu in 1994 was funded by a grant to Aubrey Cannon from the Arts Research Board of McMaster University. This support is gratefully acknowledged.

Notes

1 Ninety-three of the site total of 568 Gadidae elements were positively identified to species. Of these, eighty-nine were Pacific cod (*Gadus macrocephalus*) and only four were Walleye pollack (*Theragramma chalcogramma*).

2 The basis for considering all *Canis* specimens as domestic dog is the lack of any identified wolf remains in the Namu assemblage, and the fact that the present range of coyote does not extend to the coast.

11

THE OLD CORDILLERAN COMPONENT AT THE GLENROSE CANNERY SITE

R.G. Matson

The Old Cordilleran component at the Glenrose Cannery site, with an initial date at more than 8000 years ago, is still one of the most informative early components on the Northwest Coast. In this chapter I try to place this component into the context of this early period with reference to later developments, including the eventual development of the Northwest Coast ethnographic pattern. In doing so, information that was not available when the original monograph (Matson 1976) was written is incorporated, and certain misunderstandings that have arisen are corrected. Since much of the value of the Glenrose component is in the subsistence and seasonality fields, these aspects are particularly stressed. The Bear Cove site (C. Carlson 1979), near the northern tip of Vancouver Island, has a component that dates to approximately the same time and also has a similar artifact complex along with very interesting, and contrasting, subsistence information. Together, these two components give an estimate of the range of subsistence patterns found at the coast within this culture. Combined with artifact and distribution information from the Olcott sites to the south we can now characterize the basal culture of the Puget Sound, Gulf of Georgia, Vancouver Island region. The resulting construct is compared to contemporaneous inland variants of the Old Cordilleran Pattern and to the succeeding St. Mungo and Mayne Phases, as well as very briefly to more northern material.

THE GLENROSE SITE

The Glenrose site is located on the south side of the Fraser River, between Annacis Island and Panorama Ridge which is a highland area (Figure 1). When first occupied, Panorama Ridge was probably similar to Point Grey, a peninsula extending into the Gulf, next to the outlet of the Fraser River, with a pebble beach (Hebda 1977:141). The present Burns Bog area was probably a shallow bay, as the oldest dates for the post-marine deposits are slightly more than 5000 years BP (Hebda 1977:144). Thus, for the first component, the present relatively inland setting is misleading. The immediate environs of the site have two factors which probably conditioned its use: a more gradual slope of Panorama Ridge than is usual in that general area, and a small fresh water stream that now empties under the Glenrose Cannery buildings.

While the actually known Glenrose Cannery site is quite large, identifiable Old Cordilleran deposits were found only in Units 1/5, 4, 6, 3, 8, and 2 (Figure 2). Some of the deposits were quite deep, with the maximum depth being about 5.5 m in Unit 1, with over two-thirds of those being Old Cordilleran deposits. About 50 per cent of the artifacts for this component came from the contiguous 1-55-5 trench, and it is this portion that is the best dated. Unfortunately, preservation of non-lithic material was poor in this portion, so the best subsistence information does not correspond to the best dated or most abundant artifactual material.

The lowest deposits in the "trench" were tentatively interpreted as beach deposits, and some artifacts found there were water worn. At the time the monograph was written this interpretation was uncertain, as the most accepted relative sea level for that period was thought to be some metres below what the "beach deposits" implied (Mathews, Fyles, and Nasmith 1970). The bottom of the cultural deposit is between 2 and 3 m above modern mean sea level, and thus the interpretation of these as beach deposits suggests a relative sea level similar to that of today or up to 2 or 3 m higher. Perhaps instead of being a Fraser River beach, it was a beach of the small freshwater stream.

While the lower "trench" deposits were relatively barren of organic remains, other units, particularly 4 and 6, had abundant organic material present in this component (Figure 3). These deposits were not subject to whatever action resulted in this relatively barren sandy deposit in the trench, and included dark charcoal layers, and small, but dense shellfish deposits, as well as abundant faunal materials.

Some 614 classified artifacts (tools) were recovered from the Old Cordilleran component (Matson 1976:292) (Figure 4). In the lithic artifact class these can be divided into two categories, cobble tools and the rest. Some 269 tools, or 44 per cent, can be classified as cobble tools. Of these ninety-five (35 per cent) were unifacial chopping tools, with lesser amounts of bifacial choppers (7 per cent) and scraper planes also present (6 per cent). Twenty-four per cent (n=67) of the cobble tools were cortex spalls but they tended to be smaller and less modified than the same class found in later cultures from the BC interior. A total of thirty-two hammerstones (5 per cent) were found.

Turning to the non-cobble tool material, the leaf-shaped points so typical of the Old Cordilleran are present at Glenrose, though not in very large numbers, as a total of only four complete ones were found. In addition, a single weakly contracting stem point was found in the levels attributed to this component (Figure 4). Leaf-shaped knives (n=6) are also present, along with biface fragments, large crude bifaces, and fair numbers of unifacially re-touched flakes, and various steeply retouched flakes (scrapers) (n=68, 11 per cent) were also found. However, no end-scraper or thumbnail forms were found in scraper classes.

While some of these numbers appear to be very low, if we remove the cobble tool and core categories, the percentages become closer to what one might expect from an "Archaic" or "Lithic" component. The resulting percentages are: 2 per cent points, 2.4 per cent knives, 2 per cent biface fragments, 17 per cent retouched flakes, and 27 per cent scrapers.

A few pieces of ground stone were also found in this component, including three abrasive stones, and four pieces of miscellaneous ground stone. None of the latter fragments could be readily interpreted, but it is certain they did not come from stone tool classes common in later times.

In some ways, the tools made of bone and antler are of more interest, since they are relatively rare from deposits of this age. Eleven beam antler wedg-

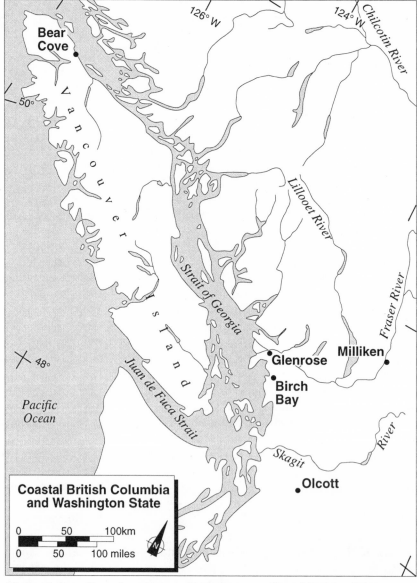

Figure 1. Location of archaeological sites mentioned in this chapter.

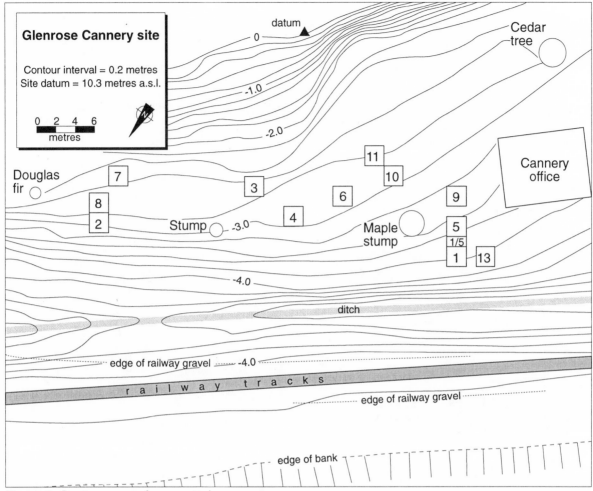

Figure 2. Contour map of excavated area.

es were recovered, along with one antler punch and a single barbed point. The latter (Figure 4g) is more likely to be a fixed barbed point than a true harpoon if one relies on the spacing of the barbs as an indicator (Clark 1975). Among the bone artifacts, three needle point awls, one ulna tool, one bone "blade" and one tooth pendant were found, along with six miscellaneous worked bone fragments.

Five dates were run on samples thought to be from the Old Cordilleran component. Four of these were from Unit 1, the deepest one:

Gak 4649   7430 ±340 BP 330 cm below surface
Gak 4650   5730 ±125 BP 360 cm below surface
Gak 4865   6780 ±135 BP 430 cm below surface
Gak 4866   8150 ±250 BP 450 cm below surface

With the exception of Gak 4649 these are in stratigraphic sequence, and Gak 4649 was the smallest sample of the four. The fifth sample was from Unit 7, which had a small amount of material

thought to be from this component. However, it resulted in a date of 3700 ±120 BP (Gak 4864). Either this date is in error, the material was introduced, or we have misclassed these levels. Peacock's analysis (1976) on "pit components" using cluster analysis and multidimensional scaling which indicates what each pit component is most similar to, is a good check on the attribution of these levels to the Old Cordilleran Component (Figure 5). In Peacock's analysis (1976:214-30), this material came out as typical Old Cordilleran (Figure 5), which suggests that the date is in error, or that some activity variant of the succeeding St. Mungo Phase has the same artifact complex as the earlier Old Cordilleran material.

While these radiocarbon assays date the older portions of this component reasonably securely, they do not date the uppermost levels well. In the original report I allowed for 1000 years between the Old Cordilleran and the succeeding St. Mungo material, although the lack of evidence for a hiatus of that

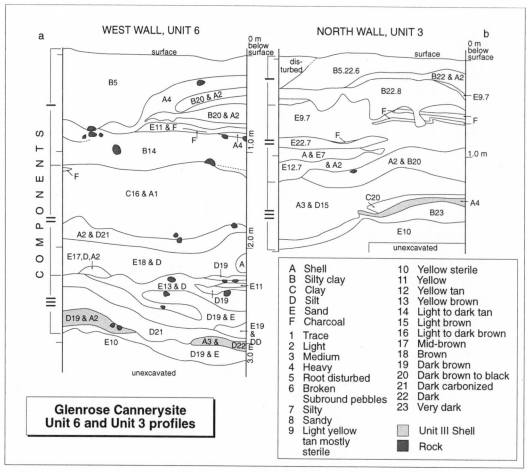

Figure 3. Profiles of Units 3 and 6 showing Old Cordilleran shell lenses.

length was also cited. I suggested a terminal date of 5500 BP (1976:19) for this component. Since then, other researchers (Leonhardy 1975) have indicated that some local variants of the Old Cordilleran lasted up until approximately 4500 years ago. I do not see any evidence that negates this possibility at Glenrose, and would now suggest that the ending date is between 4500 and 5000 BP.

Turning to the faunal remains, Imamoto (1976) identified thirty-five elements from the Old Cordilleran component, distributed between elk, deer, *canis* sp., beaver, and seal. The most abundant remains were elk and deer, followed by seal. Using the minimum number of individuals (MNI) and average usable meat results, elk was the most important, followed at some distance by deer, and seal which are calculated to have approximately equal importance. These results are in accord with what one would expect from the Old Cordilleran, as an adaptation probably oriented around large land mammals. The presence of seals is not really surprising given the seals today on Harrison Lake, far up the Fraser. It

does, however, indicate the inclusion of this species into the hunting pattern. Since both juvenile elk and deer are present, Imamoto inferred a summer seasonality for this component at Glenrose.

The fish remains, on the other hand, resulted in unexpected information (Casteel 1976). Fish remains from column samples from Units 1 and 4 (Figure 6) resulted in salmon, starry flounder, eulachon, sticklebacks, and one peamouth being identified. From Unit 1 level bags, Casteel identified both salmon and sturgeon remains. The eulachon are, of course, well known for their springtime abundance. The less well known sticklebacks are anadromous, and begin to become abundant in local freshwater streams by mid-May and continue until early summer. The abundant presence of both sticklebacks and eulachon pinpoint the occupation of this site as focused in the late spring and early summer. The procurement of a wide variety of fish during at least the early spring and summer was also part of the Old Cordilleran component at Glenrose.

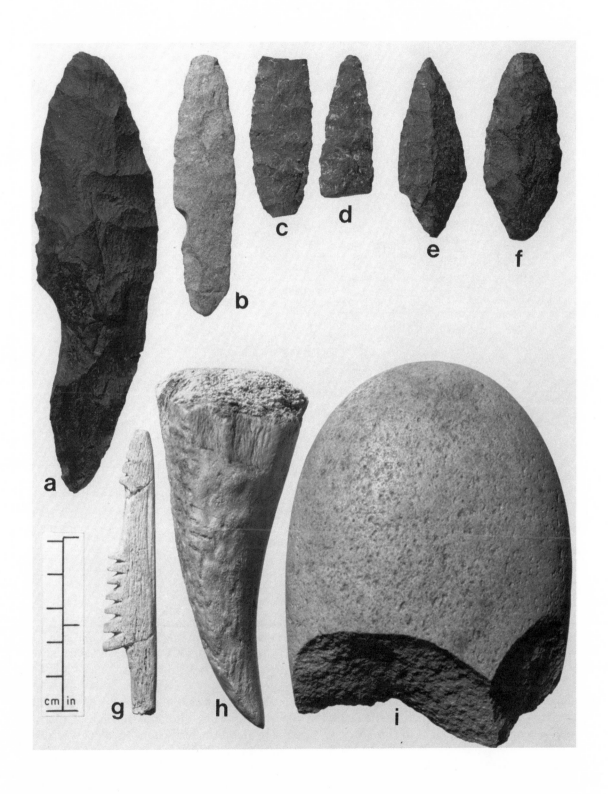

Figure 4. Glenrose Old Cordilleran artifacts: (a) leaf-shaped biface; (b, c, d, f) leaf-shaped projectile points; (e) contracting stemmed point; (g) barbed antler point; (h) antler wedge; (i) bifacial cobble chopper.

115

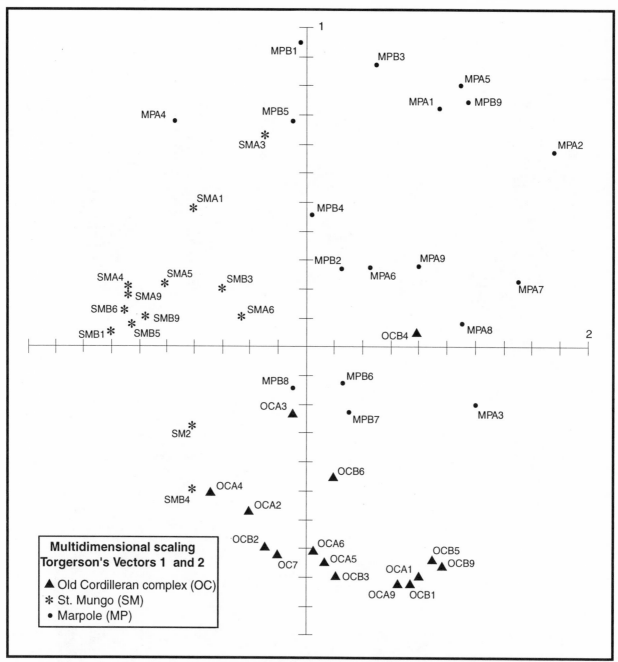

Figure 5. "Unit components" were divided into upper (A) and lower (B) halves, which were compared on the basis of the artifacts present. Closeness of entities ("Unit components") indicates relative similarity. Unit 1/5 (Figure 2) is denoted as Unit 9 on this figure.

Although no bird remains were found at Glenrose, surprising amounts of shellfish were. There were lenses of concentrated shell in the lowest portions of this component, particularly in Units 3 and 6. In all cases the shellfish was dominated by bay mussel (*Mytilus edulis*), which also occurred as small fragments in the "trench." Slightly larger amounts of shell, including some identifiable clam fragments occurred at the top-most layers in the trench. A single sealed deposit at the uppermost portion of the Old Cordilleran deposit in the trench had relatively complete mussels which Ham (1976:66) was able to determine were harvested in spring or early summer. While these shellfish deposits were present, they were only a minor constituent of this component, particularly if compared to later ones. Shellfish procurement, however, was definitely part of the subsistence pattern in the Old Cordilleran times.

	MARPOLE	ST. MUNGO	OLD CORD-ILLERAN
Salmon (*Onchorhynchus* sp.)	20%	24%	28%
Herring (*Clupea harengus*)	10%	0%	0%
Sturgeon (*Acipenser* sp.)	0%	0.31%	0%
Flounder (*Platichthys* sp.)	0%	0.16%	0.8%
Eulachon (*Thaleichthys pacificus*)	0%	7.8%	8.0%
Sticklebacks (*Gasterosteus aculteatus*)	0%	1.4%	29%
Peamouths (*Mylocheilus* sp.)	0%	0%	0.8%
Unidentified pieces	70%	66%	34%

Figure 6. Fish from column samples.

The faunal remains show a wide diversity, but indicate a subsistence pattern that was likely centred on elk, deer, and seal, but with a wide variety of less important fish and shellfish also procured. Most of the fish and shellfish could probably be obtained from the shore, with the major exception to this being the starry flounder. The seasonality inferences from the three most sensitive indicators – mussels, eulachon, and sticklebacks – are in agreement, spring and early summer. While the site may have been occupied at other times, it is clear it was regularly and intensively occupied during this season. An important question that remains is the age of both the seasonality and the faunal information.

Given that the existing dates are from the "trench" and the bulk of the faunal information is from other units, particularly Units 4 and 6, this question cannot be answered with complete confidence. In Units 3, 4, and 6, the faunal remains occurred right to the bottom; in Unit 4 they extended right to the potholes in the bottom sterile. In Unit 4, a radiocarbon date of 4240 ±110 BP (Gak 4648) was obtained for the lowest St. Mungo levels; the Old Cordilleran levels continue for 1.4 m below them. Peacock split each "pit component" into an upper and lower half, where possible, in order to look for possible mistakes in component assignments (Figure 5). Of the six split components of interest, only the lower half in Unit 4 is of questionable affiliation. Interestingly enough, the upper half of that unit is rated as a definite Old Cordilleran component (Figure 5),

which makes the position of the lower half of Unit 4 of only academic interest.

In the absence of direct dates, the only surety is that the faunal and seasonality information is older than 4500 BP. Whether or not any of it is older than, say, 6000 BP depends on the interpretation of the site formation processes. If the site was occupied all at once, then this material dates considerably older than 6000 BP. If, on the other hand, the "trench" area was occupied first, and only later were portions to the east occupied, then the faunal remains would have a later date.

Of the bone and antler tools, only the wedges are unequivocally found in the oldest dated Old Cordilleran layers. Other bone and antler tools tend to be either from deposits not directly dated or from the upper levels of the Old Cordilleran component. The barbed antler point (Figure 4), however, is from the lowest levels of Unit 3 (Figure 2), which is associated with the oldest unit components from the trench in Figure 5.

BEAR COVE

Since the Glenrose site was reported, a site with a very similar component has been reported by C. Carlson (1979) at Bear Cove at the northern tip of Vancouver Island (Figure 1). This site is also located next to a small stream, and the old component of interest is located somewhat back from the beach. It is found underneath a shellmidden beginning about 7 to 9 m above present mean sea level in a deposit which includes "poorly stratified silty loams and marine sands and gravel" (C. Carlson 1979:180). This shell-less deposit varies from 1 to 1.5 m in depth, and includes a radiocarbon date near the bottom of 8020 ±110 BP (WSU 2141). The striking similarities with the Old Cordilleran at Glenrose of "beach deposits" and the initial date is reinforced by the earliest date of the overlying shell midden which is estimated on the basis of two 4000 ± BP radiocarbon dates as around 4300 years ago. Further, water-worn artifacts are found at both sites. A distinctive difference is a black, greasy layer ranging about 20 cm in thickness at the top of this component, just below the shell midden.

A total of 137 tools are assigned to this component. Pebble tools make up 48 per cent of this number, flake or spall tools 35 per cent, bifacially flaked points or knives including fragments 6 per cent, and miscellaneous 11 per cent. The points and point fragments are interpreted as all being from leaf shaped bifaces, although one illustrated is a better contracting stem point than the one from Glenrose (C. Carlson 1979, Figure 5). Among the miscellaneous are four hammerstones, three notched stones, and two pieces of bone and antler. Most of the pebble tools are unifacial choppers, which is also the most abundant category at Glenrose. In summary, the lithic industry appears to be very similar to Glenrose in kinds of artifacts, their relative abundance, and in age.

In contrast with all these similarities with Glenrose, the faunal remains are quite different (C. Carlson 1979:188). Sea mammal remains, fish, land mammal, and bird fauna are all present, although apparently preserved only in the upper portion of this component, in the black greasy layer. The most common identifiable fish remains were those of rockfish (*Sebastes*) (72 per cent), with salmon representing 10 per cent. There were also "small quantities of pacific cod, pollock, sculpin, greenling, dogfish and ratfish" (p. 188). These fish can all be obtained in the immediate vicinity today.

Twice as many mammal bone fragments were found as compared to fish, and 78 per cent of those indentifiable were of five sea mammal categories. Fully 80 per cent of the sea mammal class were *Delphinidae* (porpoise), 9 per cent northern fur seal, 7 per cent Stellar sea lion, with the remaining 4 per cent being sea otter and harbour seal. The 22 per cent land mammals are mainly mule deer with a few pieces representing *Canis* sp. and river otter. Identified birds include ducks, gulls, loons, and murre.

Unfortunately, the age of this very interesting faunal assemblage is unclear. Like that from Glenrose, it is clearly older than 4500 BP, but, unlike Glenrose, it only represents the end of this component, as the lower portions of this component did not have any faunal remains present.

C. Carlson infers a subsistence pattern of mainly sea mammal hunting, a conclusion with which it is difficult to argue. The porpoises, in contrast with Glenrose seals, do necessitate watercraft and harpoon or equivalent techniques. C. Carlson postulates the existence of a bone and antler technology in the tradition, which is, in fact, well attested to at Glenrose, including a barbed point which may be a harpoon.

C. Carlson interprets this component as a temporary campsite on an active beach front, an interpretation very similar to that from Glenrose. While no seasonality analyses have been published, C. Carlson (personal communication) informs me that, except for the fur seal, the resources present can be obtained all year around. Thus the actual season of occupation of this site, and the likely role of the site in the annual subsistence pattern is unknown, although I think that the absence of specific seasonal indicators usually means winter occupation. The absence of elk may be explained by a local scarcity.

Together Bear Cove and Glenrose complement each other with very similar lithic assemblages and dates, but very different faunal assemblages. While Glenrose can be interpreted as a small seasonal variant on a large land-mammal oriented subsistence pattern, with no necessary specialized maritime adaptation, Bear Cove demonstrates that seasonal variants, at least of this cultural tradition, were subsisting largely on sea mammals, obtained from water craft, and using harpoons or equivalent techniques.

Although Glenrose demonstrates that a wide variety of fish were obtained, many of those could have been caught along the shore, or in small streams. The eulachon, sticklebacks and salmon all could have been obtained without getting more than one's feet wet. Only the starry flounder indicated offshore fishing, sandy bottoms, and probably quiet waters. At Bear Cove, rockfish caught along rockier shores, may also demonstrate a greater level of marine technology in addition to the porpoises. In sum, at this time, irrespective of the general subsistence pattern there were at least seasonal variants focused on foreshore resources, which included using watercraft and harpoons to obtain porpoises.

OLCOTT SITES

Although subsistence information for this time period is largely limited to that reviewed above, some additional information can be gleaned from similar lithic tool assemblages, although usually these are undated. The late G. Grabert discussed a number of such sites in a paper on pebble tool sites (1979). Here a series of sites either dominated solely by pebble tools or by pebble tools and bipointed bifaces are found at three locations around Birch Bay, and one site, the Ferndale site, along the Nooksack River, some 10 km inland from the present coast. The only date relevant to these is a date at the Ferndale site which is a minimum date for the termination of this component of 4180 ±120 BP (RL 249) (1979:169). This date is in good agreement for succeeding phases at both Glenrose and Bear Cove, as well as other initial dates for the St. Mungo Phase in the Lower Mainland area. While most of these sites are apparently found on a 9 to 11 m terrace around Birch Bay (Larsen 1971), the one most "Olcott" like, that is with the most bifaces, is found both on the above terrace and in intertidal gravels. This setting is in agreement with little sea level change from time of occupation.

These sites extend slightly the range of this coastal complex, and show that at least in one area, they are quite numerous. While easily related to the exploitation of coastal resources, including the possibility of maritime ones, these also suggest limited duration of occupation, similar to interpretations of Bear Cove and Glenrose.

Further to the south are the Olcott sites (Butler 1961, Kidd 1964). These are perhaps the first of the "bipoint and pebble tool" sites to be described. They are located well inland (about 22 to 24 km, Figure 1) and without a clear association to a coastal adaptation. There are actually quite a number of sites in this area that have a similar complex of pebble tools, leaf-shaped points and knives and spall scrapers along the south fork of the Stillaguamish River, from which numerous tools have been surface collected. In a more detailed study, Kidd (1964:27-91) reports on a number of related inland sites, including Olcott, all known from unsystematic surface collections and which share the above characteristics. Kidd's work demonstrates that the Olcott pattern is an extensive inland one, and that the description by Butler appears to be valid.

In 1961, Butler tried to associate the Olcott sites with his Old Cordilleran culture, including his postulated very early dates. Most of the Old Cordilleran culture sites that produced the first dates (and they were not the age Butler argued) did not have abundant pebble tools. So the inclusion of Olcott components with the dated Old Cordilleran culture material was questionable. Later work, however, (Bense 1972) did demonstrate that some inland Old Cordilleran components did have high percentages of pebble tools. The coastal versions of Old Cordilleran can now be seen to be a variant that does share very high numbers of pebble tools. It is also likely that the Olcott sites, at least in part, share in this cultural tradition, in spite of the lack of direct dates.

The best dated local up-river Old Cordilleran component is that at Milliken (Borden 1960, 1961, 1975) which was recently re-analyzed by Mitchell and Pokotylo. In their analysis (in this volume) pebble tools make up 11.8 per cent and 18 per cent of the

two components found there, demonstrating the presence of substantial numbers of these tools, but far less than the 44 per cent found at Glenrose and 48 per cent at Bear Cove. (The latter was probably calculated in a slightly different manner.) I have no doubt though, that the two areas are closely related in terms of lithic assemblages as there is very little that is not present in both inland and coastal sites.

Independent evidence of this close relationship has been elegantly demonstrated by Pratt (1988) since I first drafted the previous paragraph. In a paper comparing the tool assemblages and lithic source material, she compared the Milliken and Glenrose Old Cordilleran assemblages after removing the pebble tools and using a condensed seventeen class typology. The resulting ogival curve or cumulative graph (Figure 7) shows a very high similarity between the components.

The question becomes what is the use of the abundant pebble tools? Given the abundance of antler wedges in this component at Glenrose, the often suggested use as woodworking tools sounds feasible to me, as it has to many others (Grabert 1979). I have no special vision for this, and find it difficult to see why wood processing should be consistently much more important on the coast than in the interior. I do have two possible suggestions. The first has to do with the wet weather, and the relative short duration of the coastal sites. Making temporary shelters may be a constant activity for such groups. In another direction, Bordes observed people today using cobble choppers to scrape mussels off rocks. Given the evidence of mussels in parts of Glenrose,

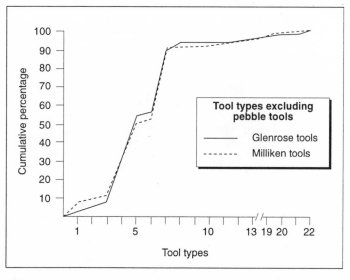

Figure 7. Comparison of Milliken and Glenrose Old Cordilleran components. Cumulative graph of lithic tool abundance, excluding pebble tools (after Pratt 1988).

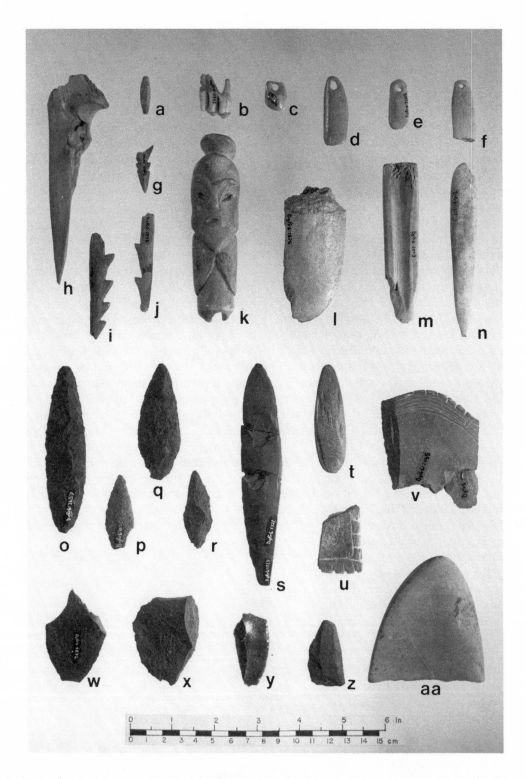

Figure 8. Glenrose St. Mungo artifacts: (a) decorative bone "grub"; (b, c) modified teeth; (d-f) bone pendants; (g) bilaterally barbed harpoon; (h) ulna tool; (i, j) unilaterally barbed antler points; (k) anthropomorphic antler figure; (l) antler wedge; (m) bone "flesher"; (n) bone awl; (o-r) projectile points; (s, t) ground stone points; (u, v) decorative ground stone; (w, x) narrow unifaces; (y, z) scrapers; (aa) abrasive stone.

Table 1. Comparison of lithic industries of St. Mungo and Old Cordilleran components at Glenrose: (a) without cores and (b) without cores or cobble tools.

	A					B				
	O.C.C.		ST.		MG	O.C.C.		ST.		MG
	#	%	#	%	%	#	%	#	%	%
Bifaces	20	4	57	12		20	9	57	14	
Narrow unifaces	43	9	90	20		43	19	90	23	
Scrapers	57	12	96	21		57	25	96	24	
Notches	13	3	14	3		13	6	14	4	
Blades, blade-like	1	0	13	3		1	0	13	3	
Stone wedges	3	1	13	3		3	1	13	3	
Utilized flakes	77	16	80	18		77	34	80	20	
Cortex spalls	67	14	12	3		--		--	-	
Hammerstones	32	7	13	3		--		--	-	
Anvil stones	2	0	1	0		2	1	1	0	
Choppers	168	34	33	7		--		--	-	
Ground stone tools	0	0	12	3		0	0	12	3	
Misc. grd. stone	4	1	5	1		4	2	5	1	
Abrasive stones	4	1	18	4		4	2	18	5	
TOTAL	491	102	457	101		224	99	399	100	
Cores	98		60			Without choppers, hammer stones and cortex spalls				

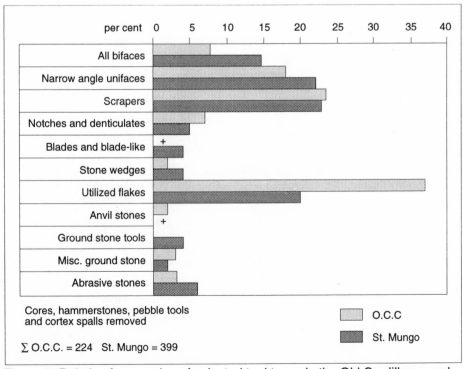

Figure 9. Relative frequencies of selected tool types in the Old Cordilleran and St. Mungo components at the Glenrose Cannery site.

121

the only component in which they were likely to preserve, this is apt to have been a regular activity, and cobble choppers may have been preserved much better than the actual mussels. Other than these, the usual suggestions for boat making, line production, and nets might also be important.

DESCENDANT CULTURES

The final topic I wish to briefly address is the relationship between the Old Cordilleran and succeeding cultures. As Table 1 and Figures 8 and 9 demonstrate, there is a close relationship at Glenrose between the Old Cordilleran and the succeeding St. Mungo component in lithic artifacts, once the abundant cobble tool assemblage is removed from the former. This as well as similarities in site use and faunal remains are convincing as evidence of an essential continuity of some sort. I have suggested that the big change between the two was in winter adaptation shifting from large land mammals to shellfish. This results in the increased use of mussels, and dense shellmiddens, and a shift from an adaptation focused in some seasons along the coast to one focused year around on the coast (Matson 1976, 1981). The evidence from Bear Cove and Birch Bay could be interpreted as indicating that year round use of the coast had already occurred in the Old Cordilleran component and that it was the intensive use of mussels in the winter that was the major change between the Old Cordilleran and descendant cultures.

I have made a similar argument for continuity in the interior plateaus between the Old Cordilleran there and at least the earliest housepit sites in the Columbia plateau. This does not mean that I believe that the Northwest Coast ethnographic pattern definitely evolved *in situ*. While there is convincing evidence for similarities between the St. Mungo and Eayem Phase, and Borden made an argument for including the Mayne Phase with them in the "Charles" culture, I think the Mayne Phase may represent a different tradition.

As I understand it, R. Carlson defined the Mayne Phase when he thought the Helen Point site had three components, with the two lowest being Marpole and Mayne Phase components (1970). The differences between the Mayne Phase and the St. Mungo phase are mainly the presence of true ground slate knives, obsidian microblades, and labrets in the former, and their absence in the latter. Since the

original work a Locarno Phase component was discovered in the compressed stratigraphy of the Helen Point site. Since all three of the differences between the St. Mungo and Mayne are well known from the Locarno Phase, I have regarded the Mayne Phase as a possible mixture of St. Mungo and Locarno, and thus perhaps not really existing. (Similar questions can be raised about other tentative occurrences of the Mayne Phase, at Crescent Beach, at Marpole, and at Duke Point.) If this is the case, then I do see continuity as basic to the Northwest Coast, with the possible exception of the Locarno Beach Phase, as Marpole clearly grades into later cultures and it is difficult to distinguish between the oldest sub-phase of the Marpole Phase and Locarno Phase components. If however, these traits do occur in the Mayne Phase, then I see the likely possibility of two streams of development in the Gulf of Georgia area, and the concurrent possibility of major dislocation.

SUMMARY

The evidence from Bear Cove, Glenrose, and Olcott sites demonstrates a widespread early coastal adaptation of a variant of the Old Cordilleran culture. Whether this is a seasonal variant of a mainly land mammal adaptation, as I argued earlier (Matson 1976), or a full-time adaptation to the coast, current evidence demonstrates use of a wide range of coastal and terrestrial resources, although no known site is indicative of much residential duration. Shellfish, flatfish, sticklebacks, eulachon, salmon, sculpin, rockfish, cod, sturgeon, and peamouth are all represented. Besides the obvious land mammals, seals, fur seals, stellar sea lion, and most amazingly, porpoises were procured. Mussels were also likely to have been extensively used. This large number of resources suggests a wide range of technologies were also known. Although the surviving lithic technology is not impressive, it may be because it was used to make the perishable technology that was used directly. The presence of numerous antler wedges at Glenrose supports this argument.

The similarities between this time and the later Mayne/St. Mungo phases indicates strong continuities, with the caveat mentioned earlier. The roots of the Northwest Coast culture appear to have grown older, stronger, and more widespread into the Old Cordilleran component in the time since the Glenrose site was first reported.

12

EARLY MARITIME CULTURE COMPLEXES OF THE NORTHERN NORTHWEST COAST

Robert E. Ackerman

The discovery of sites dated in excess of 9000 years ago on the northern Northwest Coast has provoked questions regarding the origin of the coastal pattern and the routes of southern dispersal utilized by these early coastal dwellers (Fladmark 1975, 1979b, 1983). Chard (1961) in his search for the origin of the Eskimo sea mammal hunting complex was drawn to the Okhotsk Sea region for a possible precursor. Vasil'evskii (1973, 1976, 1984), concerned with the origin of a much earlier maritime adaptation near the emergent Bering Sea platform, the Blade site complex on Anangula Island (Laughlin 1975), opted for the development of a coastal hunter-gatherer economy in the coastal region of Northern Japan, the Soviet Maritime District, Amur River estuary, Sakhalin and Kurile islands, and the margins of the Okhotsk Sea. This maritime complex then spread northward along the coastal shelf of Kamchatka, onto the southern margins of the Bering Sea platform and into the Aleutians during the period of lowered sea level (Vasil'evskii 1984:666).

Unfortunately, there are few sites that would demonstrate this hypothesis in coastal northeast Asia. Sea level rise has been relatively rapid since the close of the Late Wisconsin glacial stade. Within the Okhotsk Sea region, shorelines with depths of -24 to -21 m date to 10,500 BP (Valpeter 1983). Lower shorelines at depths of -78 to -80 m are estimated to date no earlier than 20,000 to 17,000 BP (Valpeter 1983). Along the coast of the Okhotsk and Japan seas elevated terraces between 2 to 3 and 3 to 5 m above sea level have been found, with a date range of 6790 ±90 to 3223 ±100 BP (Herschberg et al. 1983, Valpeter 1983). Similar elevated terraces 3 to 6 m high dating between 7000 and 3000 BP have also been found in the vicinity of the Anadyr River

and in the northern part of Chukotka (Valpeter 1983). Marine terraces, 5 to 10 m high, have also been located along the Chukotka coast but are apparently derived from earlier marine transgressions associated with a Late Wisconsin interstadial (Valpeter 1983). Associated driftwood and peat date from 34,600 to 33,200 ±300 BP (Valpeter 1983). No associated cultural materials have been thus far reported for the Wisconsin or Holocene age terraces.

Subsequent research on Sakhalin Island has revealed the possibility of an occupation that may date as early as 25,000 BP (Golubev 1983). This early complex from the site of Ado-Tymovo consists of discoidal cores, cobble tools, bifacial tools, large flakes, and skreblo-like tools (Golubev 1983:42). A later complex with wedge-shaped and cylindrical microblade cores, microblades, Araya burins, and polyhedral burins dates between 13,000 to 10,000 BP (Golubev 1983:48). The strong presence of cylindrical microblade cores in the second complex suggests that the microblade industries may date to a preceramic Mesolithic-Neolithic Phase rather than to an earlier Late Paleolithic assemblage. A fully maritime culture, the Okhotsk culture, has been dated on Sakhalin Island at 2530 ±35 and 2040 ±65 BP (Vasil'evskii 1973:212).

To the north of the Okhotsk Sea region, the earliest sites are those found by Dikov (1979, 1988) on the Kamchatka Peninsula and in Chukotka. The earliest level (level VII) at the Ushki 1 site, characterized by stemmed points, dates 14,300 ±200 and 13,600 ±250 BP (Dikov 1979:31). Level VI, distinguished by wedge-shaped microblade cores (a local expression of the Diuktai culture, Mochanov 1977, 1978), has been dated at 10,360 ±350, and 10,760 ±110 BP (Dikov 1977, 1979, 1988). An archaeomagnetic date of 12,300 ±300 BP for level VI suggests to Dikov (1988:14) that all of the levels in the Ushki Lake sites may be dating too recent due to sample contamination by percolating ground water. The other sites with wedge-shaped microblade cores on Chukotsk Peninsula are as yet undated (Dikov 1988).

In terms of a subsistence pattern, the Ushki Lake sites fail to provide us with insights into a maritime adaptation. The sites are located in the Kamchatka River valley, 210 km from the present mouth of the river. Here bison, mammoth, reindeer, and salmon were exploited (Dikov 1988:12). These sites would have been even further inland during the glacial maximum of the Late Wisconsin. At present, there are no Late Paleolithic coastal sites in the Soviet Far East that can be used to provide a model for Beringian coastal traditions.

It is possible that the pattern of maritime adaptation developed from a prior economy based on riverine fishing. On the emergent southern coast of the Bering Sea platform the rich resources around the estuaries of the Anadyr, Yukon, and Kuskokwim Rivers as well as the reef systems of the Aleutian Islands during lower sea levels would have been attractive to platform populations (cf., Stoker 1976, Laughlin 1980). Similar innovations appear to have occurred around the lower Amur River (Golubev 1983, Vasil'evskii 1984).

Details of the physiography of the Bering Sea platform, transgressions, and stillstands during the shift from the Late Wisconsin glacial stade through an early warming period and into the Holocene have been dealt with in another paper (Ackerman 1988b) and need not be repeated here. In brief, the general warming trend following the Late Wisconsin glacial stade was broken by cool intervals which were sufficient to temporarily halt the flooding of the platform and resulted in the creation of temporary shorelines.

Such a cooling phase occurred during the final marine transgression. This cool interval is known in Northern Europe as the pre-Boreal (dated at ca. 9600 to 9000 BP, Wendland and Bryson 1974), in western Siberia as the Perslav interval (10,000-9500 BP, Khotinskiy 1984), and in Central Siberia as the Pitsko-Ingarsk interval (9800-9300 BP, Mochanov 1978:63). During this cool interval, a stillstand in the rising sea level produced shorelines marked by the -12 to -10 m isobath (Stoker 1976, Valpeter 1983). Nunivak Island would still have been separated from the mainland, Kuskokwim and Bristol bays would have remained part of a narrow coastal plain, and there would have been a narrow coast shelf

along the Alaska Peninsula and some of the nearby Aleutian Islands (Stoker 1976, Hopkins 1979, Laughlin 1980). By approximately 6000 BP the modern shoreline conformation would have been achieved (Hopkins 1979).

The pattern of shoreline emergence and subsequent flooding along the Gulf of Alaska, Prince William Sound, the Alexander Archipelago of southern Alaska, and the coasts of British Columbia is somewhat more complex due to the effects of glaciation. The coastal shelf would have been broached in various locations by glacial lobes extending seaward from their mainland sources during the period of maximum Late Wisconsin glaciation (Denton and Hughes 1981, Mann 1986, Molnia 1986). Studies by Molnia (1986) and Mann (1986) indicate that there would have been areas along the coastal shelf that would have been ice-free. These areas of the coastal shelf may have served as possible refugia for plants and animals (Heusser 1960, Derkson 1977, Molnia 1986, Mann 1986). The coastal shelf which is presently -100 to -200 m below sea level (Mann 1986, Figure 1) would have been emergent (Molnia 1986, Figure 3) during the height of the Late Wisconsin stade, that is post 27,000 and pre-16,000 BP, and perhaps for a period of time prior to marine transgression.

Evidence for the first coastal occupation by human populations in the eastern part of the North Pacific, however, does not come from the Bering Sea region, but rather from the Northwest Coast. The oldest coastal site in the Bering Sea region is the Blade site on Anangula Island with a beginning occupation date of ca. 8500 BP (Laughlin 1975, Table 1, Aigner 1976:34). On the northern and central parts of Northwest Coast, three sites (Figure 1) – Ground Hog Bay (GHB 2) (Ackerman 1968, 1974, 1980, 1981, Ackerman et al. 1979), Hidden Falls (Davis 1984), and Namu (Hester and Nelson 1978, C. Carlson 1979) – have basal dates ranging from 9700 to 9200 BP. On the Queen Charlotte Islands Zone III of the Skoglund's Landing site and sites within the present intertidal zone may date somewhat earlier (Fladmark 1979b, 1982, Hobler 1978). Between these earliest occupations and 5000 BP, the cut-off point for this symposium, there are a number of sites in the Alexander Archipelago (Ackerman et al. 1985, Roberts 1982, Dale et al. 1989), and the Queen Charlotte Islands (Fladmark 1970a, 1970b, 1979a, 1986a) which continue the early coastal tradition.

In another paper (Ackerman 1990), I have correlated environmental with cultural changes in an attempt to provide a tentative cultural sequence for

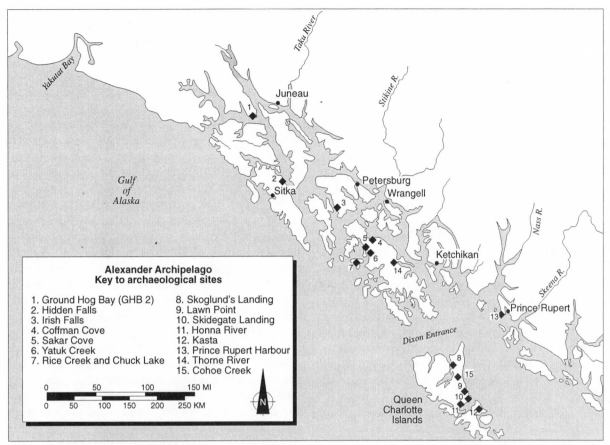

Figure 1. Archaeological site locations in coastal southeastern Alaska and northern British Columbia.

the northern part of the Northwest Coast of North America. Only the earlier part of that prehistoric record will be briefly considered here.

PERIOD I – PRIOR TO 10,000 BP

Sites reported to have been occupied possibly prior to 10,000 BP are restricted to the Queen Charlotte Islands (Figure 1). The artifactual material has been recovered from ten intertidal sites on the southern part of Moresby Island (Hobler 1978) and from raised beach deposits at the Skoglund's Landing site on Graham Island (Fladmark 1979b). The intertidal assemblages consist of large flakes and cores of andesite/argillite that have been rotated to provide multiple flaking platforms (Hobler 1978). The core reduction procedures associated with the Moresby Island intertidal sites are similar to those utilized at the GHB 2 site (Ackerman 1980). A small blade core recovered from an intertidal context may have been derived from a later component (Hobler 1978:2). The Moresby Island intertidal sites are regarded as an occupation of the shoreline when sea level was lower than present, i.e., somewhat before 10,000 BP (Hobler 1978:2). These sites were abandoned due to rising sea levels, which by 8000 BP had

reached 8 to 10 m above the present level (Hobler 1978:2). New data regarding this can be found in Chapter 13 of this volume.

The site of Skoglund's Landing is on a raised beach deposit, about 10 m above present sea level, that lies south of the village of Masset, Graham Island (Fladmark 1970a, 1990). The earliest cultural level was found in the basal gravels of Zone III and contained four pebble choppers, a pebble flake core, and three unfacially retouched flakes (Fladmark 1970a:36-7, 1979b:41, 1990:190-2). Some of the artifacts are waterworn suggesting an occupation of the beach, represented by the gravel and sand deposit of Zone III, when it was at sea level or could represent artifacts that were washed out of an earlier site occupation as sea level rose to its highest point about 8500 to 9000 BP (Fladmark 1979b:41-2, 1990:192).

There was no evidence of a microblade industry in the intertidal sites nor at the lowest level of Skoglund's Landing. Bifacial tools were similarly absent. It would be premature, however, to suggest that the flake cores derived from beach cobbles, large flakes, and cobble choppers constitute the basal industry of the northern Northwest Coast. Like the

Pasika complex to the south, the assemblage seems incomplete. Additionally, since this same industry is associated with microblade cores, microblades, bifaces, scrapers, and notches at the GHB 2 site, the limited inventory may, in the case of Skoglund's Landing, be the result of a small sample, and for the intertidal sites reflect a site feature or activity as yet not well understood. Fladmark (1990:192-3) notes that while pebble tools are not good temporal indicators, that the widespread distribution of such tools on all time levels would suggest that they were "material components of the earliest coastal occupations."

PERIOD II – 10,000 TO 8500 BP

This period is marked by rising temperatures in Europe (Boreal interval, 9300 to 8500 BP), Siberia (8900 to 8300 BP) and northern Canada (beginning 8900 BP)(Wendland and Bryson 1974, Khotinskiy 1984, Stewart and England 1983). On the Northwest Coast this is a cool, moist interval with rapid forest expansion with mountain hemlock, Sitka spruce, and alder dominant on Graham Island after 11,000 BP (Warner et al. 1982). Such a forest type appears to be present as early as 10,000 BP on Chichagof Island (Holloway 1989).

Southeastern Alaska

Raised beach deposits in southeastern Alaska containing marine shells dating between 13,000 and 9500 BP indicate "the occurrence of a widespread transgression of the sea over a landscape still depressed by the weight of late Wisconsin glaciers" (Mann 1986:257). The rates of uplift are quite variable. Stable zones such as the Ketchikan area with an uplift rate of 0.03 cm/yr can be contrasted with zones such as Glacier Bay with an uplift rate of 4 cm/yr (Hicks and Shofnos 1965, Hudson et al. 1982). Temporary stabilization or slowing of the effects of isostatic rebound may have been affected by a local glacial stillstand or readvance (Mann 1986:257). The stabilization of the 12 to 15 m terrace on which the GHB 2 site is located was probably due to a readvance of glaciers in Glacier Bay (Ackerman et al. 1979, Mann 1986:257). Subsequent uplift created lower terraces at 6.5 to 5 m (9000 to 5000 BP) and 3.5 m (3500 to 3000 BP) (Ackerman et al. 1979).

The GHB 2 and Hidden Falls sites were occupied during this time interval and represent the earliest site occupations in southeastern Alaska (Ackerman 1968, 1974, 1980, 1981, Ackerman et al. 1979, Davis 1984). Both sites are on elevated beach terraces which rest upon deposits of glaciomarine till. Both are located in small bays that presently contain a variety of intertidal, deep water, and terrestrial resources (Ackerman 1968, 1974, 1980, 1981, Ackerman et al. 1979, Davis 1984, Moss 1984, Erlandson 1984).

The diagnostic cultural traits of these two sites are (1) microblade cores, (2) microblades, (3) flake cores, (4) bifacial tools, (5) scrapers, (5) choppers, (6) notches, (7) gravers, and (8) utilized flakes, some of which may have been burinized. Artifacts recovered from the GHB 2 site will provide some insights into the cultural assemblage of these early coastal inhabitants. The microblade cores of obsidian were frontally fluted, wedge-shaped cores with platform rejuvination by retouch from either the flute face or the lateral margins (Figure 2a-c). All were made on flakes or nodules, but have a wedge or keel element that has been battered as if rested on an anvil stone or some other hard substance. Microblade cores of chert had prepared (Figure 2d) or natural platforms (Figure 2f). The chert cores have been laterally flaked to form a wedge element. Microblade cores of argillite are blocky, conical to cuboid in shape with platforms on natural or single flake scar surfaces (Figure 3a, b). Core rotation is rare to absent on the wedge shaped cores, but does occur (Figure 3b) on the cuboid shaped cores. A burinized flake (Figure 2e) with a platform created by edge retouch of the flake is similar to the Donnelly burin-scrapers of the Denali complex found in the Tangle Lakes area of central Alaska (West 1967). Microblades were relatively rare in the assemblage. Some showed evidence of retouch such as the end-burin made on a microblade (Figure 3c). Bifacial tools (Figure 3d-g) were recovered, but were rare items. Flakes were often retouched for cutting and scraping tools (Figure 3h, i). Large blade cores (Figure 4a), flake cores (Figure 4b), and cobble choppers (Figure 4c) were recovered and were found throughout the earlier cultural horizons of the site (Ackerman et al. 1979). No organic materials were recovered.

The obsidian found at the GHB 2 site was subjected to x-ray fluorescence analysis to determine the source of the raw material (Carlson 1994). Preliminary determinations suggested that the obsidian had been obtained from flows in the vicinity of Mount Edziza in the upper reaches of the Stikine River in northern British Columbia (Nelson, personal communication, 1976). Some specimens, while similar in many respects to source examples from Mount Edziza, were somewhat variant (Nelson, personal communication, 1976). Research studies (Godfrey-Smith 1987) on an obsidian source on Sumez Island on the west coast of Prince of Wales Island suggest that the anomalous obsidian

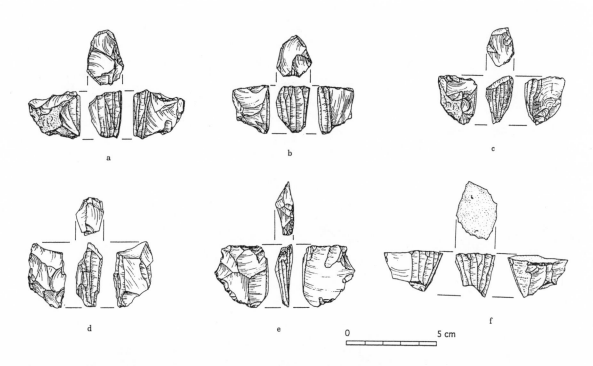

Figure 2. Microblade cores, Donnelly type burin, GHB 2 site: (a-c) wedge-shaped microblade cores, obsidian; (d, f) wedge-shaped to conoidal microblade cores, chert; (e) Donnelly type burin-scraper, chert.

specimens from GHB 2 may have been obtained from Sumez Island. The obsidian sources at Mount Edziza and Sumez Island are 550 or 350 km from Ground Hog Bay. The obsidian from the Hidden Falls site was also obtained from the Mount Edziza and Sumez Island sources. The obsidian source data thus reveals that by 9500 to 9000 years ago obsidian was already an item of long distance trade on the northern Northwest Coast. It also suggests that coastal trade with the interior was an early phenomenon.

The frontally fluted, wedge shaped type of microblade core found in the GHB 2 and Hidden Falls sites is technologically similar to those from Denali or Paleoarctic tradition (11,000 to 10,000 BP) sites in central and southwestern Alaska and from the earlier Diuktai tradition sites in northeastern Asia which date from 10,500 BP to possibly as early as 28,000 to 35,000 BP (Mochanov 1977, Dikov 1979). The cuboid to conical type microblade core found on the northern Northwest Coast may be a technological response to the different material characteristics of the local argillite rock. The cuboid to conical microblade cores types are either contemporary with the wedge shaped, frontal microblade cores or are somewhat later in time. They are additionally found in later dated site assemblages.

On Heceta Island in southeastern Alaska, we found a small site assemblage near Rice Creek. Eleven flakes were recovered from surface exposures produced by tree-throw or stream erosion. Further testing on a terrace 7.8 m above sea level resulted in the discovery of eight irregular cortex flakes, two short primary reduction flakes, two possible core platform tablets or flakes, and two irregular pieces of argillite from a gravel deposit that lay upon a glaciomarine deposit that has a provisional date of 9410 ±130 BP (Ackerman et al. 1985). I have provisionally dated the Rice Creek assemblage to 9000 BP (Figure 5). No diagnostic artifacts were recovered that would aid in identifying the cultural occupation.

At ca. 8600 BP the lower component of the Hidden Falls site was apparently overridden by a till sheet (Davis 1984). Environmental conditions following this event were possibly unfavorable locally as the site was unoccupied for the next 4000 years (Davis 1984).

Queen Charlotte Islands

Cultural Component 6 at the Lawn Point site on Graham Island of the Queen Charlotte Islands may fall within this time interval as the overlying com-

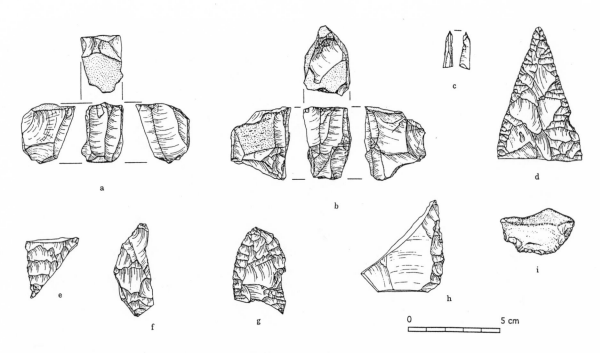

Figure 3. Microblade cores, bifaces, blade/flake tools GHB 2 site: (a, b) cuboid microblade cores, argillite; (c) angle burin on microblade, obsidian; (d) Tip of knife or projectile point, silicified slate; (e, f) fragments of obsidian bifaces; (g) chert bifacial preform; (h) edge-retouched flake, chert; (i) side-scraper, argillite.

ponent has been radiocarbon dated to 7400 ±140 and 7050 ±110 BP (Fladmark 1986a). The assemblage from Component 6 consists of pebble cores, utilized and retouched flakes, a scraper-cleaver, a hammerstone, and one microblade (see Ch. 13).

PERIOD III – 8500 TO 5000 BP

At 8500 BP there is a major break in the botanic record (Wendland and Bryson 1974, Table 7) which reflects the onset of the Atlantic interval. Lamb (1977:372) has placed the Atlantic period between ca. 8000 and 5000 BP and characterizes it as a time of maximum warming in the Holocene. Rising sea levels, occasioned by glacial meltdown, were generally offset by coastal uplift along the northwest coast of North America. The warming trend of the Atlantic period is demonstrated in the St. Elias Range of southeastern Alaska. A spruce stump dated at 8020 BP was found at an altitude of 1067 m, approximately 183 m below the current tree line (Denton and Karlén 1973:175). By 6175 to 5975 BP the tree line was higher than in the present, indicating a warmer climatic regime (Denton and Karlén 1973:175). Toward the end of this period (6000-5000 BP) there are indications of local glacial advances (Mann 1986).

Southeastern Alaska

Radiocarbon dates from Component II of the GHB 2 site indicate a continuing occupation of the site into this period (Ackerman et al. 1979). The site appears to have been in a stable relationship to rising sea levels. As noted previously, the Hidden Falls site was abandoned during this time interval.

The Chuck Lake site on Heceta Island (west coast of Prince of Wales Island, southern Alexander Archipelago) contains several isolated scatters of lithic debitage. In three locations there are also shell deposits. The cultural midden in Locality 1, dated to 8200 BP, has provided the earliest information thus far on the use of prehistoric faunal resources in the northern Northwest Coast region (Ackerman et al. 1985). The site is situated on a ridge 15 to 18 m above sea level and 1.2 km inland from the present shoreline. The midden was composed largely of shells of clams (*Saxidomus giganteus, Protothaca stamina, P. laciniata*) and mussels (*Mytilus edulis*). Cockles (*Clinocardium nuttalli*), gastropods (such as *Acmaea mitra* and *Bittium munitum*), and barnacles (*Balanus glandula, B. cariosus, B. nubilus*) were present but rare. Among the vertebrates, bottom fish (principally Pacific cod [*Gadus macrocephalus*], greenling [*Hexagrammos* sp.], sculpin [*Hemilepidotus hemilepidotus*], and rock fish [*Sebastes* sp.]) con-

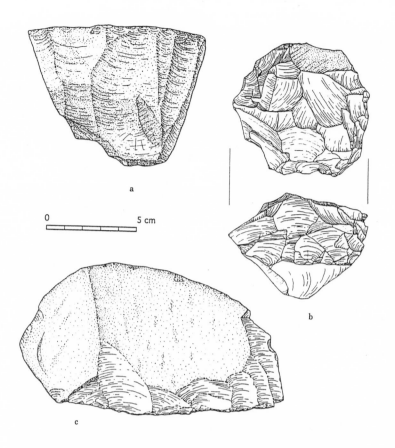

0   5 cm

Figure 4. Cores and cobble tools, GHB 2 site: (a) blade core, argillite; (b) flake core, argillite; (c) cobble chopper, andesite.

stituted 89.2 per cent of our sample (Frederick and Crockford 1987). Mammals such as beaver (*Castor canadensis*), sea lion (*Eumetopias jubata*), and deer (*Odocoileus hemionus*) or caribou (*Rangifer* sp.) made up 7.4 per cent of the sample with birds (cormorant [*Phalacrocorax* sp.], grebes [Podicipedidae], or loons [Gaviidae]) the remainder (Frederick and Crockford 1987).

The cultural inventory of Locality 1 (midden and surrounding area) of the Chuck Lake site included frontal, wedge-shaped to conical microblade cores with unretouched natural or flake scar platforms (Figures 6a-d,7a) microblades, cobble flake cores (Figure 7b-c), scrapers, hammerstones, whetstones, edge modified cobble spalls, flakes, and a fragment of a unilaterally barbed bone point (Figure 7d) (Ackerman et al. 1985). Microblades were found in the midden as well as in the overlying organic horizons. The cores are comparable to some of core types recovered from the Hidden Falls (Davis 1984) and GHB 2 sites (Ackerman 1968, 1974, Ackerman et al. 1979), Moresby tradition sites on the Queen Charlotte Islands (Fladmark 1982, 1986a, 1986b) and the Namu site near Bella Bella on the British Colum-

bia mainland (Hester and Nelson 1978; C. Carlson 1979). Obsidian recovered at the Chuck Lake site came from the Sumez Island source (Godfrey-Smith 1987). Radiocarbon dates on charcoal and shell provided dates of 8220 ±125 BP and 8180 ±130 BP respectively for an age determination of the midden. A charcoal sample from the bottom of the overlying organic horizon provided a date of 7360 ±270 BP (Ackerman et al 1985:Table 20). This suggests that a microblade industry was established on Heceta Island by 8200 years ago and continued to ca. 7000 BP.

Localities 2 and 3 of the Chuck Lake site contained thin layers of shell which provided radiocarbon dates of 5140 ±90 and 5240 ±90 BP (Ackerman et al. 1985, Table 20). No artifacts were recovered from Locality 2. In Locality 3 two microblade core reduction flakes, an edge modified cobble spall, and a possible hammerstone were recovered, but these artifacts were not directly associated with the shell deposit. It is thus not possible, at this time, to ascertain if the microblade industry continued as late as 5000 BP on Heceta Island. No other sites of this time period have been located in southeastern Alaska. On the Queen Charlotte Islands cultural events around 5000 BP would reflect the end of the Moresby tradition and the beginning of a transitional cultural complex where microblade technology was replaced by a bipolar flake technology (Fladmark 1975, 1982).

Returning to southeastern Alaska, the recently discovered Thorne River site on the eastern side of Prince of Wales Island has been dated at 7440 ±90, 7560 ±90, and 7650 ±160 BP for an average age estimate of 7520 ±59 BP (Dale et al. 1989:86). The site is on a high, south bank of the Thorne River about one mile upstream from its mouth. The site contains microblade cores, core rejuvination flakes, microblades, flake cores, flakes, pebble tools, burins, burin spalls, and "rare bifaces" (Dale et al. 1989:32-6). The major raw material from which microblade cores, burins, and bifaces were made was obsidian (Dale et al. 1989, Table 9). The microblade core types are similar to those from the GHB 2, Hidden Falls, and Chuck Lake sites.

The Irish Creek site, on a terrace 15 m above sea level that overlooks Irish Creek, Kupreanof Island, may also belong to this period. Age estimates

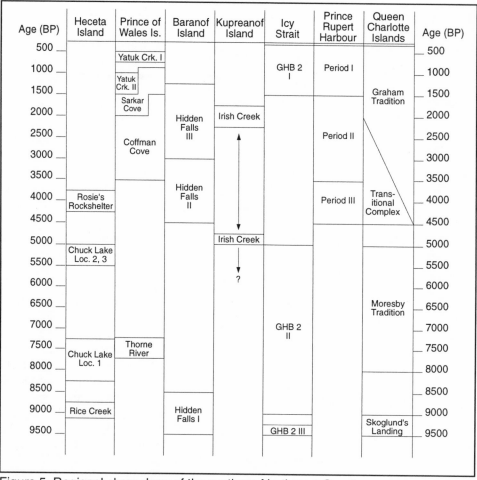

Age (BP)	Heceta Island	Prince of Wales Is.	Baranof Island	Kupreanof Island	Icy Strait	Prince Rupert Harbour	Queen Charlotte Islands	Age (BP)
500								500
1000		Yatuk Crk. I			GHB 2 I	Period I		1000
1500		Yatuk Crk. II					Graham Tradition	1500
2000		Sarkar Cove	Hidden Falls III	Irish Creek				2000
2500		Coffman Cove				Period II		2500
3000								3000
3500			Hidden Falls II					3500
4000	Rosie's Rockshelter					Period III	Trans-itional Complex	4000
4500								4500
5000	Chuck Lake Loc. 2, 3			Irish Creek				5000
5500								5500
6000				?			Moresby Tradition	6000
6500								6500
7000					GHB 2 II			7000
7500	Chuck Lake Loc. 1	Thorne River						7500
8000								8000
8500								8500
9000	Rice Creek		Hidden Falls I				Skoglund's Landing	9000
9500					GHB 2 III			9500

Figure 5. Regional chronology of the northern Northwest Coast.

for the geological formations and the downcutting of the nearby falls indicate that the site could have been occupied as early as 5000 BP (Swanston 1984). A charcoal sample collected at a depth of 28 to 30 cm provided an age estimate of ca. 2240 ±70 BP (Roberts 1982). Neither date appears satisfactory for this assemblage. I have included the Irish Creek site with other sites of the second cultural period. The site contains wedge-shaped and conical to cylindrical shaped microblade cores, flake cores, scrapers, a graver, utilized microblades, and small flakes.

Queen Charlotte Islands

Sites of the Moresby Tradition, such as the Lawn Point, Kasta, and Cohoe Creek sites on Graham and Moresby Islands, belong to this cultural period (Fladmark 1982a, 1989, Ham 1990). The Lawn Point site was discovered in a roadcut on a terrace approximately 15 m above high tide (Fladmark 1970a, 1986a). The site is stratified with six components which date 7400 ±140 and 7050 ±110 BP for Component 5, 5750 ±110 BP for Component 4, and 2005

±85 BP for Component 1 (Fladmark 1986a, Table 4). Microblade cores have been recovered from Components 2, 3, and 5 with the majority of the microblade cores recovered from Component 3 which post-dates 5750 BP (Fladmark 1986a, Table 3). Microblade cores derived from flakes or pebbles are conical to cylindrical in shape (Fladmark 1986a:45) and, as noted previously, are similar to those recovered from the Chuck Lake site. Associated with the microblade cores are microblades, pebble cores, choppers, utilized and retouched flakes, scraper-cleavers, nosed scrapers, gravers, and hammerstones (Fladmark 1986a, Table 3). Fladmark (personal communication 1988) notes that the microblade industry on the Queen Charlotte Island is present by at least 7500 BP and by 4200 BP was no longer in use. Notably missing from the assemblage are bifaces.

The Kasta site, also discovered in a newly made roadcut, is on a terrace 14 m above high tide (Fladmark 1986a:53). This site assemblage consists of microblade cores, microblades, flake cores, retouched flakes, pebble choppers, and sandstone abraders

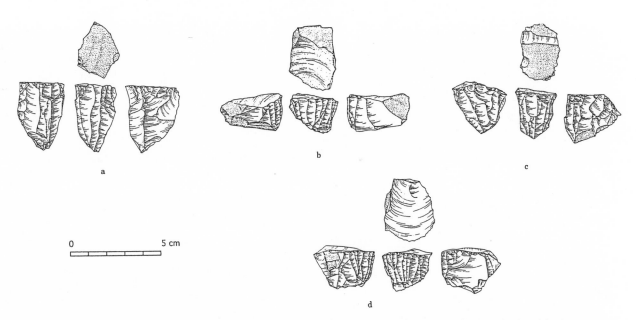

0   5 cm

Figure 6. Microblade cores, Chuck Lake site, Heceta Island: (a-d) cuboid to cylindrical microblade cores, argillite.

(Fladmark 1986a:53). Radiocarbon dates of 5420 ±100 and 6010 ±95 BP for levels 3 and 4 suggest a somewhat later initial occupation than that of the Lawn Point site (Fladmark 1986a:54). It is possible, however, that there is an earlier occupation level in the site for two water worn flakes were recovered from the gravels underlying the lowest cultural level (Fladmark 1986a:54).

The Cohoe Creek site, on Graham Island, is situated on a raised gravel beach deposit, about 15 m above present sea level (Ham 1990:199). The site was discovered during bulldozing operations prior to gravel removal. Artifacts were recovered as surface finds while the site midden was investigated *in situ*. Radiocarbon dates of 6150 ±70 and 4990 ±110 BP were obtained on charcoal samples and a date of 5715 ±90 BP from a shell sample (Ham 1990:206-7). Artifacts included pebble cores, pebble core remnants, pebble core reduction flakes, "keeled" (wedge-shaped) microblade cores made on what appear to be flakes or nodules, a microblade, a tip of a bifacial knife or point, anvil stones, abrasive stones, and ground and chipped bone points (Ham 1990). Data obtained from the shell midden indicates that the occupants of the site utilized shellfish, fish, and land mammals such as caribou and bear (Ham 1990:210-11). The data recovered from the Cohoe Creek shell midden provides the earliest evidence of resource use on the Queen Charlotte Islands and further insights into the cultural assemblage of the late Moresby tradition (Ham 1990:216).

Sites in the Prince Rupert Harbour area (Mac-

Donald and Inglis 1981) post-date cultural period III as do other sites in southeastern Alaska and the Queen Charlotte Islands (see Figure 5).

DISCUSSION

The northern Northwest Coast may have been occupied before 10,000 BP (Figure 5) if age estimates for the intertidal sites on Moresby Island, and the early levels of the Skoglund's Landing site on Graham Island prove to be correct. The artifact complexes of these sites are limited to cobble tools or cores and flakes. Sites from cultural period II (10,000 to 8500 BP) such as GHB 2 and Hidden Falls which are characterized by a microblade technology (North Coast Microblade Complex, Fladmark 1982) and associated heavy cobble chopper tool and flake core industries have beginning dates of 9000 to 9400 BP for GHB 2 (Ackerman et al. 1979) and 9000 to 9500 BP for Hidden Falls (Davis 1984). The single date of 10,180 ±800 BP for GHB 2 with its large standard deviation stands apart from the remainder of the radiocarbon date series for the site and has not been utilized as a basal date for the site (Ackerman et al. 1979). The procedures of microblade core preparation at these two sites are similar to those found in the sites of the Denali or Paleo-Arctic tradition of south central Alaska and ultimately can be derived from the Diuktai culture complex of Siberia and the Far East. The heavy chopper tool and large flake core industry is widespread around the Pacific and has a long antiquity in Asia. Both the GHB 2 and Hidden Falls sites are in coastal locations, although

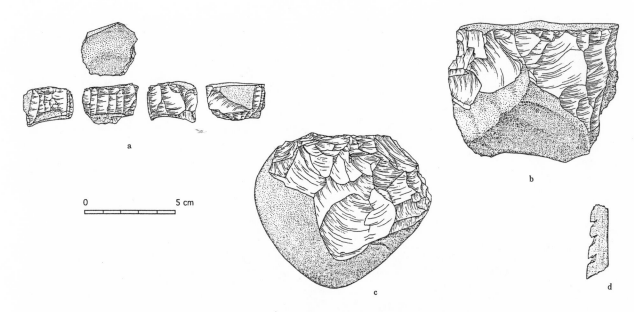

Figure 7. Cores and bone point, Chuck Lake site, Heceta island: (a) cylindrical microblade core, argillite; (b, c) cobble cores, argillite; (d) unilaterally barbed bone point fragment.

GHB 2 is on the mainland and Hidden Falls on Chichagof Island. Considering the rugged terrain of the mainland, travel by boat would have been the only economical manner of transport for this early mainland population as would it have been for the island group. It was possible at the outset to postulate the need for water craft and hence to infer the use of marine resources.

Such subsistence data were recovered from the 8200 year old midden at Locality 1 of the Chuck Lake site on Heceta Island. It was possible to clearly demonstrate that island populations of this time were fully maritime adapted and subsisted on marine resources. Heavy use was made of intertidal mollusks and bottom fish. Salmon appears to have been a relatively rare item as were terrestrial animals in the diet of Heceta Islanders. Heceta Island, as an outer island in the Alexander Archipelago of southeastern Alaska, is also exposed to the fetch of the Pacific Ocean. These early inhabitants would have had to have been competent mariners.

It is not clear how well the cultural complexes of the northern Northwest Coast correlate with climatic change. It is evident that the major thrust of early settlement appears to have occurred during a warming trend following the Late Wisconsin–Early Holocene cold period. Recent palynological investigations indicate that forest type vegetation was present by 11,000 to 10,000 BP (Holloway 1989, Warner et al. 1982). Accumulating data on plant and animal communities suggests that a sequential or-

dering of species migration is possible (Ackerman 1988a), but such data are still rather generalized. It is not clear what effect the warming trend between 8500 and 5000 BP had to do with settlement patterning. Within this interval the Hidden Falls site was abandoned, but at the GHB 2 site there is no noticeable change in the artifact inventory. There could have been a southerly expansion of the island populations for sites such as Chuck Lake and Thorne River (Figure 1) date to within this climatic interval. People who subsist on marine resources may, however, be less affected by climatic events and the population expansion may be attributable to other factors. In terrestrial terms the shift from an open to a closed canopy forest should have had a significant effect on vegetational patterns and terrestrial mammals. Unfortunately, there was little information on the use of land mammals from the Chuck Lake site. For the period between 8000 and 5000 BP there is scant information.

It is apparent from the wealth of information provided by one rather small midden at the 8200-year-old Chuck Lake site that we desperately need to focus more attention on gathering paleoenvironmental information. In this site the bones were far more informative than the artifacts.

Acknowledgments
The artifacts illustrated in Figures 2-4, 6-7 were drawn by Sarah Moore, Pullman, Washington.

EARLY PERIOD ARCHAEOLOGY IN GWAII HAANAS: RESULTS OF THE 1993 FIELD PROGRAM

13

D.W. Fedje, A.P. Mackie, J.B. McSporran, and B. Wilson

Parks Canada and the Council of Haida Nations are jointly supporting an intensive archaeological survey of Gwaii Haanas for purposes of comanagement. This survey has been carried out by a team consisting of Haida, Parks Canada and consulting archaeologists. It is projected to encompass five field seasons, the third of which was completed in 1993.

The Gwaii Haanas Archaeological Project (GHAP) has investigated a number of Early Period archaeological sites many of which appear to be no younger than 9000 years old (Fedje et al. forthcoming, Mackie and Wilson 1994). In this chapter we focus on the results of the 1993 field program on the east coast of Gwaii Haanas where research design and interpretation has developed out of an integration of paleoenvironmental and archaeological research (Fedje 1993, Mackie and Wilson 1994). More specifically, we provide a brief synopsis of the results of preliminary test excavation at two sites on Arrow Creek in Matheson Inlet, sites which are associated with raised marine deposits, and initial assessment at several intertidal lithic sites in the environs of Lyell Island. In the text below, age estimates are presented in radiocarbon years before present (BP). Tree ring calibrated calendar ages are used in calculation of the rates of deposition and sea level change. These are presented in Table 1.

Gwaii Haanas is an archipelago consisting of southern Moresby Island and adjacent smaller islands in the south of Haida Gwaii (Queen Charlotte Islands). The 1993 study area included parts of Juan Perez Sound and the environs of Lyell Island on the central east coast of Moresby Island (Figure 1). The modern coastline of the study area is densely forested with an environment ranging from wet hypermaritime in the west to subhumid maritime in the

east (rainshadow). Tidal range in this part of Haida Gwaii is approximately 6 m. In the text following, elevations are given relative to mean sea level. A 0.0 m tide is lowest low water or 3 m below mean sea level (b.m.s.l.), a 3.0 m tide is mean sealevel and a 6.0 m tide is highest high water which is 3 m above mean sea level (a.m.s.l.). Elevations were established using local tidal prediction data from the Institute of Ocean Sciences, Tides and Currents Division, corrected with reference to tidal observations and are accurate to ±10 cm.

The local environment would have been significantly different during the early to midHolocene when the Early Period Gwaii Haanas sites were occupied (Fedje 1993, Fedje et al. forthcoming). At 9000 BP the regional climate shifted from warm and moist to warm and dry. This was followed by a warm moist period at ca. 7500 BP and a cool moist period, similar to that of today, commencing ca. 5500 BP. Through the period of site occupation sea level was subject to significant change (Figure 2). Between 10,400 and 9300 BP sea level rose very rapidly. At 10,400 BP the shoreline was ca. 110 m below modern levels, by 9300 BP it was about the same as now and by 8900 BP it was 15 m higher. Relative sea levels plateaued at 15 to 13 m above current levels from 8900 to ca. 5500 BP and have been falling slowly since that time. Although the C-14 dates suggest a rise of 10 cm/yr between 10,400 and 9300 BP, calendar year corrections shows that the actual rate was only 5.4 cm/yr (12,300 to 10,240 calendar years BP).

Rapid sea level change prior to 8900 BP significantly altered the character of Gwaii Haanas. The archipelago changed from a large land mass (ca. 3000 km^2) dominated by broad low elevation plains

Table 1. Gwaii Haanas radiocarbon dates.

LOCATION AND LAB# (* = shell-wood pair)	SAMPLE #	M AMSL	MATERIAL	SPECIFIC ID	SHELL AGE	OCEAN 14C Cor-rection**	14C AGE (wood & corrected shell)	CALENDAR AGE max (median of x intercepts) min ***
Arrow Creek 1								
TO-2622	766T1	17.0	charcoal				8200 ±80	9255 (9093/7) 8991
TO-2623	766T1	17.1	charcoal				8200 ±90	9260 (9093/7) 8989
CAMS4111	766T4	15.5	charcoal				5650 ±90	6491 (6415) 6319
CAMS4112	766T4	15.7	charcoal				5650 ±70	6491 (6415) 6319
CAMS8378	766T	5.5	wood				9290 ±60	10357 (10248/3) 10147
CAMS8384*	766T	5.2	wood	hemlock cone			9150 ±80	10281 (10042) 10016
CAMS8374*	766T	5.2	shell	littleneck clam	9660 ±70	600	9060 ±70	10041 (10007) 9975
CAMS8385*	766T	3.1	wood	hemlock			9310 ±60	10366 (10233/3) 10164
CAMS8375*	766T	3.1	shell	littleneck clam	9930 ±70	600	9330 ±70	10377 (10324/3) 10206
CAMS9982*	766TM#4	2.3	wood	alder leaf			9390 ±60	10471 (10367) 10299
CAMS9983*	766tM#4	2.3	shell	mussel	9820 ±80	600	9220 ±80	10298 (10226/4) 10040
Arrow Creek 2								
CAMS8383	925TTP4	7.1	charcoal				2750 ±80	2937 (2833/2) 2763
CAMS8377	925T6C	5.5	charcoal				9010 ±160	10075 (9981) 9883
CAMS8379	925T5C	2.9	wood	conifer			1810 ±60	1816 (1715) 1626
CAMS4113	925T	2.8	wood	spruce cone			9100 ±90	10272 (10033) 9980
CAMS9987	925T5F180	2.5	charcoal				9150 ±100	10284 (10042) 9995
CAMS8380*	935T	2.7	wood	spruce cone			9150 ±60	10277 (10042) 10031
CAMS8373*	925T	2.7	shell	littleneck clam	9860 ±70	600	9260 ±60	10366 (10255/3) 10050
CAMS9984	925T2A1	2.5	shell	barnacle on flake	9810 ±190	600	9210 ±190	10375 (10265/3) 9984
CAMS10855	925T2A1	2.5	shell	barnacle on flake	9720 ±70	600	9120 ±60	10271 (10037) 10003
CAMS10599	925T5G224	2.6	wood	teredo holes			9280 ±60	10353 (10251/3) 10142
CAMS8382	925T5F231	2.6	charcoal				9840 ±100	11075 (10995) 10964
CAMS8381*	925T	2.2	wood	spruce cone			9240 ±60	10299 (10201/5) 10046
CAMS8376*	925T	2.2	shell	littleneck clam	9870 ±60	600	9270 ±60	10346 (10253/3) 10137
CAMS9986	925T5G315	1.4	wood	teredo holes			9410 ±60	10535 (10377) 10304
CAMS10600*	925T2B3	1.2	wood	spruce cone			9580 ±200	10984 (10801/5) 10362
CAMS10845*	925T2B3	1.2	shell	butter clam	9900 ±70	600	9300 ±700	10365 (10240/3) 10148
CAMS10856*	925T2B3	1.2	shell	barnacle	9930 ±60	600	9330 ±60	10374 (10324/3) 10211
CAMS10846*	925T2B4	0.8	wood	hemlock cone			9320 ±60	10370 (10300) 10205
CAMS10853	925T2B4	0.8	shell	mussel	10020 ±60	600	9420 ±60	10537 (10381) 10307
CAMS10847*	925T2B5	0.5	wood	deciduous twig			9430 ±100	10792 (10386) 10301
CAMS10848*	925T2B5	0.5	shell	mussel	10030 ±	600	9430 ±100	10792 (10386) 10301
CAMS9968*	925T2B6	o.4	charcoal				9900 ±90	11204 (11004) 10992
CAMS9969	925T2B6	0.4	shell	mussel	9970 ±70	600	9370 ±70	10436 (10359) 10222
Matheson Core 1								
CAMS10601	93M1-178	-25.1	wood	conifer, outer ring			9630 ±70	10953 (10809/2) 10560
CAMS9990	93M1-185	-26.2	wood	conifer, outer ring			9670 ±60	10963 (10924) 10623
CAMS9989	93M1-195	-26.3	wood	conifer			9780 ±60	10998 (10982) 10957
Matheson Core 4								
CAMS10816*	93M4-230	-27.3	wood	spruce needle			9030 ±50	10031 (9986) 9970
CAMS10836*	93M4-230	-27.3	shell	jingle shell	9740 ±60	600	9140 ±60	10275 (10040) 10026
CAMS10817*	93M4-238	-27.4	wood	alder			9530 ±60	10869 (10763/3) 10426
CAMS10837*	93M4-238	-27.4	shell	mussel	10200 ±60	600	9400 ±60	10532 (10372) 10302
CAMS9991*	93M4-246	-27.5	wood	deciduous twig			9530 ±60	10869 (10763/3) 10426
CAMS9992*	93M4-246	-27.5	shell	mussel	10490 ±80	600	9890 ±80	11198 (11002) 10992
Laskeek Core 92-21								
TO 3495	E9221-142	-105	wood	twig			10360 ±80	12376 (12243) 12079
TO 3735	E9221-23	-104	shell	pelesipod	10780 ±70	600?	10180 ±70	12110 (11916) 11635
Richardson Island								
CAMS9974*	1127T-1	2.5		spruce cone			8550 ±70	9529 (9490) 9450
CAMS9975*	1127T-1	2.5	wood	twig			8850 ±60	9924 (9884) 9691
CAMS9976*	1127T-1	2.5	shell	jingle shell	8850 ±60	600	8960 ±60	9987 (9967) 9907
Echo Bay								
CAMS9977*	1128T-1	2.5	wood				8550 ±60	9527 (9490) 9452
CAMS9978*	1128T-1	2.5	shell	periwinkle	9640 ±70	600	9040 ±70	10037 (9989) 9967
Dodge Point								
CAMS9979	1131T-1	15.0	charcoal				5490 ±80	6395 (6291) 6203

**Fedje et al. (forthcoming) and Southon et al. (1990);   ***calibration following Stuiver and Reimer (1993)

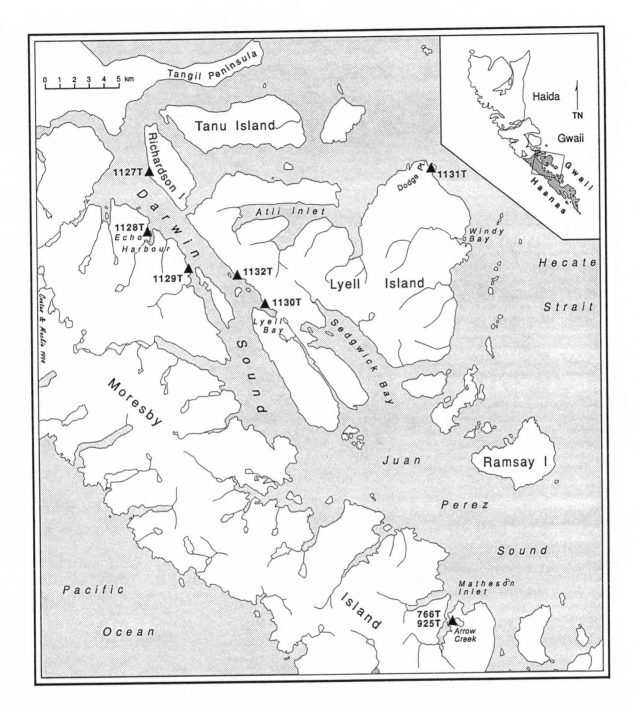

Figure 1. Gwaii Haanas study area.

with wide, low, sloping shorelines to a much smaller area (ca. 1500 km^2) with a rugged and narrow, steep shoreline (mountains sloping directly to ocean). The character of the shore zone and the rapidity of sea level change likely had significant repercussions upon availability and productivity of intertidal and anadramous resources. These repercussions were not necessarily all negative as regards resource abundance. For example, increased availability of nutrients such as iron may have spiked the lower end of the food chain (Kerr 1994), and might help explain the very abundant shellfish recovered from those parts of the Matheson Inlet cores and sections which date to this time of rapid transgression.

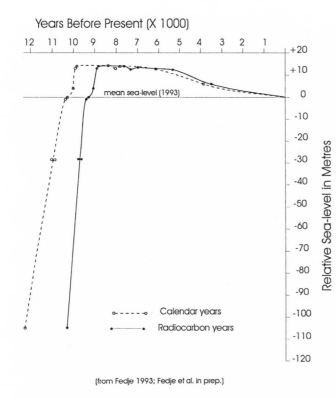

Figure 2. Gwaii Haanas sea level curve.

ARROW CREEK ARCHAEOLOGICAL SITES

The Arrow Creek sites are situated along a small creek flowing into Matheson Inlet, Juan Perez Sound on the east coast of Moresby Island (Figures 1 and 3). These sites are protected from the effect of significant winds and waves because of their position in this sheltered inlet. Fetch, even during the maximum of the Holocene marine transgression, was less than 1 km. Matheson Inlet is narrow and relatively deep (ca. 30 m) for most of its length but a late Holocene sandy sill (Josenhans et al. forthcoming) at its outlet is very shallow (ca. 5 m).

Arrow Creek 2 (925T)

The Arrow Creek 2 site was discovered in 1990 by Haida archaeologists who found stone tools lying on what appeared to be raised marine sediments (Fedje and Wanagun 1991), and was briefly revisited in 1992 (Eldridge et al. 1993). The site is situated at the head of the estuary near the modern tidal limit. The 1990 investigations were limited to the completion of a site record form and collection of a wood sample from a clay-rich stratigraphic exposure. The wood sample was dated to 9100 BP (Table 1) suggesting the sediments were laid down during the early Holocene marine transgression (Fedje 1993).

Discovery of stone tools lying on the clay-rich sediments initially suggested association with overlying mid to late Holocene (regressive) sediments.

A bear tooth and a few basalt flakes were collected in 1992; some of the artifacts were recovered from the stratigraphic exposure.

During 1993 more extensive investigations of the site were conducted as it appeared to be eroding rapidly. The objectives of the 1993 program were to define depositional history, site bounds, and interpretive potential. Fieldwork commenced with site mapping and detailed recording and sampling of the stratigraphic exposure. This was followed by shovel testing on the adjacent 7 m terrace. The final stage of fieldwork entailed the excavation of two 1 by 2 m units perpendicular to the eroding face of the lowermost terrace. In addition to terrestrial investigations, four sediment cores were collected from Matheson Inlet. The cores were collected in order to better understand the timing of marine transgression.

Stratigraphy and Dating

Stratigraphy at this site is complicated by a history of alluvial and estuarine deposition; post-depositional intrusion by burrowing mollusks; marine transgressive and regressive erosion; late Holocene (regressive) fluvial downcutting; and by differential leaching and oxidation following regression. The stratigraphic relationship of Arrow Creek 2 sediments has only become clear following detailed radiocarbon dating and the analysis of macro and microfossils (Figure 4, Table 1). The general character of sediments encountered in stratigraphic exposures and excavation profiles includes a clay-rich early Holocene (estuarine) transgressive alluvial stratum overlain, in turn, by a cobble or gravel layer (lag and coarse alluvium deposited during marine regression) and a humic loam. It appears that transgressive deposits are primarily constructional while regressive deposits are mostly erosional.

There is considerable variation in expression of the alluvial strata within these deposits, largely due to taphonomic processes (Fedje et al., forthcoming). The clay-rich alluvium exhibits considerable change, within an apparently continuous stratum, over a very short distance. At 10 m east, along the stratigraphic exposure, marine and intertidal fauna and plant material are well preserved, except in the uppermost 25 cm where the shell has been leached out, leaving casts in the clay-rich sediment. At 5 m east, only plant remains and casts of marine macrofau-

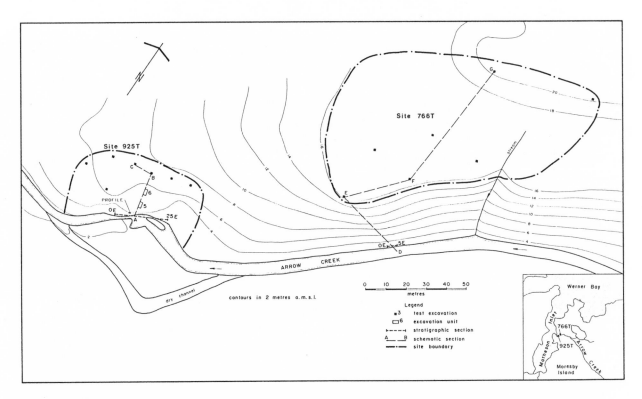

Figure 3. Arrow Creek site locations.

na are present. This indicates complete leaching. At 0 m east the laminated clays and silty sands comprising this stratum show no evidence of floral remains or marine fauna. It is unclear whether this represents leaching, oxidation, and subsequent compression or a separate alluvial unit.

Similarly, profiles in the excavations show considerable differences in character. Excavation unit 925T5 is only 2 m north of the shell-rich stratigraphic section but contains no shell. However, wood is abundant in the waterlogged clay-rich sediments. Although shellfish and marine microfauna are not present, teredo holed wood and marine microflora (diatoms and silicoflagellates) are present, thereby establishing the estuarine to marine nature of the sediments. The alluvial sediments observed in excavation unit 925T6 are currently above the permanent water table. They are subject to both oxidation and leaching. These sediments contain no shell or wood but are otherwise similar to those in 925T5 and along the stratigraphic exposure. The shovel tests exhibit alluvium with the same character as that in 925T6.

The cobble, gravel, and sand layer overlying the alluvium was most developed on the 4 m terrace (Figure 4). This layer is interpreted as a lag deposit (alluvium winnowed by tidal and/or fluvial action

during marine regression). On the lower terrace this layer appears to include coarse alluvium deposited in the late Holocene as the creek cut into the early Holocene alluvial strata. The presence of stone artifacts with sharp edges in the lower part of this layer on the 4 m terrace indicates that portion was lag rather than recent fluvial material. The downcutting interpretation is consistent with radiocarbon evidence. Carbon samples from the lag deposit on the 4 m terrace are younger than those from the 7 m terrace (Figure 4, Table 1).

It is noteworthy that ongoing erosion adjacent to the stratigraphic exposure on the lower terrace provides a good analogue for interpreting the base of the cobble-gravel layer as a lag deposit. During the recording of *in situ* artifacts in the alluvial cutbank a number of basalt flakes (n = 14) were observed in the base of the creek. These artifacts were among coarse cobbles lying directly on top of shell and clay-rich alluvium (truncated continuation of matrix observed in the stratigraphic section). They exhibited razor-sharp edges and clearly had not been transported any distance.

Dating of archaeological sites and timing of sediment deposition at Arrow Creek was established through AMS C-14 dating of plant macrofossils and shells. In Table 1 wood and charcoal dates are pre-

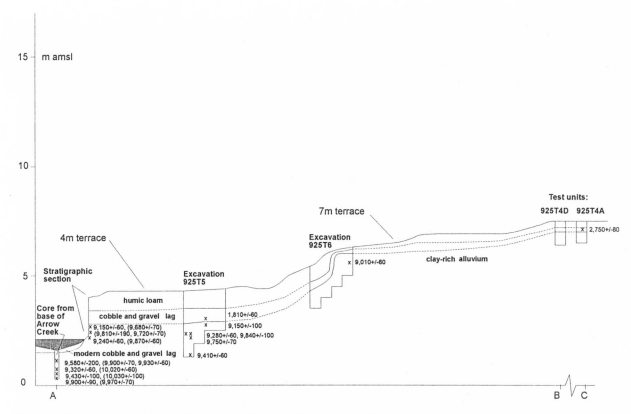

Figure 4. Schematic section of Arrow Creek 2 site (*uncorrected dates in parentheses).

sented in C-14 years BP and in calendar years BP as calibrated using the Calib 3.03 dendrochronological calibration program (Stuiver and Reimer 1993). Shell dates were corrected for the local carbon reservoir before being calibrated. In this area of the Northeast Pacific, Southon et al. (1990) have documented a ca. 700 to 800 year difference in C-14 age for shell versus wood for most of the Holocene. This difference is a consequence of the difference in the age of carbon in the atmospheric and oceanic reservoirs. Shell-wood pairs collected at Arrow Creek, Matheson Inlet, and environs during 1993 support a ca. 600 year correction for shell dates at ca. 9000 to 9500 BP. Shell is, on average, 600 years older than the wood with which it is associated. Only shell-wood pairs (n=15) that were in direct association in an estuarine or archaeological context where plant material was a maximum of about five years old at time of deposition and where shells were from shallow or surface dwelling species were used for estimating this difference.

In addition to dating the marine transgression, the C-14 record demonstrates that the Arrow Creek 2 site was occupied as early as 9300 years ago and was innundated by rising sea levels about 9000 years ago (Figure 4, Table 1). As will be discussed

further, the dates include one on barnacles (Figure 5) which adhered to an artifact 9200 years ago – clear evidence of the site's antiquity.

Lithic Artifacts and Features

Cultural remains recovered from the Arrow Creek 2 site include some 110 lithic artifacts and two possible features (Fedje et al., forthcoming). Except for a few concentrations of charcoal, all organic remains recovered during excavation and sampling appear to be non-cultural.

Lithic artifacts were recovered from both alluvial and lag deposits at this site. Approximately 80 per cent of the artifacts were excavated from early Holocene (pre-9000 BP) clay-rich alluvium. Of the remainder, all but three artifacts are from the lower part of the cobble-gravel layer and thus likely winnowed out of this same alluvium. Three flakes were recovered from the surface of the "lag" layer and could relate to late Holocene activity; however, they are situated at the base of the slope of the 7 m terrace and therefore could have slumped onto the cobble layer during final stages of fluvial downcutting.

Only one diagnostic artifact was recovered from the estuarine sediments. This is an exhausted conical microblade core manufactured from agate (Fig-

Figure 5. Selected stone tools from Arrow Creek 2.

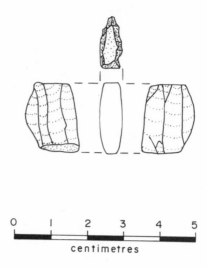

Figure 6. Microblade core from Arrow Creek 2.

ure 6). The remainder of the assemblage includes debitage and a few unifacially modified flake tools.

At Arrow Creek and all other sites discussed in this chapter, lithics appear to be of local origin. Basalt is by far the most common material with high quality stone common in exposures throughout Gwaii Haanas (Souther and Jessop 1991). Agate is readily accessible at several locations in Juan Perez Sound. We have also observed several obsidian sources in the 1993 study area.

Only two features potentially of cultural origin were observed during these preliminary excavations. These include a possible hearth feature in excavation block 925T5 and a stone wall in excavation block 925T6. A dense, roughly circular concentration of charcoal in a small depression at 2.2 m below the surface of block 925T5 may be a hearth. The charcoal, which dates to ca. 9300 BP, derives from several branch-size pieces of wood and is immediately adjacent to a number of uncharred branches, some of which are interpreted as driftwood based on the presence of teredo burrowing. Alternatively, teredos may have colonized wood, which had been deposited in the estuary, as the ocean transgressed the site. There are no artifacts in close association with the charcoal concentration. The nearest lithic artifacts are some 10 to 20 cm above this level. As such, identification as a hearth is very tentative.

An alignment of cobbles and boulders at 170 to 210 cm below unit datum in excavation 925T6 appears to be a cultural feature (Figure 7). The alignment comprises a number of large rocks with smaller cobbles carefully positioned in spaces between these so as to produce a narrow wall about 40 cm high. It extends across the 1 m wide unit and into the east and west walls of the excavation. The feature immediately underlay a charcoal sample dated to 9050 BP. The function of this feature is uncertain but it could be part of a stone-wall fish trap such as are common on estuaries throughout Gwaii Haanas, including several examples in Matheson Inlet.

Arrow Creek 1 (766T)

The Arrow Creek 1 site (Figure 3) is situated on a raised marine terrace approximately 17 m above modern mean sea level (a.m.s.l.). The site was first located in the mid 1970s and briefly reinvestigated in 1990 and 1992 (Hobler 1976, Fedje and Wanagun

Figure 7. Stone alignment at Arrow Creek 2.

1991, Fedje 1993). This large site is stratified, but based on the results of preliminary work, contains no shell or other organics except for small amounts of charcoal. The absence of organic matter likely results from the effects of several millennia in a highly acidic rainforest environment (Stein 1992).

Investigation conducted in 1991 and 1992 was limited to surface inspection and shovel testing for site bounds and some preliminary paleoenvironmental analysis. Site extent was determined from lithic artifact exposures along the eroding creek bank, in several tree-throws and from the systematic testing. The site was estimated to encompass approximately 2 hectares. Seven 50 cm square tests were excavated, including five on a 17 m a.m.s.l. terrace and two on a 20 m a.m.s.l. glacio-fluvial bench. Five of the tests produced lithic artifacts. Charcoal was recovered in association with artifacts from the basal limits of testing at two of these. These samples were radiocarbon dated to 8200 BP and 5650 BP respectively (Table 1).

Approximately forty lithic artifacts were recovered from the shovel tests and surface exposures. These are dominated by basalt and chert flakes, core

fragments, and expedient flake tools. No microblades or microblade cores were found although microlithic cores and blade-like flakes were present. Organic cultural remains were limited to small concentrations of charcoal. No formal analysis for microfossils was conducted but a soil sample from the 8200 BP level was processed for diatom analysis. Diatoms were not abundant but included both planktonic marine and benthic brackish water types. This suggests an estuarine context.

Radiocarbon dates suggest the site was occupied from at least 8200 to 5600 years BP (Table 1). This is consistent with the sea level curve obtained from the microfossil record (Fedje 1993, see below). The 1993 work at Arrow Creek 1 was limited to recording and interpreting a stratigraphic section underlying the artifact bearing sediments observed during 1990 and 1992.

Stratigraphy and Dating

The Arrow Creek 1 stratigraphic section extends from the base of a pool in Arrow Creek to about 4 m above creek level. The sediment record between this point and the edge of the 17 m terrace (ca. 8 m of sediment) is masked by colluvium and dense vegetation. Observed stratigraphy is presented schematically in Figure 8.

The base of this section is characterized by clay-rich estuarine sediments. They contain shellfish and microfossil remains (protozoa and diatoms) characteristic of a low energy brackish water environment (Fedje et al., forthcoming). These sediments are waterlogged and contain abundant plant remains. Calcareous fossils are abundant in all but the outer few centimetres of the exposed sediment and the top 10 cm of the section. Absence in the latter appears to result from percolation of acidic groundwater. Radiocarbon dating indicates the sediments were deposited between ca. 9310 and 9100 BP (Table 1).

These data suggest a period of rapid sediment accumulation (ca. 15 m) between 9300 and ca. 8200 BP and very slow accumulation thereafter. The fine sediment at the base of this section suggests deposition at the front of the receding delta (low energy environment) whereas the coarse alluvium in the upper part of the section suggests a position in the upper intertidal or supertidal zone (high energy fluvial environment). Both the 8200 and 5650 BP dates are from the sandy gravel immediately underlying the pebbly loam. This suggests a significant slowing in sediment accumulation at this time as would be expected once sea levels had begun to drop from their maximum at ca. 8900 to 8600 BP (Fedje 1993). With the lowering of the level of the estuary the

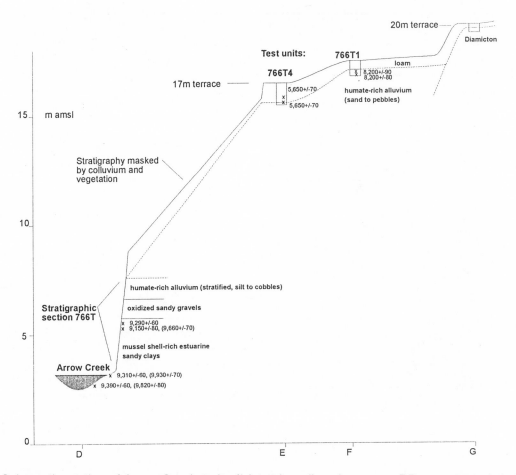

Figure 8. Schematic section of Arrow Creek 1 site (*dates in radiocarbon years BP, uncorrected shell dates in parentheses).

creek would cut into the developed fan and alluvial deposition on the 17 m terrace would decline abruptly.

INTERTIDAL LITHIC SITES

In addition to carrying out the Arrow Creek assessments, the 1993 GHAP located some 120 archaeological sites in the Lyell Island area (Mackie and Wilson 1994). Of these, twenty-three are classed as intertidal lithic sites (Table 2). These range from those with one or two isolated finds to sites encompassing over a hectare. Here we focus on intertidal sites which appear to have considerable potential in the interpretation of the Early Period in southern Haida Gwaii. These sites contain large stone tool assemblages, some of which are in association with dateable sediments. Other sites containing either diagnostic artifacts in a non-dateable context or non-diagnostic artifacts in a dateable context will be briefly noted.

The intertidal lithic sites located during 1993 consistently occupy the full range of the modern in-

tertidal zone. Dating of Holocene marine transgression and regression allows significant narrowing of the times during which this zone was accessible for human activity.

Chronology of sea level change is known in fair detail for this area (Figure 2). From this we can project that between 9000 and 2000 BP the area comprising the modern lower intertidal was subtidal and unavailable for human occupation and that between 8900 and 3000 BP the entire modern intertidal zone was subtidal. Several of the intertidal lithic sites described here extend to the lowest reaches of the modern intertidal zone. Today these are only exposed briefly a few times per year. A few centuries ago these lowest reaches were subtidal throughout the year.

Richardson Island Site (1127T)

The Richardson Island site is located on the west side of Richardson Island in Darwin Sound (Figure 1). The known area of the site is approximately 1

141

Table 2. Details of lithic scatter sites, 1993 Gwaii Haanas archaeology project.

SITE #	SIZE (m)	AREA (m^{2})	EST. # LITHICS	DIAGNOSTIC LITHICS	ELEVATION (m AMSL)	INTACT DEPOSIT
785T	1x1	1	1	no	-0.4	no
790T	55x40	2200	+10	no	-3.0 to +1.5	maybe
798T	1x1	1	1?	no	+1.0	no
805T	1x1+	1	1	no	ca +5.0	maybe
1127T	600x30	18000	+500	microblade cores, bifaces, others	-1.0 to +1.5	yes
1128T	320x200	64000	+500	bifaces, microblades/ cores, others	-3.2 to +1.5	yes
1129T	195x40	7800	+350	bifaces, cores, others	-1.0 to +2.3	maybe
1130T	150x25	3750	+100	micro-blade cores, other cores	-1.6 to +1.6	no
1131T	5x5	25	+100	no	+18.5 to 20.0	yes
1132T	55x15	825	+7	biface	-0.8 to 0.0	no
1133T	325x65	21125	+12	cores	-1.0 to +3.0	yes
1139T	1x1	1	1	no	ca +1.0	no
1145T	160x10	1600	+3	no	+0.5	no
1149T	1x1	1	1	no	ca 0.0	no
1150T	5x5	25	+3	core	ca 0.0	no
1152T	1x1	1	1	no	ca +2.0	no
1153T	30x20	600	+10	no	-1.5 to 0.0	no
1154T	5x5	25	2	no	+1.0	no
1162T	28x15	420	+12	cores	0.0 to +2.5	maybe
1164T	35x23	805	+2	cores	+0.6 to +3.1	no
1166T	1x1	1	1	no	ca 0.0	maybe
1167T	10x5	50	+4	no	ca +1.0	no
1168T	16x6	96	+7	no	+2.0 to +2.5 (fix in other files)	no
1199T	1x1	1	1	core	ca -1.0	no
1201T	120x10	1200	+3	no	-1.0	no
1209T	40x9	360	+17	no	+1.0	maybe
1223T	1x1	1	1?	no	?	no
Total		**122915**	**+1652**	**10 yes**		**4 yes, 6 maybe**

hectare, which includes the entire intertidal zone (up to 30 m wide) along a 330 m section of gravel and cobble shore. The site is exposed to significant wave action. In this context it is fortunate that any cultural record is extant. Preservation may, in part, be a result of protection of the shore zone from the full effect of wave action by kelp forests immediately offshore up until the time of the fur trade and its environmental consequences (Duggins et al. 1989, Estes et al. 1978). At present several hundred artifacts are exposed on the beach (based on observations at a 2.1 m tide). During the 1993 investigations diagnostic artifacts and a few examples of the variety of artifact types and materials present were systematically surface collected (Figure 9).

Geological Context and Chronology

The Richardson Island site extends from ca. 2.0 m a.m.s.l. to at least 1.0 m b.m.s.l. The landform on which the site sits exhibits a sharp break-in-slope about 1.0 m below low tide but otherwise exhibits gentle sloping to approximately 7.0 m a.m.s.l. at which point there is an abrupt rise to a 17 m a.m.s.l. terrace which likely represents the limit of the Holocene marine transgression. Surficial sediments at this site appear to be lag deposits produced as a result of wave and current erosion during marine transgression and regression. This interpretation is based on the absence of fines (no sediment finer than granules) and the waterworn nature of lithic artifacts. Near the southern margin of the site, however, there is a small area with sediment containing silty sand, abundant marine microfauna, macrofossils (shell and wood), and unworn lithic artifacts. The shell includes articulated butter clams in growth position. This and the C-14 dates indicate that the sediment has not been disturbed since the early Holocene marine transgression.

Two wood and two shell samples were collected from a shallow test excavated into intact sediment from ca. 1.0 m a.m.s.l. The C-14 samples are shell-wood pairs and each pair was recovered *in situ* and in close association (shell within 2 cm of its wood pair). The pairs were collected in order to provide a minimum age for the site and to provide additional data points for ocean C-14 reservoir research being undertaken by John Southon at Lawrence Livermore National Laboratory at Livermore, California.

The shell and wood dates, therefore, indicate that transgression of this site occurred earlier than 8700 BP (these shellfish would have colonized the sediments after the transgression had surpassed this elevation). The wood samples have a mean age of 8700 BP. This is a minimum age for the archaeological deposit in association as the wood was likely incorporated into the sediment at the same time or shortly before the shellfish moved in. This minimum age is consistent with an age estimate of 9400 to 9100 BP for a shoreline of this elevation using the local sea level curve (Fedje 1993, Figure 2) and from the results of the Arrow Creek 2 site investigations.

Figure 9. Richardson Island site artifacts.

The age range at Richardson Island is further supported by age limits for the diagnostic microblade cores common at this site. On the northern Northwest Coast microblade cores are not known to date more recently than ca. 5000 BP (Carlson 1990b, Davis 1990, Fladmark et al. 1990).

Lithic Artifacts

The bifaces (n=3) were manufactured from basalt and include a large relatively complete specimen, a base and a mid-section (Figure 10a, b). All exhibit large broad flake scars indicative of manufacture using antler or hardwood (e.g., yew) billets.

All collected formed tools (n=7) are basalt. These include a backed knife, two endscrapers, and four unifacially retouched billet flakes.

Utilized Flakes and Debitage

No unformed tools (n>500) or debitage were collected in 1993 although these classes of artifacts were moderately abundant in surface exposures.

All microblade cores (n=18) appear to be variations on a single type (Table 3). They are conical to cylindrical in form with simple platforms, unidirectional blade removal, and no evidence of platform rejuvenation (Figure 11a-r). The microblade cores appear to have been produced from split pebble nuclei with initial preparation by percussion flaking the circumference of the core preform. More detailed microblade core data are presented by Magne (this volume).

Percussion microcores (n=11) were at least as common as microblade cores at this site but only a small sample was collected in 1993. These artifacts have been made from split pebbles by percussion removal of blade-like flakes from the circumference of the simple platform (Figure 11u-w). Some of these may have been preforms for microblade core production. The microblade cores which had blades removed from only part of their circumference (n=11) exhibited identical characteristics on the unfluted surfaces.

One basalt macroblade core (n=1) was collected. This was prepared by removing a spall from the end of an elongate pebble.

Echo Bay Site (1128T)

This site is located on the east coast of Moresby Island about 2 km southwest of the Richardson Island site (Figure 1). The site occupies the width of the intertidal zone (ca. 50 m) in a series of small bays just north of Echo Harbour. Total site area is about 6.4 hectares but most artifacts occur in a ca. 500 m² area. Artifact concentration at this smaller area is

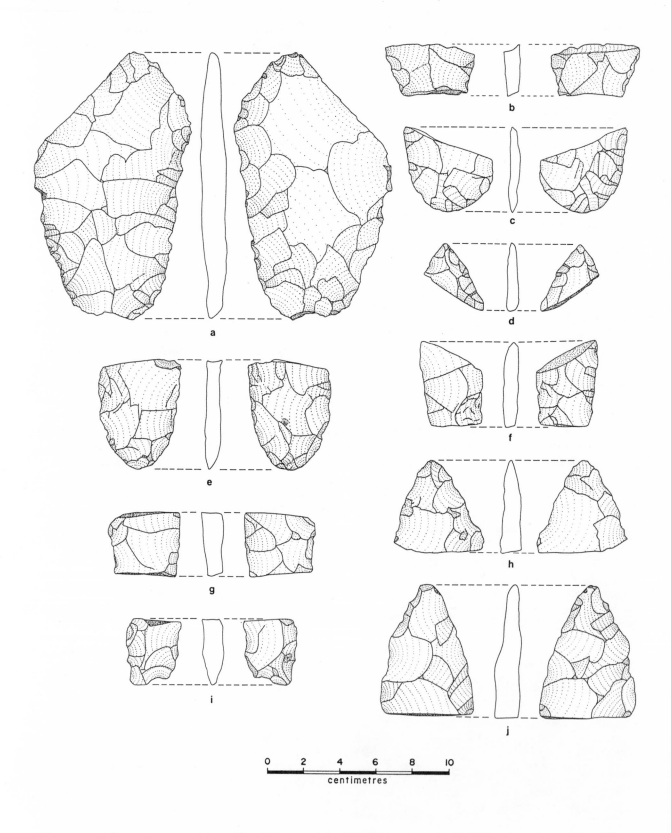

Figure 10. Bifaces recovered from Gwaii Haanas intertidal lithic sites: (a, b) Richardson Island (1127T); (c, d) Echo Bay (1128T); (e-i) Hoya Passage (1129T); (j) Shuttle Passage (1132T).

high, with a minimum of 500 pieces observed during the 1.0 m tide visit.

Geological Context and Chronology

This site is in a very protected position. The 500 m² area occupies gently sloping terrain which extends from ca. 1.5 m a.m.s.l. to below 3.2 m b.m.s.l. This area is backed by steep to vertical bedrock ridges which extend from the upper intertidal to about 8 m a.m.s.l. This context suggests that at least the upper part of the known site area must have been supertidal during occupation. Consequently, sea level must have been at least 2.5 m below that of today at that time.

For the most part, the site appears not to have been significantly affected by wave or current action during marine transgression and regression. This interpretation is based on the presence of organic-rich (marine microfauna, shell, and wood) silty to sandy sediments containing lithic artifacts (including microdebitage) in pristine condition in both surface and subsurface context.

Microfauna are dominated by subtidal marine to strong brackish formanifera (Fedje et al., forthcoming). The shell includes turban snails, periwinkles, bittium, littleneck clam, butter clam, bent-nose clam, cockle, and jingle shells. A shell-wood pair recovered *in situ* from 18 cm below surface (from a shallow test excavated into intact sediment at 1.0 m a.m.s.l.) produced a mean age of 8750 BP (Table 1). The samples were in close association (shell within 2 cm of its wood pair) and were in direct association with a basalt flake. The articulated shellfish and associated C-14 dates indicate that sediments at this part of the site have not been disturbed since the early Holocene marine transgression.

Following the arguments presented for the Richardson Island site and employing the minimum radiocarbon dates and the age limits for the sea level position indicated by the Echo Bay site's geomorphologic setting it follows that the site was occupied at ca. 9400 BP.

Lithic Artifacts

There are more than 500 lithic artifacts exposed to gentle wave action on the beach. No microblade cores were observed in 1993, however, several bifaces and cobble tools were present. During the 1993 investigations a small number of artifacts were collected, including the four diagnostic specimens described below.

The bifaces (n=4) are of basalt and include the basal half of a thin (5 mm), finely worked foliate biface, the tip of a thin (6 mm), finely worked unclas-

sified biface (Figure 10c, d), and two broken biface preforms.

Hoya Passage Site (1129T)

The Hoya Passage site is situated on Moresby Island, west of Shuttle Island (Figure 1). The site was briefly visited in 1993 and dateable material was not recovered. The site extends over most of the intertidal zone of a small bay (ca. 7800 m²), although most cultural material was observed in a few concentrations with a minimum area of 4900 m². Surface collections included a small sample of bifaces from the lower intertidal zone. The number of artifacts observed on the beach at a 3.0 m tide is estimated to be about 350.

Geological Context and Chronology

The artifact-bearing sediments at this site appear to be a lag deposit resulting from fluvial and wave and current erosion during the marine transgression and regression; however, clustering and the pristine nature of most of the artifacts suggests little horizontal movement of the coarse fraction. No intact organic deposits were observed in the stream and beach exposures but no tests were conducted and, as such, context is uncertain. The site extends from ca. 2.0 m a.m.s.l. to at least 1.0 m b.m.s.l. As with the Echo Bay site, the main concentration of lithic material is backed by steep bedrock which extends from the upper intertidal to at least 5 m a.m.s.l.

The site could not be radiocarbon dated but must date to ca. 9400 BP based on the bedrock slope constraints for a supertidal occupation area and the local sea level record (Fedje 1993, Fedje et al., forthcoming).

Lithic Artifacts

As with Echo Bay, there are abundant artifacts on the beach but no microblade cores were observed. The present sample is very small and includes the eight specimens described below.

The bifaces (n=6) include one foliate base, two mid-sections, one tip and one unclassified fragment, all of basalt, and one unclassified chert biface fragment (Figure 10e-i).

Formed tools (n=2) include a large sidescraper and a unifacially retouched macroblade.

Only a few unformed tools or debitage (n>300) were collected in 1993 although these classes of artifacts were moderately abundant in surface exposures.

Lyell Bay Site (1130T)

This site is located on southwestern Lyell Island

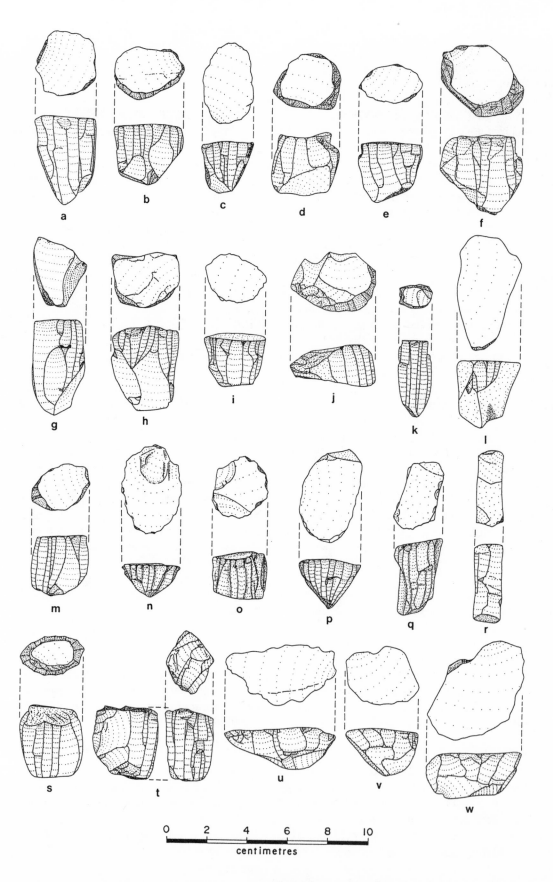

Figure 11. Microblade cores (a-t) and percussion microcores (u-w) from Gwaii Haanas intertidal lithic sites: (a-r, u-w) Richardson Island (1127T); (s, t) Lyell Bay (1130T).

146

(Figure 1). It was only briefly visited and no dateable material was recovered in association with the artifacts. The site extends across the observed tidal zone (visited at a 2.0 m tide) and includes an area of about 3500 m². Surface collections were limited to two microblade cores (Table 3) and a large macroblade core, although a variety of other artifact types are present in surface exposures along the beach. All the observed lithics were waterworn and no surviving *in situ* deposits could be located.

Geological Context and Chronology

This site is on a moderately protected beach with exposure to waves and backs onto gently sloping terrain. No subsurface tests were conducted and no lithic bearing sediments were observed. Artifacts were uniformly waterworn, which may suggest they are no longer eroding out of the beach surface. No dateable material was obtained, but the recovery of microblade cores and the sea level history constraints (Fedje 1993, Fedje et al., forthcoming) on the sites intertidal location suggests a ca. 9400 to 9100 BP age.

Lithic Artifacts

Lithic artifacts were moderately abundant at this site (ca. 100 observed at a 2.0 m tide) but only three specimens were collected.

Two basalt microblade cores were collected (Figure 11s, t). One was found in the upper intertidal at 0.8 m a.m.s.l. and one at 1.0 m b.m.s.l. The two are technologically distinct. The higher elevation artifact is a conical microblade core comparable to those recovered at the Richardson Island site (Table 3). The lower elevation core is wedge-shaped and frontally fluted. The latter core was prepared by truncating a biface and both the platform and base were prepared by pressure flaking.

One large basalt core was collected from the site. The core is unusual. It appears to have been made by splitting a cobble, removing blades and blade-like flakes from its circumference, and then reshaping the platform surface by multi-directional billet flaking. Finally, a large flake was driven off the platform using a billet. This platform preparation and flake removal sequence appears to have occurred at least twice as the macroblade scars are truncated and part of an earlier large billet flake scar is retained on one side of the core.

Other Sites

Diagnostic artifacts were observed at six other intertidal lithic sites in the 1993 study area (Table 2). One is a large biface fragment (Figure 10j) from the

Shuttle Passage site (1132T). All these sites had conical cores with simple platforms comparable to those interpreted as percussion microcores or microblade core preforms at the Richardson Island site.

A raised beach site was found at ca. 15 m a.m.s.l. at Dodge Point (1131T) on the east coast of Lyell Island. This site contained abundant cobble spalls and cobble choppers and was dated to 5500 BP.

DISCUSSION

Prior to the GHAP investigations the age of Gwaii Haanas intertidal lithic sites was uncertain. Hobler (1978) hypothesized that several likely dated to the time of the early Holocene marine transgression while Acheson (1991, personal communication 1992) questioned the case for pre-ca. 2000 BP occupation in southern Moresby Island and suggested most of the intertidal sites might be Late Period resource processing sites. A number of Gwaii Haanas archaeological sites, in both intertidal and raised marine settings, can now be unequivocally assigned to the Early Period. Preliminary investigations at these sites enables us to make a strong argument for occupation of Haida Gwaii by 9400 BP, a time when sea level was rising rapidly toward the Holocene maximum. Our understanding of lithic technology for the Early Period record in Gwaii Haanas is incomplete as much is based on field observations rather than formal analyses; tantalizing evidence for a significant change in technology exists for just prior to ca. 9000 BP, as has been observed elsewhere on the coast (Carlson, Chapter 9).

The conical microblade cores from the Richardson Island and Lyell Bay sites compare closely to those characteristic of the Anangula complex which first appears in southern Alaska around 9000 BP (Aigner 1978; see also Magne, this volume). This complex is characterized by prismatic to conical microblade cores and an absence of bifacial tools. It is suggested to originate in "the late Paleolithic/Mesolithic to Neolithic industries of northeastern Asia" (Ackerman 1992:23). Similar microblade technology is dated to ca. 8500 BP at Namu on the Central Coast, 8200 BP at Chuck Lake in southeast Alaska, and 7400 BP at Lawn Hill in northern Haida Gwaii (Carlson, Chapter 9, Ackerman et al. 1985; Fladmark 1986a). Chuck Lake and Lawn Hill do not exhibit the full range of technology seen at the Anangula type site in that they lack macroblades/cores. Ackerman (1992:22) suggests these sites may be a later manifestation of the Anangula complex. However, samples are small and may not exhibit the full range of lithic technology for the respective areas.

Table 3. Richardson Island and Lyell Bay site microblade cores.

Specimen number	Core type	Dimensions (mm)			No. of scars	blade width	Max. scar length	blade fig#
		Length	Width	Height				
1127TA1:								
1	p/c/s	28	31	43	15	3-8	43	11a
2	p/c/s	23	35	29	12	3-5	23	11b
3	p/c/s	39	25	23	20	3-7	23	11c
17	p/c/s	23	23	29	13	4-8	23	11d
20	p/c/s	31	19	29	16	2-8	28	11e
21	p/c/s	34	26	37	9	2-7	31	11f
22	p/c/s	34	21	46	6	3-6	43	11g
23	p/c/s	26	33	38	8	4-7	33	11h
25	p/c/s	22	30	24	16	3-8	24	11i
26	f/c/s	37	31	21	8	3-7	20	11j
27	p/c/s	14	10	37	13	3-6	35	11k
28	p/c/s	53	31	30	4	3-4	14	11l
29	p/c/s	27	20	30	17	2-9	28	11m
34	f/c/s	42	29	16	12	3-5	17	11n
35	p/c/	9	29	22	16	3-7	21	11o
37	p/c/s	40	26	22	12	3-6	19	11p
39	p/c/s	36	19	32	9	3-6	31	11q
40	p/c/s	37	14	28	3	3-7	21	11r
1130TA1:								
1	p/r/fa	27	23	35	9	3-10	34	11s
3	p/c/s	12	20	35	14	3-9	35	11t

Core type (attributes):
    p: split pebble nuclei   f: flake nuclei
    c: conical to cylindrical   r: rotated, subprismatic
    s: simple platform   fa: faceted platform

The wedge-shaped microblade core from Lyell Bay compares closely to those characteristic of Denali technology which was present in central and southern Alaska from ca. 10,700 until 9000 BP (Ackerman 1992). Denali technology compares closely to that of the Diuktai complex of northeast Asia which dates from 35,000 to 10,500 BP. The Denali complex is characterized by frontally fluted wedge-shaped microblade cores and by biface and blade-like flake technology (West 1967). With only one wedge-shaped specimen this connection is most tenuous. It may simply be that both core preparation techniques were known and used dependent upon need or proficiency.

At first blush, the Richardson Island site association of microblade cores and bifaces would appear to belie the case for a biface-free Early Coast Microblade Tradition (Fladmark 1990, Fladmark et al. 1990). However, except for the Echo Bay and Hoya Passage sites which date to ca. 9400 BP, the Gwaii Haanas early Holocene lithic sites can only be dated to a general 9400 to 9000 BP period. As such, the association of bifaces, blade cores, and the two microblade core types is uncertain. Ackerman's re-

search would suggest this is a time of technological transition. It may be that the Richardson Island and Lyell Bay sites are multicomponent sites spanning this key time. Their geological setting provides only a 9400 to 9000 BP temporal constraint for deposition of cultural material (the modern beach was intertidal to supertidal during this time range). In this vein it is noteworthy that the very rich Echo Bay and Hoya Passage sites are geologically constrained such that occupation must date to ca. 9400 BP. During the preliminary investigations of 1993 these sites produced several bifaces but no microblade cores.[1] Recovery of a wedge-shaped microblade core from Lyell Bay is intriguing as it was from the lower intertidal and could date to the earliest part of the record, however, it may fall in the range of variation for the later period as well (Magne, this volume).

This record appears to compare well to that seen at Namu (but see endnote 1) where the early deposits contain a biface and cobble tool tradition, and where microblade core technology does not appear until after 9000 BP (Carlson, Chapter 9). The significance of the differences suggested between the tentative early biface tradition and the Moresby

Tradition as defined by Fladmark (1989) cannot be determined with our present very limited data.

As with the early coastal complexes in the Bering Sea and Southeast Alaska, Haida Gwaii economies at this time were necessarily maritime oriented. The position of sites on the shore of small islands in an archipelago tens of kilometres from the BC mainland, even during the late Wisconsian to earliest Holocene period of depressed sea levels, necessitated the use of watercraft to access any variety of resources. By 10,000 BP the lands were densely forested. Gwaii Haanas terrestrial fauna was insular and probably (as today) exhibited little diversity. Mammals native to this area, until recently, were limited to bears, martin, ermine, otters, mice, and, possibly, small numbers of caribou in the subalpine. At the same time, marine and intertidal fauna were present and likely abundant, even during the period of rapid marine transgression (Fedje 1993, Fedje et al., forthcoming). The Richardson Island site, for example, is on a small island with very limited intertidal resources and no anadromous or significant terrestrial resources. Inhabitants would have had to cross more than a kilometre of open water to reach Moresby Island and its more abundant resources.

The archaeological record from the Gwaii Haanas intertidal sites and from the Arrow Creek 2 site extends to at least 9400 BP. In concert with the results of marine geological research, these data suggest the possibility of a much longer record, now drowned, on earlier shorelines (Fedje et al., forthcoming, Josenhans et al., forthcoming). The palynological and geological records suggest much of the continental shelf along the Northwest Coast, including the environs of Haida Gwaii, was suitable for human occupation by ca. 14,000 BP (Barrie et al. 1994, Fedje 1993, Mobley 1988, Warner et al. 1982, 1984). Fladmark's hypothesis for a late Wisconsian movement of early peoples between Beringia and southern North America via a coastal route gains further credence with these data (Fladmark 1979a, 1983, Easton 1992).

Rejection of the coastal migration model based on a lack of evidence for pre-11,000 BP occupation along the Pacific Coast south of the Wisconsian ice-sheets (Workman, quoted in Busch 1994) is a *non sequitur*. The 18,000 to 11,000 BP shorelines upon which these people would have lived are currently under more than 50 m of ocean waters (Fairbanks 1989, Garrison 1992, Dunbar et al. 1992) and have received little archaeological attention.

There is strong evidence to suggest coalescence of the Laurentide and Cordilleran ice masses between 21,000 and 12,000 BP (Burns 1993, Duk-Rodkin and Jackson 1993, Rains et al. 1990, White et al. 1985, Young 1993). The west coast would have provided a viable route for early humans to move between Beringia and southern North America at a time when the Ice-free Corridor was not yet passable. This is not to say, however, that people did not move into southern North America prior to the Wisconsian maximum via either or both routes or, that the coastal margin was impassible even during the late Wisconsian maximum.

It should be kept in mind that Haida oral history maintains they originated in this area and that both archaeology and paleoecology fit well to this history. Examples include correspondence between sea level change and paleoecology. Tradition tells of islands rising out of the sea, the flood at Cape Ball, and people walking across what is now open ocean. Oral descriptions also speak of a time when this country was all grass and when the first tree arrives (Swanton 1905). Recent palynological research has shown that the then much larger area of Haida Gwaii was covered by herbs, grasses, and, later, shrubs from at least 14,000 BP to ca. 12,000 BP when the first conifers moved in (Fedje 1993, Mathewes 1989).

Results of the 1993 survey demonstrate the need for a strong focus on the intertidal zone and on raised beaches. The early 1980s systematic survey only occasionally examined the lower intertidal zone and did not survey to 15 m elevation raised beaches (Acheson, personal communication 1993). Similarly, the early GHAP surveys only examined "higher potential" beaches with less than 20 per cent surveyed to below half-tide (Zacharias and Wanagun 1992, Eldridge et al. 1993).

Finally, integration of paleoecological and geological evidence with our, albeit limited, knowledge of Early Period human adaptation should allow more effective survey and interpretation here and elsewhere on the Northwest Coast. We now know where to look for Early Period archaeological remains in Gwaii Haanas and should be able to conduct much more cost-effective survey for such sites. Preservation of sites such as these, which have been subject to marine transgression and regression, offer considerable hope for eventual discovery of the now submerged much older sites in the Hecate Strait area.

D.W. Fedje, A.P. Mackie, J.B. McSporran, and B. Wilson

Acknowledgments

This work was supported by Parks Canada and the Council of Haida Nations. The 1993 field crew included the authors, Allen Brooks, Tanya Collinson, Edana Fedje, John Kelly, Andrew Mason, Fred Seiber, Ian Sumpter, and Jordan Yeltatzie. We worked co-operatively with Heiner Josenhans of the Geological Survey of Canada in the Matheson Inlet coring operation. Special thanks go out to John Southon and the CAMS group at Lawrence Livermore National Laboratory, California with whom we are co-operating in C-14 reservoir research. Rick Lalonde prepared the artifact drawings. The authors: D.W. Fedje and J.B. McSporran, Parks Canada, Calgary T2P 3H8; A.P. Mackie, Millennia Research, Victoria V8L 3X9; B.Wilson, Council of Haida Nations, Skidegate VOT 1S1.

Note

1 In May 1994 the Gwaii Haanas Archaeology crew conducted systematic surface collection and preliminary excavations for purposes of detailed site assessment of the Echo Bay site. In excess of 1800 lithic items have been recovered, including a large number of bifaces, macroblades, a wedge-shaped microblade core, microblades, cobble tools, as well as a variety of other tools, debitage, and a small amount of bone. Analysis was not complete at the time of writing

14 COMPARATIVE ANALYSIS OF MICROBLADE CORES FROM HAIDA GWAII

Martin P.R. Magne

Recent research in South Moresby National Park Reserve/Gwaii Haanas (see Fedje et al., this volume) has greatly supplemented our knowledge of the archaeology of the Queen Charlotte Islands (Haida Gwaii). Three years of intensive survey have succeeded in recording nearly 200 additional Aboriginal sites, including Haida villages, middens, intertidal lithic sites, and others. One of the prominent areas of focus has been the early Holocene occupations of the Gwaii Haanas archipelago, where paleoenvironmental reconstructions are strongly linked to relative sea level locations of archaeological sites. Intertidal lithic sites, whose existence was once debatable, can now at times be clearly related to relative sea levels over the past 10,000 years. Two intertidal lithic sites with microcores discussed here (Richardson Island and Lyell Bay, Figure 1) strengthen existing concepts concerning early settlement of Haida Gwaii, in particular those complexes related to the Northwest Microblade Tradition.

Fladmark's research at the Lawn Point and Kasta sites (Fladmark 1986a), as well as at Skidegate Landing and other locations discussed below, was pivotal in reinforcing his theory concerning the potential for a coastal route for the peopling of the Americas following or during the later parts of the Pleistocene. While these particular sites do not date to much before 8000 BP, (the microblade component at Lawn Point dates to 7000 to 7500 BP, and there is an earlier, undated, non-microblade component; Kasta dates to 5500 to 6000 BP) and they are on dry land today, they do prove human presence on Haida Gwaii at a time when sea levels were actively rising, then stabilizing. The intertidal sites demonstrate occupations below current sea levels and therefore extend our knowledge at least partly into

an area many including myself (cf., Ives et al. 1989) have said may be too difficult to examine productively – the offshore shelf.

Microblade technology, being so widespread and at the same time so distinctive, has been examined in some detail for some time, and has seen several synthetic discussions, quantitative and qualitative analyses, and even assignments to ethnic affiliations. Clark (1981) provides the most complete overview of the Northwest Microblade Tradition. It includes such sites as Denali, Campus, Onion Portage, Anangula, and other sites from Alaska. I and perhaps others (e.g., Greaves 1991) would extend it to southern interior British Columbia (Lehman, Hat Creek, Highland Valley). LeBlanc and Ives' (1986) Bezya site in northeastern Alberta is clearly within the tradition as well (see also Pyszczyk 1991 and Stevenson 1981 for other microcores in northern Alberta). Ackerman et al. (1985) define a northern Northwest Coast Microblade Tradition, within which they include the Lawn Point and Kasta sites of Fladmark's Moresby Tradition. I use Clark's general scheme here, also placing the Lawn Point and Kasta sites within the Northwest Microblade Tradition (NWMT), which is a fairly long-term (11,000 to perhaps 4,500 or later BP) tradition over the northwest from Alberta to Alaska and the northern west coast. The distinctiveness of microblade/core subtraditions or complexes within the general tradition focuses on core manufacturing techniques, principally treatment of the core platform. The cores of the NWMT are relatively small, in relation to some other microcore complexes of the Pacific Rim (although see Fladmark 1985 and Smith 1974 regarding the large cores from the Mount Edziza area). Some authors have indicated that sizes appear to

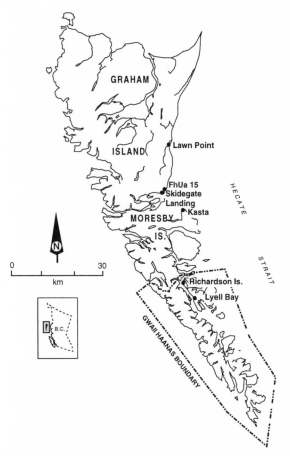

Figure 1. Haida Gwaii showing microcore sites discussed in text.

ticular, both studies indicated trends across major complexes within each tradition in terms of major size attributes as well as platform preparation sequences.

The available sample of materials from sites in Haida Gwaii included fifteen cores found in the intertidal zone on the west side of Richardson Island, and two from Lyell Bay (see Fedje et al., this volume for core illustrations). The Lawn Point sample consists of ten cores, Kasta has eighteen, Skidegate Landing eight, and there is one additional core from FhUa 15. These cores were measured and examined by myself at Simon Fraser University, courtesy of Knut Fladmark. The total sample of fifty-four Haida Gwaii cores was analyzed first-hand. These data, in addition to those available from Morlan's (1970) analyses, as well as more recent reports concerning the Campus (Mobley 1991) and Chuck Lake sites (Ackerman et al. 1985), represent a sizable sample of microcores within which major temporal and geographic trends should be detectable. I should note that other microcores are known from Haida Gwaii but were not available for study (see, for example, Ham 1990).

ANALYSES

The purpose of the analyses is to seek patterns in metric variation of microcores to allow preliminary placement of the Gwaii Haanas cores within the historical patterns demonstrated by Fladmark and others. Relying on identification of strong patterns in assemblages of known affiliation, some with definite age determinations, the Gwaii Haanas cores are then compared directly against these patterns. Multivariate analytic techniques allow the entire sample, and subsets of it, to be analyzed simultaneously.

The analyses reported here are based primarily on a limited set of variables: core platform length and width, core height and chord, maximum length of blade scars, number of blade scars, core angle, and manufacturing sequence (P1, F1, Pd; see Figure 2). All of these were measured on all cores from Haida Gwaii, however, published measures for other NWMT cores did not always include these. Most of the final results rely on platform length, platform width, or chord length, and core height or blade length.

In addition to direct measures from those cores, I used measures published by Morlan (1970) for the several sites he assigns to Anangula, Brooks Range 1 and 2; Healy, Denali, southwest Yukon, and Lehman complexes; the Hat Creek cores I examined in 1979; the Chuck Lake, Alaska, cores published by

vary in some predictable ways and, along with other morphological trends, may be directly related to the particular lithic raw materials available.

Morlan (1970) analyzed a large number of microblade cores from the NWMT as well as from the Arctic Small Tool Tradition (ASTT), concluding that major distinctions are observable in the manufacturing sequence of the core platform and core faces, these being known as P1 and F1 sequences respectively. Differences attributable to the morphology of the raw material are in terms of the Pd sequence. Morlan's paper was seminal in its geographic coverage and assemblages examined, but also in its use of a suite of statistical tests of independence across the data set. In an unpublished paper (Magne 1979) I employed Morlan's data in comparison to microcores and microblades from Upper Hat Creek Valley, BC (Pokotylo 1978, Ludowdoicz 1983, Greaves 1991). In addition to revealing interesting patterns with respect to the relationship of the Hat Creek assemblage, multivariate analyses supplemented Morlan's interpretations of patterns within his entire sample of NWMT and ASTT assemblages. In par-

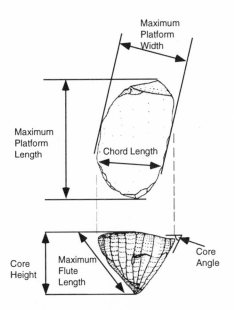

Figure 2. Microcore variables. Core weight and number of blade scars were also recorded.

Ackerman et al. (1985); and the Campus cores from Mobley's (1991) publication. When not reported, chord length was obtained from platform width, and core height was obtained from maximum blade length, directly, with no conversion indices. The Haida Gwaii analyses are based mainly on metrics for individual cores, while the analyses comparing these to the other NWMT assemblages are based on mean measures (see Morlan 1970 for his use of mean assemblage measures). Given known dates for the Lawn Point, Kasta, and Chuck Lake assemblages, an estimated 9000 BP sea level based age for Richardson Island and Lyell Bay, and "known" complex associations from published works, test hypotheses can be presented for the Gwaii Haanas assemblages and the Haida Gwaii assemblages generally:

(1) Richardson Island and Lawn Point cores will be similar to each other;

(2) Kasta and Skidegate Landing cores will be more similar to each other than to Richardson or Lawn Point;

(3) Lyell Bay cores will tend to associate more strongly with Richardson but being a small sample may not show clear association;

(4) The early Haida Gwaii cores will closely resemble those from Chuck Lake; and

(5) The Haida Gwaii cores generally will be distinct within the NWMT complexes.

HAIDA GWAII ANALYSES

In general appearance, the cores from Richardson Island and Lyell Bay are mostly wedge- or boat-shaped and are in most respects immediately similar to those from Lawn Point. The Gwaii Haanas cores show some variety, in that a cylindrical core is present at Richardson Island and one Lyell Bay core has a prepared platform; both wide and thin wedge-shaped and "tongue-shaped" cores are present. The cores from Lawn Point, Kasta, and Skidegate Landing are also similarly varied. Some of these are quite tabular in overall shape. Note that none of the Richardson Island or Lyell Bay cores exhibits platform rejuvenation, a feature almost completely lacking in the other Moresby Tradition assemblages as well. These are clearly not "Campus" cores, where platform rejuvenation is very common. Figure 3 illustrates the three main core morphologies that were studied during the course of these analyses.

The Kasta and Skidegate cores are cruder in appearance generally, with more battering of bases and platforms (33 per cent of Kasta, 50 per cent of Skidegate), although interestingly, 60 per cent of Richardson, but only 20 per cent of Lawn Point cores exhibit battering (Table 1). Almost half of the Richardson cores have battered bases, but only two of ten Lawn Point cores, four of the eighteen from Kasta, and four of eight from Skidegate Landing. Basal damage or battering is an interesting occurrence that has not been systematically studied to date. It originates from methods used to place some cores while detaching blades, perhaps seating them on an anvil, or from using the core for some other purpose, perhaps as a wedge. The amount of damage observed is not consistent, and often seems like more than what should result from removing blades. However, some platforms are heavily damaged as well (Table 1). Through time in the Moresby Tradition, Fladmark noted a distinct trend in microblade production techniques: from early, prepared cores to later, bipolar cores. There may be a direct relationship between the damage seen on certain cores and bipolar means of blade detachment.

The Richardson Island and Lawn Point cores are the large ones in the group (Figure 4), with Lyell having a small and a mid-size core, in terms of platform length and width. This is apparent in univariate (Figure 4) and bivariate (Figure 5) graphs. Thus the "early" Haida Gwaii cores are in the large range, with Skidegate Landing showing long flute length in relation to platform length or chord. The Kasta cores are also nearly equal in this ratio. This is attributable to the "tabular" nature of several of these

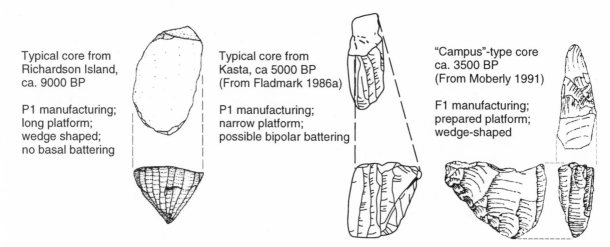

Typical core from Richardson Island, ca. 9000 BP

P1 manufacturing; long platform; wedge shaped; no basal battering

Typical core from Kasta, ca 5000 BP (From Fladmark 1986a)

P1 manufacturing; narrow platform; possible bipolar battering

"Campus"-type core ca. 3500 BP (From Moberly 1991)

F1 manufacturing; prepared platform; wedge-shaped

Figure 3. Examples of "Richardson" and "Kasta" – cluster cores and "Campus" type core, illustrating major differences between each.

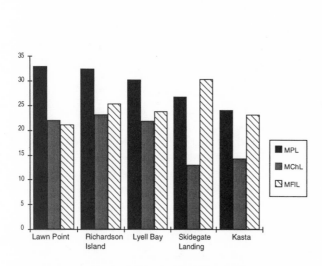

Figure 4. Haida Gwaii microcore complexes mean platform length, mean chord length, and mean flute length (millimetres). Note platform length of Lawn Point, Richardson Island, and Lyell Bay cores and short chord length of Skidegate Landing and Kasta cores. Note in addition that a ratio of flute length to chord length would be much greater in the Skidegate landing and Kasta samples.

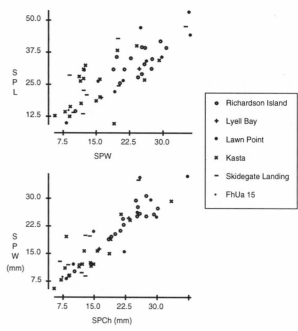

Figure 5. Scatterplots of platform length (SPL), platform width (SPW), and platform chord (SPCH) of Haida Gwaii microcores. As in previous figure, note relative length of Lawn Point and Richardson Island cores, although a small number of other cores are relatively large as well. The Richardson Island and Lawn Point assemblages also contain a few small cores. In the lower graph, an expected strong relationship is shown between platform width and platform chord; however, groupings are evident of Richardson Island and Lawn Point cores in opposition to Kasta and Skidegate Landing cores.

Table 1. Frequency and location of battering on Haida Gwaii microcores.

| Site | Location of Battering | | | | |
	Base	Base& Plat.	Platform	None	Total
FhUa 15	1	0	0	0	1
Kasta	4	0	3	11	18
Lawn Point	2	0	0	8	10
Lyell Bay	1	0	1	0	2
Richardson Is.	7	1	1	6	15
Skidegate	4	0	0	4	8
Total	**19**	**1**	**5**	**29**	**54**

While these patterns only partly support the hypothesis of close association of early and later Gwaii Haanas cores, multidimensional scaling of the same distance matrix (not shown here) when seen in the first three dimensions reveals even stronger patterns, closely linking Lawn Point with Richardson Island, with the more weakly linked Lyell core falling within the "early" distribution. These analyses are not complete at the time this chapter was being prepared.

cores, which I believe reflects either the choice or availability of different raw material sources and possibly easier ways of making microblades. Several of the tabular Kasta cores have battered bases.

Q-mode cluster analysis was applied to the Haida Gwaii cores using Ward's Method on Euclidean distance matrices derived from the unstandardized metric data (Figure 6). This analysis shows clear groupings of Haida Gwaii microcores when seven metric variables are employed (platform length, platform width, platform chord, core height, core angle, blade length, and number of blade scars). Two distinct clusters represent groupings based primarily on Kasta or Richardson Island cores. Skidegate Landing cores are most similar to Kasta cores, and Lawn Point cores only slightly more similar to Richardson cores.

NORTHWEST MICROBLADE TRADITION ANALYSES

Mean assemblages measures are used to compare fifteen "complexes" (note that Morlan's "complexes" already include mean measures obtained from several sites within each "complex"). This limits the number of variables that can be employed, for the sake of comparability. For all cores, only measurements of mean platform length, chord length, and flute length were employed. For the assemblages where chord length was not reported, as noted above, chord length was taken as equal to platform width, and core height as equal to maximum blade length. I also recorded core manufacturing sequence using Morlan's scheme, since his work showed microcore patterning along the lines of reduction sequence, mainly differing in terms of face first or platform first

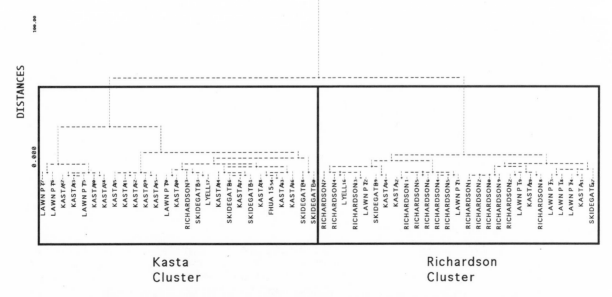

Figure 6. Haida Gwaii microcores seven variable cluster analysis. This analysis clearly forms two major clusters, one dominated by Kasta cores, the other by Richardson Island cores. Most of the Lawn Point cores fall in the Richardson Island cluster while the Skidegate Landing cores mostly occur in the Kasta Cluster. Note the split occurrence of the two Lyell Bay cores.

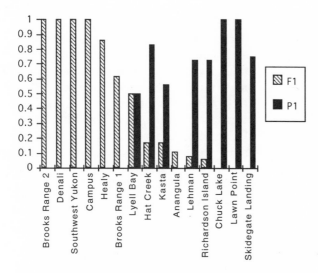

Figure 7. Relative frequency of F1 and P1 manufacturing sequences in Northwest Microblade Tradition complexes. The assemblages have been arranged along the X-axis in decreasing percentage of F1 (Face-first) manufacturing sequence. The Brooks Range 2, Denali, southwest Yukon, and Campus complexes exhibit 100 per cent F1 manufacturing, while the Chuck Lake, Lawn Point, and Skidegate complexes exhibit none. The Gwaii Haanas assemblages exhibit a mix of F1 and P1 manufacturing, although F1 is not frequent. The Lyell Bay assemblage here shows 50-50 F1 to P1 sequences, but the sample size is two cores. Also notable is the apparent pattern that apart from Anangula, the more southern complexes are predominantly P1 sequence.

techniques. Graphs of the proportional frequency of F1 and P1 (Figure 7) show that the Haida Gwaii assemblages are predominantly P1, while the early Denali and later Campus ones are F1. There is a strong trend for the Northwest Coast and southern interior British Colulmbia assemblages to be P1, while the extreme northwest assemblages are predominantly F1. This may point to a subtradition of NWMT technologies, and this may be related to raw materials.

Bivariate graphs (Figure 8) show interesting but not immediately interpretable patterns. A graph of the three metrics shows that Anangula, Brooks Range 1, and Hat Creek assemblages are the largest in most respects. Knowing the context of the Hat Creek assemblage fairly well, I think that the large size of those cores supports a notion that raw material avail-

ability has a great deal to do with core morphology. This is an area with excellent, fine grained basalt available in quantity. The Haida Gwaii assemblages show strong patterning, grouping very strongly as predicted. The Chuck Lake assemblage closely resembles the Lawn Point and Richardson Island ones, and Kasta and Skidegate are also very similar to each other.

The cluster analysis (Figure 9) of the NWMT complexes (using the same method employed above) is not surprising at this stage, since it is based only on three variables. Here it is very clear that the early Denali and Campus assemblages are fairly distinct with Healy Lake and southwest Yukon assemblages grouping overall with the "later" Kasta and Skidegate sites, while assemblages from Richardson, Lawn Point, Lyell Bay, and Chuck Lake group strongly together with Hat Creek. Anangula and Brooks Range 1 form their own group.

However, the preceding analyses are based on mean measures for complexes that Morlan created by grouping sites thought to belong to them. Since site-specific variability may be masked, the Haida Gwaii cores were also compared to the mean values for individual sites in Morlan's sample, using only those sites with three or more cores (Table 2). This

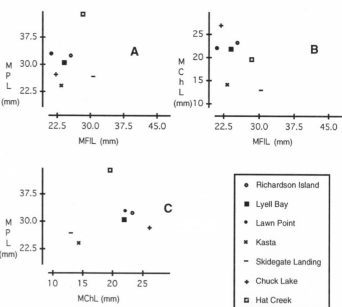

Figure 8. Scatterplots of mean platform length (MPL), mean platform width (MFIL), and mean platform chord (MChL) of Northwest Microblade Tradition microcores. Haida Gwaii and Hat Creek cores labeled for comparison. The Haida Gwaii cores group in all graphs, with Kasta and Skidegate Landing as "outliers." Note in A and B the short flute lengths of the Chuck Lake and Lawn Point assemblages; in C, note the short chord lengths of Kasta and Skidegate cores.

gives a sample of eighteen sites, including those from Haida Gwaii. Indeed, in this cluster analysis (Figure 10) the previous patterns are shown very strongly again: the measures of mean platform, chord, and flute lengths strongly discriminate the various sites within their assignment to various complexes.

Thus it would appear that expectations with respect to the Richardson Island and Lyell Bay cores are met in relation to other Northwest Microblade Tradition complexes, while the distinctiveness of the Haida Gwaii assemblages applies primarily to the early or supposedly early ones. As an aside, the placement of the other southern British Columbia cores, those from Hat Creek and the Lehman site, may have bearing on their relative ages as well. The Hat Creek cores group very closely to the "early" Haida Gwaii and Chuck Lake cores, and share many characteristics, while the Lehman cores occur quite closely grouped with the "later" Haida Gwaii assemblages.

Table 2. Data employed in cluster analysis based on Haida Gwaii and Hat Creek assemblages and individual site assemblages analyzed by Morlan (1970).

Morlan complex	SITE	MPL	MChl	MFl
Anangula	Anangula	45.0	28.4	42.7
Brooks Range 1	Onion Portage	41.1	17.0	53.8
Healy	RaEc 1	17.8	11.8	26.4
Healy	RaEc 2	19.7	9.6	3.9
Denali	Campus-Morlan	23.0	9.0	22.3
Denali	Mt. Hayes 5	26.7	11.0	26.7
Denali	Mt. Hayes 95	21.7	8.9	20.6
Denali	JgVf 2	23.6	9.0	19.7
SW Yukon	JiVs 1	23.9	10.7	21.6
SW Yukon	IeSh 1	20.5	11.1	30.5
Interior BC	Lehman	25.3	17.7	24.9
Interior BC	Hat Creek	44.4	19.6	28.4
NWC Early	Chuck Lake	27.4	26.7	22.1
NWC Early	Lawn Pt.	33.0	22.1	21.1
NWC Late	Kasta	24.1	14.3	23.2
NWC Late	Skidegate	26.8	13.0	30.4
NWC Early	Richardson Is.	32.5	23.2	25.4
NWC Early	Lyell Bay	30.3	21.9	23.9

CONCLUSIONS

Microblade cores recovered from intertidal contexts in Gwaii Haanas have compared to others from the northern Northwest Coast, particularly other as-

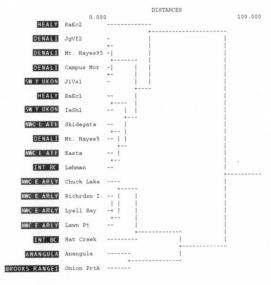

Figure 10. Northwest Microcore assemblages cluster analysis (Euclidean distance, Ward's method): Morlan's NWMT sites, Hat Creek, Haida Gwaii. In this analysis individual site assemblages from Morlan's "complexes" are employed. Note again the tight grouping of the "early" Haida Gwaii cores and their separation from Kasta and Skidegate cores.

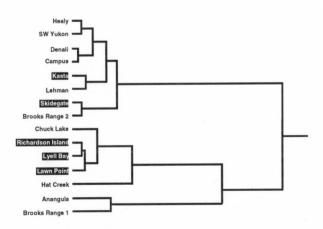

Figure 9. Northwest Microblade Tradition assemblages: three variable cluster analysis (platform length, chord length, core height), using Euclidean distance and Ward's method. Note the tight clustering of Richardson Island, Lyell Bay, and Lawn Point cores with Chuck Lake. The Kasta and Skidegate Landing cores do not cluster as tightly, but are found in a cluster separate from the earlier Haida Gwaii cores.

semblages from Haida Gwaii. Metric analyses clearly differentiate the earlier, ca. 7000 to 9000 BP, technologies from the later, ca. 5000 to 6000 BP, technologies. Cores from Richardson Island are closely related to those from Lawn Point while Kasta and Skidegate Landing cores are clearly different from those. The ca. 8300 BP Chuck Lake cores from coastal Alaska in turn strongly resemble the early Haida Gwaii cores. As a group, the early Haida Gwaii cores are very distinct, when compared to a series of other Northwest Microblade Tradition sites and complexes. Non-metric characteristics also differentiate assemblages and appear to indicate development of less-specialized lithic technology through time. Interestingly, very strong discrimination of major complexes or subtraditions can be obtained with three metric measures: platform length, chord length, and flute length. Future studies of microcores, including microcore assemblages without firm dates, may benefit from these strong patterns. The analyses demonstrate a very strong likelihood of a 7000 to 9000 year range for the Richardson Island and Lyell Bay microcores.

Acknowledgments

I would like to thank Knut Fladmark for access to the Lawn Point, Kasta, Skidegate Landing, and FhUa 15 assemblages. This chapter is modified from a paper presented at the 1994 meetings of the Canadian Archaeological Association in Edmonton, Alberta.

15 THE EARLY PREHISTORIC OCCUPATION OF KITSELAS CANYON

Gary Coupland

The prehistoric human settlement of northwestern British Columbia and southeastern Alaska covers at least the last 9000 years. The early man "hot spots" of this area are the islands of southeast Alaska, the Queen Charlotte Islands, and less certainly, the area around Mount Edziza. This north coast region is a vast area of dense, mountainous rainforest and rugged coastline. It is drained by a series of east-to-west running rivers, the main ones being the Taku, the Stikine, the Nass, and the Skeena. The Skeena is the largest of these rivers. Draining an area of over 42,000 km² (Farley 1979:39), the Skeena is second in size only to the Fraser among Canada's west coast rivers. Yet, despite its apparent prominence as a corridor for early human settlement, the earliest dated site components from the Skeena are ca. 5000 BP, 2000 to 4000 years later than the earliest components from southeastern Alaska and the Charlottes. The lack of early Holocene sites in the Skeena area is not for want of looking – although it may be for want of looking in the right places. In the last twenty years, major archaeological investigations have been conducted at Prince Rupert Harbour near the mouth of the Skeena (MacDonald 1969, 1983, MacDonald and Inglis 1981), at Kitselas Canyon, 150 km upriver from the mouth (Allaire 1978, 1979, Coupland 1985a, 1985b, 1988), and at Hagwilget Canyon, 150 km upriver from Kitselas (Ames 1979). The evidence collected thus far indicates initial occupation at each of these localities about 5000 years ago. In this chapter, I discuss the early human occupation at Kitselas Canyon in the context of early Skeena and early north coast prehistory.

Kitselas Canyon is a 2 km long constriction of the Skeena River, the first such constriction encoun-

tered as one proceeds upriver from the coast (Figure 1). It is situated near the present cultural boundary between Coast Tsimshian and Gitksan territory, and near the ecotonal boundary between the coast and boreal forest environments. Archaeological investigations began at Kitselas Canyon in 1968 as part of the North Coast Prehistory Project, with excavations at Gitaus (Allaire 1978, 1979). This site yielded three prehistoric components, the lowest of which is dated at 4100 BP (Allaire 1979:29).

Archaeological investigation continued at Kitselas Canyon from 1981 to 1983. This time the focus of attention was the Paul Mason site. Three prehistoric cultural components were identified at this site, the lowest of which has a radiocarbon date of 5050 ±40 BP (SFU 259) (Coupland 1985a:214). This component yielded an entirely lithic artifact assemblage that included microblades. The lower component at Gitaus did not yield microblades.

THE BORNITE PHASE

The presence of microblades in the early component at the Paul Mason site clearly distinguishes it from all other components at Kitselas Canyon. The 5000 BP date places this component almost 1000 years earlier than the early component at Gitaus. On the basis of these technological and chronological differences, I have identified the early component at the Paul Mason site as a discrete cultural unit, calling it the Bornite Phase (Coupland 1985a:322-6, 1988:221-2). The Bornite Phase takes its name from a local mountain, and its cultural identity from the presence of an obsidian-based microblade industry. The dates range from 5000 to 4300 BP.

In terms of physical stratigraphy, the Bornite Phase component at the Paul Mason site is associ-

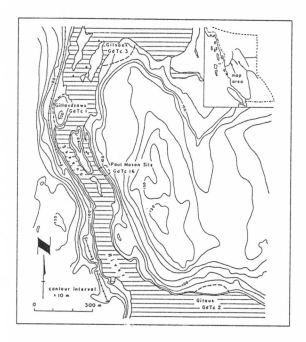

Figure 1. Kitselas Canyon archaeological sites.

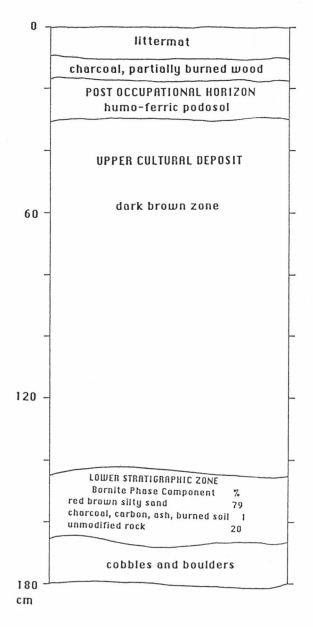

Figure 2. Schematic stratigraphic profile of the Paul Mason site.

ated with a discrete soil horizon (Figure 2), reddish-brown in colour, clearly distinct from the overlying dark brown soil zone. The reddish-brown zone averages about 25 cm thick, and is in direct contact with bedrock and glacial till underneath.

The artifact assemblage of the Bornite Phase component at the Paul Mason site includes 215 stone tools (Figure 3). The lithic technology is represented mainly by two core reduction techniques, including microblade cores and cobble flake cores. Two bipolar cores were also recovered. There is only minimal evidence of stone grinding and production of bifaces. Wood, antler, and bone tool industries may have existed, but have not been preserved.

The microblade industry is represented by 116 microblades and two microblade core rejuvenation flakes (56.2 per cent of the Bornite Phase assemblage) (Figure 4). No complete microblade cores were recovered so it is impossible to reconstruct the shape of the cores. But the rejuvenation flakes were clearly removed from microblade cores. One, made of , is a mid-section fragment of the fluted surface of a microblade core. Five parallel blade scars are present, each 7 to 8 mm wide. The other, made of chert, is a thin flake from the fluted surface of the core, with four parallel blade scars present.

The microblades are triangular or trapezoidal in cross-section. Retouch or use wear, in the form of microflaking or polish, is present on about half of the microblades (see Table 1). Where present, retouch and use wear were restricted to the lateral edges of the implements, suggesting that they functioned as cutting tools. Two blades show evidence of nicking and tiny flake scars along one edge, while the other edge is rounded and polished. These blades may have been side-hafted and used as knives. There is no evidence of end wear or retouch on any microblade that might suggest use as points.

160

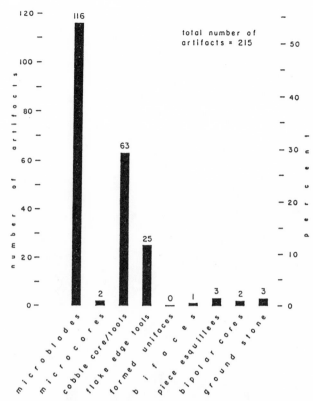

Figure 3. Bornite Phase artifact assemblage profile.

Only sixteen complete microblades were recovered. Undoubtedly many were broken accidentally before, during, or after use. But, in light of the possible evidence of hafting, it is also likely that many blades were purposely broken to create relatively short, straight sections.

Obsidian, chert, and quartz were all used in the manufacture of Bornite Phase microblades. Obsidian was by far the most frequently used raw material (n=106; 91.4 per cent). There is no local obsidian source. The closest known sources are Mount Edziza, 400 km north of Kitselas, and Anahim Peaks, 330 km to the south. Two microblades from the Bornite Phase component and three obsidian flakes from the overlying dark brown soil zone were analyzed using x-ray fluorescence (Godfrey-Smith 1984). The microblades were made from Anahim obsidian; the other three flakes, from Mount Edziza obsidian. Kitselas Canyon may have been at the crossroads of northern and southern obsidian trade routes at this time.

The Bornite Phase cobble flake core industry is represented at the Paul Mason site by sixty-three cobble core tools (30 per cent of the assemblage), and twenty-five flake tools (11.9 per cent of the assemblage) (Figure 5). The cobble flake core industry is distinct from the microblade industry in terms of raw material selection and core reduction techniques.

The favoured raw material was argillite (n=51; 81.4 per cent). The local argillite is fine-grained, relatively easily flaked, and available as water-smoothed cobbles in the beds of the Skeena River and nearby creeks.

Cobble flake cores were reduced in either of two ways (Figure 6). The most common technique (n=49; 77.8 per cent of all cobble flake cores) was the systematic removal of flakes from one end or one side. This reduction resulted first in the removal of a small number of cortex-backed flakes, then in the removal of flakes in which the leading cortical edge of the core was used as a ready-made striking platform. The angle between the cortex and the core face ranged between 45 and 90°. Many of the cores were obviously rotated, so that they were flaked from opposing cortical surfaces. This was probably done to maintain a desired flaking angle of close to 90°. Flakes removed from the cores were typically wide and thin, with at least one acute edge of less than 45°. These flakes appear to have been used as cutting implements with little or no edge retouch.

The other, less common (n=14; 22.2 per cent of all cobble flake cores), reduction technique involved relatively unsystematic flaking at various locations on the core, resulting in the removal of most or all of the cortex. The desired product of this reduction technique may have been large, acute-angled, cortex-backed spalls, of which three with evidence of edge wear were recovered. These spalls, with naturally sharp edges, were likely used as cutting tools.

Any of the cobble flake cores may have been used as core tools at some time during the reduction stage, but clear evidence of wear, was seen on twenty-two cores (34.9 per cent of all cobble flake cores). All core tools had been systematically reduced from one end or one side. Invariably, the wear present on these tools was located on an edge formed by the intersection of the core face and the cortex surface. Most of these implements (n=18; 81.8 per cent of all core tools) had steep working edge angles, between 60 and 75°, with rough, heavy-duty wear undercutting both intersecting surfaces.

Four core tools have edge angles slightly less than 45°. The edge wear on these implements is also rough and undercut. They may have been used as choppers, but the edge angle makes them similar in form to tools identified as "scraping planes" by Matson (1976:145) at the Glenrose site.

The remaining Bornite Phase assemblage includes three groundstone tool fragments – one possible abrader, and two miscellaneous pieces of ground slate – a small bifacially worked piece of obsidian, three pièces esquillées, and two bipolar cores.

Table 1. Metric measurements of Bornite Phase microblades and rejuvenation flakes.

Rejuvenation Flakes (all measurements in mm)

	Cases	Mean	Range
Weight	2	1.4	0.8-2.0
Length	2	17.0	13.8-20.2
Width	2	14.8	11.6-17.9
Thickness	2	4.8	4.8-4.8

Microblades (all measurements in mm)

Unmodified Microblades

	Cases	Mean	Median	Range	Std Dev	Quartiles
Length	5	19.2	17.9	17.5-24.0	2.7	17.6-21.5
Width	55	5.9	5.8	3.3-9.8	1.4	5.0-6.8
Thickness	55	1.6	1.5	0.8-3.4	0.6	1.1-2.0

Retouched Microblades

	Cases	Mean	Median	Range	Std Dev	Quartiles
Length	1	24.5				
Width	4	6.7	7.1	4.0-8.4	1.9	4.8-8.1
Thickness	4	1.5	1.2	1.1-2.5	0.7	1.1-2.2

Utilized Microblades

	Cases	Mean	Median	Range	Std Dev	Quartiles
Length	10	20.7	19.8	9.6-34.1	7.2	15.5-25.3
Width	57	6.5	6.6	4.0-10.4	1.4	5.4-7.3
Thickness	57	1.7	1.6	0.7-3.5	0.6	1.2-2.1

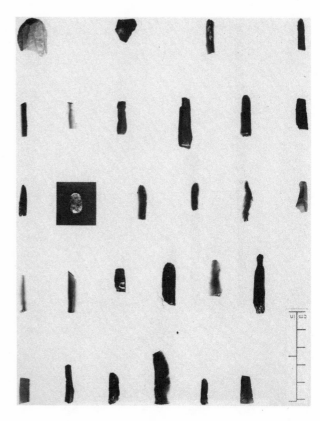

Figure 4. Microblades and rejuvenation flakes from the Bornite Phase.

INFERENCE OF SITE FUNCTION

Bornite Phase material was only recovered from excavations in the northeast part of the Paul Mason site. Given the limited diversity of the tool assemblage, the lack of curated implements, and the apparently small size of the component, a reasonable inference is that the Paul Mason site functioned as a short-term seasonal camp for small groups at this time.

The lack of faunal material precludes any conclusive statement of seasonality, but a reasonable speculation would be mid-summer to early fall, which coincides with the maximum abundance of Skeena-run salmon in the canyon (Aro and Shepard 1967:296-9). Kitselas Canyon was (and is) a critical salmon fishing location. Escapement figures show that approximately 83.4 per cent of all Skeena-run sockeye, pink, coho, and chinook pass through Kitselas Canyon annually (Aro and Shepard 1967:296-9).

The absence of a land mammal hunting tool kit – projectile points, bifaces, scrapers – suggests that terrestrial fauna did not constitute an important resource category at Kitselas Canyon during the Bornite Phase, although land mammals may have been hunted outside Kitselas Canyon at this time.

REGIONAL COMPARISONS
Lower Skeena/Prince Rupert Harbour Sites

The Bornite Phase at Kitselas Canyon is contemporaneous with a number of components in the lower Skeena/Prince Rupert Harbour area (Figure 7). At Prince Rupert Harbour, the Dodge Island, Kitandach, Ridley Island, Boardwalk, and Lachane sites all have radiocarbon dates in the 5000 BP range. The early components from these sites represent MacDonald and Inglis's (1981) Period III (5000-3500 BP), which overlaps with the Bornite Phase and the subsequent Gitaus Phase (4300-3600 BP) at Kitselas Canyon. Period III components at Prince Rupert Harbour lack any evidence of microblade manufacturing, and are therefore distinctly different from the Bornite Phase. The remainder of the Period III lithic assemblage shows some similarities and some differences to the Bornite Phase assemblage. The similarities are high proportions of cobble core tools and acute-edge flake tools. The Period III site components are small and shallow, like the Bornite Phase component, and lack evidence of large permanent structures. The differences, in addition to the absence of microblades at Prince Rupert Harbour, are the presence in Period III of a developed bone tool industry, including barbed points, awls, harpoons, and wedges; chipped stone bifaces, including rare lanceolate projectile points (MacDonald and Inglis 1981:45); and groundstone implements, including abraders and slate points (Fladmark, Ames, and Sutherland 1990:232). Bone tools, lanceolate chipped points, and slate points are not present in

Figure 5. Bornite Phase cobble core tools.

the Bornite Phase. The bone tools in the Period III components appear to date to the earliest occupation of Prince Rupert Harbour, coeval with the Bornite Phase. However, the bifaces and groundstone tools may date to the latter part of Period III, which would likely make them contemporaneous with the Gitaus Phase. Chipped stone bifaces and groundstone tools are present in the Gitaus Phase, and lanceolate points are common in the subsequent Skeena Phase at Kitselas Canyon (3600-3200 BP) (Allaire 1979:46).

Chipped stone bifaces are also common in Zone A at GhSv 2 at Hagwilget Canyon, where Ames (1979:208) has suggested an initial occupation of as early as 5000 BP, based on a 3500 BP date from the top of Zone A. The Zone A assemblage is more similar, however, to the Skeena Phase assemblage than to the Bornite Phase. Microblades were not recovered at GhSv 2, but lanceolate points, bifaces, and formed unifaces are all common in Zone A.

Elsewhere in the lower Skeena area, microblades have been recovered from a site near Hagwilget Canyon, GgSw 5 at Skeena Crossing (Acheson 1977). Only two microblades were recovered, however, they are manufactured from chert, and were surface collected.

The Northern Northwest Coast Area

Outside the lower Skeena/Prince Rupert Harbour area, the Bornite Phase is most similar to the north coast sites that define the Microblade Tradition (Carlson 1979, 1983a, Fladmark 1982) (Figure 7). These include Lawn Point (components 2 to 5), and Kasta on the Queen Charlotte Islands (Fladmark 1970a, 1979b, 1986a), and Groundhog Bay 2 (component II) (Ackerman 1968, 1974, Ackerman et al. 1979), Hidden Falls I (Davis 1984), the Chuck Lake site (Ackerman et al. 1985), the Thorne River site (Holmes 1988), and possibly the Irish Creek site (Roberts 1982) in southeastern Alaska. These sites range in age from 9000 to 5000 BP, and have lithic assemblages defined by microblade core and cobble flake core industries, with groundstone and chipped stone bifaces rare or absent.

Somewhat farther afield, Namu zone II has yielded microblades and radiocarbon dates ranging between 9000 and 5000 BP (Luebbers 1978, R.L. Carlson 1979, this volume). Zone IIb, Period 2 with dates ranging between 6500 and 5000 BP (R.L. Carlson 1979:214), corresponds closely to the Bornite Phase.

Finally, there are the sites in the Mount Edziza area of northwestern British Columbia (Smith 1971, 1974; Fladmark 1982). Most of these sites have uncertain dates, but one site with microblades, securely dated between 5000 and 4000 BP is the Grizzly Run site (Fladmark 1982:253-81).

I compared the Bornite Phase assemblage to those sites mentioned above for which complete assemblages have been reported – Chuck Lake, Groundhog Bay, Hidden Falls, Thorne River, Irish Creek, Lawn Point, Grizzly Run, and Namu (Table 2, Figure 8). There is general similarity in the assemblage profiles among these sites; the main source of variability being the proportion of microblades in each component. The Bornite Phase, Chuck Lake, and Grizzly Run have the highest proportions of microblades – over half the assemblage in each case. The high proportion of microblades at Grizzly Run may be attributed to the proximity of the site to a major obsidian source. According to Fladmark 1982:279), the early occupation of this site was devoted almost entirely to lithic manufacturing. The Paul Mason and Chuck Lake sites are different in that neither is located close to an obsidian source. At these two sites, the high proportions of microblades are probably functionally associated with fishing. This inference is clear for Chuck Lake, where a lithic assemblage dominated by microblades is associated with a faunal assemblage dominated by fish bones (Ackerman et al. 1985:125-6). At the Paul

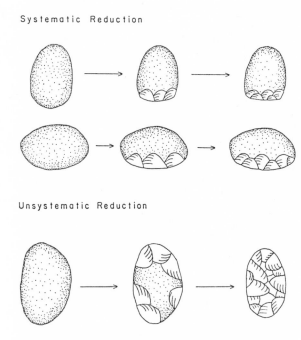

Figure 6. Schematic of systematic reduction and unsystematic reduction of Bornite Phase cobble flake cores.

Mason site fishing is inferred because of the location of the site in Kitselas Canyon.

Groundhog Bay, Hidden Falls, Thorne River, Irish Creek, Lawn Point, and Namu all have lower proportions of microblades than the Bornite Phase, but are generally similar in the proportions of cobble core tools and flake tools.

The microblade and cobble-flake industries combined constitute over 95 per cent of the Bornite Phase assemblage at the Paul Mason site. This probably attests to the importance of food-processing and woodworking. These may well have been the only activities conducted at the Paul Mason site during the Bornite Phase. At Chuck Lake, Thorne River, Lawn Point, and Groundhog Bay, the combined microblade core and cobble flake core industries constitute over 90 per cent of the assemblages; at Namu and Irish Creek, 80 per cent of the assemblages. Only Component I at Hidden Falls differs markedly in this regard. Here, the microblade core and cobble flake core industries constitute only 61.4 per cent of the total lithic assemblage. The high proportion of formed unifaces at this site distinguishes it from other north coast components. The location of the Hidden Falls site argues for a coastal adaptation.

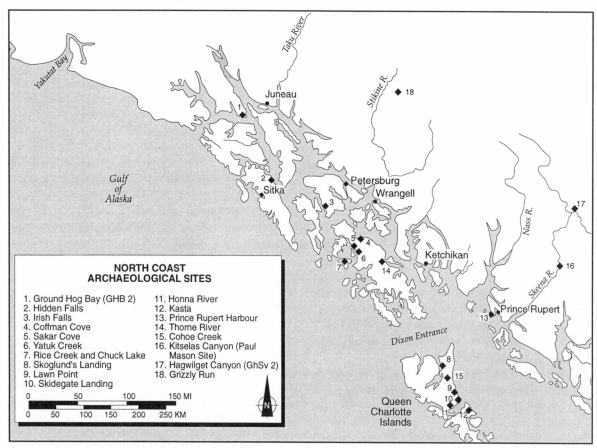

Figure 7. North coast archaeological sites.

The unifaces include a variety of scrapers, gravers, and denticulates, which suggest the performance of a greater diversity of activities than at the other sites. Perhaps Hidden Falls was used as a base camp at this time.

Despite the general similarities among these components in the combined contribution of the two main lithic industries, there is important inter-assemblage variability in terms of how frequently each industry occurs. This is especially apparent for the northern coastal sites, Chuck Lake, Irish Creek, Lawn Point, Groundhog Bay, and Hidden Falls. The microblade industry constitutes almost 90 per cent of the Chuck Lake assemblage, 44 per cent of the Irish Creek assemblage, 35 per cent of the Lawn Point assemblage, 34 per cent of the Thorne River assemblage, and 12 per cent of the Groundhog Bay and Hidden Falls assemblages respectively. With the exception of Hidden Falls, the proportions of cobble core and flake tools at these sites are inversely related to the proportions of the microcores and blades. Thus, while the same sets of activities were likely conducted at these sites, they may not have been conducted with the same frequency.

What is surprising about these figures is the great range in the proportions of microblades. Only at the Chuck Lake site do microblades "swamp" the assemblage. Microblades are important at Lawn Point, Thorne River, Groundhog Bay, Irish Creek, and Namu, but not overwhelmingly so. The Bornite Phase is somewhere in the middle, somewhat closer to Chuck Lake in the proportion of microblades. The significance of this distribution may be reflected in the faunal assemblages from Chuck Lake and Namu. At Chuck Lake and Grizzly Run, fish bones constitute 95 per cent of the faunal assemblage by Number of Identified Species (NISP). At Namu, fish bones, including salmon, are abundant in Period 2 deposits but constitute a much lower proportion of the faunal assemblage than in later periods (Cannon 1991:33). From this we may infer a positive correlation between fishing and the frequency of microblades.

CONCLUSIONS

The Microblade Tradition of the northern Northwest Coast is characterized by microblades, cobble core tools, flake edge tools, rare bifaces, and rare groundstone implements (Carlson 1979, 1983a, Fladmark 1982). The Bornite Phase at Kitselas Canyon clearly fits within this tradition. With its high proportion of microblades, the Bornite Phase assemblage at Kitselas Canyon is most similar to the Chuck Lake site assemblage in southeastern Alaska, where a

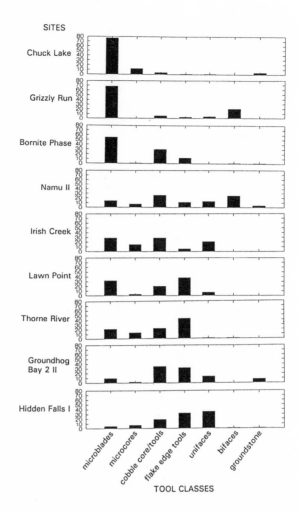

Figure 8. Relative percentage of tool classes in north coast archaeological assemblages. Namu frequencies based on 1978 data only.

fish-dominated faunal assemblage is present. It is most likely that the Paul Mason site was also an important fishing location during the Bornite Phase.

To date, the Bornite Phase is the only example of the Microblade Tradition in the lower Skeena/Prince Rupert Harbour area. The early components at Prince Rupert Harbour, Kitselas Canyon, and Hagwilget Canyon are all distinctly different from each other. These differences may yet be the result of sampling or differences in site use. At present, however, I do not believe that the evidence reflects the existence of a single, unified cultural system in the lower Skeena/Prince Rupert Harbour area at ca. 5000 BP. This raises an important question. What are the origins of the Bornite Phase? There are two possibilities here. First, with its basic similarities to other Microblade Tradition components, especially the Chuck Lake site, we may look to southeastern Alaska, or possibly the Queen Charlotte Islands for the origins of the Bornite Phase. The problem with this hypothesis is the absence of microblades at Prince Rupert Harbour. With microblade components to the north, west, and east, how could Prince Rupert Harbour have been missed?

A second possibility is that the origins of the Bornite Phase lie not to the north, but to the south, perhaps at Namu. There are basic assemblage similarities between Kitselas Canyon and Namu in terms of the microblade core and cobble flake core industries, and a strong similarity between the two areas in terms of the use of Anahim obsidian to produce microblades. Salmon fishing became increasingly important at Namu, beginning about 5000 BP

(Cannon 1991), which coincides with the beginning of the Bornite Phase. Conceivably, a small group from the central coast area moved to the Kitselas Canyon area at this time, perhaps via Douglas Channel and the Kitimat-Kitsumkalum Trench, which provide a virtually direct route to Kitselas Canyon. This would explain the absence of microblades at Prince Rupert Harbour. Once at Kitselas Canyon, the people took advantage of a prime salmon fishing location.

At present, this argument is speculation. More work is needed to understand the origins and development of early human settlement in the lower Skeena area.

Table 2. North Coast artifact assemblages.

		Microblades	Microblade cores	Cobble core/tool	Flake edge tools	Formed unifaces	Bifaces and projectile points	Ground stone	Total	Sources
Chuck Lake	#	58	9	3	1	1		3	75	Ackerman et. al. 1985
	%	77.3	12.0	4.0	1.3	1.3		4.0		
Grizzly Run	#	55		5	2	3	16		81	Fladmark 1985
	%	67.9		6.1	2.5	3.7	19.8			
Bornite Phase Paul Mason	#	116	2	63	25		1	3	210	Coupland 1985a
	%	55.2	1.0	30.0	11.9		0.5	1.4		
Namu II*	#	60	28	113	49	57	105	15	427	R.L.Carlson 1979, this volume
	%	14.1	6.6	26.5	11.0	13.3	24.6	3.5		
Irish Creek	#	10	5	10	2	7			34	Roberts 1982
	%	29.4	14.7	29.4	5.8	20.5				
Lawn Point (Comp's 2-5)	#	167	16	102	195	38			518	Fladmark 1986a
	%	32.2	3.1	19.7	37.6	7.3				
Thorne River	#	125	74	128	256	7	3	0	593	Holmes 1988
	%	21.1	12.5	21.6	43.2	1.2	1	0		
Groundhog Bay 2	#	6	1	22	20	9	0	5	63	Ackerman 1968
	%	9.5	1.6	34.9	31.7	14.3	0	7.9		
Hidden Falls I	#	9	14	37	62	68	1	2	193	Davis 1989
	%	4.7	7.2	19.2	32.1	35.2	0.5	1.0		

(*based on 1978 data only)

16

THE NAMU OBSIDIAN INDUSTRY

W. Karl Hutchings

I must admit to a certain fascination with obsidian. Its translucency, as well as its variety of colour and patterning, and its unique workability in the production of flaked stone tools, has an aesthetic appeal that I suspect reaches back through prehistory for countless thousands of years. At the same time, however, its physical properties and the geographic localization of sources, combine to impose important constraints within the design of any technological system from which it is a part. Consideration of these constraints was a very real aspect of the prehistoric use of obsidian, and must comprise a significant role in its analysis.

Excavations at Namu since the late 1960s have produced a cultural assemblage which includes a relatively large number of obsidian artifacts and debitage. Aesthetic appeal aside, a technological analysis of this material offers an opportunity to assess the problematic role of obsidian microblades, as well as provide an outline of an obsidian industry spanning ten thousand years.

THE SITE

The Namu site (ElSx 1) on the Central Coast of British Columbia, is a deep, stratified shell midden located on the mainland shore of Fitzhugh Sound, less than 3 miles south of the entrance to Burke Channel (51° 51' 32" North lat., 127° 51' 50" West long.) (see Chapter 9). The midden deposits lie on the north side of the Namu River mouth, partially beneath a large abandoned bunkhouse built in 1946 as part of a cannery owned by British Columbia Packers Ltd. (Luebbers 1978). The deposits extend from the shoreline to beyond a bedrock outcrop more than 60 m from the river's edge.

The Namu deposits were first tested in 1968 by James Hester (University of Colorado) who undertook a major program of excavations in 1969 to 1970 (Hester and Nelson 1978). Further excavations in 1977, 1978, and 1994 were directed by Roy L. Carlson (1979; and Chapter 9). The material described and analyzed here is the obsidian assemblage recovered by both the Hester and Carlson excavations, and includes both the Early and Late Period material, although the emphasis is on the former.

TEMPORAL RELATIONSHIP

A temporal framework has been assigned (Chapter 9) to the various strata within the cultural deposits based on radiocarbon dates and stratigraphic integrity. This sequence has been divided into six major temporal periods as follows:

Period 1a:	10,000 – 9000	years BP
Period 1b:	9000 – 8000	years BP
Period 1c:	8000 – 6000	years BP
Period 2:	6000 – 5000	years BP
Period 3:	5000 – 4500	years BP
Period 4:	4500 – 3500	years BP
Period 5:	3500 – 2000	years BP
Period 6:	2000 – contact	years BP

The relative frequency of obsidian artifacts and debitage for each period is presented in Figure 1.

CLASSIFICATION

The assemblage consists of 1053 microlithic obsidian artifacts and debitage. Of these, 1037 pieces with assignable provenience were analyzed and divided into ten major classes based on general morphology:

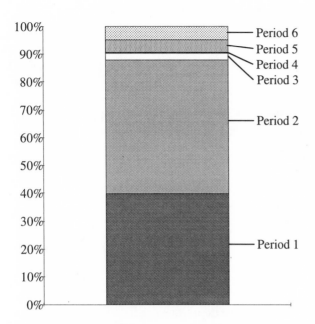

Figure 1. Relative frequency of Namu obsidian artifacts and debitage by period.

Bipolar core	Microblade (complete)
Bipolar flake	Proximal microblade
Flake medial	Microblade
Microcore	Distal microblade
Microflake	Other

These major classes were then further sub-divided based on attributes of utilization, retouch, and lack of utilization and retouch, for a total of thirty major classes and subclasses of combined artifacts and debitage. Incomplete or fragmentary pieces were classified with complete specimens with the exception of microblades, as outlined above. Additional minor classes were identified within the major class "Other" and include: Microblade Cores and fragments, Microblade Core Platform Rejuvenation Flakes, Blades, (Macro) Cores, Perforators & Borers, and Bifaces. Distributional data are presented in Table 1.

The assemblage was examined under low-power magnification (6.3x to 40x) for evidence of retouch or utilization. It was evident from use-wear traces on many of the pieces that several types of activities were being performed with the obsidian tools. These pieces were studied and attempts made to replicate and identify the wear patterns. Organic residue traces were also noted on several of the pieces; these too were examined, though briefly, and will be discussed below.

ARTIFACT CLASSES AND DEFINITIONS

An artifact was considered to be retouched if it exhibited flake scars that appeared to result from intentional finishing of the piece that was spatially restricted, of consistent dimension and patterning, used to create a notch or isolate a tip, or any combination of these characteristics, or if the piece appeared to be ground (e.g., an edge that had been purposefully dulled or backed).

An artifact was classified as utilized if it exhibited: small, patterned, scalar flake scars that were not necessarily uniform in dimension; removal of flake scars primarily from a single face; as well as spatial restriction of these characteristics. Utilization then, was recognized as being distinct from retouch by differences in flake size and shape, uniformity, and consistency of patterning.

If a piece carried neither of the characteristics of retouch or utilization then it was classified as no use/retouch. The presence of residues on pieces that were recognized as neither retouched nor utilized through wear analysis raises an interesting question: How much, and what kind of utilization is necessary to produce identifiable use-wear on microlithic obsidian? Only eleven (30.6 per cent) of the thirty-six pieces carrying residues were classified as retouched (n=6) or utilized (n=5). This may suggest that a large portion of the material classified as "no use/retouch" may actually have been used, but not to the extent where it is visually recognizable. Alternatively, it may simply suggest that artifacts discarded in middens may pick up erroneous residues not necessarily from use, but from contact with decaying organic matter.

Bipolar Cores

Bipolar cores (Figure 2i and j) were classified according to Crabtrees's (1982) definition, and with the aid of replicative experiments and comparative collections. The attributes considered in the identification of bipolar cores were opposing negative flake scars, sheared cone of force (near absent negative bulb of percussion), and opposing crushed impact points.

The Namu obsidian bipolar cores appear to have been worked to their useful limit. There are no large bipolar cores (none exceed approx. 4 cm³ volume). In fact, it appears that bipolar obsidian reduction, as practiced at Namu, may have been a last resort effort to secure a maximum amount of working edge from material that would otherwise have been unworkable because of its small size. While this implies that bipolar reduction was used solely on small fragments, this may not have been the case; if larger

Table 1. Distribution of Early Period Namu obsidian artifacts and debitage from major excavation units by Period. Pieces recovered from auger probing etc. have not been included.

Unit	Rivermouth trench				Main trench*		Test pits
Period	1A	1B	1C	2	1	2	2
Major classes							
Bipolar core	0	31	38	28	3	18	2
Bipolar flake	0	11	20	17	2	15	1
Flake	2	11	11	13	2	32	7
Microcore	1	8	6	10	0	6	4
Microflake	0	41	57	54	5	49	33
Microblade (complete)	0	2	7	7	7	8	8
Proximal microblade	0	9	21	24	4	19	7
Medial microblade	0	7	14	11	1	16	3
Distal microblade	0	2	4	6	1	10	5
Other	2	18	31	19	7	36	1
Minor classes							
Microblade core frag.	0	2	2	4	0	1	0
Microblade core rej. flk.	0	2	1	2	0	1	0
Core	0	2	1	2	0	3	2
Blade	0	0	0	1	0	0	0
Perforator/borer	0	0	1	2	0	0	0
Biface	0	0	0	1	0	0	0
Microblade/frag**	0	0	10	7	0	0	0
Period totals/unit	5	146	224	208	32	214	74

* Materials recovered from the main trench include those from the University of Colorado excavations and have not been subdivided into Periods 1A, 1B, and 1C as with the Rivermouth trench.
** "Microblade/frag." does not constitute a minor class. These pieces were unavailable for study and so could not be assigned to major classes

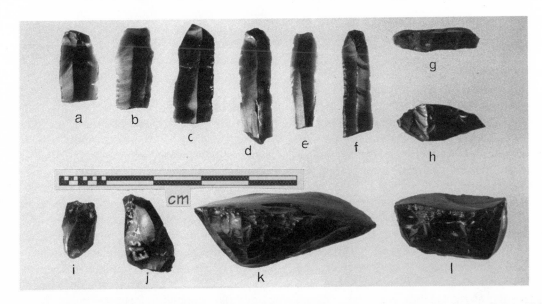

Figure 2. Examples of obsidian artifacts from Namu: (a) backed proximal microblade fragment, #3626g; (b) backed medial microblade fragment, #3605; (c) backed medial microblade fragment, #3771; (d) utilized proximal microblade fragment, #3839; (e) proximal microblade fragment, #3538; (f) proximal microblade fragment, #3536; (g) microblade core platform rejuvenation flake, #3737; (h) microblade core platform rejuvenation flake, #3785; (i) bipolar core, #3796; (j) bipolar core, #3692; (k) microblade core, #3752; (l) microblade core, #3549. Both microblade cores appear to have been utilized, perhaps as scrapers, since the removal of the last microblades.

cores were reduced in this manner they have been subsequently reworked so that the original core size is impossible to predict.

The large number of bipolar cores present in the sample (n=133; 12.8 per cent of the total obsidian assemblage) suggests that a relatively high level of conservation was practiced with respect to the reduction and use of obsidian at the Namu site. Presumably, exhausted cores or otherwise unusable, small nodules were reduced by bipolar percussion in order to extract a maximum amount of usable cutting edge. This conservatism most likely resulted from procurement costs related to source distance, accessibility, and transportable size restrictions (see Hayden 1980). Artifact numbers 1711c, 3504, 3539w, and 3581c are microblade cores which have been further reduced by the bipolar technique. Bipolar core number 3562d may also have been a microblade core at one time. These, as well as artifact number 1077a, a flake further reduced by bipolar percussion, are fine examples of obsidian conservation at Namu.

This phenomenon furnishes a possible explanation for the relative lack of microblade cores at Namu. Despite the recovery of 231 microblades and microblade fragments, only nine obsidian microblade cores and fragments were recovered from the Namu excavations, suggesting that these cores may have been routinely reduced using the bipolar technique.

Bipolar Flakes

Bipolar flakes were also classified according to Crabtrees's (1982) definition, and also with the aid of replication and comparative collections. The attributes considered in the identification of bipolar flakes were: opposing positive flake scars, sheared cone of force (near absent positive bulb of percussion), ridge back or wedge (orange section) shape, overall flatness, opposing "ventral" faces, and opposing crushed impact points.

Considering the quantities of bipolar cores in the sample (n=133), it seems odd that there should be so few bipolar flakes (n=79). Hayden (1980) has suggested that the bipolar technique is often utilized for expedient tool manufacture and may be related to fish and small-game butchery. If this were the case at Namu, I suggest that exhausted bipolar flakes may have been discarded with the waste products of these activities, perhaps in the intertidal zone. This may explain why they appear to be under-represented in the stratified deposits.

Flakes

Flakes and microflakes were distinguished from each other by assigning an arbitrary boundary, or "sectioning point," for division of size ranges based on ventral surface area. A sectioning point of approximately 1.5 to 2 cm^2 was chosen to define the boundary between the two classes, with microflakes falling into the range below this point. Morphologically, flakes were defined as exhibiting positive bulbs of percussion, ventral face, a striking platform, erailure scars, radiating fissures, or any combination of these characteristics.

The flake/microflake sectioning point seemed to work very well. Familiarity with the medium suggests that control over flake size is readily attainable such that one could intentionally create a primary flake or a microflake with relative ease, and that the obvious difference in size between these classes within the Namu assemblage is most likely intentional and highly relevant.

Since most of the obsidian flakes from the excavations are fragmentary, the actual size, for purposes of classification, was often extrapolated from either length, width, thickness, bulb and platform size, or various combinations depending on which of these dimensions were present on the fragment. Despite their classification as flakes, the largest of these pieces is approximately 30 mm in length, indicating that either the original cores were relatively small, or that larger flakes were in turn further reduced, perhaps again by bipolar percussion.

Flakes (n=112) represent the only major artifact class whose relative frequency increases substantially during the Late Period (Figures 3 and 4).

Microblades

Microblades are defined as small, parallel-sided bladelets, usually less than 1 cm wide, exhibiting one or (usually) two dorsal arrises, and produced via the pressure technique from a prepared core (Figure 2a-f). Obsidian was by far the material of choice for microblade production at Namu (see Chapter 9). As explained previously, the Namu microblades (n=231) were divided into complete, proximal, medial, and distal classes. Indications of use, where present, rarely extend to the ends of the fragments indicating that complete microblades were often intentionally snapped to form several individual segments in preparation for use or retouch. Other microblades, neither used nor retouched, may have broken during manufacture (which was found to often be the case with replicated pieces), or through subsequent depositional processes. Considering only complete pieces and proximal fragments, a mini-

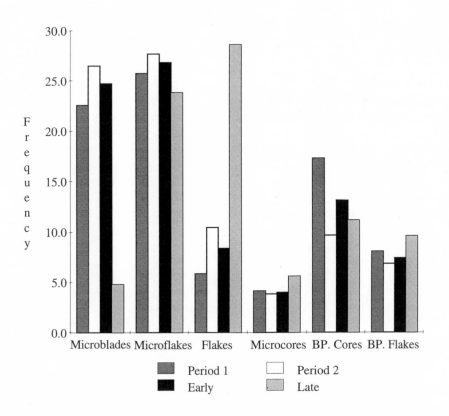

Figure 3. Relative frequencies of Namu obsidian artifact classes by Period (Early vs. Late). Note that individual data are also presented for Periods 1 and 2, which together constitute the Early Period.

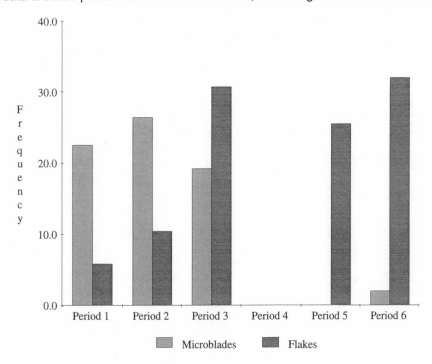

Figure 4. Relative frequency of total Namu obsidian versus microblades and flakes by period.

mum number of 129 individual microblades are represented in the assemblage; casual attempts at refitting of fragments, however, have not been successful, suggesting that the number is much higher. For statistical purposes, all microblade classes have been grouped together and are discussed herein as a single class.

The high proportion of retouched microblades (27.7 per cent of the microblades class) was surprising; Owen (1988:72) suggests that frequencies between 3 and 15 per cent are most common among microblade assemblages. Notably, however, 27 per cent of the microblades recovered from the Bezya site in northeastern Alberta exhibit retouch (Le Blanc and Ives 1986:76).

I had initially suspected that microblades may have, among other functions, been used as fish or small-game butchering tools and had, therefore, expected to find significantly more "utilized" than "retouched" pieces. My suspicions were based upon Flenniken's (1981) work with replications of hafted vein-quartz microliths based on excavated materials from Hoko River. In addition to "working edge" retouch, six microblades (artifact numbers 1222, 1712b, 3626g, 3626i, 3748, 3771, and possibly number 3605) were found to exhibit steep retouch and/or edge grinding and are best characterized as backed microblades (Figure 2a-c). The edge ground pieces appear to represent a task for which the microblades were grasped rather than hafted.

Examination of the microblade cores and core fragments (Figure 2g, h, k, l), as well as the distal portions and overall form of the microblades, suggests that at least three forms of microblade cores were produced at Namu: a tabular core, an oval, or boat-shaped core, and a conical core. Both the tabular core, and the conical core were identified by Jeffrey Flenniken whose examination of the microblades from the 1977 to 1978 excavations pro-

Figure 5. Replications of Namu obsidian microblade cores by Jeffrey Flenniken: (a) tabular core; (b) conical core.

duced the replications seen in Figure 5 (Carlson, personal communication 1990).

Microcores

Microcores were loosely defined as those cores whose flake scars represent the removal of microflakes. These cores (n=43) seldom exceed a volume of 3 to 5 cm³. Some of these pieces may represent the exhausted end-product of larger core reduction sequences, though the general expression of material conservation suggests that most were reduced from small nodules.

It may be possible in some cases that the classification microcore has been applied to fragments of bipolar cores where the fragment is not complete enough to distinguish the characteristics of bipolar percussion.

Microflakes

As discussed for the flakes classification, microflakes were defined as exhibiting less than 1.5 to 2 cm² ventral surface area, and as having the same general morphological characteristics as outlined for flakes.

This class represents the largest (26.4 per cent) within the obsidian assemblage at Namu, and includes such items as bifacial thinning flakes (artifact numbers 1225 and 1818b), and at least three resharpening or pressure thinning flakes (artifact numbers 1922b, 3662i, 3539l, and possibly number 3587a).

Of the obsidian assemblage exhibiting residues, more than 45 per cent is represented by the combined microflake (30.6 per cent) and microcore (16.7 per cent) classes.

Like the microblades mentioned previously, two microflakes exhibit backing by edge grinding, and may represent tools which were intended to be grasped, perhaps with the application of relatively large amounts of pressure directed through the backed surface. Also noteworthy is the fact that microflakes exhibit the second highest (behind microblades) incidence of retouch and/or utilization; 30.3 per cent of the Namu obsidian microflakes exhibit these characteristics.

Other

This class contains 182 artifacts including: three bifaces from Period 6, one from Period 5, and one from Period 2; six microblade core platform rejuvenation flakes (three from Period 2, and three from Period 1); two burins; three perforators or borers; fourteen cores and core fragments; and miscellaneous debitage and shattered obsidian. Several piec-

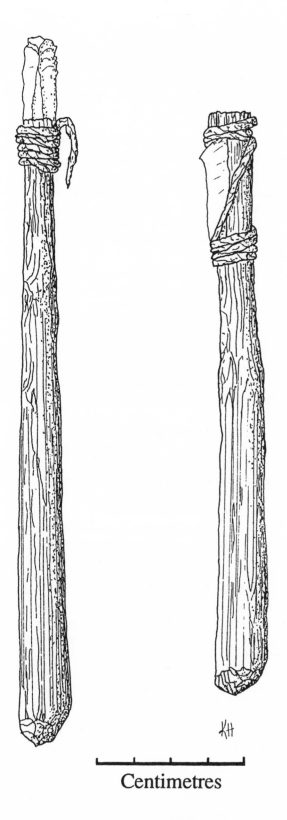

Centimetres

Figure 6. Examples of end-hafted and side-hafted obsidian microblades used during replication and use-wear experiments. In both hafting models the microblade segments are set into the split end of a cedar haft which is bound with spruce root.

es (12.6 per cent) within this class exhibit retouch and/or utilization.

EXPERIMENTS

Prior to analysis I had expected to find a larger proportion of utilized microblades relative to those that exhibited intentional retouch; however, this proved not to be the case. My expectations were based on the assumption that microblades or microblade sections were side-hafted for use as fish or small game butchering tools, as suggested by Flenniken's (1981) work (see also Luebbers 1978:40, Sanger 1968b:201). To discover why the Namu microblades exhibit retouch and not merely evidence of utilization, several experiments were conducted to investigate the cutting properties of obsidian microblades using hafted and non-hafted microblade segments. Hafted microblade segments were used only for fish butchering. Two hafting methods were used. The first method utilized a microblade segment set into the side of a cedar haft near the tip. The second method utilized a microblade segment set into, and projecting from, the tip of a cedar haft (Figure 6). Both hafting methods were friction-based, and no mastic was used.

Unlike Flenniken's (1981) hafted vein-quartz microliths, the obsidian microblades performed poorly for fish processing purposes. The worst of both hafting styles was that inspired by Flenniken's (1981) research (i.e., side-hafted). This style proved highly inefficient and required frequent cleaning to avoid being "gummed-up" when various tissues adhered to the leading edge, causing the tool to ride over the remaining flesh without cutting.

The second hafting style (i.e., end-hafted) avoided this problem by keeping the haft away from the material to be cut and allowing a higher attack angle between the tool and target material, thereby also increasing the cutting efficiency. In addition, this style has the added benefit of two usable cutting edges rather than one, without having to disassemble the tool and re-haft the blade.

The major problem for both experimental hafting styles, however, lies in protecting the cutting edge from dulling too quickly. The extremely thin edges of the microblade segments were quickly dulled and broken from contact with fish scales, which are surprisingly tough and abrasive, and from contact with bony elements of the fish, or simply from accidental contact with the wooden working surface.

The results of the fish butchering experiments strongly suggest that obsidian microblades are not nearly as practical as Flenniken's (1981) tougher-edged bipolar vein-quartz tools. R.L. Carlson (1979:216) reports that 610 milky quartz microflakes, cores and other fragments were recovered during the 1977 to 1978 Namu excavations. These pieces may have fulfilled the butchering duties suggested for the replicated Hoko River side-hafted knives. The presence of these pieces coupled with the findings of these experiments, suggest that obsidian microblades used for butchering small game and fish would represent costly, redundant, and inferior technology relative to bipolar quartz tools known to be used by the inhabitants of the Namu site.

Ironically, since this research was initiated (originally in 1986 as an analysis of the combined University of Colorado and 1977-78 Simon Fraser University obsidian assemblage), further excavations at the Hoko River wet/dry site have recovered an end-hafted, quartz crystal microblade. The microblade is set in a cedar haft and bound with cherry bark (see Croes 1987, Figure 9).

Further tests were performed to identify tasks more suited to the cutting capabilities of the obsidian microblades. The presence of backed microblades and microflakes suggests both the hafting and grasping of these tools, therefore a series of tests were performed with un-hafted microblades and repeated with basalt and obsidian flakes for comparative purposes.

In sum, it was found that basalt flakes, or practically any available flake, though not as inherently sharp, are much better suited to cutting sinuous flesh than are obsidian microblades. The microblades are well suited for cutting thin leather and hide, splitting and trimming thin pieces of soft woods such as cedar, and may be useful in the preparation and finishing of basketry and cordage materials. The sharp, thin, and straight edges of the microblades make them generally superior to basalt flakes and marginally superior to un-hafted obsidian flakes for precision cutting of any soft or pliable material. When end-hafted, however, the utility of the obsidian microblade increases many-fold. These composite knives are in fact comparable to modern razor knives used for delicate, precision craft work, and may have served a similar function prehistorically. Considering the evidence for personal adornment and beautification from later periods of Northwest Coast prehistory, it may not be unreasonable to suggest that obsidian microblades may have also been used to cut and trim hair, or for intentional scarification.

S.E.M. AND WEAR ANALYSIS

A scanning electron microscope (S.E.M.) provided by Simon Fraser University was used to examine both the residues and the cutting edges from both the Namu and experimentally produced assemblages to identify the tasks associated with various tool classes. Unfortunately, S.E.M. access time was limited and the results of the study are incomplete, and consequently only a brief outline of these analyses is presented.

Examination of residues (e.g., artifact number 1195a) suggested only that they were indeed organic, as determined by the identification of preserved bacteria on the suspected residual material and its absence from the rest of the surface of the piece. Identification of the residue itself, however, was inconclusive.

Under low-power magnification, and sometimes with the unaided eye, one type of residue appears to have an iridescent quality similar in appearance to that left after handling and processing fish. The other appears similar to scraped bone or antler residues reproduced experimentally. Notably, none of the residues occurs on microblades, but only on bipolar materials, microflakes, flakes, and microcores.

The S.E.M. was also used in conjunction with replication experiments and techniques of microwear analysis as outlined by Del Bene (1979), Diamond (1979), Fedje (1979), Kamminga (1979), Keeley (1980), and others, to aid in identification of the tasks performed by the retouched and utilized portion of the assemblage.

Use-wear identified by S.E.M. and low-power studies fall into four basic categories: incising, cutting, scraping, and sawing. Artifact number 1045, a utilized burin spall which would otherwise be classified as debitage, exhibited use-wear which indicated that it had been used to incise a shallow groove or line, probably in bone, or possibly in softened antler. The piece was apparently hand-held and repeatedly drawn toward its user in a unidirectional fashion, as indicated by unidirectional, microscopic flake removal. Several other pieces from the Namu collection exhibit intentionally isolated tips that may have been used for similar tasks.

Scraping use-wear appears on almost all classes including some microblades. Replication experiments suggest that it is the result of rapid, bidirectional scraping of hard materials such as bone, antler, and hardwood. This type of use was subsequently identified on pieces exhibiting suspected bone or antler residues.

Cutting use-wear most often occurred on microflakes, but was also common on microblades. It appears similar to the scraping wear described above, but is more uniform, resembling light, intentional retouch. It was found that cutting soft woods such as cedar (especially when green) or cutting barks, pliable roots, or fresh plant materials in general produced similar use-wear. While experimental cutting of hair was not part of the original research design, it should definitely be considered in future research.

I consider sawing use-wear to be the least reliable of the identified categories. Sawing wear is almost exclusively restricted to the obsidian microblades. Unfortunately, it can also be similar to certain long-term trampling damage on microblades due to the delicate nature of the thin edges. While in use, small fragments of obsidian are broken from the edge of the obsidian blade, these become lodged in the material being sawn and act to abrade and fracture the remaining blade edge. Although the result can be surprisingly similar to trampling damage, it is sometimes possible to distinguished the two by the presence of angular, sometimes bidirectional, microscopic flake scars, and striations which run parallel with the working edge.

SUMMARY AND DISCUSSION

Only a very small quantity of obsidian is found within the earliest deposits (Period 1A) at Namu, prior to 9000 BP. There is a steady increase in the use and deposition of obsidian during the Early Period, 10,000 BP to 5000 BP, peaking in Period 2 (6000 BP to 5000 BP) of the Early Period (Figures 1 and 7). Approximately 48 per cent of the total obsidian recovered was deposited during Period 2 with approximately 12 per cent of the total obsidian assemblage deposited after 5000 BP. Only three pieces of obsidian were recovered from Period 4 deposits (4500 to 3500 BP).

Microblades occur within the Early Period shortly after 9000 BP, and upon their appearance immediately comprise a significant portion, over 15 per cent, of the obsidian tool inventory, increasing to more than 26 per cent by Period 2. Despite the drastic decline in obsidian deposition in Period 3 (refer to Figure 1), microblades still comprise a large proportion (over 19 per cent) of the component (cf., Hester 1978:101, and Chapter 9). Note, however, that the Period 3 obsidian component is relatively small and that Strata 3 (Period 3) intrusions which reach into underlying Period 2 depos-

its may have caused some mixing. Although obsidian begins to reappear during Late Periods 5 and 6, obsidian microblades do not. The single microblade that appears after Period 3 (i.e., after 4500 BP), is associated with Period 6 (2000 BP to contact), and appears to be an anomaly, perhaps intrusive.

The significance of large relative proportions of microblades within an assemblage may seem problematic. The production technology is such that once the core is prepared, large numbers of microblades may be quickly and easily produced (cf., Clark 1992), and therein lies the problem: are we observing punctuated accumulation resulting from relatively rare activities, or a slow, but steady accumulation resulting from relatively common or punctuated activities? The stratified, microblade bearing deposits at Namu attest to a technological tradition passed across countless generations over several millenia. Artifact spatial distribution and relative frequencies suggests that microblades were manufactured on a relatively continual basis, but in very small quantities to meet immediate needs.

Interestingly, the relative frequency of flakes may fluctuate in opposition to that of microblades (Figure 4), remaining relatively low during the Early Period, peaking at the beginning of the Late Period (Period 3), and remaining relatively high throughout. One interpretation is that flakes and microblades may represent alternative solutions to a

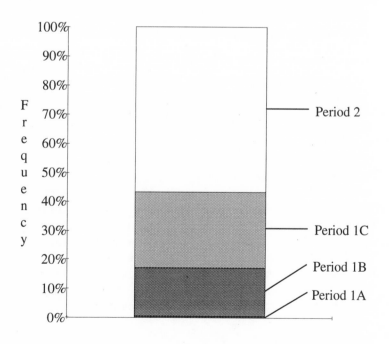

Figure 7. Relative frequencies of Namu obsidian deposition during the Early Period (1a to 2).

common functional requirement, though perhaps not the only function attributable to each tool type. This change over time may, therefore, represent a changing economic situation, or simply a change in technological organization. Alternatively, and more befitting the present data, both tool types represent different technologies. Changes occurring after the beginning of the Late Period, perhaps the disruption of trade or transportation routes affecting obsidian procurement, induced the abandonment of obsidian microblade use. Such a scenario may explain the near complete lack of obsidian at Namu for an entire millenium (Period 4) between 4500 BP and 3500 BP. The absence of microblades in the Late components once obsidian reappears suggests either that obsidian microblades represent, at least by that time, a non-essential technology, or that their role within the technological system was successfully replaced sometime around 4500 BP.

The microlithic nature of the assemblage and the high proportion of retouched and utilized pieces suggests that a great deal of conservation of raw materials use was practiced; to the point of smashing exhausted microblade cores and retouching pieces which exhibit as little as 0.5 cm^2 surface area. This practice seems to be related to procurement costs resulting from quarry distance and accessibility. Several of the quarry sources have been identified through trace element analyses, these include: Obsidian Creek (Anahim Peak), Central Coast, McKenzie Pass, and the Ilgachuz Mountains, within the Coastal Range of central British Columbia, and reaching as far south as the Newberry Craters in Oregon by the Late Period (R.L. Carlson 1979:220).

From the experimental results of this investigation I feel that the microblade class of the Namu assemblage does not reflect a technological component directed toward fish or game processing in any way similar to the Hoko River fish knives as first suspected. Instead, obsidian microblades appear to represent a technology based not only around material conservation resulting from the economics of procurement, but also, and perhaps most importantly, around edge sharpness, and designed as a replaceable lithic component in a composite hafted tool. In particular, obsidian microblades are simply too fragile to perform any but the most delicate cutting tasks if the edges are to be preserved, and the conservation-conscious nature of the assemblage

suggests that this may have been a concern. Their utility in the performance of certain tasks related to craft work has been noted. Used as simple tools to perform the tasks ascribed to microflakes, bipolar flakes, and various other microliths, obsidian microblades would represent expensive, disposable, and redundant technology.

R.L. Carlson (1990b:67, see also 1983:19-20, and Figure 1:3 extreme right) suggests that microblade technology offers an alternative solution to the production of bifacial projectile points and knives. He has suggested that microblades and microblade sections may have been hafted as insets or side-blades in grooved bone and antler shafts to form composite cutting and piercing implements implying ties with the Old World Mesolithic of Northeast Asia (see also Carlson 1990b:67) and, specifically, the northeast Asian blade tradition. Interestingly, technological studies conducted on bladelet components of composite tools and projectile armatures from the Epipaleolithic of the Levant (e.g., Kukan 1978:161-9), have noted that the hafted margins of microliths are purposefully retouched as an aid to friction-based hafting. Specifically, that the increased surface area of a retouched margin serves to increase friction between the microlith and the mastic used to secure the piece within a slotted haft. In addition, the arrises on a retouched margin may aid in dispersing excess impact energy incurred during use, prolonging the life of these lithic components.

In this light, the steep backing observed on some of the Namu microblades, notably all from the Early Period, lends support to Carlson's (1983a) proposal that at least some microblades and microblade sections may have formed the lithic side-blade components of composite bone and antler cutting and piercing implements. From a design perspective (Hutchings 1991, n.d.), one might expect to find this type of technology in an environment where a lance-type of weapon may have been used to dispatch harpooned or otherwise trapped or wounded game. The diversity of microblade retouch and wear, however, combined with the presence of bifaces within the Early Period at Namu, and the hafted quartz crystal microblade from Hoko River (Croes 1987), which admittedly occurs much later, suggest that this was not the only function for microblades during the Early Period on the Northwest Coast.

17 THE EARLY PREHISTORY OF THE MID FRASER-THOMPSON RIVER AREA

Arnoud R. Stryd and Michael K. Rousseau

This chapter reviews what is known about human history and adaptation in the Mid Fraser-Thompson River drainage area of south-central British Columbia for the time span between deglaciation, ca. 12,000/11,000 BP, and the establishment of the Shuswap Horizon ca. 3500 BP.[1] It summarizes the available archaeological evidence, and offers a revised culture-historical model for this period.

The southern interior of British Columbia can be divided into a number of archaeological regions based on modern environmental characteristics and what appear to be distinctive, albeit related, archaeological sequences (e.g., Fladmark 1982a:Figure 8, Stryd 1973:Figure 5, Richards and Rousseau 1987:Figure 4). This chapter is concerned with three of these regions (Figure 1): (1) the Mid Fraser region, consisting of the Fraser River drainage from south of Lytton to Big Bar; (2) the Thompson River region, consisting of the Thompson River drainage between Lytton and Kamloops; and (3) the Thompson-Shuswap region, consisting of the drainage of the South Thompson River, Shuswap Lake, and the North Thompson River as far north as about Clearwater.

PERIODS IN MID FRASER-THOMPSON RIVER AREA PREHISTORY

During his pioneering archaeological research in the Mid Fraser region, David Sanger divided the archaeological past into four periods: a Late Period, dating from 2000 BP to the historic period ca. 150 BP; an Upper Middle Period, from 3500 to 2000 BP; a Lower Middle Period, from 5000 to 3500 BP; and an Early Period, from 7000 to 5000 BP (Sanger

---

[1] All dates expressed in radiocarbon years BP.

1970:106). The intent of defining these periods was to "facilitate the ... discussion of cultural events through time," and to offer "a means of shorthand reference to segments of time" (Sanger 1970:106).

Archaeological periods, while primarily segments of time, should also, whenever possible, reflect archaeological content. In such instances, each period represents a particular segment of time and a particular configuration of archaeological traits. Sanger's four-period scheme, established primarily as a descriptive device in the mid 1960s, does not reflect, as accurately as it could, current knowledge about the content of the archaeological record for the Mid Fraser-Thompson River area. In order to better reflect what is presently known about changes in archaeological content, the following three-period scheme is used in this chapter: Early Period, ca. 11,000 to 7000 BP; Middle Period, ca. 7000 to 3500 BP; and Late Period, ca. 3500 to 200 BP. The evidence on which this periodization is based is discussed below.

SANGER'S CULTURE-HISTORICAL MODEL

The initial culture-historical model for the Mid Fraser-Thompson River area developed by David Sanger in the 1960s was based primarily on excavations at the Lochnore-Nesikep locality on the Fraser River between Lillooet and Lytton. This model was constructed around two major archaeological units: the Lochnore complex and Nesikep Tradition. The Lochnore complex was thought to represent a poorly understood northward migration of people from the Columbia Plateau between 7000 and 9000 years ago, and was manifested archaeologically by leaf-shaped bipoints, macroblades, edge-battered

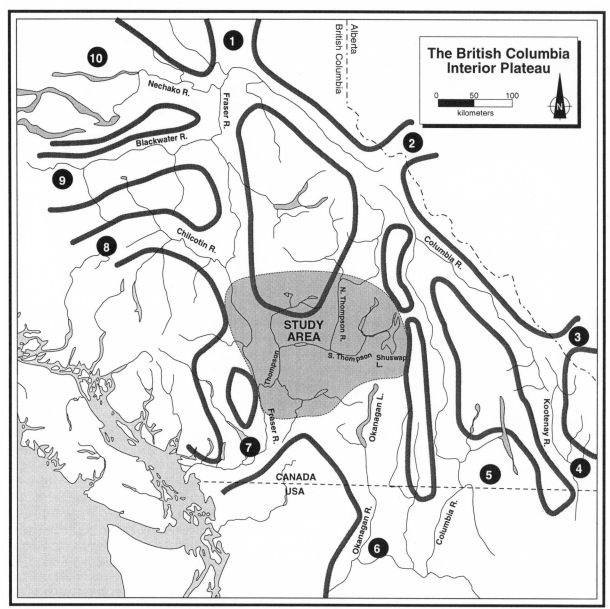

Figure 1. Location of the study area and possible major early travel corridors leading into the Mid Fraser-Thompson River drainage area. Route (1) from the Peace River District via the upper Fraser River; (2) from the Northern Plains via the Yellowhead Pass; (3) from the Plains via Kickinghorse and Sinclair Passes; (4) from the Plains via Crowsnest Pass and the East Kootenays along the upper Columbia River; (5) from the Columbia Plateau via the Arrow Lakes region; (6) from the Columbia Plateau via the Okanagan and Similkameen Valleys; (7) from the south coast via the Fraser River; (8) from the central coast via the Chilcotin River; (9) from the central coast via the Blackwater River; and (10) from the central coast via the Nechacko River.

cobbles, cobble choppers, concave-ended unifaces, and an absence of microblades (Sanger 1969:192). Sanger (1969:192) considered the Lochnore complex to be a "late regional expression" of Borden's (1969) Protowestern Tradition.

According to Sanger (1969:194-7), the Nesikep Tradition was a 7000-year long cultural continuum representing an early population movement from the central interior of British Columbia which ended with the ethnographic Interior Salish of the south central interior. This tradition is manifested archaeologically by a continuity in projectile point styles, the use of microblades until about the time of Christ, a "related chipping technique," and a consistent preference for the use of dark grey to black vitreous basalt (Sanger 1969:194-6). Around 3500 BP, the semi-subterranean pithouse came into use (Sanger 1969: 196). With regards to subsistence, Sanger states (1969:196) that "there is nothing ... to suggest that throughout the entire span of the Nesikep Tradition the subsistence pattern noted in early historic times (1800) did not prevail."

Sanger's model was used, with minor changes, throughout the 1970s. In the 1980s, however, there was a reassessment of his model. Several researchers questioned both the validity of the Nesikep Tradition and the age and duration of the Lochnore complex (Carlson 1983a, Fladmark 1982: 127-8, Richards and Rousseau 1987:11, Arcas Associates 1986), and some of Sanger's conclusions regarding cultural continuity and prehistoric subsistence have been challenged (Arcas Associates 1985:21, Fladmark 1982; Richards and Rousseau 1987). This reassessment, along with new field work near Ashcroft (Arcas Associates 1985, Rousseau 1991, Rousseau et al. 1991a), near Lillooet (Hayden et al. 1986, 1987), in the Highland Valley (Arcas Associates 1986), and near Monte Creek (Wilson 1991, Wilson et al. 1992), have led to

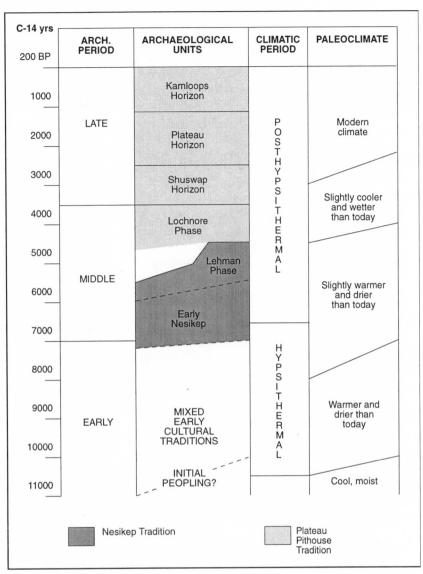

Figure 2. Revised archaeological sequence for the Mid Fraser-Thompson river drainage area.

the development of a revised archaeological sequence – and a revised culture-historical model – for the Mid Fraser-Thompson River area (Figure 2). This model, and the evidence on which it is based, is discussed below. The discussion excludes developments in the Late Period; these have already been presented in Richards and Rousseau (1987).

A REVISED CULTURE-HISTORICAL MODEL

In the revised culture-historical model, Sanger's Nesikep Tradition and Lochnore complex and Richards and Rousseau's (1987) Plateau Pithouse Tradition, are redefined. A new archaeological unit, the Lehman Phase, is introduced. In addition, evidence for the presence of several widespread, early, tradi-

tions is noted. The following discussion is organized by archaeological period, starting with the Early Period. Within each period, the archaeological evidence is presented by archaeological unit, preceded by a review of environmental conditions.

The Early Period

The Early Period, as used here, covers the time span from deglaciation, ca. 12,000/11,000 BP, to the end of the Hypsithermal climatic period, ca. 7000 BP (Hebda 1982). The initial peopling of the Mid Fraser-Thompson River drainage probably began ca. 11,000/10,000 BP, shortly after deglaciation and establishment of flora and fauna (see below). Dated archaeological remains are limited to three sites occupied in the latter half of this period (see below).

Information for the initial part of this period is based entirely on surface finds in museum and private collections.

Diagnostic artifact types in surface collections from the area display attributes that suggest affiliation with several widespread, early, technological traditions. Several distinctive bifacial knives and/or projectile points that closely resemble those recovered from investigated Plano Tradition, Early Coast Microblade Complex, Early Stemmed Point Tradition, Old Cordilleran Tradition, and Western Fluted Point Tradition components in adjacent culture areas. While there are no excavated occupation sites on the Canadian Plateau that can be firmly related to any of these technological traditions, there is little reason to doubt their presence. For presentation purposes, the evidence is summarized using these well-known early tradition monikers.

Environmental Conditions

Paleoenvironmental studies indicate that vast parts of the Mid Fraser-Thompson River area were deglaciated and supporting pioneering grasslands by at least 11,500 BP (Clague 1981, Hebda 1982, 1983, Mathewes 1984, Mathewes and Rouse 1975). Between ca. 11,500 and 10,500 BP, communities of pine, alder, and poplar occupied valley sides and upland areas, whereas sagebrush and grasses occupied well-drained valley-bottom areas, indicating a cool and moist environment (Hebda 1982, 1983). Around 10,500 BP, a notable decrease in pine species and an increase in Douglas-fir, grasses, and sages, indicated the beginning of a major period of warmer and drier climatic conditions (Mathewes 1984) known as the Hypsithermal (Hebda 1982) or "early Holocene xerothermic interval" (Mathewes and Heusser 1981, Mathewes 1984). Characterized by increased summer temperatures and drought (Mathewes and King 1989), this warm and dry episode persisted until ca. 7000-6500 BP, climaxing between ca. 10,000 and 8000 BP (Hebda 1982). These grassland habitats may have supported a mixture of late Pleistocene and early Holocene fauna suitable for human predation. Examples of such fauna, but not in archaeological contexts, include an extinct bison (Bison occidentalis) skull in a late Pleistocene glacial lake delta in the North Okanagan region (Fulton 1971:199), and a mixture of smashed moose and mountain sheep remains from Lochore Creek in the Mid Fraser region radiocarbon dated to 11,285 ±1000 BP (Ryder 1978:63, Clague 1980, Table 4, Ryder, personal communication, 1992).

Western Fluted Point Tradition

Although components of the Western Fluted Point Tradition have been uncovered north and south of the study area at Charlie Lake Cave in north-central British Columbia (Fladmark et al. 1988; Fladmark, this volume; Driver, this volume), and on the Columbia Plateau near the city of Wenatchee (Mehringer 1988), no conclusive evidence for the presence of this tradition has yet been found in the Mid Fraser-Thompson River drainage. The most convincing evidence is a point in a surface collection from Shuswap Lake (Figure 3). It is a large, complete, lanceolate, chalcedony biface exhibiting a classic Clovis point outline, and it bears multiple basal thinning flake scars on both faces similar to those observed on Western Fluted Point variants dated to ca. 10,500 BP (Carlson 1991c, Fladmark 1981, Fladmark et al. 1988, Gryba 1985, Driver, this volume). However, basal margin edge grinding, a typical trait, is absent.

Intermontane Stemmed Point Tradition

Stemmed points dominated regional point assemblages at two different times. The first dates to the early Middle Period, and is called the Intermontane Stemmed Point Tradition (Chapter 1, this volume). The second dates to the Shuswap Horizon of the Late Period (Richards and Rousseau 1987:25-7).

Some researchers (e.g., Bryan 1980, Choquette 1987b) have hypothesized that the Intermontane Stemmed Point Tradition may predate the Fluted Point Tradition, originating in the Great Basin ca. 14,000 BP, and subsequently spreading northward as the ice sheets decayed. If so, this may be culturally related to the Early Ushki culture of eastern Russia (Dikov 1979, 1988), having entered North American ca. 15,000 to 13,5000 BP (Carlson 1983a:82). On the other hand, Musil (1988) and Carlson (1991c:86) have argued that stemming is a logical and probable technological derivative of fluted point technology. Radiocarbon dates from the Columbia Plateau and Great Basin indicate an age of between ca. 10,500 and 8000 BP for the Early Stemmed Point Tradition, supporting the latter model.

Evidence for the Intermontane Stemmed Point tradition in British Columbia is currently sparse. A number of bifaces resembling specimens from the Great Basin (Bryan 1980) and Columbia Plateau (Leonhardy and Rice 1970, Rice 1972, Moody 1978, Carlson 1983a) have been found in surface collections from the Mid Fraser-Thompson River area (Figure 4), and in the nearby Kootenay area (Cho-

Figure 3. A large biface found on Shuswap Lake provisionally assigned to the western Fluted Point Tradition.

quette 1987a, and this volume). The age of the local surface finds are not known, but the use of stemmed points in the study area was probably introduced ca. 10,500/10,000 BP from the Columbia Plateau to the south.

Plano Tradition

Numerous well-made, lanceolate, stemmed, and foliate projectile points found in surface collections throughout the study area exhibit striking stylistic and technological similarities to various point forms from the Plano Tradition of the Northwest Plains (Wormington 1964, Wormington and Forbis 1965, Frison 1978, 1983). Specifically, similarities with Alberta, Scottsbluff, Agate Basin, Eden, Lusk, and Hell Gap forms are present (Figure 5).

Sanger (1970:119) noted that the Clinton Museum has a "Scottsbluff-like" point in its collections, whereas Grabert (1974:67) reported that Scottsbluff/Eden-like points have been found in low frequencies

in the Shuswap Lakes area by local collectors. Grabert speculated that there was a northward extension of early populations across the Columbia Plateau shortly after the retreat of glacial ice, and that these people were probably influenced by Plains cultures, including, presumably, Plano biface technology (Grabert 1974).

Early Coast Microblade Complex

In the Mid Fraser-Thompson River area, microblades occur primarily in Middle Period contexts (see below). However, at least two Early Period sites have yielded small assemblages containing microblades: the Pre-Mazama component at the Landels site near Ashcroft (Rousseau et al. 1991a, Rousseau 1991) and the unexcavated Drynoch Slide site on the Thompson River near Spences Bridge (Sanger 1967). Radiocarbon dates place these assemblages at ca. 8400 and 7500 BP respectively (see below). Presumably there is historical continuity between microblade use in the Early and Middle Periods.

Sanger (1968a) placed all microblade assemblages from the southern interior into a technological tradition which he called the Plateau Microblade tradition. The age, archaeological affiliation, contexts, and culture-historical significance of microblade use in interior British Columbia have been the subject of considerable discussion since Sanger's pioneering work (e.g., Fladmark 1982:128-9, Carlson 1983a, 1983b, Ludowoicz 1983, Richards and Rousseau 1987:57-8, Campbell 1985, Arcas Associates 1986:153-6), but are still only poorly known.

Early Period microblade technology probably derived from the north or northern coast where microblades occur relatively early. Microblades have been reported for Alaska at ca. 11,000 BP (Carlson 1983b:20) and the northern Northwest Coast at ca. 10,000/9000 BP (Ackerman et al. 1979, Fladmark 1979b). To the south, on the Columbia Plateau, microblades occur at ca. 7000 BP (Campbell 1985:299), and in the Fraser Canyon on the southern coast they appear ca. 3000 BP (Eldridge 1981). Early microblade assemblages on the Northwest Coast have been termed the "Early Coast Microblade Complex" (Fladmark 1982), the "Microblade Tradition" (Carlson 1983b), and the "Early Boreal Tradition" (Borden 1969).

As Carlson (1983b:20) and others have noted, there is a north to south cline in the commencement date for microblade technology from Alaska to the coast of British Columbia north of Vancouver Island. This cline appears to continue inland through the southern interior of British Columbia into the Co-

Figure 4. Selected bifaces provisionally assigned to the Intermontane Stemmed Point Tradition: specimen (a) Lillooet locality; (b) Cache Creek locality; (c) EdRa 1; (d) Chase locality; (e) EeQw 6; (f) Bridge Lake; (g) Shuswap Lake.

Figure 5. Selected bifaces provisionally assigned to the Plano Tradition: specimen (a) Lytton locality; (b) Pavilion locality; (c-f) Chase locality; (g) EdRk 8.

lumbia Plateau. Fladmark (1982:128) sees the Plateau Microblade Tradition as being related to the Early Coast Microblade Complex, having been introduced from the coastal regions to the west rather than from the Yukon before ca. 7000 BP. Since there is no evidence for early microblades on the south coast of British Columbia, Fladmark presumably meant that they were introduced from the central coast via the Skeena River and Chilcotin region (Figure 1).

Old Cordilleran Tradition

The Old Cordilleran Tradition is an early cultural manifestation found in the Columbia Plateau and along the southern and central Northwest Coast

(Carlson 1983b; Fladmark 1982). It has been called the Old Cordilleran Culture (Butler 1961, 1965) or Pattern (Matson 1976, Fladmark 1982), the Protowestern Tradition (Borden 1969, 1975), and the Pebble Tool Tradition (Carlson 1983a, 1983b, Chapter 1 this volume). Its origins are unclear at present, and both southern and Asiatic derivations are possible (Carlson 1983b). Several regional expressions of the Old Cordilleran have been defined, including the Cascade Phase of the Lower Snake River region (Leonhardy and Rice 1970, Bense 1972), the Milliken and Mazama Phases of the Lower Fraser Canyon (Borden 1975), and the provisional Indian Dan and Okanagan Phases of the Okanagan Valley (Grabert 1974).

Sanger (1969) thinks that the Lochnore Complex of the Mid Fraser-Thompson River drainage is a late manifestation of the Old Cordilleran, and this argument also has been made by others (e.g., Fladmark 1982:127, Eldridge 1974, Arcas Associates 1985:20-1). More recently, it has been suggested (Arcas Associates 1986) that the Lochnore Complex, called the Lochnore Phase in this report, is a Middle Period archaeological manifestation derived from the Old Cordilleran of coastal British Columbia, rather than from either an Early Period Old Cordilleran regional variant or a Middle Period continuation of such an Early Period variant (see discussion under Middle Period).

There is at present no conclusive evidence for an Early Period Old Cordilleran Tradition in the Mid Fraser-Thompson River area. The main problem in identifying potential Early Period Old Cordilleran sites in this area is that the primary diagnostic indicators – large and medium-sized foliate bifaces and pebble choppers/cores – persist in small numbers throughout the entire archaeological sequence. Some of the foliate bifaces and pebble choppers/cores present in surface collections from throughout the study area (Figure 6) may belong to an early Old Cordilleran Tradition, but no such dated sites have yet been identified.

Investigated Early Period Sites
Landels Site

The Landels site (EdRi 11) is located ca. 13 km southwest of Ashcroft in the Oregon Jack Creek Valley of the Thompson River region (Figure 7). Excavations revealed the presence of an intact component lying beneath, and intermixed with, Mazama tephra (Figure 8) (Rousseau et al. 1991a, Rousseau 1991). Seventeen tools were secured from this Pre-Mazama component, including thirteen nearly complete or fragmented microblades, two utilized flakes, an unformed uniface, and a core fragment. Fragmented deer bone was recovered, as was a bone fragment from a muskrat-sized rodent.

The vertical distribution of cultural materials in the Pre-Mazama component indicates two brief occupation episodes. The most recent occupation, in the bottom of the tephra layer (Figure 8), is marked by a sparse scattering of lithic waste flakes, a few microblades, fragmented faunal remains, and a right distal deer humerus with cut marks. The deer humerus provided a radiocarbon date of ca. 7700 BP. Remains from an older occupation were encountered 10 to 25 cm below the tephra. These include most of the microblades in the Pre-Mazama component as well as scattered deer bone fragments radiocarbon dated to ca. 8400 BP.

While the sample of cultural materials recovered from the Pre-Mazama component is small, it is at present the earliest excavated and dated component on the Canadian Plateau. It also provides the earliest direct evidence for use of microblade technology in this area. Lithic and faunal remains reflect intensive deer hunting and processing, which is consistent with data from younger components at the site. The cultural affiliation of the Pre-Mazama component is unknown. It may relate to the Early Coast Microblade Tradition, or perhaps the beginning of the Nesikep Tradition.

Gore Creek Site

A well-studied Early Period site in the area is the Gore Creek "burial" (EeQw 48) found near the community of Pritchard in the South Thompson River Valley (Figure 7) (Cybulski et al. 1981). It is currently the earliest conclusive evidence for human occupation of the study area. The burial consists of the post-cranial remains of a young adult male accidentally killed in a mud slide. No artifacts or other cultural remains were associated with the skeleton. Recovered from beneath Mazama tephra (Figure 9), the skeleton yielded a radiocarbon date of 8250 ±115 BP (Cybulski et al. 1981).

The skeleton exhibits a tall, lineal body build with strong lower limb development, a form typical of an inland hunting adaptation (Cybulski et al. 1981). A larger sample of human remains from this period is necessary before it can be determined if this individual is typical of the local population at that time. A carbon isotope value of -19.4 per mil was initially thought to indicate that this individual relied exclusively on protein derived from terrestrial sources (Chisholm and Nelson 1983); however, a subsequent re-evaluation of the data suggests that about 8 ±10 per cent of his dietary protein may have come from marine fish (i.e., salmon and steelhead) (Chisholm 1986).

If one assumes that the Gore Creek individual's marine protein intake was typical for an adult prior to ca. 8000 BP, then human adaptation in the study area appears to have been characterized by a primarily hunting subsistence that was likely supplemented to some degree by floral resources. The Gore Creek individual suggests that salmon was of minor dietary importance to the early occupants of the Thompson River area.

Drynoch Slide Site

The Drynoch Slide site (EcRi 1) is located south of Spences Bridge in the Thompson River Valley (Fig-

Figure 6. Selected large foliate bifaces resembling those found in Old Cordilleran Tradition components: specimens (a-c) Lytton locality; (d-e) Dutch Lake near Clearwater.

ure 7). A detailed account of the geological slide is presented in Anderton (1965). The eastern portion of the site contains an artifact-bearing stratum of aeolian sand overlain with tons of slide deposits (Figures 10 and 11). Slumpage of the southern face of the slide has exposed the site. Charcoal associated with the cultural materials produced a radiocarbon date of 7530 ±270 BP (Sanger 1967). A more recent date of 3175 ±150 BP comes from the river bank and is not associated with the material beneath the tephra. Cultural materials collected over the last two decades from the sand beneath the tephra include: a medium-sized, asymmetrical, resharpened, basalt point or knife (Figure 12); three microblades (Apland personal communication 1986, Hobler personal communication 1987, Sanger 1970, Figure 28g); unifacial and unretouched flake tools; and the remains of elk, deer, and fish. The fish may be salmon (Sanger personal communication 1985), but no definite identification has been made yet. The faunal

remains from the site indicate a reliance on large ungulates, and also that river fishing, presumably for salmon, was established on at least a relatively small scale by at least 7500 BP along this part of the Thompson River. The Drynoch Slide site is of unknown archaeological affiliation. The presence of microblades and the use of relatively fine-grained basalt for tools may indicate that this site should be assigned to the early Nesikep Tradition, but such an assignment would, in our opinion, be premature.

The Middle Period

The Middle Period, as used here, covers the time span from the commencement of the Nesikep Tradition at end of the Hypsithermal climatic period, ca. 7000 BP, to the establishment of the Shuswap horizon, ca. 3500 BP. Two cultural traditions, the Nesikep Tradition and the Plateau Pithouse Tradition, have been previously defined for this period and are revised slightly in this chapter.

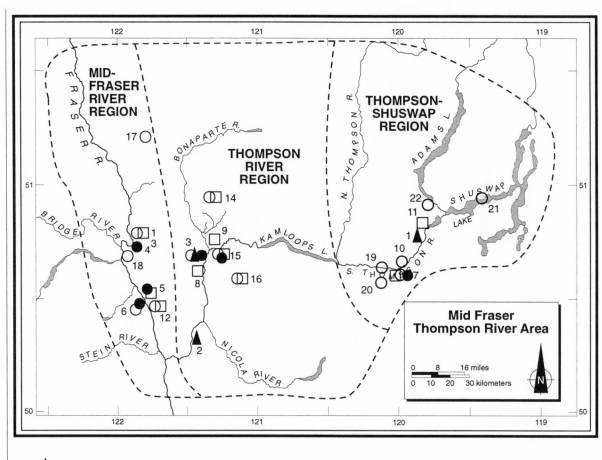

▲ Early Prehistoric Period Components
● Early Nesikep Components
□ Lehman Phase Components
○ Lochnore Phase Components

Figure 7. Investigated sites predating ca. 3500 BP: (1) Gore Creek (EeQw 48); (2) Dry-noch Slide (EcRi 1); (3) Landels (EdRi 11); (4) Fountain (EeRl 19); (5) Lehman (EdRk 8); (6) Nesikep Creek (EdRk 4); (7) EdQx 42; (8) Oregon Jack Creek (EdRi 6); (9) Cache Creek (EeRh 3); (10) Moulton Creek (EeQx 5); (11) Green Acres (EeQw 6); (12) Loch-nore (EdRk 7); (13) Keatley Creek (EeRl 7); (14) Hihium Lake (EgRg 4); (15) Rattle-snake Hill (EeRh 61); (16) EcRg 1, EcRg 2, EcRg 4, and EdRg 2; (17) EiRm 7; (18) Terrace (EeRl 171); (19) EdQx 41; (20) Baker (EdQx 43); (21) EfQt 1; and; (22) EfQw 2.

Environmental Conditions

The Middle Period is associated with a climatic trend toward progressively cooler and wetter conditions following the Hypsithermal maximum. Throughout much of the Middle Period, the Mid Fraser-Thompson River area was probably characterized by continuous mesic grasslands at low and mid elevations, with sagebrush less abundant than in the preceding xeric grasslands of the Hypsithermal (Hebda 1982). Douglas fir and ponderosa pine became established as major forest species, and forests descended to elevations perhaps 100 m or so above today's grassland/forest transition (Hebda 1983:

251). The fauna of the mesic grasslands was probably dominated by open, arid grassland species such as elk, antelope(?), and bighorn sheep (Hebda 1983:251). The effect of reduced water levels on local fish populations and salmon runs is not known, but the Thompson River may have supported greater numbers of freshwater mollusca. By ca. 4500 BP, Douglas fir and ponderosa pine had expanded to below today's grassland/forest transition, and a modern fauna, with deer replacing elk as the dominant ungulate, would have existed in the study area (Hebda 1982, 1983).

Figure 8. A post-excavation view of the south walls of the main excavation block at the Landels site (EdRi 11) near Ashcroft in the Thompson River Valley. Note thick Mazama tephra layer near the bottom of the units.

Nesikep Tradition (ca. 7000 to 4500 BP)

The Nesikep Tradition was originally defined by Sanger (1969:194-7) as a 7000-year long cultural continuum representing an early population movement from the central interior of British Columbia, and ending with the ethnographic Interior Salish of the south central interior. Concerns about various aspects of this tradition have been expressed by several researchers (see above), and in this chapter the Nesikep Tradition is redefined.

The oldest unequivocal Nesikep Tradition assemblage, Zone II at the Lehman site (EdRk 8), is dated at 6650 ±110 BP (Table 2), and is the basis for a commencement date of ca. 7000 BP for this tradition. However, the commencement date may be older if the Early Period Drynoch Slide site or the Pre-Mazama component at the Landels site are eventually assigned to the Nesikep Tradition.

In our view, the Nesikep Tradition represents an adaptive pattern that emerged from the melding of peoples and cultures belonging to a number of early cultural traditions in response to increasing cooler and wetter environmental conditions during the terminal Hypsithermal and early Post-Hypsithermal. In the Nesikep Tradition, people subsisted primarily on deer and elk, supplemented by rabbits, rodents, freshwater mollusca (mostly during the latter part), salmon, freshwater fish, small birds, and plant resources (Sanger 1969:196, 1970, Stryd 1972, Arcas Associates 1985:92-4). There is no evidence for the intensive utilization of anadromous salmon during this tradition (Arcas Associates 1985:93), and Sanger's assertion (1969:196) that the basic ethnographic subsistence pattern has a 7000-year antiquity is, in our opinion, not supportable.

There is evidence for at least technological and stylistic artifact change within the Nesikep Tradition during its ca. 2500 year existence. It is anticipated that this tradition will eventually be divided into a number of named archaeological phases which will reflect these changes and, possibly, changes in settlement and subsistence as well. At present, only one phase – the Lehman Phase, comprising the later part of the Nesikep Tradition and dated to ca. 6000 to 4500 BP – has been defined. The interval prior to the Lehman Phase is simply referred to at this time as the early Nesikep Tradition.

Early Nesikep Tradition

Excavated early Nesikep Tradition sites are restricted to two sites in the Lochnore-Nesikep locality, two sites near Ashcroft, one site near Lillooet, and one

Figure 9. The Gore Creek "burial" site near Pritchard in the South Thompson River Valley, looking west. The lower arrow indicates Mazama tephra ca. 6800 BP, and the upper arrow indicates Mount St. Helens "Y" tephra ca. 3200 BP. The human remains were recovered from below the Mazama tephra.

1985:80-1), is now considered to be an early Nesikep component. Also near Ashcroft, the Landels site (EdRi 11) contains a sparse occupation in the bottom of Stratum II that may belong to the early Nesikep (Rousseau et al. 1991a:103, Rousseau 1991:7). Zone I at EdQx 42 near Monte Creek appears to be a mixed early Nesikep and Lehman Phase component although it was not identified as such by the excavator (Wilson 1991). The basal component (Component 3) at the Fountain site (EeRl 19) near Lillooet (Stryd 1972) is also assigned to the early Nesikep (Arcas Associates 1985:85). Four radiocarbon dates are presently available for the early Nesikep (Table 2). Early Nesikep projectile points identified in surface collections throughout the area (Figure 14) (e.g., Sanger 1970:121, Figure 43), indicate that remains of this tradition are relatively common.

Based on the above excavations, the following traits are characteristic of the early Nesikep Tradition: well-made, lanceolate, corner-notched, and barbed projectile points (see below) which, according to Sanger (1970:119), may be "distantly related technologically to the projectile points of the Plano tradition"; a high incidence of formed unifaces; a microblade technology using wedge-shaped microblade cores (Sanger's Plateau Microblade Tradition); antler wedges; ground rodent incisors; bone points and needles; red ochre; and small oval scrapers (formed unifaces), some with bilateral side notches (Arcas Associates 1985, Sanger 1970, Stryd 1972). Fauna from these components include large quantities of deer remains, as well as elk, salmon, steelhead trout, bird, and freshwater mollusca (Arcas Associates 1985, Sanger 1970, Stryd 1972).

Early Nesikep Tradition projectile points appear to represent variations on a basic formal theme. Most are consistently well-made, relatively thin, lanceolate in outline, and have straight or recurved lateral margins and thin lenticular cross-sections. An occasional point has serrated blade margins (Figure 14m, y). Diagnostic attributes include: (1) V-shaped corner notching (and occasionally basal notching) forming pronounced to slight lateral barbs and parallel to slightly expanding basal-lateral margins; (2) straight or convex basal margins; and (3) slight to pronounced edge grinding along both the basal-lat-

site near Monte Creek (Table 1). The basal component (Zone VII) of the Nesikep Creek site (EdRk 4) (Figure 13) yielded a cultural assemblage that Sanger (1970:47) maintains is at least 7000 years old, although it yielded a radiocarbon date of 5635 ±190 BP (Table 2). Zone II at the Lehman site (EdRk 8) contains both early Nesikep and Lehman Phase material, but reports of Lochnore Phase projectile points (Arcas Associates 1985, Table 15) are in error. Zone IV at the Rattlesnake Hill site (EeRh 61) near Ashcroft, which was initially (but provisionally) assigned to the Lehman Phase (Arcas Associates

Figure 10. Drynoch slide in the Thompson River valley. Arrow indicates deeply buried archaeological deposits to ca. 7500 BP (looking north).

eral and basal margins. Intentional basal thinning by removal of multiple, elongate, pressure flakes from both faces is also quite common (e.g., Figure 14a, r, y).

It appears that early Nesikep Tradition projectile points were frequently resharpened. The large, well-barbed points with recurved lateral blades (e.g., Figure 14b) probably represent the initial unmodified form of these points, with the shorter points with small barbs and shoulders (e.g., Figure 14l) resulting from blade margins having been resharpened.

Projectile points similar to early Nesikep forms have not been noted in any neighbouring culture areas. As a result, the early Nesikep Tradition is viewed as a cultural manifestation that probably developed in the study area out of a mix of Early Period traditions. It should also be pointed out that some early Nesikep corner-notched points resemble some point forms found in the much later Plateau Horizon (ca. 2400 to 1200 BP) (Richards and Rousseau 1987:35). However, the latter can usually be distinguished on the basis of differences in size, form, raw material, notching, and absence of basal edge grinding.

Lehman Phase

The Lehman Phase was initially defined as a result of excavations at the Rattlesnake Hill site near Ash-croft (Arcas Associates 1985) and in the Highland Valley (Arcas Associates 1986). A number of Lehman Phase components have been excavated so far in the Mid Fraser-Thompson River area (Table 1). Major components occur at three sites: Lehman (EdRk 8), Zone II (Sanger 1970; Arcas Associates 1985:84-6); Rattlesnake Hill (EeRh 61), Zones IIB and III (Arcas Associates 1985); and Oregon Jack Creek (EdRi 6) (Rousseau and Richards 1987).

The dates for this phase are preliminary. Based on five accepted radiocarbon dates (Table 2) and other considerations, we propose a commencement date of ca. 6000 BP and a termination date of ca. 4500 BP for this phase.

The following traits, among others, are typical of this phase: thin, pentagonal projectile points with obliquely-oriented, V-shaped corner or side notches known as Lehman obliquely-notched points (Figure 15a-r); lanceolate knives with straight cortex-covered bases; elliptical (or leaf-shaped) knives with prominent striking platforms at their bases; tabular circular scrapers at least 5 mm thick with continuous unifacial marginal retouch (Figure 15s, t); "horseshoe-shaped" convex endscrapers; multi-direction flake cores with medium to large flake scars; large but often thin direct percussion flakes; unifacially retouched flakes with cortex or retouch backing; a high incidence of fine- and medium-grained

Figure 11. Closeup view of the Drynoch Slide site geologic profile. Arrow indicates location of Mazama tephra. Cultural materials have been secured from the aeolian stratum below the tephra (looking northwest).

Figure 12. Basalt biface collected from the early component at the Drynoch Slide site.

Figure 13. The Nesikep Creek site (EdRk 4) (indicated by arrow) in the mid-Fraser River region (looking west).

basalts; and an apparent lack of microblade technology (Arcas Associates 1985, Figures 19 to 22). Many of the points and lanceolate knives exhibit striking platforms at their distal ends.

Deer and elk were hunted during the Lehman Phase. Freshwater mollusca were collected in the Thompson (and possibly South Thompson) Valley, sometimes in large numbers. Turtle remains from the mixed Zone 1 assemblage at EdQx 42 in the South Thompson Valley may indicate turtle consumption. The main rivers were fished for salmon (species unknown) as well as an unidentified fish species. There is, however, no evidence for an intense utilization of salmon at this time. The mid elevation location of EgRg 4 at Hihium Lake (Gehr 1976) and unexcavated EcRg 2 in the Highland Valley suggest that upland lake fishing may have been practised at this time, although these shoreline sites could have been occupied for other purposes such as waterfowling and the pursuit of beaver. No storage pits or evidence for plant collecting has yet been reported, but the presence of fire-altered rock at several sites suggests the practise of food boiling, or the use of underground ovens during this phase.

There is no evidence for use of the semi-subterranean winter pithouse during this phase. Presum-ably people were relatively nomadic year round, using only portable shelters.

No human remains have yet been found in association with Lehman Phase artifacts. Internment in mounds may have been practised, as Lehman obliquely-notched points were collected from a now destroyed burial mound (EbRj 22) near Lytton . Two extended burials from Clinton dated to 4950 ±170 BP may belong to the Lehman Phase, but the relatively high proportion of salmon in the diet of these individuals (37 ±10 per cent and 38 ±10 per cent [Chisholm 1986:147]) indicates that they probably should be assigned to the more riverine-oriented Lochnore Phase (see below).

The Lehman Phase appears, on the basis of continuity in projectile point, scraper, and knife styles, and continuity in certain technological traits such as heavy point base grinding, to represent a development out of the early Nesikep Tradition cultures of the area (see Discussion below).

Lochnore Phase

The Lochnore Phase was defined as a result of excavations in the Highland Valley east of Ashcroft (Arcas Associates 1986). This phase includes those assemblages formerly attributed to the Lochnore

Figure 14. Selected early Nesikep Tradition projectile points: specimen (a) Lytton locality; (b-e) EdRk 4; (f-m) EdRk 8; (n-p) EeRl 19; (q) EfRl 16; (r) EfRl 26; (s) EfRl 3; (t-u) Dutch Lake locality; Clearwater; (v) Chase locality; (w) EeQw 3; (x) EdRa 7; (y) EfQw 1.

complex as originally defined by Sanger (see above). At least fifteen sites with Lochnore Phase components have been excavated (Table 1), and Lochnore Phase artifacts have been found in surface collections throughout the area (e.g., at EfRk 1, EfRl 3, and EfRl 5 [Stryd and Hills 1972:198, Figure 3a and 3p]). Major components are: Lochnore Creek (EdRk 7), Zone III (Sanger 1970); Terrace (EeRl 171), Component 2 (Richards 1978); Rattlesnake Hill (EeRh 61), Zone IIA (Arcas Associates 1985); Valley Mine (EcRg 1), Component II (Arcas Associates 1986); Landels (EdRi 11), Stratum II (Rousseau et al. 1991a, Rousseau 1991); Moulton Creek (EdQx 5), below tephra (Eldridge 1974); and Baker (EdQx 43), Zone 3 (Wilson et al. 1992).

The dating of this phase is preliminary. Based on a number of radiocarbon dates and other considerations, we propose a commencement date of 5500 BP and a termination date of 3500 BP (Table 2).

The following traits, among others, are found in this phase: leaf-shaped to lanceolate, unbarbed projectile points with wide side notches, heavy basal grinding, and pointed or convex bases, named the Lochnore side-notched point (Figure 16a-c, f-h); leaf-shaped to lanceolate points made predominantly on end-struck flakes (Figure 17), often bipointed, some with plano-convex cross-sections; oval bifaces; round to oval scrapers on relatively thin flakes with almost continuous retouch (Figure 16j, k); concave-edged endscrapers on silicas; possibly a macroblade technology; microblade technology at some sites; end and/or side scrapers on large blade-like flakes; unifacially-backed flake scrapers; crescentic flake scrapers (Sanger 1970,Figure 33s, x); tear-shaped (elliptical) bifaces, with plano-convex cross-sections but no edge grinding (Sanger 1970, Figure 31a-c); flake scrapers with an obliquely-oriented straight scraping edge; edge-battered cobbles; unifacial cobble choppers; red and yellow ochre; notched pebbles, possibly used as net sinkers (Figure 16d, e); a chipping technique which results in sinuous and, at times, almost denticulate artifact edges; predominant use of non-vitreous basalts for artifact manufacture; possibly elliptical (or leaf-shaped) knives with a prominent striking platform, consisting of a single large flake scar, located at the base slightly offset from the long axis of the implement; and introduction and use of pithouses (at least in the latter part of the Phase).

Recent excavations at three sites (EdQx 41, 42, and 43) near Monte Creek have considerably enlarged the Lochnore Phase trait list, particularly regarding artifacts made of materials other than stone

(Wilson 1991, Wilson et al. 1992). Included are: bone splinter unipoints (fish hook barbs?), formed bone unipoints, bone splinter awls, metapodial awls, bone needles (single eyed), antler flakers, antler wedges, unilaterally barbed antler points, worked rodent incisors, drilled animal tooth pendants, eagle claw pendants (?), *Olivella* shell beads, limpet shell beads, orange ochre, abraders, and bipolar lithic technology. Both bone and antler industries are present, although the latter is not extensive. The known inventory of the Lochnore Phase will be enlarged even further if it can be demonstrated that all materials from below the volcanic tephra at the Moulton Creek site (EeQx 5) should be attributed to this Phase.

Some of the Lochnore side-notched points are relatively narrow and have parallel-sided denticulate blade margins, creating a lanceolate outline. Unlike the thin Lehman Phase projectile points, all Lochnore side-notched points are moderately to relatively thick, having lenticular (biconvex) to almost diamond cross-sections. The leaf-shaped and lanceolate points in some Lochnore Phase assemblages have the same general formal outline as unnotched Lochnore side-notched points. The proportion of notched to unnotched types appears to vary considerably. At most sites, the majority of leaf-shaped/lanceolate points are of one type or the other. In some cases, only one or two examples of the "other type" are present among the leaf-shaped/lanceolate points, and in at least one case, all the points were of one type (unnotched) in a reasonably large assemblage (EeQx 5). At EdQx 43, another site reputed to have only unnotched lanceolate points (Wilson et al. 1992), a single Lochnore side-notched point was recovered from Zone 2 and probably is associated with Zone 3 which yielded the large number of unnotched lanceolate points. The reasons for this variability in the proportion of notched to unnotched leaf-shaped/lanceolate points in assemblages of reasonable size are not known, but temporal, geographic, and functional factors may be involved. Firstly, notched leaf-shaped/lanceolate points appear to be more common in the first half of the Lochnore Phase, with unnotched forms more frequent in the latter half. Also, assemblages dominated by notched leaf-shaped/lanceolate points seem to be more frequent along the mid Fraser and Thompson Rivers than in the South Thompson area where unnotched points predominate, but this may be a reflection of sampling error. Lastly, unnotched forms may also be more frequent in sites such as EeRl 171 where the production of bifacial preforms was an important activity.

Figure 15. Selected Lehman Phase bifaces (a-r) and tabular circular scrapers (s-t): specimens (a-b) Lytton locality; (c-g) EdRk 8; (h) EeRl 1; (i) EfRl 3; (j) Hat Creek valley; (k) EeRl 7; (l-m) EgRg 4; (n-o) EeRh 61; (p) EeRf 4; (q) EjRa 1; (r) EeQw 6; (s-t) EdRk 8.

Originally, microblades were reported as being absent in this phase (Arcas Associates 1986:170). However, large numbers of microblades have recently been recovered at several Lochnore Phase assemblages: underneath Housepit 7 at the Keatley Creek site (EeRl 7) (Hayden et al. 1987); Stratum II at the Landels site (EdRi 11) (Rousseau et al. 1991a, Rousseau 1991); Zones 2 and 3 (and possibly Zone 1) at EdQx 41 (Wilson 1991); Zones 2 and 3 (and possibly part of mixed Zone 1) at EdQx 42 (Wilson 1991); and Zone 3 at the Baker site (EdQx 43) (Wilson et al. 1992). The microblade assemblages of the Late Period Quiltanton Complex in the Highland Valley (Arcas Associates 1983, 1986) may, in fact, be of Middle Period age (Arcas Associates 1986:159-60), and could possibly be of Lochnore Phase affiliation since some are mixed with Lochnore material.

Pithouses were initially reported as absent in this phase (Arcas Associates 1986:170), not appearing until the following Shuswap Horizon. However, a group of three pithouses was recently exposed at the Baker site (EdQx 43) near Monte Creek in the South Thompson Valley (Wilson et al. 1992), and Eldridge (personal communication 1993) thinks that the assemblage from below the volcanic tephra at nearby EeQx 5 could have come from a pithouse. The small EdQx 43 dwellings (maximum horizontal dimension between about 3.0 and 4.5 m) are round or oval in plan, in pits between 35 and 50 cm deep, with steep side walls and very shallow saucer-shaped floors. The dwellings are thought to have consisted of conical or square-topped mat lodges with a conical framework of light poles, possibly with a single central support, set over a shallow excavation. Grav-

Figure 16. Selected early Lochnore Phase bifaces (a-c), net sinkers (d-e), and scrapers (j-k): specimens (a-b) EdRk 8; (c-e) EeRh 61; (f- k) EeRl 7. The net sinkers are one-half actual size.

Figure 17. Selected bone, antler, and tooth artifacts (left), and foliate bifaces (right) recovered from the late Lochnore Phase (ca. 4300 BP) component at site EdQx 43 near Monte Creek.

el and cobble rims appear to have held down the bark mats. A side entrance is reported for one structure (House 1), and all three houses contained a large storage or refuse pit (see below), a large hearth off-set from the floor centre, and, in two cases, single boulder seats near the hearths. Hearths consist of fire-cracked rocks, charcoal, and other material in bowl-shaped pits measuring 75 to 110 cm, maximum horizontal dimension and between 18 and 25 cm deep. Radiocarbon dates (Table 2) place these structures between 4450 and 3950 BP in the latter part of the Lochnore Phase.

There is evidence in the Lochnore Phase for hunting (deer, elk, beaver, bear, marmot, muskrat, porcupine, rabbit, turtle); fowling (duck, Cooper's hawk, loon, hawk, goshawk, eagle, goose); fishing (salmonid, sucker, peamouth chub, northern squaw-fish, burbot, whitefish); and the collecting of fresh-water mollusca (Richards 1978, Sanger 1969:194, Eldridge 1974:49, 58, Arcas Associates 1983, 1986, Wilson 1991, Wilson et al. 1992). Domestic dogs are present at EdQx 43 (Wilson et al. 1992). No evidence for plant collecting has yet been recovered.

Evidence for food storage in this phase takes the form of several pits inside the three pithouses at the Baker site (EdQx 43) (Wilson et al. 1992). These pits are described as roughly circular, oval, and some-what rectangular in plan, and "bowl and basin-shaped" in cross-section. They attain maximum

horizontal dimensions of 127 cm and maximum depths of 45 cm. Each house contained one large pit (maximum horizontal dimension >80cm); House 3 also possessed several smaller pits. These pits contain refuse, including, in some cases, articulated salmonid vertebrae, and they have been interpreted as food storage pits (Wilson et al. 1992).

The presence of pithouses, probable food storage pits, a possible fish smoking pit, and the relative frequency of salmonid remains at EdQx 43 suggests seasonal sedentism, at least in the South Thompson Valley during the latter part of the Lochnore Phase. This was made possible by an increased reliance on anadromous salmon and the advent of fish preservation. These recent findings are consistent with the results of carbon isotope analyses indicating that marine fish contributed between 40 and 60 per cent of protein in the human diet in the subsequent Late Period (Chisholm 1986). Furthermore, isotope analysis of two possible Lochnore Phase skeletons from EiRm 7 near Clinton, dated at 4950 ±170 BP (McKendry 1983, Stijelja and Williams 1986), indicates that marine fish contributed 37 ±10 per cent and 38 ±10 per cent of the protein consumed by those individuals (Chisholm 1986:147). These data suggest that salmonid utilization was already quite intensive in the Lochnore Phase, although not as important as in the following Late Period.

Trade, or some sort of interaction with peoples on the coast, is indicated by an *Olivella* shell bead at EdQx 42 and EdQx 43 and twelve keyhole limpet beads at EdQx 43 (Wilson 1991:103, Wilson et al. 1992). The presently known distribution of Oregon obsidian suggests that Oregon obsidian at EeRl 171 near Lillooet (Stryd 1980:12) may also indicate trade or social interaction with coastal groups.

Human remains from the Lochnore Phase are limited to five teeth and a toe bone from the Baker site (EdQx 43) (Wilson et al. 1992) and, possibly, the two individuals from EiRm 7 near Clinton (McKendry 1983, Stijelja and Williams 1986). The scattered nature of the EdQx 43 remains led Wilson et al. (1992:93) to suggest that tree or elevated burial may have been in use. This typically coastal burial practice is not known either ethnographically or archaeologically in the study area. At EiRm 7, both individuals were interred in extended position without grave goods in a dry watercourse, a practise more consistent with interior burial practices, and, therefore, more likely to have been in use in the Lochnore Phase than the practice of tree or elevated burial.

There are indications of geographic variation within the Lochnore Phase, although the number of well documented and reasonably-sized assemblages remains small. These variations include a greater emphasis on cryptocrystalline raw material in the South Thompson Valley, at least at some sites (e.g., EdQx 41 and 42, EeQx 5); the exploitation of a wider range of freshwater fish species in the South Thompson River; the virtual absence of freshwater mollusc exploitation along the Mid Fraser River; and possibly greater emphasis on unnotched types of leaf-shaped/lanceolate points in the South Thompson area. The bone and antler industry may be more extensive along the South Thompson River than elsewhere, but this is uncertain, and variability exists among the South Thompson sites (Wilson 1991, Wilson et al. 1992). Pithouses may be absent in the Mid-Fraser and Thompson River Valleys, but we suspect that their apparent lack is a sampling problem.

The geographic distribution of the Lochnore Phase probably extends beyond the Mid Fraser-Thompson River area. To the north, a possible Lochnore assemblage with microblades, leaf-shaped and lanceolate points, and two possible Lochnore side-notched points in an undated context was recovered by Mitchell from Horn Lake Southwest (EkSe 1) on the western Chilcotin Plateau (Mitchell 1970). To the south, small assemblages from EbQr 1, EcQt 2 (Zone 2), and EcQv 4 in the north Okanagan (Grabert 1974) may be of Lochnore affiliation, but no other definite Lochnore assemblages have been identified. In the south Okanagan Valley of Washington State, several sites have yielded assemblages exhibiting a relatively high degree of similarity with Lochnore Phase assemblages (Grabert 1974). Recently Wilson et al. (1992) have drawn attention to similarities between the Lochnore Phase assemblage at EdQx 43 in the South Thompson Valley and Indian Dan/late Kartar Phase sites in the upper Columbia River drainage.

The apparent existence of geographic variation within the Lochnore Phase, and the possible relationship of the Lochnore Phase to sites south and north of the study area, suggests that the Lochnore Phase may eventually be redefined as an archaeological horizon spanning a large geographic area similar to the horizons of the Late Period (Richards and Rousseau 1987). A number of local or regional phases may perhaps then be defined for the "Lochnore Horizon" to reflect geographic variation.

As presently defined, the Lochnore Phase spans about 2000 years. Not unexpectedly, there are some differences in the traits of the early and later parts of the Phase. Most obvious among these is the presence of pithouses and pithouse villages, and the more intensive utilization of salmon in the later part of the phase. Furthermore, notched leaf-shaped/lanceolate points may be more common in the first half of the phase, with unnotched forms more frequent in the later half. The absence of certain traits early in the Lochnore Phase may be a sampling problem. Future research could result in a division of this phase into two sequential phases or horizons. The origin of the Lochnore Phase, and its relationship to the Lehman Phase and Plateau Pithouse Tradition are discussed below.

The Late Period

The Lochnore Phase is followed by the Shuswap Horizon, the first of three archaeological horizons that together comprise the Late Period of the Mid Fraser-Thompson River area. Continuity in artifact types, lithic technology, use of pithouses, and increased importance of salmonids indicate that the Lochnore Phase is ancestral to the Late Period. Many of the traits formerly thought to be unique to the Late Period, such as use of pithouses, existence of semi-permanent pithouse villages, and intensive salmon utilization, are now first evident in the latter part of the preceding Lochnore Phase. The differences between the later Lochnore Phase and Late Period seem to be mainly one of scale and intensity, with larger pithouse villages, more intensive salmon utilization, a greater reliance on salmon storage, a better developed salmon procurement technology, and more trade with the coast characterizing the Late Period.

Originally, the Shuswap Horizon was thought to have commenced between ca. 4000 and 3500 BP (Richards and Rousseau 1987:22). There are, however, no unequivocal Shuswap Horizon components in the Mid Fraser-Thompson River area dated earlier than 3000 BP except for a problematic date of 3900 ±800 BP from House 11 at EeRb 10 in Kamloops (Richards and Rousseau 1987, Rousseau and Richards 1988), and two dates of 3220 ±90 and 3280 ±125 BP on a single sample (which also yielded dates of 2605 ±140 and 2680 ±100 BP) from House 2 at the Lochnore Creek site (EdRk 7) south of Lillooet (Sanger 1970:103-4). Given these data, we propose that the commencement date of the Late Period and Shuswap Horizon be placed (for now) at 3500 BP, with the understanding that it may eventually be revised closer to 3000 BP.

PLATEAU PITHOUSE TRADITION

The Plateau Pithouse Tradition (PPT) was originally defined by Richards and Rousseau (1987) to express basic similarities evident between the three prehistoric cultural horizons of the Late Period. The PPT is seen as being characterized by a lifeway generally similar to that described for the ethnographic Interior Salish of the Canadian Plateau (Richards and Rousseau 1987:49). Central to the definition of the PPT are: use of semi-subterranean pithouses as winter dwellings in semi-permanent villages; a semi-sedentary, logistically organized, seasonally regulated subsistence and settlement strategy; and a hunting and gathering subsistence with a strong emphasis on salmon fishing and use of food storage pits. Other significant cultural elements/patterns characterizing the Plateau Pithouse Tradition are presented in Richards and Rousseau (1987:50-1).

Recent excavations at the Baker Site (EdQx 43) near Monte Creek in the South Thompson River valley (Wilson et al. 1992) indicate that the PPT can be further extended back in time to at least 4300 BP, corresponding with the latter half of the Lochnore Phase. The currently available data suggest that the general adaptive pattern characterizing the PPT probably emerged on the Canadian Plateau sometime around 4500 BP, and was firmly established by at least 4300 BP. This is consistent with data from the Columbia Plateau to the south, where the earliest investigated housepits date to about the same time (Chatters 1989). Considering this, we are hereby formally revising the commencement date of the PPT to ca. 4500 BP, with the understanding that it

may be pushed back several hundred years more if future data allow.

DISCUSSION AND SUMMARY
The Early Period

The initial peopling of the Mid Fraser-Thompson River drainage area appears to have involved peoples belonging to or participating in a regional variant of a number of different well-known archaeological traditions found in the Pacific Northwest. There are several major travel routes connecting this area with adjacent physiographic areas (Figure 1). These routes would have permitted easy human movement and interaction throughout most of the Intermontane Period (see also Borden 1979:Figure 2).

The earliest occupants may have been affiliated with the western variant of the Fluted Point Tradition, who could have easily entered the area shortly after deglaciation (ca. 11,000 BP) from the Peace River District, Northern Plains, and/or Columbia Plateau. There is, however, no conclusive evidence for the presence of the Fluted Point Tradition in the study area. Between ca. 10,500 and 8000 BP, peoples participating in the Early Stemmed Point Tradition of the Columbia Plateau, the Plano Tradition of the Northern Plains, the Early Coast Microblade Complex of the Northwest Coast, and the Old Cordilleran Tradition (Pebble Tool Tradition) of the Columbia Plateau and Northwest Coast ventured into the study area.

In the Early Period, initial cool and wet postglacial conditions were quickly replaced by hot and dry conditions resulting in xeric grasslands in much of the study area. During this period, a reliance on hunting and a subsistence pattern characterized by an ever-broadening foraging spectrum involving greater and more efficient exploitation of small plants and animals are inferred (see also Ames 1987). Fishing seems to have been a minor subsistence activity along the Mid Fraser and Thompson Rivers.

The Middle Period

At the beginning of the Middle Period, ca. 7000 BP, there emerged a distinctive, southern interior ungulate-hunting culture called the Nesikep Tradition. Its origins appear to lie in the mix of regional early traditions. The Lehman Phase is the final manifestation of the Nesikep Tradition.

About 5500 BP, evidence for the Lochnore Phase appears. In our view, this phase represents a riverine and Douglas fir forest adaptation that emerged as a result of Coast Salish peoples moving into the southern interior to exploit improving salmon and humid forest resources toward the end of the mesic grassland period and the onset of cooler and wetter climatic conditions. The identification of these people as Salishan is based on the continuity between this tradition and the historic Salish-speakers of the area. Furthermore, Elmendorf (1965) identifies the northwestern part of present Interior Salish territory, particularly the Lillooet Lake and Thompson River areas, as the most probable homeland of the proto-Interior Salish, an area more or less consistent with that of the Lochnore Phase.

It is our view that the origins of the Lochnore Phase are not to be found in the Nesikep Tradition. Several technological and behavioural differences between the Lehman Phase and Lochnore Phase indicate that the latter is not a development out of the former. Instead, the origins of the Lochnore Phase probably lie in the Old Cordilleran of coastal British Columbia, notably from the river valleys on the Coast and Cascade Mountains from Puget Sound north (Suttles and Elmendorf 1963). Furthermore, the Old Cordilleran appears to be closely associated with the history of salmon (Carlson 1983b), which would have pre-adapted these people for the more intensive exploitation of anadromous resources made possible by changing climatic conditions, particularly if they came from an area with a long established tradition of riverine salmon exploitation.

Two aspects of the culture-historical model presented in this chapter were recently questioned on the basis of excavations at three sites in the South Thompson Valley. Firstly, Wilson (1991:vi, 123) suggests that the Lehman and Lochnore Phases are not distinct archaeological entities, because of the co-occurrence of Lochnore and Lehman material on a knoll at EdQx 41 (Wilson 1991:123) and because "Lochnore and Lehman components are typically mixed" (Wilson 1991:22). He proposes that they be combined into a single unit, but rejects the idea that Lochnore and Lehman material reflect "different specialized activities" (Wilson 1991:vi, 123). Instead, he "prefer[s] the simplest explanation ... that is, Lochnore and Lehman are likely variants of the same culture rather than related to different cultures or language groups" (Wilson 1991:123), and, for reasons not entirely clear to us, concludes that "the suggestion that a Lochnore phase movement of salmon fishing Salish into the area occurred at the beginning of the Middle Prehistoric Period is rejected" (Wilson 1991:vi).

Secondly, Wilson et al. (1992) propose more recently that the Lochnore Phase of the South Thompson Valley represents a northward movement into the Canadian Plateau of people from the Columbia drainage of Washington State. This proposal is based primarily on similarities in housepit and projectile point styles between the Baker site (EdQx 43) near Monte Creek and Indian Dan/late Kartar Phase sites in the upper Mid Columbia region. The idea that developments in the South Thompson Valley may be different from those further to the west is first suggested in Wilson's 1991 study. There, based on the presence of large amounts of cryptocrystallines at EdQx 41 and nearby EdQx 42, he states that "apparent differences in raw material selection between the mid Fraser/Thompson and the South Thompson archaeological areas may argue for different cultures being present in each area" (Wilson 1991:119, 49, 82).

At this point in time, we maintain our belief in the integrity of both the Lochnore and Lehman Phase concepts. Although the precise trait content of each phase needs clarification and undoubtedly some revision, there are notable typological and technological differences between the two phases. The knoll at EdQx 4, a deflationary environment with mixed Lochnore and Lehman material, is not a sound basis for suggesting that the two phases are not distinct. It should also be noted that Lochnore and Lehman assemblages are *not* typically mixed (Table 1). Furthermore, the fact that some components contain both Lochnore and Lehman material does not necessarily mean that the material is *mixed*; instead, it could be the results of deflationary factors, or the excavator may not have distinguished between the two assemblages – a real possibility with Sanger's work at EdRk 8 (Zone II) and Gehr's excavation at EgRg 4.

We have already commented on the existence of geographic variability within the Lochnore Phase, and the possibility that the Lochnore Phase manifestation might be treated in the future as a cultural horizon with regional phases (see Richards and Rousseau 1987:5-7). Furthermore, the use of cryptocrystallines in the South Thompson Valley varies considerably among Middle Period sites, with moderately high values (>20 per cent) at EdQx 41, EdQx 42, and EeQx 5, but very low (<3 per cent) at EdQx 43 (Eldridge 1974, Wilson 1991, Wilson et al. 1992). It is important to note that readily available cryptocrystalline lithic materials are far more common in the South Thompson Valley than in the Thompson River and Mid Fraser regions where high quality glassy basalts are more accessible. Regardless of the relative proportions of different lithic material, it is our view that this is not sufficient grounds for establishing the presence of different cultures in the Mid Fraser–Thompson region and the South Thompson Valley.

With regard to the hypothesized Upper Mid Columbia origin of the South Thompson variant of the Lochnore Phase, it should be noted that while there are some similarities between the Baker site and Indian Dan/late Kartar Phase sites, there are also some important differences, notably an apparent lack of emphasis on salmon exploitation and the absence of fish storage (Chatters 1989). Wilson et al. (1992:166) themselves note that "similarities between the Kartar phase housepits of the Columbia River and those of EdQx 43 should not be overdrawn." Furthermore, when Baker site housepit radiocarbon dates (the only Lochnore Phase housepits excavated so far on the Canadian Plateau) are compared with dates from the five earliest housepit sites in the Upper Mid Columbia (Chatters 1989, Table 1), no significant difference is evident, and at this point in time it is uncertain whether this type of housepit, if the same, is earlier along the South Thompson or Upper Mid Columbia River. It is, therefore, our view that the apparent similarities between these two regions should not be overlooked, but that it is premature to conclude that these similarities reflect a northward movement of Indian Dan/Kartar Phase people or a southward movement from the Canadian Plateau.

It also remains our view that the Nesikep and Plateau Pithouse Traditions represent different ethnic groups of different linguistic affiliation, with the Nesikep Tradition representing a non-Salishan indigenous people and the latter a Salishan intrusion. In our model, the newly-arrived Lochnore Phase people at first co-existed with, and then absorbed, presumably both culturally and genetically, the indigenous Lehman Phase people, over a 1000-year long period, thereby bringing to an end the Nesikep Tradition around 4500 BP. Such a sequence of events, while admittedly somewhat speculative, would have been possible if the two groups were not in constant direct competition. There is a precedent in this area for such a scenario in the case of the Athapaskan-speaking Nicola-Similkameen Indians

who, living primarily by hunting in the Nicola Valley in the nineteenth century, were eventually absorbed through intermarriage and warfare by neighbouring Salish-speaking Indians after the valley became of value to them following the introduction of the horse (Kennedy and Bouchard 1975).

The Plateau Pithouse Tradition represents a fundamental continuity in culture and adaptive behaviour in the Mid Fraser-Thompson River area. This continuity spans approximately four and a half millennia, and encompasses the latter part of the Lochnore Phase and the Shuswap Plateau, and Kamloops Horizons. It concludes with the Interior Salish indigenous peoples of the historic period. This suggests that the Interior Salish have probably occupied the study area for at least that length of time. The Salishan movement into the British Columbia interior from the coast would have taken place early in the post Hypsithermal at a time of increasingly cooler and wetter conditions and expanding pine and Douglas fir forests. Such a scenario is generally consistent with Elmendorf's models of Interior Salish origins and migrations based on linguistic considerations (e.g., Suttles and Elmendorf 1963, Elmendorf 1965, Suttles 1987, Kinkaide 1990, Thompson and Kinkaide 1990).

We posit that Salish peoples began venturing up the Fraser and Thompson river drainages around 5500 years ago on a seasonal basis to hunt and collect plants, and secondarily to fish. These incursions would have taken place primarily in the summer when salmon fishing was relatively poor on the coast and lower Fraser Canyon. During the fall, these Salishan groups would have returned to villages in the lower Fraser Canyon and elsewhere to harvest salmon. Such a pattern of regular seasonal use of the interior by coastal and Fraser Canyon Salish groups may have persisted for a millennia until ca. 4500 BP, and is represented archaeologically by the first half of the Lochnore Phase. After ca. 4500 BP, salmon populations were sufficient in upper drainages to allow these Salish groups to establish permanent residence and to engage in the logistically organized subsistence and settlement strategy that characterizes the Plateau Pithouse Tradition.

Table 1. Investigated Early and Middle Period sites of the Mid Fraser-Thompson River area.

Site number	Component	Reference	Comment
EARLY PERIOD SITES			
EcRi 1	–	Sanger 1967	not excavated, but a small dated collection was recovered from an exposure
EdRi 11	Stratum V and VI	Rousseau et al. 1991a, Rousseau 1991	small sample indicates microblade use at ca. 8400 BP
EeQw 48	–	Cybulski et al. 1981, Chisholm and Nelson 1983	skeleton of man caught in mud slide; no associated artifacts
MIDDLE PERIOD SITES			
Early Nesikep			
EdQx 42	Zone 1	Wilson 1991	mixed with Lehman Phase and possible Lochnore Phase material in deflationary knoll-top setting
EdRi 11	Stratum II	Rousseau et al. 1991a, Rousseau 1991	small assemblage; possible early Nesikep; mixed with Lochnore Phase material
EdRk 4	Zone VII	Sanger 1970	
EdRk 8	Zone II	Sanger 1970	zone also contains Lehman Phase material; possibly mixed
EeRh 61	Zone IV	Arcas Associates 1985	
EeRl 19	Comp. 3	Stryd 1972	
Lehman Phase			
EcRg 1A	Comp. III	Arcas Associates 1986	possible Lehman Phase
EdQx 42	Zone 1	Wilson 1991	mixed with early Nesikep material in deflationary knoll-top setting
EdRi 6	Area 1	Rousseau and Richards 1988	single occupation; well represented
EdRk 7	Zone II	Sanger 1970	
EdRk 8	Zone II	Sanger 1970	zone also contains early Nesikep material; possibly mixed
EeQw 6	–	Johnson-Fladmark 1973	single Lehman point in larger assemblage from multi-component housepit village; point probably not associated with housepits
EeRh 3	–	Lawhead 1979	isolated find in larger assemblage
EeRh 61	Zone IIB and III	Arcas Associates 1985	
EeRl 7	–	Hayden et al. 1987	single Lehman point in Lochnore Phase assemblage below Housepit 7
EgRg 4	–	Gehr 1976	materials from several phases present and possibly mixed
Lochnore Phase			
EcRg 1A	Comp. II	Arcas Associates 1986	mixed with Quiltanton Complex and, possibly, with Lehman Phase material
EcRg 1B	Comp. II	Arcas Associates 1986	
EcRg 2	–	Arcas Associates 1986	
EcRg 4C	Comp. II	Arcas Associates 1983	mixed with Quiltanton Complex material

Table 1. Investigated Early and Middle Period sites of the Mid Fraser-Thompson River area (continued).

Site number	Component	Reference	Comment
EdQx 41	Zone 2 and 3	Wilson 1991	Zones 2 and 3 one component; Zone 1 could be more recent
EdQx 42	Zone 2 and 3	Wilson 1991	Zones 2 and 3 considered here one component
EdQx 43	Zone III	Wilson et al. 1992	late Lochnore Phase housepits
EdRg 2	Comp. III	Arcas Associates 1986	possible Lochnore Phase component
EdRi 11	Stratum II	Rousseau et al. 1991a, Rousseau 1991	mixed with possible early Nesikep material
EdRk 4	Zone V	Sanger 1964, 1966, 1970	assemblage could contain some intrusive material
EdRk 7	Zone III	Sanger 1966, 1969, 1970	assemblage may contain some intrusive material (Sanger 1966:8)
EeQx 5	Below ash	Eldridge 1974	Lochnore Phase materials may also occur above ash; not certain if all material below ash belongs to this phase
EeRh 61	Zone IIA	Arcas Associates 1985, 1986	
EeRl 7	–	Hayden et al. 1987	large assemblage of points and microblades below Housepit 7 and smaller assemblage below Housepit 5.
EeRl 171	Comp. II	Richards 1978	river cobble reduction station and small task camp; specialized assemblage
EfQt 1	Area A Comp. I	Rousseau et al. 1991b	possible Lochnore Phase
EfQw 2	–	The Midden 1992	possible Lochnore Phase
EgRg 4A	–	Gehr 1976	materials from several phases present and possibly mixed

Table 2. Early and Middle Period archaeological radiocarbon dates from Mid Fraser-Thompson River area.

Site number	Provenience	Date in C-14 Date BP*	Calibrated number	Laboratory	Material	Source/Comment
EARLY PERIOD						
EdRi 11	Stratum VI	8400 ±90	**	SFU-867	bone***	Rousseau et al. 1991a; Rousseau 1991; below Mazama tephra ca. 6800 BP
EeQw 48	–	8250 ±115	**	S-1737	bone	Cybulski et al. 1981
EdRi 11	Stratum V	7670 ±80	8541 (8423) 8383	SFU-866	bone	Rousseau et al. 1991a; Rousseau 1991; associated with Mazama tephra ca. 6800 BP
EcRi 1	–	7530 ±270	8559 (8363) 8039	GSC-530	charcoal	Sanger 1967; from below Mazama tephra ca. 6800 BP
MIDDLE PERIOD						
Early Nesikep						
EdRk 8	Zone II	6650 ±110	7589 (7496) 7429	I-2367	bone	Sanger 1970: association with early Nesikep not certain; could be associated with Lehman Phase material
EdRi 11	Stratum II	6000 ±80	6988 (6882,6874, 6852), 6742	SFU-886	bone	Rousseau et al. 1991a; Rousseau 1991; possible early Nesikep; mixed with Lochnore Phase material
EdQx 42	Zone 1	5920 ±130	6889 (6782,6774, 67440), 6635	AECV-1318c	freshwater shell carbonate	Wilson 1991; mixed with Lehman Phase material; actual age of shell probably more recent; possibly Lehman Phase date
EeRh 61	Zone IV	5870 ±500	7274 (6728) 6189	SFU-384	charcoal	Arcas Associates 1985: Table 17
EdRk 4	Zone VII	5635 ±190	6669 (6418) 6289	GX-408	bone	Sanger 1970
Lehman Phase						
EeRh 61	Zone IIB	6290 ±120	7299 (7187) 7093	SFU-398	freshwater shell carbonate	Arcas Associates 1985: Table 17; date considered too old, possibly by about 1500 years; charcoal date Riddle-572 from same layer
EeRh 61	Zone III	5940 ±120	6942 (6841,6836, 6790) 6669	SFU-397	freshwater shell carbonate	Arcas Associates 1985: Table 17; date considered too old, possibly by about 1500 years; charcoal date SFU-386 from same layer
EdQx 42	Zone 1	5920 ±130	6889 (6782,6774, 6744) 6635	AECV-1318c	freshwater shell carbonate	Wilson 1991; mixed with early Nesikep Tradition material; actual age of shell probably more recent; possibly early Nesikep Tradition date
EdRi 6	Pit Feature	4850 ±100	5726 (5594) 5470	Beta-11453	bone	Rousseau and Richards 1988

Table 2. Early and Middle Period archaeological radiocarbon dates from Mid Fraser-Thompson River area (continued).

Site number	Provenience years BP	Date in C-14 Date BP*	Calibrated number	Laboratory	Material	Source/Comment
EeRh 61	Zone IIB	4470 ±110	5299 (5212,5195, 5051) 4875	Riddl-572	bone	Arcas Associates 1986:163; accelerator method; from same layer as shell date SFU-398
EeRh 61	Zone III	4470 ±400	5639 (5212,5195, 5051) 4549	SFU-386	charcoal	Arcas Associates 1985: Table 17; from same layer as shell date SFU-397
Lochnore Phase						
EdQx 42	Zone 2/3	6290 ±100	7289 (7187) 7159	AEVC-1319c	freshwater shell carbonate	Wilson 1991; from transition between Zones 2 and 3; both zones here considered to be Lochnore Phase; actual age of shell more recent
EdRg 2	Component III	5510 ±90	6410 (6304) 6203	Beta-14483	bone	Arcas Associates 1986: Tables 8 and 17; accelerator method; possibly Lochnore Phase
EcRg 1B	Component II	5490 ±190	6469 (6299) 5997	Riddl-249	bone	Arcas Associates 1986: Table 8; possibly Lochnore Phase; accelerator method
EdRi 11	Stratum II	5480 ±70	6399 (6297) 6197	Beta-37977	bone	Rousseau et al. 1991a; Rousseau 1991; from middle and lower Stratum II; mixed with possible early Nesikep material; possibly terminal early Nesikep date
EdQx 41	Zone 2	5480 ±100	6406 (6297) 6189	AECV-1316c	freshwater shell carbonate	Wilson 1991; actual age of shell probably somewhat more recent
EcRg 1B	Component II	5390 ±90	6297 (6192) 5997	Beta-14482	bone	Arcas Associates 1986:Table 8; possibly Lochnore Phase; accelerator method
EdQx 41	Zone 3	5100 ±110	5981 (5906,5787, 5775) 5729	AECV-1317c	freshwater shell carbonate	Wilson 1991; actual age of shell probably somewhat more recent
EcRg 1B	Component II	4750 ±190	5724 (5560,5531, 5472) 5289	Riddl-250	bone	Arcas Associates 1986:Table 8; accelerator method
EdQx 43	Zone 3	4450 ±100	5289 (5045,5002, 4997) 4873	AECV-1566c	charcoal	Wilson et al. 1992; from House 2
EdQx 43	Zone 3	4350 ±90	5043 (4962,4956, 4873) 4851	AECV-1561c	charcoal	Wilson et al. 1992; from House 2
EdQx 43	Zone 3	4260 ±90	4962 (4852) 4652	AECV-1564c	charcoal	Wilson et al. 1992; from smudge pit
EdQx 43	Zone 3	4240 ±120	4967 (4841) 4575	AECV-1562c	charcoal	Wilson et al. 1992; from House 1
EdQx 43	Zone 3	4200 ±90	4863 (4829,4747, 4731) 4571	AECV-1563c	charcoal	Wilson et al. 1992; from House 1
EeRl 171	Component 2	4145 ±205	4962 (4815,4758, 4720, 4673,4647, 4621,4618) 4419	I-9724	charcoal	Stryd 1980:Table 1; Richards 1978:12
EdQx 42	Zone 3	3950 ±260	4832 (4417) 3993	AECV-1616c	charcoal	Wilson et al. 1992; from House 3
EcRg 1B	Component II	3930 ±100	4526 (4413) 4249	Beta-13352	bone	Arcas Associates 1986:Table 8
EdRi 11	Stratum II	3520 ±70	3897 (3832) 3698	SFU-626	bone	Rousseau et al. 1991a; Rousseau 1991; from upper StratumII; presumably dates terminal Lochnore Phase

* dates calibrated using Stuiver and Reimer (1987), cited at one sigma

** date too old to calibrate

*** all bone dates are from bone collagen

18

COQUITLAM LAKE: AN EARLY LITHIC COMPONENT IN THE LOWER MAINLAND

Milt Wright

Coquitlam Lake serves the needs of over 200,000 residents of the lower mainland in its current capacity as a fresh water reservoir. It would appear that this lake has been serving the needs of human populations for the last several thousand years, based on the discovery of lithic assemblages recovered from the eroding lakeshore margins (Wright and Williams 1982). These stone tool assemblages are notable both for the variety of lithic materials employed and the range of lithic technologies in evidence. However, the primary significance of the Coquitlam Lake sites remain their location, and the fact that they represent the first substantive prehistoric site discoveries from the high elevation coastal mountain lakes north of the lower mainland (Figure 1). These upland lakes may have figured in the early human exploitation of the area for they would have been among the first areas to become ice free (Souch 1989). In addition, such upland lakes would have been unaffected by the fluctuations in sea level that marked the onset and early history of the Holocene period along the coast. It is also possible that the resources available in Coquitlam Lake provided a variety and seasonal abundance that was unavailable in lower mainland settings. Thus the setting and resource base of upland lakes such as Coquitlam Lake may well have played a role in the early human settlement of British Columbia.

The discovery of early prehistoric archaeological sites will probably always remain a combination of good luck and methodical archaeological fieldwork. Certainly the association between landform and human settlement patterning is well demonstrated in the archaeological record and regional surveys can be guided using geomorphic criteria. In the case of early prehistoric sites these landform associations may be difficult to discern following shifts in drainage patterns, lake and sea level changes, and mantling of formerly open terrain by dense vegetation. Some authors have recently argued that landform may have exercised only a limited role in early human movement and that terrestrial mammal distribution and movement were key considerations (Kelley and Todd 1988). However, it can be argued that both human and animal movement is governed in part by landscape features and that human settlement pattern is therefore correlated with landform, but simply as a consequence of predictable game movements. Unfortunately not all areas reveal the ancient landforms, and only rarely do modern developments provide access to and exposures of these specific locales (e.g., Wilson, this volume).

It is not surprising, therefore, that most early prehistoric sites recorded to date in British Columbia occur as basal deposits of multicomponent coastal and lower mainland village sites (e.g. Namu, Bear Cove, Glenrose). These sites are invariably associated with current sea levels and recent river courses, but researchers have noted the fact that the onset of early human settlement may well be associated with former sea levels and long abandoned, or at least significantly removed lacustrine and riverine settings (R.L. Carlson 1979, Fladmark 1982). These shorelines and drainage features are not readily apparent in the British Columbia landscape. Indeed, some of the former shorelines in question are likely within present tidal zones, while the land-based locales are mantled by coastal forest cover. These considerations have led some authors to suggest (Fladmark 1982) that the current inventory of early prehistoric sites in British Columbia is biased and

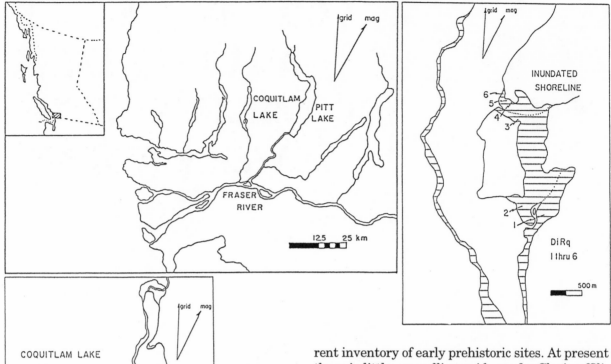

Figure 1. Study area and site locations on Coquitlam Lake.

rent inventory of early prehistoric sites. At present there is little compelling evidence for Clovis affiliated sites in the coastal or lower mainland regions of British Columbia and some authors suggest that this largely plains adapted culture may not have been capable of adopting a coastal lifestyle (Carlson 1983a). It is also conceivable that the coastal and lower mainland areas were not available for settlement during very early time horizons due to raised sea levels (Souch 1989), suggesting that other regions of the province may contain evidence of early immigrants. If the lower mainland and coastal zones were inundated then the elevated shores of north-south trending lakes and inlets which penetrate the coastal mountain range immediately north of the lower mainland may have been attractive and available to early populations. The upland lakes include Seymour, Coquitlam, and Stave Lakes, all of which are virtually unknown archaeologically.

The lakes north of the lower mainland are steep sided and narrow with exceptionally deep north basins and shallow south basins, reflecting glacial scouring of the former and massive deposition of sediments in the latter. Many of the lakes have been dammed and artificial reservoirs created, both for water supply to the lower mainland and generation of hydroelectric power. Despite the raised lake levels many of the reservoirs retain a semblance of the original lake configuration, owing to the precipitous nature of their shorelines (Figure 1).

Coquitlam Lake (490 m a.m.s.l.) was artificially raised in 1913 to a point 23 m above its original

that further discoveries may yet be made identifying earlier occupations to the currently recognized Microblade, Pebble Tool, Stemmed, and Fluted Point Traditions (Carlson 1983a). That many gaps exist in the present record of early occupation sites is best exemplified by the recent discoveries of large Clovis sites in Oregon and Washington (Willig and Aikens 1988, Mehringer 1988). This is not meant to suggest that Clovis is necessarily the earliest cultural manifestation that will be found on the Northwest Coast, but simply to indicate the shortcomings in the cur-level. The substantial age of the reservoir, which houses one of Canada's National Water Land Marks, prompted the reinforcement of the earthen dam structure with rip rap during the summer of 1979. This construction necessitated the draining of the reservoir to near original lake level and this happily coincided with the conduct of a local survey of historical resources (Wright 1980). Foot survey of the exposed reservoir margins recorded the presence of three historic and six prehistoric sites. The historic sites relate to the logging of the basin prior to its inundation and camps associated with the construction of the earthen dam and diversion tunnel to the Indian Arm Power Generating Station.

All of the prehistoric sites are located within the active zone of the reservoir, that being the area of maximum wave activity and annual drawdown fluctuations. Those portions of the reservoir which would have been the original lakeshore were obscured by mass wasting of the reservoir margins. Six prehistoric sites, all defined by eroded surface finds, were located along the southeast margins of the reservoir. None of these sites could be deemed to be in association with the prereservoir shoreline but they did cluster around an area where two creeks formerly entered the lake from the east. Some of these sites were single finds but a dense cluster of artifacts was found on a bedrock projection (DiRq 5). In prehistoric times DiRq 5 would have been 22 m above the lake level atop a bedrock shelf rising vertically from the lakeshore. Access to the lakeshore would have been difficult and it is unlikely that water craft would have been used in Coquitlam Lake as neither the inlet nor outlet is navigable. During the onset of the Holocene, Coquitlam Lake was inundated and thus presented a marine adaptation for part of its early history (ca. 13,000 to 12,000 years ago, Clague 1981; Souch 1989). This inundation event is evinced by marine clays within the basal sediments of DiRq 5; however, there is no evidence so far to suggest that the site was occupied during this time.

The assemblage of artifacts (Figures 2, 3) recovered from the bedrock shelf on Coquitlam Lake includes 149 surface finds and 81 excavated remains for a total of 230 lithic items. The excavations at the Coquitlam Lake site consisted of three 1 m squares excavated to depths of 50 cm whereupon either bedrock or sterile marine clays were encountered. Notable absences from the assemblage include bone, antler, and ground or pecked stone tools. The absence of organic remains is likely taphonomic, while the absence of ground stone tools could be either functional or a factor of site chronology. The surviving lithic inventory from the site is diverse and includes the ubiquitous pebble tool/flake core tool residues, a series of biface points and thinning flakes, and microblades with microcores. A range of raw materials was employed in the manufacture of these artifacts indicating the use of local sedimentary cobbles and igneous materials derived from the Garibaldi area. There is also evidence of a new lithic material and it too is thought to be derived from the Garibaldi Mountains (Souther, personal communication 1979). The grey lustrous material is described as aphanatic (microcrystalline) volcanic rock with amphiboles of hornblende and feldspar. Despite the excellent flaking properties exhibited by this material it has yet to be documented in coastal or lower mainland site assemblages, suggesting that the affiliation of the Coquitlam Lake site may be inland. The lithic technologies recorded at Coquitlam Lake are interesting in that they include pebble tool technology, bipolar technology, biface production, and microcore and blade manufacture.

Current syntheses of British Columbia prehistory identify the Early Coast Microblade complex and the Old Cordilleran (Pebble Tool Tradition) as the two major players in the coastal and lower mainland areas respectively. The primary distinction between the later two resides in the absence of microblades within Old Cordilleran components. Peripheral to these latter groups are the Stemmed Point and Fluted Point Traditions, which dominate to the south and east of the study area. Neither of the latter two traditions have demonstrated a significant presence within the study area, but this may be a consequence of sampling bias.

The microblade and microcore inventory at Coquitlam Lake includes eleven core fragments and twenty-four fragmentary microblades (Figures 2 and 3). None of the cores is whole and all reveal platform rejuvenation flake removal via bipolar percussion. Only one microblade is complete, the remainder are distal and proximal portions and most were made from the Garibaldi igneous material. Other materials used in the production of microblades include andesite and Garibaldi obsidian. Unfortunately the fragmentary nature of the microcores precludes discussion of core form but they are similar to the Namu cores in that both were rejuvenated and ultimately exhausted using bipolar technology (Figure 3a).

The pebble tool and flake core industry (Figure 3d) at Coquitlam Lake is indistinguishable from assemblages found in lower mainland sites. The production of bifaces is evinced by fifty-one bifacial thinning flakes and five bifaces (Figure 3c). Included in this inventory are bipointed projectiles, a stemmed point, a point mid-section, and a point of

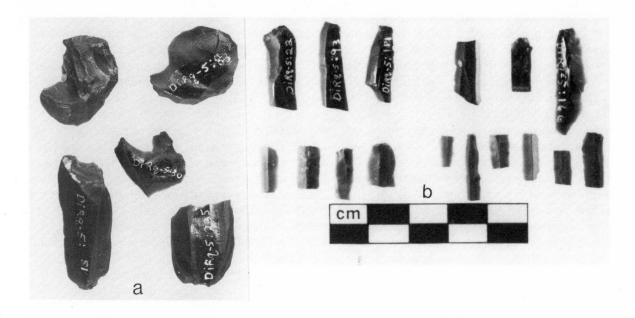

Figure 2. (a) Microblade core and (b) microblade fragments from the Coquitlam Lake site (DiRq 5).

contention. The bipointed specimens are readily comparable to points recovered from coastal and lower mainland locations. The single stemmed point is missing its base but the indentation of the ground stem margins are clear. The best examples of the lithic technicians art are evinced by a near complete point and a mid-section fragment. The mid-section fragment is quite thin and exhibits collateral flaking. Neither of these latter attributes are known to be common in bipoint assemblages.

The final specimen is formed from a porphyritic basalt and has been variously identified as either a fluted point or a bipoint that has been tip impact fractured (Fladmark 1982:106). The context of this artifact and the associated assemblage suggest that the protracted discussion of the affiliation of one tool is neither warranted nor ultimately productive. There is simply insufficient archaeological evidence to substantiate the presence of fluted point technology at the Coquitlam Lake site and the comments of several colleagues and an anonymous reviewer have convinced me not to enter into a debate of whether fluting or impact fracture is indicated for this specimen (DiRq 5:233; Figure 4). Suffice it to say that I find the features of the medial flake removed from this specimen intriguing and view the explanation of a bipoint tip impact fracture as being parsimonious. If this medial flake scar was the result of an impact fracture, it is somewhat curious that no attempt was made to repair the damaged tip and thereby salvage the near complete projectile. The lithic assemblage at DiRq 5 contains portions of discarded projectile points and ample evidence of bifacial reduction, both of which suggest that tool repair was one activity being conducted at this site. The near complete point is likely to remain a "point of contention" and I leave it to the reader to form his or her own opinion as to the mechanism that created the medial flake scar on this specimen.

Further inspection of the eroding site surface will no doubt yield additional artifacts but only excavated specimens in datable context will ultimately resolve the chronology and regional context of the Coquitlam Lake site. Excavations to date have only tested the inundated portions of the site, and while lithic items are found at depths of 35 cm below the surface the sedimentary context is highly complex. The excavation profile indicated a predicable history of forest fires in the lake basin with burned root channels infiltrating the artifact bearing matrices. Further excavation should be directed toward the non-inundated portions of the site whereby the association and stratigraphic succession of the site assemblage may be identified. The presence of massive boulders and mature tree stands will impede excavation and it may prove difficult to identify discrete and intact episodes of site formation. In the absence of intact site deposits with datable context the Coquitlam Lake site may remain an enigmatic association of potentially early culture markers.

Figure 3. Platform rejuvenation flakes from (a) microblade cores, (b) bi-polar pieces, (c) projectile points and fragments, (d) pebble tools and flake cores. DiRq 5(a, b), DiRq 4, 5, 6 (c, d).

If the coastal mountain lakes have always provided a connection between the lower mainland and the interior they would be a logical point to discover early lithic components with a mixture of coastal and lower mainland traits. Ethnographic documentation (Suttles 1955) and inferences derived from the pictograph panels on Harrison Lake suggest that these mountain lakes and marine inlets provided important routes of communication and trade between inland and coastal/lower mainland areas. Perhaps the Coquitlam Lake site is the first indication of this kind of hybrid artifact assemblage, but supportive evidence will be needed from several more sites. The distribution of lithic raw material types may provide important clues to help resolve this question. It is curious that the raw material used to manufacture the microblade cores, though of excellent quality, has yet to be identified in lower mainland sites. This is even more baffling when you consider that the source is likely to be in the same region as the clearly inferior Garibaldi obsidian which does appear in lower mainland sites.

If the Coquitlam Lake site assemblage is the spurious amalgamation of eroded individual and chronological separate site deposits, its contribution to the study of British Columbia prehistory will be simply one of demonstrating prehistoric use of the coastal mountain lakes region. However, if the artifact assemblage is in fact a single contemporaneous artifact deposit its composition stands in marked

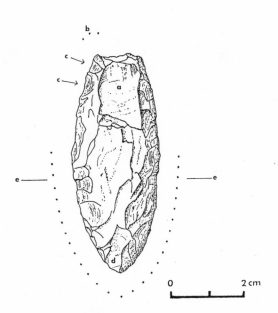

Figure 4. The "point of contention," artifact no. 233 from DiRq 5. Medial flake scar on one face only (a). Dots (b) indicate extent of marginal abrasion/ grinding. Fresh flake scars (c). Diagonal flake scar (d). Horizontal lines (e) indicate location of shoulders.

contrast to any other British Columbia site and one which could conceivably date to a very early level. The basic problems remain that the site is undated, and is probably undatable, it contains a mix of technologies and artifact types that have yet to be recognized on coastal or interior sites, and it also reveals the use of a high quality lithic material which does not appear in nearby lower mainland assemblages.

It has already been inferred, based upon lithic material types, that the affinities of the Coquitlam Lake site assemblage reside with inland, rather than coast settings. Unfortunately there are few early prehistoric sites documented for the interior regions of the province (Fladmark 1986b) and their relationship, if any, with coastal zones has yet to be evaluated. The presence of the high quality lithic material at Coquitlam Lake may provide a means for identifying such regional site affinities. At the very least it should be possible to verify that the upland lakes north of the lower mainland have provided a means of transit between the interior and the coast. This upland and interior linkage may have provided a valued option to the communication and commercial conduit provided by the Fraser River. It is hoped that further research in the interior dealing with extant collections may help to shed some light on this dimly known aspect of British Columbia prehistory.

Acknowledgments

Research at Coquitlam Lake was supported by the Heritage Conservation Branch, Provincial Government, and the Department of Archaeology, Simon Fraser University. Access to the restricted reservoir area was granted by the Greater Vancouver Water District and staff at the reservoir facility are thanked for their assistance, particularly Mike Vanachuk. The British Columbia Hydro and Power Authority supplied archival records pertaining to the construction and maintenance of the Coquitlam Lake reservoir. Jean Williams ably assisted in the survey and test excavation of the reservoir sites and Knut Fladmark assisted with surface surveys and offered many helpful comments on site interpretations. Lithic material identifications were provided by Jack Souther, Geological Survey of Canada.

19

EARLY SURFACE COLLECTIONS FROM THE ALBERNI VALLEY

Alan D. McMillan

Following two seasons of excavation at the Shoemaker Bay site, at the head of Alberni Inlet on western Vancouver Island, a survey of the surrounding area was undertaken in 1975. Part of that survey focused on the rivers that drain the Alberni Valley (McMillan 1975). The Sproat and Stamp Rivers, flowing from Sproat Lake and Great Central Lake respectively, join to form the Somass River, which 8 km later flows into the head of Alberni Inlet (Figure 1). Despite its limited extent, the Somass is rich in archaeological remains, with twenty-five sites recorded along or near its banks. Extensive residential and industrial disturbance has raised site visibility but also contributed to site destruction.

As part of the survey, an attempt was made to locate early sites by investigating areas of disturbance, such as road-cuts and modern gravel quarries, at elevated locations above the river. In total, nine such sites have been recorded, all consisting exclusively of lithic artifacts and detritus, often heavily weathered and patinated, found in disturbed gravel contexts at up to 30 m elevation above the modern river. None has yielded any organic material or has any obvious remaining buried deposits, and no dates are available. Yet the elevated site locations, nature of the deposits, and artifact types suggest considerable antiquity.

Microblade technology is evident at six of the nine sites, which have yielded twenty-three microblade cores and over thirty microblades (Figure 2). Cores are frequently made of a locally available micro-crystalline argillite, although examples of basalt and chert are also found (Table 1). Wedge-shaped, cylindrical and tabular cores, in the categories defined by Morlan (1970), all occur. Several are small core remnants. Particularly common are those

based on tabular blocks with well-defined bedding planes. Little preparation of the striking platform is evident, a feature probably related to the nature of the raw material. Core rotation to find new platforms is fairly common, and often only a few blades were removed. Extensive post-depositional weathering on many examples has obscured evidence of microblade removal.

Microblades are triangular to trapezoidal in cross-section, with a clear bulb of percussion when the proximal end is present. Only seven are complete; most are proximal or medial sections, with the curved distal end being broken or snapped off (Table 2).

Bifacial leaf-shaped points co-occur with microblades at three of these sites (Figure 3). In addition, retouched cortex spalls and other large flake tools are fairly common. Pebble tools and cores are relatively rare but appear at several sites. Chipping detritus is abundant.

Table 1. Microblade cores.

Attribute	No.	Range	Mean	s.d.
height	23	16-38 mm	27.3 mm	6.8 mm
width	23	13-49 mm	25.6 mm	8.5 mm
thickness	23	5-41 mm	19.5 mm	8.8 mm

Table 2. Microblades.

Attribute	No.	Range	Mean	s.d.
length	7	17-26 mm	20.3 mm	3.1 mm
width	32	6-10 mm	7.7 mm	1.0 mm
thickness	32	1-3 mm	1.9 mm	0.5 mm

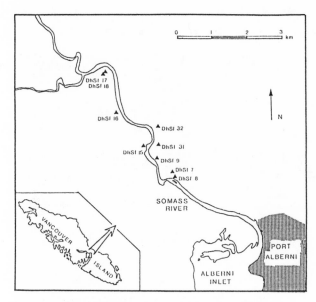

Figure 1. The Alberni Valley showing the location of possible early sites.

Figure 2. Microblades and cores from DhSf 32.

Aside from the occurrence of sandstone abraders at several sites, the only ground stone artifact is a fragment of ground and incised siltstone (Figure 4). A border design is formed by an incised line, with short perpendicular strokes joining it to the intact edge. Very similar examples have been reported for the St. Mungo phase at the Glenrose and St. Mungo sites (Borden 1983, Figure 8-4, Matson 1976, Figure 8-11a). The location of the Alberni find, at one of the less elevated sites, may indicate a somewhat later time period.

It is argued here that elevation serves as a guide to chronological ordering of sites in the Alberni Valley, rather than simply reflecting different activities. Sites at roughly 15 to 30 m elevation yielded almost exclusively chipped-stone artifacts, with the microblade technology well represented. At less elevated sites, microblade cores and cortex spall tools still occur, but these are joined by stemmed projectile points or knives, and occasional ground stone tools such as celts. Finally, late period sites along the modern river edge are marked by fire-cracked rock, ground slate artifacts, and occasional small basalt points. Some were fishing stations occupied into historic times.

Post-Pleistocene emergence of the land relative to the sea has been considerable in the Alberni Valley, with marine sediments evident up to about 90 m above the modern sea level, compared to about 150 m on eastern Vancouver Island and about 30 m on the outer west coast (Fyles 1963, Holland 1964, Mathews et al. 1970, Clague et al. 1982). Specific studies of sea level changes are lacking for the immediate area. On the adjacent east coast of the island, organic materials from geologic deposits formed during the latter half of the uplift have radiocarbon ages of 11,500 to 12,350 years (Fyles 1963:xiii, 93). After initial Holocene highs, sea levels rapidly dropped to below the modern position by about 9000 BP (Clague et al. 1982), gradually rising to near-modern levels by roughly 5000 BP (Fyles 1963:xiii, Clague et al. 1982:608). On the outer west coast, wood from marine silts at 25 m elevation has been dated to 13,000 BP (Clague et al. 1982:611). After early Holocene submergence, sea levels appear to have attained a height of 2.4 to 3.4 m above modern levels by about 5100 BP, then, after a thousand year standstill, have dropped gradually to present levels (Friele 1991).

The only radiocarbon dates for the Alberni Valley come from the excavated Shoemaker Bay site (McMillan and St. Claire 1982), which is clearly associated with modern sea levels. Initial occupation is dated at 4000 radiocarbon years, with the major

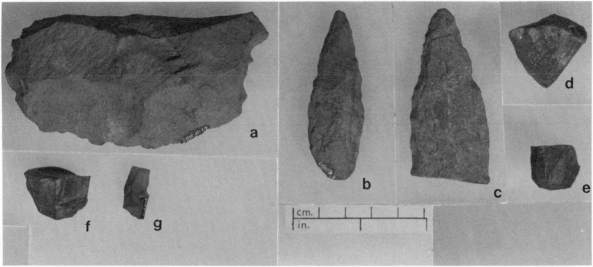

Figure 3. Artifacts from DhSf 31: (a) retouched cortex spall tool; (b, c) chipped bifaces; (d-f) microblade cores; (g) microblade fragment.

site build-up beginning by 2800 BP. Early levels yielded abundant quartz crystal microblades, comparable to those of the temporally equivalent Locarno Beach and Marpole phases in the Gulf of Georgia and distinct from the earlier industry in the Alberni Valley.

The lack of dateable material or in-context information for the presumed early sites hampers any broad comparisons. Such comparisons must be limited to technological considerations; data required to assess other concerns, such as prehistoric subsistence patterns, are absent.

Obvious broad parallels exist with what has been variously termed the "Microblade Tradition" by Carlson (1979, 1983a, 1983b, 1990b), the "Early Coast Microblade Complex" by Fladmark (1975, 1982), and the "Early Boreal Tradition" by Borden (1969, 1975, 1979). Characterized by lithic artifacts, including a well-developed microblade industry, particularly in outer coast locations, such sites are earliest and best known in the north. In southeastern Alaska, they include Ground Hog Bay 2 and Hidden Falls, where microblades appear about 9000 years ago (Ackerman 1968, 1980, Ackerman et al. 1979), and Chuck Lake, at about 8200 years (Ackerman et al. 1985). Ackerman's (1980) description of Ground Hog Bay 2 microblade cores, commonly of local material such as argillite, with little platform preparation, platforms frequently based on natural cleavage planes or single flake scars, and frequent core rotation, could equally well apply to the Alberni examples. General similarities also exist with microblade sites on the Queen Charlotte Islands

reported by Fladmark (1982, 1986a), and placed by him in the Moresby Tradition dated between ca. 7400 and 5500 BP. However, the Queen Charlotte cores frequently are based on split pebbles and seem more carefully prepared than most Alberni examples.

At equivalent time periods, the south coast, particularly the Gulf of Georgia region, was occupied by bearers of a culture known as "Old Cordilleran" by Matson (1976) and others, the "Pebble Tool Tradition" by Carlson (1979, 1983a, 1983b, 1990b), and "Protowestern" by Borden (1969, 1975, 1979). Typical traits include bifacially-flaked, leaf-shaped projectile points, pebble tools, and cores, cortex spall tools, and other large flake implements, with an absence of the microblade technology. On northern Vancouver Island, the Bear Cove site yielded such an assemblage from early levels radiocarbon dated to 8000 years (C. Carlson 1979).

Borden (1975, 1979) has speculated that these two early cultural traditions met and merged somewhere in the vicinity of northern Vancouver Island, with their fusion providing the basis for subsequent development of Northwest Coast cultures. No evidence for such an occurrence is evident at Bear Cove. On the central coast, however, Carlson (1979, 1983a) sees a blending of the two traditions at sites such as Namu. There, leaf-shaped points and pebble tools were found in the earliest levels, dated to about 9700 BP, with microblades joining the assemblage after about 8500 BP. The resultant artifact inventory resembles that found in the early Alberni Valley sites. Small numbers of bifaces and pebble tools also oc-

Figure 4. Artifacts from DhSf 18: (a) abrasive stone; (b,c) retouched flake tools; (d) chipped biface; (e) microblade; (f, g) microblade cores; (h) ground and incised siltstone fragment.

cur in the southeastern Alaska microblade sites, although bifaces of any kind are apparently lacking from the Moresby tradition on the Queen Charlotte Islands. Merger of two cultural traditions is not necessarily a precondition for the co-occurrence of these artifact types.

In summary, the early Alberni sites provide evidence of a more southerly distribution of early microblade producing cultures than was previously known. Such sites are now recorded from southeast-ern Alaska to western Vancouver Island, with a time range of about 9000 to 5000 BP. The early Alberni sites are assumed to fall within this time range, although probably within the last half. Such sites are crucial to our understanding of early coastal population movements. However, in areas lacking the extensive disturbance of the Alberni Valley, such elevated and forested site locations may pose major problems for archaeological detection.

THE LATER PREHISTORY OF BRITISH COLUMBIA

20

Roy L. Carlson

What is the relationship between the archaeological remains of the Early Period, 10,500 to 5000 BP, and the Native population resident in British Columbia at the time of European contact in the late eighteenth century? The aboriginal population at that time has been conservatively estimated at 74,400 people (Borden 1954:189). Diseases introduced from Europe may have already reduced the population from higher prehistoric numbers. On the northern coast, but mostly in the Alaska panhandle and the immediate hinterland were the Tlingit speaking peoples, and on the Queen Charlotte Islands were their remote linguistic relatives, the Haida. In the interior of Alaska and the Yukon, and throughout the northern interior of British Columbia south to the Chilcotin and Nicola were peoples speaking Athabascan languages which are also remotely related to Tlingit. On the Nass and Skeena and adjacent coastline were Tsimshian speaking peoples whose language may or may not be related to Penutian, a family of languages spoken by peoples of Washington, Oregon, and California. Further south on the coast were the Wakashan (Kwakiutlan-Nootkan) speaking peoples – the Heiltsuk, the many groups of northern Vancouver Island and the adjacent mainland such as the Nimkish – who spoke languages of the Kwakiutlan group, and the Nuu-chah-nulth of the west coast of Vancouver Island who spoke Nootkan. In the Bella Coola valley and adjacent coast, along the Strait of Georgia and lower Fraser River region, and throughout the southern interior of British Columbia were Native peoples who spoke languages belonging to the Salishan family. The Kutenai spoke their own language which is not clearly related to any other in the world. (See Helm [1981] and Suttles [1990] for detailed cover-

age of the Native peoples and languages.) Using language as a guide, there are then five groups of related peoples (Figure 1) whose prehistory is embodied in the archaeological record: Tlingit-Haida-Athabascan (although not all linguists agree that these languages are related), Tsimshian, Wakashan, Salishan, and Kutenai. What is the historic relationship between these peoples and the five early cultural traditions described in preceding chapters? The most economical hypothesis is that these peoples are descendants of the peoples bearing these early cultural traditions.

There is difficulty in linking archaeological assemblages with particular ethnic groups. Much of this difficulty stems from the incompleteness of the surviving archaeological record and much from the leveling of technological differences through the processes of acculturation and borrowing evident throughout the prehistoric period. By the time of European contact the basic technology and material culture of the ethnographic peoples were quite similar throughout the province except for differences between coastal and interior cultures related to environmental factors, and some differences in style. The most marked differences among the ethnographic peoples are the differences in language mentioned above. Languages do not survive in the archaeological record in the absence of writing. In order to investigate linkages between archaeological assemblages and known peoples, it is necessary to go back to the distribution of cultures during the Early Period, the period of initial settlement, and see how the distributions of these early cultural traditions correlate with the distribution of Native peoples at the end of the prehistoric period. The logic of this approach is that the Early Period is the only

Figure 1. Map of native language groups of the ethnohistoric period.

time when populations were small and relatively isolated, and acculturation at a minimum.

The Fluted Point Tradition and its probable derivatives – the Plano Tradition and the Internontane Stemmed Point Tradition – are so minimally represented in the archaeology of British Columbia that correlation with the ancestors of any ethnolinguistic group is even more problematical than with the other traditions, although using spatial propinquity as the sole criterion, the isolated Kutenai would logically be the descendants of people bearing the Stemmed Point Tradition. The earliest prehistory of the Tsimshian region is unknown. The earliest known occupants there, who date to about 5000 BP, used coastal pebble tool and microblade technologies (Chapter 17). Later, between 3600 and 3200 BP (Coupland 1985a), projectile points and scrapers with a vaguely Plano resemblance are found, but this is very late to be Plano derived even under conditions of exceptional cultural lag. Both the linguistic and archaeological pictures indicate that Tsimshian culture is an amalgamation of elements from many sources (see Ives 1990) and deriving it from a single early cultural tradition is highly improbable.

The Pebble Tool Tradition is the most widespread early cultural tradition in British Columbia.

It is earlier on the coast (Chapters 7 to 11) and some of its elements such as pebble tools and foliate bifaces are found in later periods up the Fraser River (Chapter 17). Its distribution correlates best with the distribution of Salishan and Wakashan speaking peoples although it is also present at a very early time period in the Queen Charlotte Islands and is probably the earliest cultural tradition there. The early prehistory of the Nootkan speaking Nuu-chahnulth on the west coast of Vancouver Island is unknown, although the assemblages closest to their territory are assemblages of the Pebble Tool Tradition – the beach assemblages from Quatsino Sound at the northern end of Vancouver Island (Apland 1982), and the typologically early Somass River assemblages (Chapter 19) which look like later variants of this same tradition with the addition of microblade technology. The ancestors of the Salishan and Wakashan speakers may well have shared a common technology. The inference generated by the data at hand is that the ancestors of the Salishan speakers spread down the coast and settled in river valleys such as the Bella Coola and along the protected waters of the Strait of Georgia, and were soon followed by the ancestors of the Wakashan speakers who settled the outer coast. The Salishan ancestors later moved up the Fraser into the interior.

The early distribution of the Microblade Tradition correlates best with the distribution of peoples speaking the Tlingit-Haida-Athabascan group of languages. Microblade technology is present in sites in central Alaska from 10,700 years ago (Hoffecker et al. 1993), in northeastern British Columbia at Charlie Lake Cave from 9500 years ago (Chapter 2), in the Alaska Panhandle and in the Queen Charlotte Islands by 9000 years ago (Chapter 12), at Namu 8500 years ago (Chapter 16), at the Landels site on the Thompson River about 8500 years ago (Chapter 17), and further south at Kettle Falls on the Columbia River earlier than the deposition of a layer of volcanic ash from Mount Mazama about 6700 years ago (Chance and Chance 1985). The question is, how did this spread take place? The most economical hypothesis is that the Microblade Tradition before 9000 BP represents the culture of the ancestors of the Tlingit-Haida-Athabascan speaking peoples, and from them microblade technology spread south to their neighbours.

The limited nature of the archaeological remains of the pre-5000 BP period makes it difficult to put much of a "human face" on these early peoples who left behind traces of their presence. We know that they faced incredible difficulties in populating a new land, that they successfully adapted to the changing environments of the post-glacial period, and that their populations grew in numbers. The correlations presented above that the Pebble Tool Tradition represents the ancestors of the Salish and Wakashan speakers, the Microblade Tradition the Tlingit, Haida, and Athabascan speakers, the Intermontane Stemmed Point Tradition possibly the Kutenai speakers, and that Tsimshian represents a very ancient amalgamation from various sources agrees in general with what the Native peoples have always said: our ancestors have lived here since time immemorial. It should be noted that the archaeological record of the Early Period does look quite different from that of the Native cultures known ethnographically. It is not until the Middle Period between 5000 and 2000 BP that the archaeological remains become increasingly indicative of the customs and social institutions known more fully from ethno-historic accounts. This development is summarized below.

COASTAL CULTURAL DEVELOPMENT DURING THE MIDDLE AND LATE PERIODS – 5000 BP TO CONTACT

In the Middle Period it is possible to move away from culture history couched in terms of types of stone tools. Stone was still used for tools and technology did shift from one based on the flaking to one based on grinding, polishing, and sawing stone, but more important are other kinds of data which bear on art, religion, and the nature of society. The improved data base is the result of more known and excavated sites, of the vastly improved preservation of bone in the many coastal shell middens, and of culture growth attributable to both population expansion and outside influences. Unfortunately, the archaeological record is never complete, nor do all archaeological sites of the same time period and cultural affiliation yield information on the same aspects of culture, so it is still necessary to generalize from the small samples of past human behaviour actually recovered to the customs and beliefs of entire populations. Since culture represents shared, habitual behaviour these generalizations should have considerable validity. The development of the coastal cultural system is shown in Figure 2. Some of these same developments took place in those parts of the interior where the inhabitants had access to abundant salmon. The most significant coastal assemblages dating to the early part of this period were found at Namu (Hester and Nelson 1978) on the central coast, Blue Jackets Creek (Fladmark et al. 1990) in the Queen Charlotte Islands, and Pender Canal (Carlson and Hobler 1993) in the Gulf Islands. Data for the later part come from Yuquot (Dewhirst 1980) at Friendly Cove on Vancouver Island, and from sites around Prince Rupert Harbor (MacDonald 1983) and near the mouth of the Fraser River (Borden 1983), although there is some information from all parts of the coast.

Certain events necessary to the elaboration of culture during the Middle Period had already taken place during the Early Period. The most significant was colonization of the rivers by salmon following the retreat of glacial ice. Knowledge of fishing had undoubtedly been brought by the earliest peoples, but we can only guess at the particular techniques used at that time. The 6500- to 5000-year-old bone barbs for composite fish hooks from Namu (Chapter 9) have already been mentioned, as have the frequencies of salmon bones (Chapter 10) which indicate the considerable importance of this fish by this time. Cannon's (1991) quantitative assessment of the relative frequencies of the different animal and fish bones from Namu indicates that in the deposits dating between 5000 and 4200 years ago salmon outnumbered all other species combined and reached their highest relative frequency. This situation persisted throughout the Middle Period deposits at that site. Since the inhabitants of Namu were making such use of salmon at this time, it is highly probable that the other coastal peoples were doing the same. Part of the problem is discovering and excavating sites where salmon were actually processed and the bones left behind rather than thrown into the river or disposed of in some other manner. Carbon isotope studies of a large sample of human skeletons from the coast spanning the last 5000 years have demonstrated that with minor exceptions, 90 per cent or more of the protein in the diet was derived from the sea (Chisholm 1986). While salmon cannot be differentiated from sea mammals and shellfish in this type of analysis, the Namu data on relative bone frequency do argue that salmon were more important than all other marine genera. Artifact types indicative of subsistence activities are shown in Figure 3.

Recent discoveries of the bones of land-locked salmon directly dated by C-14 to 15,500 and 18,000 years ago at Kamloops Lake (C. Carlson and K. Klein 1995) indicate that salmonids predate evidence of human presence in the Pacific Northwest. However, it is the anadramous salmon which returns from the sea and goes up the rivers to spawn and can be harvested at predictable times in huge numbers, that was the catalyst leading to a preserved, stored food surplus and the sedentism necessary for the elaboration of culture during the Middle Period. The earliest anadramous remains have not yet been found.

Catching and eating salmon when available would not have been enough to change the way of life of peoples who must have been organized originally as small bands of nomadic people who fished and hunted. The nomadic way of life severely limits the acquisition of material goods, whereas sedentism fosters such behaviour. The requirements for ac-

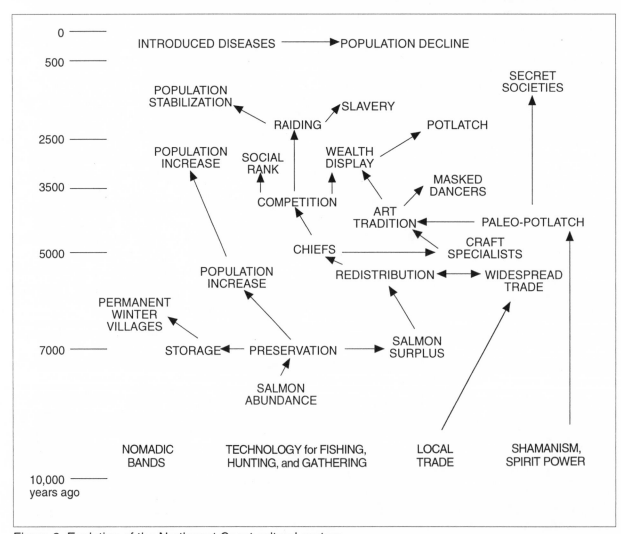

Figure 2. Evolution of the Northwest Coast cultural system.

218

cumulating goods beyond the necessities of day-to-day subsistence are a stable food surplus which can be preserved and stored for use during the lean months and a permanent home base for storage. Surpluses in food and material goods also require someone to manage them and an exchange or trade system for their distribution. The step following mastery of preservation and storage in the evolution of the system of culture as it is known among the historic Indians was in all probability the development of specialists, individuals who did not have to spend all or most of their time participating in the food quest. Such individuals would then be free to put their energy into politics, religion, war, arts and crafts, or whatever was dictated as important by the society of which they were a part. There is evidence that this development did take place during the Middle Period.

At some time in the Middle Period the cedar plank house, which served as a permanent locus for storage of food surpluses as well as a natural smoke house for preserving fish hanging from its ceiling, must have developed. This event is not well documented in the archaeological record. There is evidence for an increase in quantity and quality of specialized woodworking tools (Figure 4) – antler splitting wedges, and adzes and chisel blades of bone and ground stone – in the millenium between 4000 and 3000 years ago, and it is possible that the plank house was part of this development. The record of tree pollen preserved in stratigraphic sequences in bogs indicates climax forests of cedar, the single most important natural resource for utensils, houses, and clothing of the ethnographic coastal peoples, were available from 5000 years ago onward (Hebda and Mathewes 1984). At Kitselas Canyon on the Skeena River there is evidence of a permanent village of two rows of houses dating between 3200 and 2700 years ago (Coupland 1985a). At the Pender Canal site stone slab boxes for storage and holes for posts occur in a black floor-like deposit at 2500 years ago (Carlson and Hobler 1993). Eventually the plank house became the standard coastal dwelling from Alaska to northern California. Remains of the earliest houses have not yet been found.

Food surpluses alone do not lead to the better things in life. For benefits to accrue they must be concentrated in the hands of a leader or management specialist with the authority to dispose of them in a productive manner. It is probable that a head

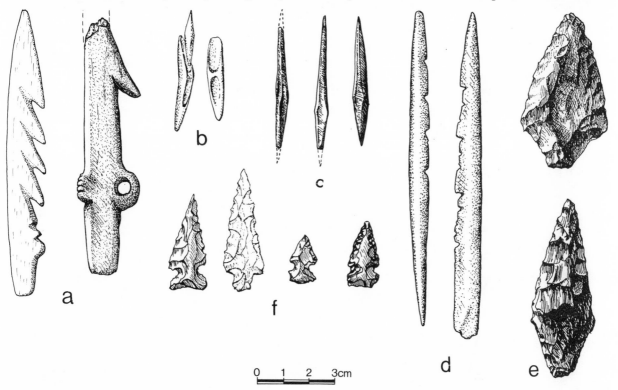

Figure 3. Artifacts related to subsistence: (a) harpoon heads used in sea mammal hunting; (b) salmon harpoon head; (c) barbs for composite fish hooks; (d) barbed bone arrow points; (e) chipped stone spear points; (f) chipped stone arrow points. Various sites; (a, e) Middle Period; (b, c, d, f) Late Period.

of an extended family or lineage filled this role during the Middle Period and maximized surpluses for the benefit of the kin group with, of course, the head as chief. The presence of luxury goods indicates personal wealth and leisure time and the goods themselves are sometimes clues to craft specialization and social rank. Social differentiation can sometimes be inferred from differential wealth in grave goods, although since blankets and wood carvings and similar luxuries normally perish in the coastal climate, such inferences are somewhat equivocal. Particular kinds of graves and grave goods can also indicate individual status. Cross-cultural studies have shown that complexity of design of art objects is an indicator of social structure: the greater the number and degree of interlocking of figures portrayed on an art object, and the less the amount of open space, the greater the probability that the art object was a product of a ranked, non-egalitarian society in which important people were differentiated from others (Fisher 1961).

The archaeological assemblage from the midden deposits at the Pender Canal site in the Gulf Islands, which date between 4000 and 2500 years ago, indicates the development of a society with luxury goods, craft specialists, and a social hierarchy during this period (Carlson 1991a). Adult burials range from simple interments of individuals placed on their sides with their knees drawn up and no accompanying wealth objects to the same type of interment with wealth objects, to individuals who were seated in stone slab cists and ritually fed with elaborate carved antler spoons or clam shell dishes. Some of the spoons are well carved and indicative of the work of a craftmaster, and some are so similar in style that they were probably the work of an individual who specialized in their manufacture. The carvings on the spoon handles are composed of two to four human and animal figures carved three-dimensionally with little open space, not unlike totem poles and house posts of the historic period. A range of simple to complex soapstone lip ornaments (labrets) and different sizes of ear spools were found scattered throughout the burial area, as were other types of standardized soapstone ornaments (Dahm 1994). The range in labret types suggests that these ornaments were not simple luxuries, but necessities for marking differences in social rank. Among the historic period Haida women of the Queen Charlotte Islands the larger the labret the higher the social rank of the wearer (Keddie 1981).

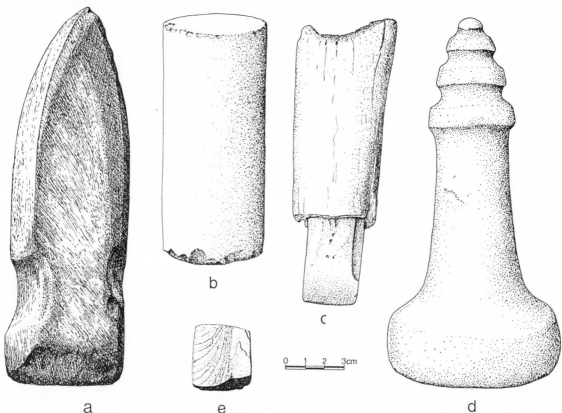

Figure 4. Woodworking Tools: (a) splitting adze; (b, d) hand mauls; (c) hafted nephrite adze blade; (e) mussel shell adze blade. Various sites, Late Period.

Evidence of labrets first appears near the beginning of the Middle Period at three sites – Pender Canal, BlueJackets Creek, and Namu. Labrets at that time were worn by some men and some women. There is some suggestion from the latter two sites that the males may have been sea mammal hunters which suggests further that the female wearers were their wives. If so, it may be further inferred that they constituted the top echelon of society. Although salmon were probably the most important food resource, the hunting of sea mammals may have been the most prestigeful occupation. The earliest labrets at Blue Jackets, Namu, and Pender are small, simple one-piece ornaments. Later forms known mostly from Pender are larger and some are elaborate composite affairs. Large ear spools were also used in the Gulf Islands and on the adjacent mainland between 3000 and 2500 years ago. The sequence of labret types may mark the evolution of a progressively more rigid and precise system of social ranking during the Middle Period. If so, this system continued on the northern coast until historic times, whereas on the southern and central coasts labrets went out of use toward the end of the Middle Period, and were replaced by artificial head deformation as a visible mark of high status. Artifacts indicative of complex society and ceremonialism are shown in Figure 5.

Craft specialization may be inferred from the uniformity of products found over a continuous geographic area and from the presence of high quality, well designed artifacts of any sort. Several of the ritual spoons from Pender were certainly made by the same artist. The uniformity of nephrite adze blades throughout the Strait of Georgia and lower Fraser beginning between 3000 and 2500 years ago strongly suggests that they were made by specialists. It is probable that they were also used by specialists. The technical requirements of dugout canoe manufacture, for example, are such that it seems likely it was a group activity. Evidence for weaving (Figure 6) is mostly from the Late Period. Full-time craft specialists may well have been few. Salmon-based subsistence promotes periods of leisure time during the winter months after the food supplies have been preserved and stored, and it seems probable that this was the time craftspeople produced their wares. During the historic period this season was also the time of ceremonies, and there is considerable inferential evidence for this activity during the Middle Period.

Potlatches were the most widespread ceremonies of the historic period. They took many forms and were undertaken for various reasons, but their common features were feasting and the distribution of property. They were the basis for the legal system, and their main function was the public validation of rights and privileges. The most widespread type of potlatch was the memorial potlatch, a feast for the dead which took place after an interval of mourning. The earliest glimmerings of this institution are found at the BlueJackets Creek site (Severs 1974, Murray 1981) where three burials dating between 5000 and 4000 years ago found in a seated position suggest the beginning of the custom of seating the important dead as part of their memorial services. At the Pender Canal site between 4000 and 3000 years ago not only were some of the dead found in a seated position, they also had either a spoon placed at the mouth or a large clamshell bowl in the hand or near the body. Why feed the dead? Rituals in which the dead are fed are probably a reflection of the social importance of gifts of food to the living which are in turn one of the most basic ingredients of the potlatch. Some of the carvings on the handles of the spoons depict masks similar to those used in potlatches during the historic period. All of these facts indicate potlatching-type behaviour and the development of the memorial potlatch, if not other types, between 4000 and 3000 years ago.

The earliest evidence for a religious specialist, the shaman, also occurs at this time although the nearly worldwide distribution of this specialization indicates it has great antiquity and may already have been present in the Early Period. During the historic period human and animal masks were used by some coastal peoples not only in potlatches, but in spirit dances, secret society performances, and shamanic rituals, all divergent aspects of the religious system based on a belief in spirits both as helpers and as a source of illness. The shaman had the ability to diagnose illness and to cure it (although a theatrical theme runs throughout shamanism which may in some cases have been more important than curing). Evidences of this system appear in Middle Period assemblages with carvings of miniature masks of long-beaked birds, wolves, mountain goats, and humanoids as well as representations of owls, serpents, salamanders, and other creatures who were probably spirit helpers. Some of these creatures exhibit joint marks, ribs, and backbones, indicators of the shamanic power of rebirth from bones (Eliade 1964). Certainly shamanism, the belief in animal spirit helpers, and the custom of representing them in art were present early in the Middle Period. Whether spirits and art had yet been brought into the service of the elite as among the historic period peoples of the northern and central coast with their

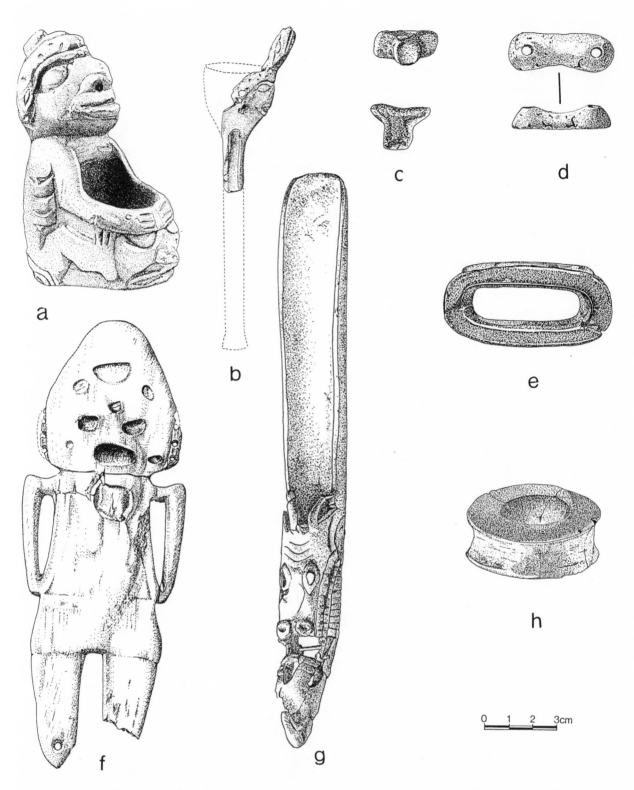

Figure 5. Artifacts indicative of social and ceremonial customs: (a) seated human figure bowl; (b) tubular pipe; (c) simple, early labrets; (d) part of a composite labret; (e) soapstone lip spool; (f) antler figurine; (g) antler ritual spoon with carved goat and eagle masks; (h) soapstone ear spool. Sites and periods: (a) pithouse village near Lytton, Late Period; (b) surface find from near Saanich, Late Period; (c, d, e, g, h) Pender Canal site, Middle Period; (f) Kwatna, Late Period.

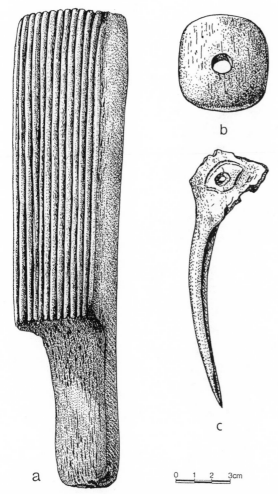

Figure 6. Artifacts associated with weaving: (a) bark beater; (b) spindle whorl; (c) blanket pin. Various sites, Late Period.

the headwaters of the Stikine. Anahim obsidian also reached Prince Rupert Harbour from points east, as did Edziza obsidian from the north. The latter is also found across Hecate Strait at the Blue Jackets Creek site on Graham Island. Seashells are found in Interior sites and constituted part of the goods moving in the opposite direction. Obsidian and shells must have been only a small part of much larger trading networks.

Raiding was an integral part of historic period coastal culture since it brought in slaves to help produce the wealth necessary for the potlatch and the maintenance of high status. Hand to hand fighting and the taking of trophy skulls were part of the system. Warrior weapons are known earliest from Blue Jackets Creek where two fancy bone daggers with geometric designs were found buried with an adult male dated at 4900 years ago (Fladmark et al. 1990, Figure 7q, Severs 1974). At Namu an adult male dated to 4400 years ago had been buried with his dagger and sea hunting equipment of walrus ivory; the blade of a bone dagger or spear head was found wedged in his backbone. Skeletons from Prince Rupert Harbour and Pender Canal show healed fractures of the lower forearm presumably the result of hand to hand fighting. Stone war clubs (MacDonald 1983) of elaborate design from the Queen Charlottes and the Skeena testify to the social importance of warfare and to the integration of spirit beliefs as part of the war complex. Isolated skulls have been found at many sites and could be war trophies. A cache of warrior weapons including copper wrapped rod armour dating to 2500 years ago was excavated from a site in Prince Rupert Harbour (MacDonald 1983). The large lanceolate stone points from Strait of Georgia sites dating about 2500 years ago and younger may actually be daggers (Figure 7). At Tsawwassen near Vancouver two skeletons buried away from other people bear cut marks indicative of scalping (Curtin 1992).

The fortress at Kitwanga on the Skeena River has been extensively excavated, and shows both late pre-contact and early historic period components (MacDonald 1979). Kitwanga was one of a string of five forts situated near the junctions of trails linking the headwaters of the Iskut, Nass, and Skeena. All fortress sites dated so far fall at the end of the Middle Period and in the Late Period, including those in southeast Alaska (Moss and Erlandson 1992). All in all there is considerable evidence for warfare.

When did institutionalized slavery begin? Slavery is likely to evolve in societies with a strong sense of social rank and a propensity for raiding. The type

totem poles, family crest ownership, and secret societies cannot be determined, but certainly the ingredients for this evolution were there.

Whereas the potlatch may have begun to function as a means of redistribution of goods on the local level, there is also evidence of long distance trade in obsidian (Carlson 1994). On southern Vancouver Island and in the Gulf Islands almost all the obsidian found came from eastern Oregon, although a small percentage came from a source in the volcanic area opposite northern Vancouver Island and an even smaller amount from Mount Garibaldi near Squamish. At Namu and at adjacent sites on the central coast almost all obsidian came from the same sources as in the Early Period – Anahim Peak and the Rainbow Mountains up Burke Channel and along the Mackenzie Trail to the east – but lesser amounts found their way from eastern Oregon, northern Vancouver Island, and Mount Edziza on of historic period cultural system in which slavery was integrated with warfare, wealth, and the potlatch, and the production of craft and food surpluses evolved during the Middle Period. In spite of the lack of direct evidence, slavery was probably part of the evolution. The effects of warfare and slave raiding on population growth could have been population stasis and stabilization of the entire cultural system. Indeed, by the end of the Middle Period there is evidence for the presence of most of those complexes which together make up Northwest Coast culture, and little evidence for changes other than in style during the succeeding Late Period.

At Namu, at Prince Rupert Harbour, and at Yuquot at Friendly Cove on Vancouver Island culture continued with little change from the Middle Period to historic times, whereas on the lower Fraser and Strait of Georgia several sequent phases of culture are present which led some researchers (see Beattie 1985) to postulate population replacement and the movement of peoples out of the Interior. Since these earlier phases were spread over the same geographic region as the historic central Coast Salish, it seems more probable that these phases mark poorly understood changes in the archaeological record of the resident population rather than major population replacements. The most pronounced changes in the environment of the Strait of Georgia were changes in sea level which would have destroyed those parts of archaeological sites close to the shoreline (Carlson and Hobler 1993) and thus altered the types of archaeological samples discovered by archaeologists.

At the beginning of the Late Period were the cultures just described and at its end were the various Indian peoples known from the ethno-historic record and to whom it is possible to attach real names (Figure 1). On the Strait of Georgia and probably also in Wakashan territory head deformation replaced the wearing of labrets as a sign of high rank. In the Salish area tubular pipes for smoking tobacco came into use. On the middle and lower Fraser a shamanic cult using stone bowls carved to represent a seated human figure embellished with snakes and other reptiles became prominent. The replacement of midden burial along most of the coast by burial in rock shelters or trees also altered the nature of the Late Period sample of archaeological remains since, although few burial caves have been excavated, many middens have been.

Although the overall social and subsistence system of the Middle Period seems largely self-gener-

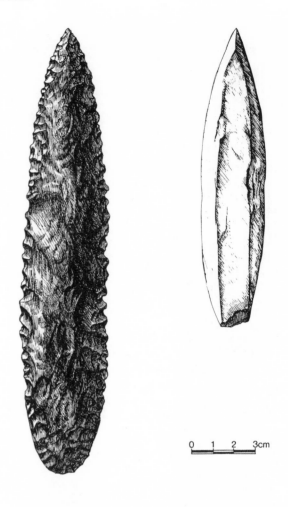

Figure 7. Daggers, Helen Point site, ca. 2000 BP.

ated, there are some evidences of external influences (Carlson 1989). Labrets and bilaterally barbed styles of harpoon heads occur even earlier on Kodiak Island to the north, and much earlier in the Soviet Maritime district and on the Kamchatkan Peninsula in Asia. Ground slate daggers have much the same distribution, but are a thousand years later. Spoons and animal masks and the rib and socket or x-ray style of shamanic art also show a general north Pacific continuity, and the copper wrapped rod armour found at Prince Rupert Harbour is Asiatic in style. These distributions indicate that coastal British Columbia was receiving cultural influences from Asia via the Aleutian Islands or Alaska throughout the Middle Period. Although these external influences are discernable, evolution of the social system of which they became a part could not have taken place without the sedentism permitted by the winter village and stored surpluses.

INTERIOR CULTURAL DEVELOPMENT DURING THE MIDDLE AND LATE PERIODS – 5000 BP TO CONTACT

The interior is a much larger area than the coast and is usually divided into a northern or Cordilleran portion including the upper Fraser drainage north of Quesnel, and a southern or plateau portion covering the region occupied by the middle Fraser, Arrow Lakes, and upper Columbia drainages. During the historic period Athapascan speaking peoples centred to the north and Salishan speaking to the south of this approximate boundary (Figure 1). The peoples of the Pacific drainage of both regions had access to salmon whereas those in the Arctic drainage did not and relied mostly on hunting. Much less is known about the Middle Period in the northern than in the southern interior.

Assemblages from the Middle Period of the northern interior (Clark 1981) are known from the Callison site almost on the Yukon border, Charlie Lake Cave and the Farrell Creek site near Fort St. John, sites near Mount Edziza, the Natalkuz Lake site in Tweedsmuir Park at the headwaters of the Nechako River, and several sites including Tezli and Punchaw Lake on the Mackenzie Trail between the Fraser and Mackenzie Pass. Technologies originating from different cultural traditions are found in these sites, but it is not always clear whether they are contemporaneous or sequent, and if the latter, the correct chronological order. Charlie Lake Cave (Chapter 2) is the only excavated well-stratified site in the region. Fluted points and points of the Plano tradition are unknown after the Early Period, and are followed about 6000 years ago by large side-notched points of the Plains Archaic. These continue throughout the sequence until replaced by arrow points in the Late Period. At Mount Edziza (Fladmark 1985) microblade industries are present by 4900 years ago; younger assemblages there in the 4000 to 3000 BP period have large lanceolate and expanding-stem "fishtail" bifaces which may be belated derivatives of the Plano Tradition. Similar points occur in the Yukon and in Alberta and on the Upper Skeena. The interfingering in time and space of three technologies – microblades from the north and west, fishtail and lanceolate vaguely Plano points from the east, and notched Archaic points from the south – seems to be characteristic of the northern interior between 6000 and 4000 years ago. In cultural-historical terms these distributions could indicate either amalgamation of various groups, interaction or shifting boundary areas between groups, or periodic movement into the area by hunting peoples of diverse ancestry.

Much of the Late Period archaeological research in the border areas between Athapascan speakers and Salish speakers has been aimed at answering the question of which of these peoples first occupied the middle and upper Fraser. Archaeological research at Eagle Lake (Magne and Matson 1982) supports the model of a late southward movement of Athapascans whereas research on the Blackwater (Donahue 1975) does not.

On the upper Fraser (Richards and Rousseau 1987) between 4000 and 3000 years ago villages indicating a shift from a nomadic to a semisedentary way of life began to be established along rivers and lakeshores. At Tezli on the Blackwater River the earliest date on a circular pithouse is 3850 years ago; at Nakwantlun near Anahim Lake the earliest date on such a house is 3500 years ago; at Punchaw Lake the earliest occupation from below the floor of a surface dwelling is dated at 3980; at Natalkuz Lake a C-14 date of 2415 years ago was obtained on charcoal from the central hearth of a surface dwelling with a microblade industry and a corner notched point. All of these sites also have more extensive Late Period occupations. At no Middle Period sites in the northern interior is there evidence for the development of any of those institutions dependant on the accumulation of a large surplus.

The southern interior as far east as the Arrow Lakes is better known archaeologically in the Middle Period than is the northern interior. At about 7000 years ago the culture of this region looks like an amalgamation of earlier biface and microblade technologies with the retention of a nomadic life style (Chapter 17). The bearers of this culture were primarily hunters of deer and elk, although some salmon remains are found. Between 7000 and 5000 years ago flaked stone artifacts similar to those of the Pebble Tool Tradition of the coast with its leaf-shaped points and pebble choppers begin to show up in sites on the Mid Fraser and Thompson rivers. This event probably marks the up-river movement of coastal peoples following the salmon as these fish developed spawning runs further and further up the river systems. This change is actually better documented for the Columbia River system. At Kettle Falls (Chance and Chance 1985), just over the border in Washington, the earliest assemblage pre-dates 6800 years ago and contains notched sinkers for nets and salmon bones as well as stone tool types originating with various early cultural traditions: pebble tools, a microblade industry, and projectile points of leaf-shaped and stemmed types. By 4000 years ago winter villages of circular pithouses made their appearance on both the Fraser and upper Columbia drainages, and in some respects cultural development began to parallel that of the coast (Richards and Rousseau 1987, Hayden and Spafford 1993).

The earliest evidence for increased salmon consumption in the interior comes from two skeletons excavated near Clinton and dated 4950 years ago. Isotopic analysis indicated 37 to 38 per cent marine protein in the diet (Chisholm 1986). Later skeletons show even higher values of 40 to 60 per cent. Notched pebbles probably used as net sinkers are the earliest evidence of fishing technology. River molluscs were extensively used. Evidence of storage pits is not present until 4000 years ago.

Eighteen sites (Richards and Rousseau 1987) in the region between Williams Lake on the north, the Arrow Lakes on the east, Lillooet on the west, and the Okanagan River on the south have revealed evidence of Middle Period occupations between 4000 and 2400 years ago. Twelve of these sites are pithouse villages and the rest are surface scatters of flaked stone tools. The beginning of use of the pithouse occurs slightly after the advent of a phase of cooler and wetter climate. This climatic change may have been responsible not only for a presumed shift to warmer winter dwellings, but for an increased presence of salmon in the Fraser River system which would have contributed to the development of winter villages with storage facilities, surpluses, and the general elaboration of culture. The pithouses tend to be large, 7.6 to 16 m in diameter, with internal storage pits and hearths; their size indicates they were multi-family dwellings. Fishing implements including harpoons, and wood working tools including wedges and nephrite chisels or adze blades occur. Luxury goods are not common although bone bracelets, pendants, and beads have been found in limited numbers. Art work is also present in limited amounts. For example, the end of a pecked stone maul or pestle shaped into the form of a bear's head was discovered. Trade with the coast is indicated by a dentalium shell and another marine shell ornament from a site at Kamloops. Obsidian is surprisingly rare. Its near absence is possibly an indicator of hostile relationships with peoples just to the north between the mid Fraser and the obsidian sources of the Rainbow Mountains. All of the complexes of this period are more elaborate in the Late Period and are known from many more excavated sites. Keatley Creek (Hayden and Spafford 1993) is the most fully excavated site .

The Kootenai region (Choquette 1984) remained somewhat distinct from the rest of the southern interior during the Middle Period. Pithouses have not been found and sites are generally unstratified thin scatters of debris and flaked stone tools. Hunting remained the primary subsistence activity. The chronology is based partly on changes in the preferred type of stone for tools. Between 5000 and 3000 years ago large spear points with expanding stems made of Kootenai argillite are characteristic, and archaeological sites are situated with reference to present day hydrological features. Notched pebbles for fish nets are also present. A site near the confluence of the Wildhorse and Kootenay rivers yielded a C-14 date of nearly 4000 years for the middle of the occupational span. Top-of-the-world chert was preferred for tool making from 3000 years ago onward.

Throughout the interior small side-notched arrow points replace larger points for the spear thrower after about 1500 BP. In the interior, as on the coast, the final two millenia of prehistory witness few changes in culture.

SUMMARY

Although archaeological, ethnological, and linguistic facts provide evidence of the history and prehistory of peoples and cultures, such facts do not speak for themselves and to be meaningful must be integrated into a cultural-historical model. The method employed in this volume on the first 5000 years of prehistory in British Columbia has been to provide such a framework in the introductory chapter, to organize the data-bearing chapters in the body of the work according to this model, and to summarize data from later periods in this final chapter. The overall model is that between 10,500 and 9000 years ago the province was colonized by peoples bearing several different cultural traditions who are the ancestors of the Native peoples living in British Columbia at the time of contact. These original inhabitants were organized as small nomadic bands who brought with them the knowledge of flaked stone tools and of hunting and fishing, small boat building, and hide working – all ingredients of an arctic survival kit – and probably shamanism to deal with the spirit world. Explicit in this model is that the earliest people differed in language as well as in the technology which serves to differentiate them from each other archaeologically, and that *core* territory and *core* language features were maintained throughout later prehistory in spite of considerable acculturation and possible shifts in the peripheries of language areas. The primary achievement of the Early Period was the development of salmon-based subsistence which was basic to the later elaboration of culture.

REFERENCES

Acheson, S.
1977   Test Excavations at GgSw 5, Kitsegukla/
        Skeena Crossing. Unpublished report
        submitted to the Heritage Conservation
        Branch. Victoria.

1991   In the Wake of the ya'aats; xaatgaay
        ('Iron People'): A Study of Changing
        Settlement Strategies among the
        Kunghit Haida. Ph.D. dissertation,
        University of Oxford. Oxford.

Ackerman, R.E.
1968   Archeology of the Glacier Bay Region,
        Southeastern Alaska. *Washington State
        University, Laboratory of Anthropology,
        Report of Investigations* 44.

1974   Post Pleistocene Cultural Adaptations of
        the Northern Northwest Coast. Pp. 1-20
        in Proceedings, International Conference
        on the Prehistory and Paleoecology of
        the Western Arctic and Sub-Arctic. S.
        Raymond and P. Schledermann eds.
        University of Calgary Archaeological
        Association. Calgary.

1980   Microblades and Prehistory: Technologi-
        cal and Cultural Considerations for the
        North Pacific Coast. Pp. 189-97 in Early
        Native Americans: Prehistoric Demogra-
        phy, Economy and Technology. D.L.
        Browman ed. Mouton. The Hague.

1981   Perspektivy Izucheniia Technologu
        Kamennoi Industrii Severnoi Chasti
        Severo-Zapadnogo Poberezh'ia (techno-
        logical Perspectives on the Stone Indus-
        try of the Northern part of the North
        West Coast). Pp. 42-7 in Dreunie
        Kultury Sibiri i Tikhhokeanskogo
        Basseina. Izdatel'stovo "Nauka."
        Novosibirsk.

1988a   Early Subsistence Patterns in Southeast
        Alaska. Pp. 175-89 in Diet and Subsist-
        ence: Current Archaeological Perspec-
        tives. B.V. Kennedy and G.M. LeMoine
        eds. University of Calgary Archaeologi-
        cal Association. Calgary.

1988b   Settlements and Sea Mammal Hunting
        in the Bering-Chuckchi Sea Region.
        Arctic Anthropology 25(1):52-79.

1990   Prehistoric Cultures of the Northern
        Northwest Coast. Pp. 67-78 in Tradi-
        tional Cultures of the Pacific Societies:
        Continuity and Change. Han Sang-bok
        and Kim Kwang-ok eds. Selected papers
        of the 16th Pacific Science Congress,
        Seoul National University Press. Seoul.

1992   Earliest Stone Industries on the North
        Pacific Coast of North America. *Arctic
        Anthropology* 29:18-27.

1994   The Early Prehistory of Southwestern and Southeastern Alaska. Paper presented at the 45th Arctic Science Conference. Anchorage.

Ackerman, R.E., T.D. Hamilton, and R. Stuckenrath
1979   Early Cultural Complexes on the Northern Northwest Coast. *Canadian Journal of Archaeology* 3:195-209.

Ackerman, R., K. Reid, J. Gallison, and M. Roe
1985   Archaeology of Heceta Island: A Survey of 16 Timber Harvest Units in the Tongass National Forest, Southeastern Alaska. *Washington State University Center for Northwest Anthropology Project Report* 3. Pullman.

Aigner, J.S.
1976   Early Holocene Evidence for the Aleut Maritime Adaptation. *Arctic Anthropology* 13(2):32-45.

1978   The Lithic Remains from Anangula, an 8,500-year-old Aleut Coastal Village. Universitat Tubingen, Institute fur Urgeschichte, *Urgeschichtliche Materialhefte* 3. Tubingen.

Alden, W.C.
1953   Physiography and Glacial Geology of Western Montana and Adjacent Areas. *U.S. Geological Survey Professional Paper* 231.

Alexander, H.C.
1974   The Association of Aurignacoid Elements with Fluted Point Complexes in North America. Pp. 21-31 in International Conference on the Prehistory and Paleoecology of the Western North American Arctic and Subarctic. S. Raymond and P. Schledermann eds. University of Calgary Archaeological Association. Calgary.

Allaire, L.
1978   L'archaeologie des Kitselas d'après le site stratifié de Gitaus (GdTc 2) sur la rivière Skeena en Columbie Britannique. *Canada. National Museum of Man. Mercury Series. Archaeological Survey Paper* 72. Ottawa.

1979   The Cultural Sequence at Gitaus: A Case of Prehistoric Acculturation. Pp. 18-52 in Skeena River Prehistory. R. Inglis and G. MacDonald eds. *Canada. National Museum of Man. Mercury Series. Archaeological Survey Paper* 87. Ottawa.

Ames, K.M.
1979   Report of Excavations at GhSv 2, Hagwilget Canyon. Pp. 181-218 in Skeena River Prehistory. R. Inglis and G. MacDonald eds. *Canada. National Museum of Man. Mercury Series. Archaeological Survey Paper* 87. Ottawa.

1987   Early Holocene Adaptations on the Southern Columbia Plateau. Paper presented at the 20th annual meeting of the Canadian Archaeological Association. Calgary.

Ames, K.M. and A.G. Marshall
1980   Villages, Demography, and Subsistence Intensification on the Southern Columbia Plateau. *Northern American Archaeologist* 2(1):25-52.

Ames, K.M., J. Green, and M. Pfoertner
1981   Hatwai (10NP143) Interim Report. *Boise State University Archaeological Report* 9.

Anderson, D.D.
1970   Microblade Traditions in Northwestern Alaska. *Arctic Anthropology* 7(2):2-16.

Anderton, L.J.
1965   Quaternary Stratigraphy and Geomorphology of the Lower Thompson Valley, British Columbia. M.A. thesis, University of British Columbia. Vancouver.

Andrews, J.T., and R.M. Retherford
1978   A Reconnaissance Survey of Late Quaternary Sea Levels, Bella Bella/Bella Coola Region. Central British Columbia Coast. *Canadian Journal of Earth Sciences* 15:341-50.

Apland, B.
1982 Chipped Stone Assemblages from the Beach Sites of the Central Coast. Pp. 13-63 in Papers on Central Coast Archaeology. P.M. Hobler ed. *Simon Fraser University Department of Archaeology Publication* 10. Burnaby.

Arcas Associates
1983 Bethlehem Copper Corporation Lake Zone Development Heritage Mitigation Study. Authors: Arnoud H. Stryd and Stephen Lawhead. Consultants report on file, Resource Management Branch. Victoria.

1985 Excavations at the Rattlesnake Hill Site (EeRh 61), Ashcroft, BC. Authors: Stephen Lawhead and Arnoud H. Stryd. Consultants report on file, Resource Management Branch. Victoria.

1986 Archaeological Excavations at Valley Mine, Highland Valley, BC. Authors: Stephen Lawhead, Arnoud H. Stryd, and A.J. Curtin. Consultants report on file, Resource Management Branch. Victoria.

Archer, D.J.
1980 Analysis of Spatial Patterns at a Prehistoric Settlement in the Lower Fraser Canyon, BC. M.A. thesis, University of Victoria. Victoria.

Aro, K., and M. Shepard
1967 Pacific Salmon in Canada. Spawning Populations of North Pacific Salmon. International North Pacific Fisheries Commission. Vancouver.

Baichtal, J.F.
1994 An Update on the Pleistocene and Holocene Fauna Recovered from the Caves on Prince of Wales and Surrounding Islands. Paper presented at the 21st Annual Meeting of the Alaska Anthropological Association. Juneau.

Ball, B.F.
1978 Heritage Resources of the Northeast Coal Study Area 1977-1978. Heritage Conservation Branch. Victoria.

Banfield, A.W.F.
1974 The Mammals of Canada. University of Toronto Press. Toronto.

Bard, E., B. Hamelin, R.G. Fairbanks, and A. Zindler
1990 Calibration of the 14C Timescale over the Past 30,000 Years Using Mass Spectometric UTh Ages from Barbados Corals. *Nature* 234:405-9.

Barrie, J.V., K.W. Conway, R.W. Mathewes, H.W. Josenhans, and M.J. Johns
1994 Submerged Late Quaternary Terrestrial Deposits and Paleoenvironment of Northern Hecate Strait, British Columbia Continental Shelf, Canada. *Quaternary International* 20:123-9.

Beattie, O.
1985 A Note on Early Cranial Studies from the Gulf of Georgia Region: Long-Heads, Broad-Heads and the Myth of Migration. *BC Studies* 66:28-36. Vancouver.

Bedwell, S.F.
1973 Fort Rock Basin: Prehistory and Environment. University of Oregon Books. Eugene.

Bense, J.
1972 The Cascade Phase: A Study in the Effect of the Altithermal on a Cultural System. Ph.D. dissertation in anthropology, Washington State University. Pullman.

Benson, L.V.
1978 Fluctuation in the Level of Pluvial Lake Lahontan during the Last 40,000 Years. *Quaternary Research* 9:300-18.

Binford, L.R.
1981 Bones, Ancient Men and Modern Myths. Academic Press. New York.

Blackman, M.B.
1981 Window on the Past: The Photographic Ethnohistory of the Northern and Kaigani Haida. *Canada. National Museum of Man. Mercury Series. Ethnology Service Paper* 74. Ottawa.

Blaise, B., J.J. Clague, and R.W. Mathewes
1990 Time of Maximum Late Wisconsin Glaciation, West Coast of Canada. *Quaternary Research* 34:282-95.

Bonnichsen, R., and K. Turnmire eds.
1991 Clovis Origins and Adaptations. Centre for the Study of the First Americans. Oregon State University. Corvallis.

Borden, C.E.
1954 Distribution, Culture, and Origin of the Indigenous Population of British Columbia. Pp. 186-96 in *Transactions of the 7th British Columbia Natural Resources Conference*. Victoria.

1960 DjRi 3, an Early Site in the Fraser Canyon, British Columbia. *National Museum of Canada Contributions to Anthropology Bulletin* 162. Ottawa.

1961 Fraser River Archaeological Project: Progress Report. *National Museum of Canada Anthropological Papers* 1. Ottawa.

1962 West Coast Crossties with Alaska. Pp. 9-19 in Prehistoric Cultural Relations between the Arctic and Temperate Zones of North America. J.M. Campbell ed. *Arctic Institute of North America Technical Paper* 11.

1965 Radiocarbon and Geological Dating of the Lower Fraser Canyon Archaeological Sequence. *Proceedings of the Sixth International Congress on Radiocarbon and Tritium Dating*. Pullman.

1967 People of the Canyon: An Introduction to Lower Fraser Canyon Prehistory. Unpublished manuscript. Laboratory of Archaeology, University of British Columbia. Vancouver.

1968a A Late Pleistocene Pebble Tool Industry of Southwestern British Columbia. Pp. 55-69 in Early Man in Western North America. C. Irwin-Williams ed. *Eastern New Mexico University Contributions in Anthropology* 1(4).

1968b The Prehistory of the Lower Mainland. Pp. 9-26 in Lower Fraser Valley: The Evolution of a Cultural Landscape. A. Siemans ed. *B.C. Geographical Series* 9.

1968c New Evidence of Early Cultural Relations between Eurasia and Western North America. *Proceedings of the 8th International Congress of Anthropological and Ethnological Sciences* 3:331-7. Tokyo and Kyoto.

1969 Early Population Movements from Asia into Western North America. *Syesis* 2:113.

1970 DjRi 7-1970 Notes Terrace 1 Including House Pit; Charcoal Sample Forms. Unpublished Records, Vol. N22. University of British Columbia. Vancouver.

1973 New Evidence Concerning Late Pleistocene and Early Holocene Population Movements from Asia into the New World. Pp. 201-5 in The Bering Land Bridge and its Role for the History of Holarctic Floras and Faunas in the Late Cenozoic. Academy of Sciences, USSR. Far Eastern Scientific Centre. Khabarovsk.

1975 Origins and Development of Early Northwest Coast Culture to about 3000 BC. *Canada. National Museum of Man. Mercury Series. Archaeological Survey Paper* 45. Ottawa.

1979 Peopling and Early Cultures of the Pacific Northwest: A View from British Columbia, Canada. *Science* 203(4383):963-71.

1983 Prehistoric Art of the Lower Fraser Canyon. Pp. 131-66 in Indian Art Traditions of the Northwest Coast. R.L. Carlson ed. Archaeology Press, Simon Fraser University. Burnaby.

Browman, D.L., and D.A. Munsell
1969 Columbia Plateau Prehistory: Cultural Development and Impinging Influences. *American Antiquity* 34(3):249-64.

Bryan, A.L.
1980   The Stemmed Point Tradition: An Early
        Technological Tradition in Western
        North America. Pp. 77-107 in Anthropo-
        logical Papers in Memory of Earl H.
        Swanson Jr. L.B. Harten, C.N. Warren,
        and D.R. Tuohy eds. Special Publication
        of the Idaho State University Museum of
        Natural History. Pocatello.

1988   The Relationship of the Stemmed Point
        and Fluted Point Traditions in the Great
        Basin. *Nevada State Museum Anthropo-
        logical Papers* 21:53-74. Reno.

Burley, D.V.
1980   Marpole: Anthropological Reconstruc-
        tions of a Prehistoric Northwest Coast
        Culture Type. *Simon Fraser University
        Department of Archaeology Publication*
        8. Burnaby.

Burns, J.A.
1986   A 9000-year-old Wapiti (*Cervus elaphus*)
        Skeleton from Northern Alberta, and Its
        Implications for the Early Holocene
        Environment. *Geographie Physique et
        Quaternaire* 40:105-8.

1993   Don't Look Fossil Gift Horses in the
        Mouth: They Too Have Tongues of Ice. P.
        A-14 in *Geological Association of Canada
        Meetings Abstracts*.

Busch, L.
1994   A Glimmer of Hope for Coastal Migra-
        tion. *Science* 263:1088-9.

Butler, B.R.
1961   The Old Cordilleran Culture in the
        Pacific Northwest. *Occasional Papers of
        the Idaho State College Museum* 5.
        Pocatello.

1965   The Structure and Function of the Old
        Cordilleran Culture Concept. *American
        Anthropologist* 67:1120-31.

Campbell, S.K.
1985   Sedimentary Sequence at Excavated
        Sites and Regional Paleoenvironmental
        Reconstruction. In Summary of Results,
        Chief Joseph Dam Cultural Resources
        Project. S.K. Campbell ed. Office of
        Public Archaeology, University of Wash-
        ington. Seattle.

Cannon, A.
1988   Radiographic Age Determination of
        Pacific Salmon: Species and Seasonal
        Inferences. *Journal of Field Archaeology*
        15:103-8.

1991   The Economic Prehistory of Namu.
        *Simon Fraser University Department of
        Archaeology Publication* 19. Burnaby.

1993   The Ratfish and Marine Resource Defi-
        ciency on the Northwest Coast. Paper
        presented at the 25th Annual Meeting of
        Canadian Archaeological Association.
        London, Ontario.

Carlson, C.C.
1979   The Early Component at the Bear Cove
        Site, BC. *Canadian Journal of Archaeol-
        ogy* 3:177-94.

Carlson, C. and K. Klein
1995   Late Pleistocene Salmon of Kamloops
        Lake. Paper presented at the 28th
        annual meeting of the Canadian Ar-
        chaeological Association, Kelowna, BC.

Carlson, R.L.
1970   Excavations at Helen Point on Mayne
        Island. Pp. 113-25 in Archaeology in
        British Columbia, New Discoveries. R.L.
        Carlson ed. *BC Studies* 6-7.

1972   Excavations at Kwatna. Pp. 41-58 in
        Salvage '71. R.L. Carlson ed. *Department
        of Archaeology Simon Fraser University
        Publication* 1. Burnaby.

1979   The Early Period on the Central Coast of British Columbia. *Canadian Journal of Archaeology* 3:211-28.

1983a   The Far West. Pp. 73-96 in Early Man in the New World. R. Shutler Jr. ed. Sage Publications. Beverly Hills.

1983b   Prehistory of the Northwest Coast. Pp. 13-32 in Indian Art Traditions of the Northwest Coast. R.L. Carlson ed. Archaeology Press, Simon Fraser University. Burnaby.

1983c   Method and Theory in Northwest Coast Archaeology. Pp. 27-40 in The Evolution of Maritime Cultures on the Northeast and the Northwest Coasts of America. *Department of Archaeology Simon Fraser University Publication* 11. Burnaby.

1989   Circum-Pacific Drift and Coastal British Columbia. In Proceedings of the Circum-Pacific Prehistory Conference. Washington State University. Pullman.

1990a   Cultural and Ethnic Continuity on the Pacific Coast of British Columbia. Pp. 79-90 in Traditional Cultures of the Pacific Societies, Continuity and Change. Sang-bok Han and Kwang-ok Kim eds. Paper presented to the Pacific Science Association 16th Congress. Seoul National University Press. Korea.

1990b   Cultural Antecedents. Pp. 60-9 in Handbook of North American Indians, 7, Northwest Coast. W. Suttles ed. Smithsonian. Washington.

1991a   The Northwest Coast before A.D. 1600. Pp. 111-35 in The North Pacific to 1600. E. Crownhart-Vaughn ed. *Proceedings of the Great Ocean Conference* 1. Oregon Historical Society Press. Portland.

1991b   Appendix B: Namu Periodization and C-14 Chronology. Pp. 85-95 in The Economic Prehistory of Namu, by Aubrey Cannon. *Simon Fraser University Department of Archaeology Publication* 19. Burnaby.

1991c   Clovis from the Perspective of the Ice Free Corridor. Pp. 81-90 in Clovis Origins and Adaptations. R. Bonnichsen and K.L. Turnmire eds. Center for the Study of the First Americans, Oregon State University. Corvallis.

1994   Trade and Exchange in Prehistoric British Columbia . Pp. 307-61 In Prehistoric Exchange Systems in North America. T. Baugh and J. Ericson eds. Plenum Publishing. New York.

Carlson, R.L., and P.M. Hobler
1993   The Pender Canal Excavations and the Development of Coast Salish Culture. Pp. 25-52 in Changing Times: British Columbia Archaeology in the 1980s. K. Fladmark ed. *BC Studies* 99.

Casteel, R.
1976   Fish Remains from Glenrose. Pp. 82-7 in Prehistoric Adaptations at the Glenrose Cannery Site (DgRr 6) Fraser Delta, BC. R.G. Matson ed. *Canada. National Museum of Man. Mercury Series. Archaeological Survey Paper* 52. Ottawa.

Chance, D.H., and J.V. Chance
1977a   Kettle Falls 1972 Salvage Archaeology in Lake Roosevelt. *University of Idaho Anthropological Research Manuscript Series* 31. Moscow.

1977b   Kettle Falls 1976 Salvage Archaeology in Lake Roosevelt. *University of Idaho Anthropological Research Manuscript Series* 39. Moscow.

1979   Kettle Falls 1977 Salvage Archaeology in Lake Roosevelt. *University of Idaho Anthropological Research Manuscript Series* 53. Moscow.

1982   Kettle Falls 1971 and 1974 Salvage Archaeology in Lake Roosevelt. *University of Idaho Anthropological Research Manuscript Series* 69. Moscow.

1985   Kettle Falls 1978 Further Archaeological Excavation in Lake Roosevelt. *University of Idaho Anthropological Research Manuscript Series* 84. Moscow.

Chance, D.H., J.V. Chance, and J.L. Fagan
1977   Kettle Falls 1972 Salvage Archaeology in Lake Roosevelt. *University of Idaho Anthropological Research Manuscript Series* 31. Moscow.

Chard, C.S.
1959   Old World Sources for Early Lithic Cultures. Pp. 314-20 in *Actas del 33rd Congreso Internacional de Americanistas.*

1961   Time Depth and Culture Process in Maritime Northeast Asia. *Asian Perspectives* 5(2):213-16.

Chatters, J.
1989   Resource Intensification and Sedentism on the Southern Plateau. *Archaeology in Washington* 1:3-19.

Chisholm, B.S.
1986   Reconstruction of Prehistoric Diet in British Columbia Using Stable-carbon Isotope Analysis. Ph.D. dissertation in archaeology, Department of Archaeology, Simon Fraser University. Burnaby.

Chisholm, B.S. and D.E. Nelson
1983   An Early Human Skeleton from South Central British Columbia: Dietary Inference from Carbon Isotopic Evidence. *Canadian Journal of Archaeology* 7(1):396-98.

Choquette, W.
1982   An Early Culture Complex in the Kootenay Region. Paper presented at the 40th Annual Plains Conference. Calgary.

1983   Results of Archaeological Salvage Excavations at the LeVesque Site, DgQa 6, Moyie Valley, BC. Report on file at the Heritage Conservation Branch. Victoria.

1984   A Proposed Cultural Chronology for the Kootenai Region. Pp. 303-16 in Cultural Resources Investigations of the Bonneville Power Administration's Libby Integration Project, Northern Idaho and Northwestern Montana. S. Gough ed. *Eastern Washington University Reports in Archaeology and History* 100-29.

1985   A Proposed Cultural Chronology for the Kootenai Region. *The Thunderbird* 5(4):2-5 and 5(5):2-5. Pullman.

1987a   Archaeological Investigations in the Middle Kootenai Region and Vicinity. Pp. 57-119 in Prehistoric Land Use in the Northern Rocky Mountains: A Perspective from the Middle Kootenai Valley. A. Thoms and G. Burtchard eds. *Washington State University Center for Northwest Anthropology Project Report* 4. Pullman.

1987b   Typological Visibility and the Stemmed Point Tradition. Paper presented at the Canadian Archaeological Association Conference. Calgary.

Christensen, O.
1971   Banff Prehistory: Prehistoric Subsistence and Settlement in Banff National Park, Alberta. *National Historic Sites Service Manuscript Report* 67. Ottawa.

Churcher, C.S. and M. Wilson
1979   Quaternary Mammals from the Eastern Peace River District, Alberta. *Journal of Paleontology* 53:71-6.

Cinq-Mars, J.
1979   Bluefish Cave I: A Late Pleistocene Eastern Beringian Cave Deposit in the Northern Yukon. *Canadian Journal of Archaeology* 3:1-32.

Clague, J.J.
1980   Late Quaternary Geology and Geochronology of British Columbia, Part 1: Summary and Discussion of Radiocarbon Dated Quaternary History. *Geological Survey of Canada Paper* 80-13.

1981   Late Quaternary Geology and Geochronology of British Columbia, Parts 1 and 2: Summary and Discussion of Radiocarbon Dated Quaternary History. *Geological Survey of Canada Paper* 80-13 and 80-35.

Clague, J., J.R. Harper, R.J. Hebda, and D.E. Howes
1982   Late Quaternary Sea Levels and Crustal Movements, Coastal British Columbia. *Canadian Journal of Earth Sciences* 19:597-618.

Clark, D.W.
1992A   Microblade Production Station (KbTx-2) in the South Central Yukon. *Canadian Journal of Archaeology* 16:3-23.

1981   Prehistory of the Western Subarctic. Pp. 107-29 in Handbook of North American Indians, 6, Subarctic. J. Helm ed. Smithsonian Institution. Washington.

Clark, D.W. and A.M. Clark
1994   Batza Tena Trail to Obsidian. *Canada. National Museum of Civilization. Mercury Series. Archaeological Survey Paper* 147. Ottawa.

Clark, D.W. and R.E. Morlan
1982   Western Subarctic Prehistory: Twenty Years Later. *Canadian Journal of Archaeology* 6:79-94.

Clark, J.G.D.
1975   The Earlier Stone Age Settlement of Scandinavia. Cambridge University Press.

Conover, K.
1978   Matrix Analyses. Pp. 67-99 in Studies in Bella Bella Prehistory. J.J. Hester and S.M. Nelson eds. *Simon Fraser University Department of Archaeology Publication* 5. Burnaby.

Cook, J.
1969   The Early Prehistory of Healy Lake, Alaska. Ph.D. dissertation in anthropology. University Microfilms, University of Michigan. Ann Arbor.

Coupland, G.
1985a   Prehistoric Cultural Change at Kitselas Canyon. Ph.D. dissertation in anthropology, University of British Columbia. Vancouver.

1985b   Household Variability and Status Differentiation at Kitselas Canyon. *Canadian Journal of Archaeology* 9:39-56.

1988   Prehistoric Economic and Social Change in the Tsimshian Area. Pp. 211-43 in Prehistoric Economies of the Pacific Northwest Coast. B.L. Isaac ed. *Research in Economic Anthropology, Supplement* 3. JAI Press. Greenwich.

Crabtree, D.E.
1982   An introduction to Flintworking. 2nd edition. *Occasional Papers of the Idaho Museum of Natural History* 28. Pocatello.

Cressman, L.S.
1977   Prehistory of the Far West: Homes of Vanished Peoples. University of Utah Press. Salt Lake City.

Cressman, L.S., D.L. Cole, W.A. Davis, T.M. Newman, and D.J. Scheans
1960   Cultural Sequences at the Dalles, Oregon, A Contribution to Pacific Northwest Prehistory. *Transactions of the American Philosophical Society, New Series* 50(10). Philadelphia.

Cressy, G.B.
1928   The Indiana Sand Dunes and Shorelines of the Lake Michigan Basin. *The Geographical Society of Chicago Bulletin* 8. Chicago.

Croes, D.R.
1987   Locarno Beach at Hoko River, Olympic Peninsula, Washington: Wakashan, Salishan, Chimakuan or Who? Pp. 259-83 in Ethnicity and Culture. R. Auger et al. eds *Proceedings of the 18th Annual Conference of the Archaeological Association of the University of Calgary.* Calgary.

1988   Review of *British Columbia Prehistory* by Knut Fladmark. *BC Studies* 77:73-5.

Curtin, A.J.
1984   Human Skeletal Remains from Namu (ElSx 1): A Descriptive Analysis. M.A. thesis in archaeology, Simon Fraser University. Burnaby.

1992   Scalping and Slavery in Marpole Times: Evidence from the Tsawwassen Site. Paper presented at the 45th Northwest Anthropology Conference, Simon Fraser University. Burnaby.

Cybulski, J.S., D.E. Howes, J.C. Haggarty, and M. Eldridge
1981   An Early Human Skeleton from Southcentral British Columbia: Dating and Bioarchaeological Inference. *Canadian Journal of Archaeology* 5:59-60.

Dale, R.J., C.E. Holmes, and J.D. McMahan
1989   Archaeological Mitigation of the Thorne River Site (CRG177). Prince of Wales Island, Alaska. Forest Highway No. 42 (DT-FH70-86-A-00003). *Alaska Department of Natural Resources Division of Parks and Outdoor Recreation Office of History and Archaeology Report* 15. Anchorage.

Dahm, I.R.
1994   Cultural and Social Dimensions of the Gulf Island Soapstone Industry. M.A. thesis in archaeology, Simon Fraser University. Burnaby.

Damon, P.E. , C.W. Fergusson, A. Long, and E.I. Wallick
1974   Dendrochronologic Calibration of the Radiocarbon Time Scale. *American Antiquity* 39:350-66.

Dansie, M.
1984   Human and Carnivore Modification of Small Mammals in the Great Basin. *First International Conference on Bone Modification Abstracts*, pp. 8-9.

Daugherty, R.D.
1956   Archaeology of the Lind Coulee Site, Washington. *Proceedings of the American Philosophical Society* 100:233-78.

1962   The Intermontane Western Tradition. *American Antiquity* 28:2:144-50.

Davis, E.L.
1968   Early Man in the Mohave Desert. Pp. 42-7 in Early Man in Western North America. C. Irwin-Williams ed. *Eastern New Mexico Contributions in Anthropology, part* 4. Portales.

Davis, S.D.
1990   Prehistory of Southeastern Alaska. Pp. 197-202 in Handbook of North American Indians, 7, Northwest Coast. W. Suttles ed. Smithsonian. Washington.

Davis, S.D. ed.
1984   The Hidden Falls Site, Baranof Island, Alaska. Ms. on file, Chatham Area Office, Tongass National Forest, USDA Forest Service. Sitka.

1989   The Hidden Falls Site, Baranof Island, Alaska. *Alaska Anthropological Association Monograph Series.* Fairbanks.

Del Bene, T.A.
1979   Once upon a Striation: Current Models of Striation and Polish Formation. Pp. 167-78 in Lithic Use-Wear Analysis. B. Hayden ed. Academic Press. New York.

Denton, G.H., and S. Karlen
1973   Holocene Climatic Variations: Their Pattern and Possible Cause. *Quaternary Research* 3(2):155-205.

Denton, G.H., and T.J. Hughes (eds.)
1981   The Last Great Ice Sheets. John Wiley & Sons. New York.

Derevianko, A.P.
1990   Paleolithic of North Asia and the Problem of Ancient Migrations. Academy of Sciences of the USSR. Novosibirsk.

Derkson, S.J.
1977   Glacial Geology. Pp. 1-32 in Dixon Harbour Biological Survey: Final Report on the Summer Phase of 1975 Research. G.P. Streveler and I.A. Worley eds. National Park Service. Juneau.

Dewhirst, J.
1980   The Indigenous Archaeology of Yuquot, A Nootkan Outside Village. The Yuquot Project. Vol. 1. W.J. Folan and J. Dewhirst eds. *Canada National Historic Parks and Sites Branch History and Archaeology* 39. Ottawa.

Diamond, G.
1979   The Nature of So-Called Polished Surfaces on Stone Artifacts. Pp. 159-66 in Lithic Use-Wear Analysis. B. Hayden ed. Academic Press. New York.

Dikov, N.N.
1977   Arkheologicheskie Pamiatniki Kamchatki, Chukotki i Verkhnei Kolymy. (Archeological Monuments of Kamchatka, Chuktka and the Upper Koloyma). Izdatel'stvo "Nauka." Moscow.

1979   Dreunie Kultury Severo-Vostochnoi Azii (Ancient Cultures of Northeastern Asia). Izdatel'stvo "Nauka." Moscow.

1988   On the Road to America. *Natural History* 1:10-14.

Dixon, E.J.
1976   The Pleistocene Prehistory of Arctic North America. In Colloque 17, IX Congrès, Union Internationale des Sciences Préhistoriques et Protohistoriques. Nice.

1993   Quest for the Origins of the First Americans. University of New Mexico Press. Albuquerque.

Doll, M., and R.S. Kidd
1978   Fluted Points in Alberta. Poster Session, American Quaternary Association International Conference. Edmonton.

Donahue, P.
1975   Prehistoric Relationships between the Plains, Boreal Forest and Cordilleran Regions. Pp. 83-92 in Prehistory of the North American Sub-Arctic: The Athabascan Question. J.W. Helmer, S. Van Dyke, and F.J. Kense eds. *Proceedings of the Ninth Annual Chac Mool Conference.* Calgary.

Driver, J.C.
1982   Early Prehistoric Killing of Big Horn Sheep in the Southeastern Canadian Rockies. *Plains Anthropologist* 27:265-72.

1988   Late Pleistocene and Holocene Vertebrates and Palaeoenvironments from the Charlie Lake Cave Site, Northeast British Columbia. *Canadian Journal of Earth Sciences* 25:1545-53.

1990   Meat in Due Season: The Timing of Communal Hunts. Pp. 11-33 in Hunters of the Recent Past. B.O.K. Reeves and L.B. Davis eds. George Allen and Unwin. London.

Duggins, D.C., C.A. Simenstad, and J.A. Estes
1989   Magnification of Secondary Production by Kelp Detritus in Coastal Marine Ecosystems. *Science* 245:170-3.

Duk-Rodkin, A., and L. Jackson
1993   Late Wisconsinan Glaciation and the Ice-free Corridor. P. A-25 in *Geological Association of Canada Meetings Abstracts.*

Dumond, D.E.
1980   The Archaeology of Alaska and the Peopling of America. *Science* 209(29):984-91.

Dunbar, J.S., S.D. Webb, and M. Faught
1992   Inundated Prehistoric Sites in Apalachee Bay, Florida, and the Search for the Clovis Shoreline. In Paleoshorelines and Prehistory: An Investigation of Method. L.L Johnson and M. Stright eds. CRC Press. Ann Arbor.

Easton, N.A.
1992   Mal de Mer above Terra Incognita, or "What Ails the Coastal Migration Theory." *Arctic Anthropology* 29:28-42.

Eldridge, M.
1974   Recent Archaeological Investigations near Chase, B.C. *Cariboo College Papers in Archaeology* 2. Kamloops

1981   The Hope Highway Archaeological Salvage Project. Pp. 53-110 in *Annual Research Report 1, Activities of the Heritage Conservation Branch for the Year 1978*. B.O. Simonsen, R. Kenny, J. McMurdo, and P. Rafferty eds. Heritage Conservation Branch. Victoria.

Eldridge, M., A. Mackie, and B. Wilson
1993   Archaeological Inventory of Gwaii Haanas National Park Reserve, 1992. Report on file, Parks Canada. Calgary.

Eliade, M.
1964   Shamanism: Archaic Techniques of Ecstasy. Pantheon Books.

Elmendorf, W.W.
1965   Linguistic and Geographic Relations in the Northern Plateau Area. *Southwestern Journal of Anthropology* 21:63-78.

Erlandson, J.M
1984   Faunal Analysis of the Invertebrate Assemblage. Pp. 151-79 in The Hidden Falls Site, Baranof Island, Alaska. S.D. Davis ed. Manuscript on file, Chatham Area Office, Tongass National Forest, USDA Forest Service, Sitka.

Estes, J.A., N.S. Smith, and J.F. Palmisano
1978   Sea Otter Predation and Community Organization in the Western Aleutian Islands. *Ecology* 59:822-33.

Fairbanks, R.G.
1989   A 17,000-year Glacio-Eustatic Sea Level Record: Influence of Glacial Melting Rates on the Younger Dryas Event and Deep-Ocean Circulation. *Nature* 342:637-42.

Farley, A.
1979   Atlas of British Columbia. University of British Columbia Press. Vancouver.

Fawcett, I.
1991   Appendix C: Faunal Analysis of Matrix Samples. Pp. 97-100 in The Economic Prehistory of Namu: Patterns in Vertebrate Fauna, by Aubrey Cannon. *Simon Fraser University Department of Archaeology Publication* 19. Burnaby.

Fedje, D.W.
1979   Scanning Electron Microscopy Analysis of Use-Striae Pp. 179-88 in Lithic Use-Wear Analysis. B. Hayden ed. Academic Press. New York.

1983   An Early Prehistoric Surface Find from Site 349R. Note on file, Archaeological Research Services, Canadian Parks Service. Calgary.

1986   Banff Archaeology 1983-1985. Pp. 25-62 in Eastern Slopes Prehistory Selected Papers. B. Ronaghan ed. *Archaeological Survey of Alberta Occasional Paper* 30. Edmonton.

1988a   The Norquay and Eclipse Sites: Trans-Canada Highway Twinning Mitigation in Banff National Park. *Environment Canada Parks Service Microfiche Report Series* 395. Ottawa.

1988b   Banff Prehistory, in Banff National Park Resource Description and Analysis. Manuscript on file, Environment Canada Parks Service.

1993   Sea-Levels and Prehistory in Gwaii Haanas. M.A. thesis in archaeology, University of Calgary.

Fedje, D.W., A. Mason, and J.B. McSporran
n.d.   Preliminary Investigations at the Arrow Creek Sites in Gwaii Haanas. Paper in preparation.

Fedje, D.W., and Wanagun (R. Wilson)
1991   1990 Archaeological Inventory and Impact Assessment in Gwaii Haanas. Report on file, Parks Canada. Calgary.

Fedje, D.W., and J. White
1988   Vermilion Lakes Archaeology and Paleoecology. Trans-Canada Highway Mitigation in Banff National Park. *Environment Canada Parks Service Microfiche Series* 463. Ottawa.

Ferguson, A., and L.V. Hills
1985   A Palynological Record, Upper Elk Valley, British Columbia. Pp. 355-69 in Climatic Change in Canada: Critical Periods in the Quaternary Climatic History of Northern North America. C.R. Harington ed. *Syllogeus* 55.

Fisher, J.L.
1961   Art Styles as Cultural Cognitive Maps. *American Anthropologist* 63:79-93.

Fladmark, K.R.
1970a   Preliminary Report on the Archaeology of the Queen Charlotte Islands: 1969 Field Season. Pp. 18-45 in Archaeology of British Columbia: New Discoveries. R.L. Carlson ed. *BC Studies* 6, 7.

1970b   Preliminary Report on Lithic Assemblages from the Queen Charlotte Islands, British Columbia. Pp. 117-36 in Early Man and Environments in Northwest North America. R.A. Smith and J.W. Smith eds. University of Calgary Archaeological Association. Calgary.

1975   A Paleoecological Model for Northwest Coast Prehistory. *Canada. National Museum of Man. Mercury Series. Archaeological Survey Paper* 43. Ottawa.

1978   The Feasibility of the Northwest Coast as a Migration Route for Early Man. Pp. 19-128 in Early Man in America from a Circum-Pacific Perspective. A.L. Bryan

ed. *University of Alberta Department of Anthropology Occasional Papers* 1. Edmonton.

1979a   Routes: Alternate Migration Corridors for Early Man in North America. *American Antiquity* 44:55-69.

1979b   The Early Prehistory of the Queen Charlotte Islands. *Archaeology* 32:38-45.

1981   Paleoindian Artifacts from the Peace River District. Pp. 124-35 in Fragments of the Past: British Columbia Archaeology in the 1970s. K.R. Fladmark ed. *BC Studies* 48.

1982   An Introduction to the Prehistory of British Columbia. *Canadian Journal of Archaeology* 6:95-156.

1983   Time and Places: Environmental Correlates of Mid-to-Late Wisconsinan Human Population Expansion in North America. Pp. 13-41 in Early Man in the New World. Richard Shutler Jr. ed. Sage Publications. Beverly Hills.

1985   Glass and Ice: The Archaeology of Mt. Edziza. *Simon Fraser University Department of Archaeology Publication* 14. Burnaby.

1986a   Lawn Point and Kasta: Microblade Sites on the Queen Charlotte Islands, British Columbia. *Canadian Journal of Archaeology* 10:37-58.

1986b   British Columbia Prehistory. National Museums of Canada. Ottawa.

1989   The Native Culture History of the Queen Charlotte Islands. Pp. 199-222 in The Outer Shores. G. Scudder and N. Gessler eds. Queen Charlotte Museum Press. Skidegate.

1990   Possible Early Human Occupation in the Queen Charlotte Islands. *Canadian Journal of Archaeology* 14:183-97.

Fladmark, K.R., D. Alexander, and J. Driver
1984   Excavations at Charlie Lake Cave (HbRf 39), 1983. Manuscript report on file, Heritage Conservation Branch. Victoria.

Fladmark, K.R., K. Ames, and P. Sutherland
1990   Archaeology of the Northern Coast of British Columbia. Pp. 229-39 in Handbook of North American Indians, 7, Northwest Coast. W. Suttles ed. Smithsonian. Washington.

Fladmark, K.R., J.C. Driver, and D. Alexander
1988   The Paleoindian Component at Charlie Lake Cave (HbRf 39), British Columbia. *American Antiquity* 53(2):371-84.

Flenniken, J.
1981   Replicative Systems Analysis: A Model Applied to the Vein Quartz Artifacts from the Hoko River Archaeological Site. *Washington State University Laboratory of Anthropological Reports of Investigations* 59. Pullman.

Frederick, G.C., and S. Crockford
1987   Report on Vertebrate Faunal Remains from Rosie's Rockshelter (CRG-236) and Forward (Chuck) Lake (CRG-237), Alaska. Contract Report in conjunction with Ackerman et al. 1985, USDA Forest Service. Ketchikan.

French, D.
1973   Nelson Archaeological Project: Results of the Investigation of a Stratified Campsite, DiQi 1 near Taghum, BC. Report on file Archaeology Branch. Victoria.

Friele, P.A.
1991   Holocene Relative Sea-Level Change: Vargas Island, British Columbia. M.Sc. thesis in geography, Simon Fraser University. Burnaby.

Frison, G.C.
1973   The Wardell Buffalo Trap 48SU301: Communal Procurement in the Upper Green River Basin, Wyoming. *University of Michigan Museum of Anthropology Paper* 48.

1977   Paleoindian Sites and Economic Orientations in the Big Horn Basin. Pp. 97-116 in Paleoindian Lifeways. E. Johnson ed. *Museum Journal* 17. West Texas Museum Association. Lubbock.

1978   Prehistoric Hunters of the High Plains. Academic Press. New York.

1983   The Western Plains and Mountain Region. Pp. 109-24 in *Early Man in the New World*. R. Shutler Jr. ed. Sage Publications. Beverly Hills.

Frison, G., and D. Stanford
1982   The Agate Basin Site. Academic Press. New York.

Fulton, R.J.
1971   Radiocarbon Geochronology of Southern British Columbia. *Geological Survey of Canada Paper* 7:1-37.

Fyles, J.G.
1963   Surficial Geology of Horne Lake and Parksville Map-areas, Vancouver Island, British Columbia. *Geological Survey of Canada Memoir* 318. Ottawa.

Garrison, E.G.
1992   Recent Archaeogeophysical Studies of Paleoshorelines of the Gulf of Mexico. In *Paleoshorelines and Prehistory: an Investigation of Method*. L.L. Johnson and M. Stright eds. CRC Press. Ann Arbor.

Gehr, K.D.
1976   The Archaeology of the Hihium Lake Locality, British Columbia. Manuscript on file with the author.

Godfrey-Smith, D.
1984   Obsidian X-ray Fluorescence Analysis of Five Samples from the Paul Mason Site. Manuscript, Laboratory of Archaeology, University of British Columbia. Vancouver.

1987   Obsidian Artifact Analysis-Chuck Lake Site, Heceta Island, Alaska. Contract Report in conjunction with Ackerman et al. 1985, USDA Forest Service. Ketchikan.

Golubev, V.A.
1983   K Vosprosy o Pervonochal'nom Zaselenii Ostrova Sakhalin (The Question of the Initial Settlement of Sakhalin Island). In Pozdnepleistotsenovye i Runnegolotsenovye Kul'turnye Sviazi Azii iAmerihii. Otvetstvennyi Redaktor, R.S. Vasil'evskii, str. 41-8, Izdatel'stvo "Nauka," Sibirskoe Otdelenie, Novosibirsk.

Gough, S. ed.
1984   Cultural Resource Investigations of the Bonneville Power Administration's Libby Integration Project, Northern Idaho and Northwestern Montana. *Eastern Washington University Reports in Archaeology and History*. Archaeological and Historical Services. Cheney.

Grabert, G.
1974   Okanagan Archaeology. *Syesis* 7, Supp. 2.

1979   Pebble Tools and Time Factoring. *Canadian Journal of Archaeology* 3:165-76.

Grayson, D.K.
1984   Quantitative Zooarchaeology: Topics in the Analysis of Archaeological Faunas. Academic Press. Orlando.

Greaves, S.
1991   The Organization of Microcore Technology in the Canadian Southern Interior Plateau. Ph.D. dissertation in anthropology, University of British Columbia, Vancouver.

Gruhn, R.
1961   The Archaeology of Wilson Butte Cave, Southcentral Idaho. *Idaho State College Museum Occasional Papers* 6. Pocatello.

Gryba, E.
1983   Sibbald Creek: 11,000 Years of Human Use of the Alberta Foothills. *Archaeological Survey of Alberta Occasional Paper* 22. Edmonton.

1985   Evidence of the Fluted Point Tradition in Alberta. Pp. 22-38 in Contributions to Plains Prehistory: The 1984 Victoria Symposium. D. Burley ed. *Archaeological Survey of Alberta Occasional Paper* 26.

1988   An Inventory of Fluted Point Occurrences in Alberta. Report on file, Archaeological Survey of Alberta. Edmonton.

Haley, S.D.
1981   Evidence for a Bipolar Technology at the South Yale Site, BC. *The Midden* 13(2): 9-11.

1982   A Second Look at the Pasika Complex. Paper presented at the 35th Annual Northwest Anthropological Conference. Burnaby.

1983a   New Radiocarbon Estimates for the South Yale Site, BC. *The Midden* 15(2):7-10.

1983b   The South Yale Site: Yet Another Point. *The Midden* 15(5):3-5.

1987   The Pasika Complex: Cobble Reduction Strategies on the Northwest Coast. Ph.D dissertation in archaeology, Simon Fraser University. Burnaby.

Ham, L.C.
1976   Analysis of Shell Samples from Glenrose. Pp. 42-78 in Prehistoric Adaptations at the Glenrose Cannery Site (DgRr 6) Fraser Delta, BC., R.G. Matson ed. *Canada. National Museum of Man. Mercury Series. Archaeological Survey Paper* 52. Ottawa.

1990   The Cohoe Creek Site: A Late Moresby Tradition Shell Midden. *Canadian Journal of Archaeology* 14:199-221.

Harrison, J.E.
1976   Dated Organic Material below Mazama (?) Tephra: Elk Valley British Columbia. *Geological Survey of Canada Paper* 76-10:169-70.

Hart, J.L.
1973   Pacific Fishes of Canada. *Fisheries Research Board of Canada Bulletin* 180. Ottawa.

Hartwig, F., and B.E. Dearing
1979   Exploratory Data Analysis. Sage University Paper Series on Quantitative Applications in the Social Sciences, 07106. Beverly Hills.

Hayden, B.
1980   Confusion in the Bipolar World: Bashed Pebbles and Splintered Pieces. *Lithic Technology* 9 (1):2-7

Hayden, B., D. Alexander, K. Kusmer, D. Lepofsky, D. Martin, M. Rousseau, and P. Friele
1986   Report on the 1986 Excavations at Keatley Creek: A Report of the Fraser River Investigations into Corporate Group Archaeology Project. Report on File, Department of Archaeology, Simon Fraser University. Burnaby.

Hayden, B., J. Breffitt, P. Friele, M. Greene, W.K. Hutchings, D. Jolly, I. Kuijt, K. Kusmer, D. Lepofsky, B. Muir, M. Rousseau, and D. Martin
1987   Report on the 1987 Excavations at Keatley Creek: A Report of the Fraser River Investigations into Corporate Group Archaeology Project. Report on File, Department of Archaeology, Simon Fraser University. Burnaby.

Hayden, B. and J. Spafford
1993   The Keatley Creek Site and Corporate Group Archaeology. Pp. 106-39 in Changing Times: British Columbia Archaeology in the 1980s. K. Fladmark, ed. *BC Studies* 99.

Haynes, C.V.
1991   Geoarchaeological and Paleohydrological Evidence for a Clovis-Age Drought in North America and Its Bearing on Extinction. *Quaternary Research* 35(3):438-51.

Hebda, R.J
1977   The Paleoecology of a Raised Bog and Associated Deltaic Sediments of the Fraser Delta. Ph.D. dissertation, University of British Columbia. Vancouver.

1981   Palaeoecology of Bluebird Pond, Rocky Mountain Trench, British Columbia. Report on file, Royal British Columbia Museum. Victoria.

1982   Postglacial History of Grasslands of Southern British Columbia and Adjacent Regions. Pp. 157-94 in Grassland Ecology and Classification, Symposium Proceedings, June 1982. A.C. Nicholson, A. McLean, and T.E. Baker eds. BC Ministry of Forests. Victoria.

1983   Postglacial Environment History, Highland Valley and Surrounding Areas. In Bethlehem Copper Lake Zone Development Heritage Mitigation Study, by A. H. Stryd and S. Lawhead (Arcas Associates), Appendix II. Consultants 1984. Report on file, Resource Management Branch. Victoria.

Hebda, R., and R. Mathewes
1984   Holocene History of Cedar and Native Indian Cultures of the North American Pacific Coast. *Science* 255:711-13.

Helm, J. ed.
1981   Handbook of North American Indians, 6, Subarctic. Smithsonian. Washington.

Herschberg L.B., A.A. Riazantsev, and A.V. Mechetin
1983   Ancient Shorelines of the Last Postgacial Transgression and their Mapping on the Shelves of the Sea of Japan and the Sea of Okhotsk In *XI Congress, International Union for Quaternary Research, Abstracts* 3:108. Moscow.

Hester, J.J.
1978　Conclusions: Early Tool Traditions in Northwest North America. Pp. 101-12 in Studies in Bella Bella Prehistory, J.J. Hester and S.M. Nelson eds. *Simon Fraser University Department of Archaeology Publication* 5. Burnaby.

Hester, J.J., and S.M. Nelson eds.
1978　Studies in Bella Bella Prehistory. *Simon Fraser University Department of Archaeology Publication* 5. Burnaby.

Heusser, C.J.
1960　Late-Pleistocene Environments of North Pacific North America. *American Geographical Society Special Publications* 35. New York.

Hicks, S.D., and W. Shofnos
1965　The Determination of Land Emergence from Sea Level Observations in Northeastern Alaska. *Journal of Geophysical Research* 70(14):3315-20

Hobler, P.M.
1976　Archaeological Sites on Moresby Island, Queen Charlotte Islands. Report on file, BC Archaeology Branch. Victoria.

1978　The Relationship of Archaeological Sites to Sea Levels on Moresby Island, Queen Charlotte Island. *Canadian Journal of Archaeology* 2:1-14.

Hoffecker, J.F., W.R. Powers, and T. Goebel
1993　The Colonization of Beringia and the Peopling of the New World. *Science* 259:46-53.

Holland, S.S.
1964　Landforms of British Columbia: A Physiographic Outline. *British Columbia Department of Mines and Petroleum Resources Bulletin* 48. Victoria.

Holloway, G.P.
1989　Analysis of Botanical Material. Pp. 57-86 in The Hidden Falls Site, Baranof Island, Alaska. S.D. Davis ed. Manuscript on file, Chatham Area Office, Tongass National Forest. Sitka.

Holmes, C.E.
1988　Archaeological Mitigation of the Thorne River Site (CRG-177), Prince of Wales Island, Alaska. *Alaska Department of Natural Resources Office of History and Archaeology Report* 15. Fairbanks.

Holmes, C.E., and J.D. McMahan
1979　The Thorne River Archaeological Mitigation Project, An Interim Progress Report. Abstracts, 15th Annual Meeting of the Alaska Anthropological Association. Fairbanks.

Hopkins, D.M.
1979　Landscape and Climate of Beringia during Late Pleistocene and Holocene Time. Pp. 15-41 in The First Americans: Origins, Affinities and Adaptations. W.S. Laughlin and A.B. Harper eds. Gustav Fisher. New York.

Hudson, T., K. Dixon, and G. Plafker
1982　Regional Uplift in Southeastern Alaska. Pp. 132-35 in the U.S. Geological Survey in Alaska: Accomplishments during 1980. W.L. Coonrand ed. *Geological Survey Circular* 844. Washington.

Hutchings, W. K.
1991　The Nachcharin Composite Projectile: Design Theory and the Study of Hunting Systems Technology at Mugharet en-Nachcharini in the Post-Natufian Levant. M.A. thesis in anthropology, University of Toronto. Toronto.

n.d.　Un-Designing the Past: Design Theory, Technology, and Archaeological Explanation. Manuscript in possession of the author.

Imamoto, S.
1976　An Analysis of the Glenrose Faunal Remains. Pp. 21-41 in Prehistoric Adaptations at the Glenrose Cannery Site (DgRr 6) Fraser Delta, BC. R.G. Matson ed. *Canada. National Museum of Man. Mercury Series. Archaeological Survey Paper* 52. Ottawa.

Irving, W.N., and J. Cinq-Mars
1974   A Tentative Archaeological Sequence for
        Old Crow Flats, Yukon Territory. *Arctic
        Anthropology* 2 (supplement):65-81.

Ives, J.W.
1980   The Prehistory of the Boreal Forest of
        Northern Alberta. Paper presented to
        the Annual Meeting of the Archaeologi-
        cal Society of Alberta, Lethbridge.

Ives, J.W., A.B. Beaudoin, and M. Magne
1989   Evaluating the Role of a Western Corri-
        dor in the Peopling of the Americas. In
        Routes into the New World. Reprint
        Proceedings of the Circum-Pacific Pre-
        history Conference. R.E. Ackerman ed.
        Washington State University. Pullman.

Jennings, J.D.
1983   Ancient North Americans. W.H. Free-
        man. San Francisco.

Johnson, E.
1987   Late Pleistocene Cultural Occupation on
        the Southern Plains. *International
        Union for Quaternary Research XII
        International Conference Abstracts* 195.

Johnson-Fladmark, S.
1973   Shuswap Lakes Archaeological Project.
        Manuscript on file, Resource Manage-
        ment Branch. Victoria.

Josenhans, H.W., J.V. Barrie, K.W. Conway,
        R.T. Patterson, R.W. Mathewes, and G.J.
        Woodsworth.
1993   Surficial Geology of the Queen Charlotte
        Basin: Evidence of Submerged Proglacial
        Lakes at 170 m on the Continental Shelf
        of Western Canada. Current Research,
        Part A, *Geological Survey of Canada
        Paper* 93-1A:119-27.

Josenhans, H.W., D.W. Fedje, K.W. Conway, and
        J.V. Barrie
in   Post Glacial Sea-levels on the West-
press   ern Canadian Continental Shelf: Evi-
        dence for Rapid Change, Extensive
        Subareal Exposure and Early Human
        Occupation. *Marine Geology*.

Kamminga, J.
1979   The Nature of Use-Polish and Abrasive
        Smoothing on Stone Tools. Pp. 143-58 in
        Lithic Use-Wear Analysis. B. Hayden ed.
        Academic Press. New York.

Keddie, G.R.
1981   The Use and Distribution of Labrets on
        the North Pacific Rim. *Syesis* 1(4):59-80.

Keeley, L.H.
1980   Experimental Determination of Stone
        Tool Uses. University of Chicago Press.
        Chicago.

Kelley, C.C., and W.D. Holland
1961   Soil Survey of the Upper Columbia River
        Valley. *British Columbia Soil Survey
        Report* 7. Victoria.

Kelley C.C., and P.N. Sprout
1956   Soil Survey of the Upper Kootenay and
        Elk River Valleys in the East Kootenay
        District of British Columbia. *British
        Columbia Soil Survey Report* 5. Victoria.

Kelly, M.K.
1984   Microblade Technology and Variability
        in the Chehalis River Region, Southwest
        Washington. M.A. thesis, Department of
        Anthropology, Washington State Univer-
        sity. Pullman.

Kelly, R.L.
1988   The Three Sides of a Biface. *American
        Antiquity* 53:717-34.

Kelly, R.L., and L.C. Todd
1988   Coming in to the Country: Early
        Paleoindian Hunting and Mobility.
        American Antiquity 53:231-44.

Kennedy, D.I.D., and R. Bouchard
1975   Indian History and Knowledge of the Merritt to Surrey Lake Corridor of the Proposed Coquihalla Highway. Appendix 1. In Coquihalla Highway Project, Merritt Bypass to Surrey Lake, BC, Detailed Heritage Resource Inventory and Impact Assessment by S. Lawhead (Arcas Associates). Consultants report on file, Resource Management Branch. Victoria.

Kerr, R.A.
1994   Iron Fertilization: A Tonic, but No Cure for the Greenhouse. *Science* 263:1089-90

Khotinskiy, N.A.
1984   Holocene Climatic Change. Pp. 179-200 in Late Quaternary Environments of the Soviet Union. A.A. Velichko ed. (English language edition edited by H.E. Wright Jr. and C.W. Barbosky). University of Minnesota Press. Minneapolis.

Kidd, R.S.
1964A   Synthesis of Western Washington Prehistory from the Perspective of Three Occupation Sites. M.A. thesis in anthropology, University of Washington. Seattle.

Kinkaide, M.D.
1990   Prehistory of Salishan Languages. Pp. 197-208 in *Papers of the 25th International Conference on Salish and Neighbouring Languages.* University of British Columbia. Vancouver.

Klein, R.G.
1973   Ice-Age Hunters of the Ukraine. University of Chicago Press. Chicago.

Kukan, G.J.
1978   A Technological and Stylistic Study of Microliths from Certain Levantine Epipaleolithic Assemblages. Ph.D. dissertation in anthropology, University of Toronto. Toronto.

Kunz, M.L., and R.E. Reanier
1994   Paleoindians in Beringia: Evidence from Arctic Alaska. *Science* 263:660-2.

Kusmer, K.D.
1986   Microvertebrate Taphonomy in Archaeological Sites: An Examination of Owl Deposition and the Taphonomy of Small Mammals from Sentinel Cave, Oregon. M.A. thesis in archaeology, Simon Fraser University. Burnaby.

Lamb, H.H.
1977   Climate, Present, Past and Future. Vol. 2. Methuen. London.

Larsen, C.
1971   An Investigation into the Relationship of Change in Relative Sea Level to Social Change in the Prehistory of Birch Bay, Washington. M.A. thesis in anthropology, Western Washington State College. Bellingham.

Laughlin, W.S.
1975   Aleuts: Ecosystem, Holocene History and Siberian Origin. *Science* 189 (4202):507-15.

1980   Aleuts: Survivors of the Bering Land Bridge. Holt, Rinehart and Winston. New York.

Lawhead, S.
1979   Salvage Archaeology Project 1978: Investigations at 6 Locations in British Columbia. Manuscript on file, Resource Management Branch. Victoria.

Layton, T.N.
1972   Lithic Chronology in the Fort Rock Valley, Oregon. *Tebiwa* 15:1-21.

LeBlanc, R., and J.W. Ives
1986   The Bezya Site: A Wedge-Shaped Core Assemblage from Northeastern Alberta. *Canadian Journal of Archaeology* 10:59-98.

LeClair, R.
1976   Investigations at the Maurer site near Agassiz. Pp. 33-42 in Current Research Reports. R.L. Carlson ed. *Simon Fraser University Department of Archaeology Publication* 3. Burnaby.

Leonhardy, F.C.
1975   The Lower Snake River Culture Typology –1975, Leonhardy and Rice Revisited. Abstract of a paper presented at 28th Annual Meeting, Northwest Anthropological Conference. *Northwest Anthropological Research Notes* 10:61.

Leonhardy, F.C., and D.G. Rice
1970   A Proposed Culture Typology for the Lower Snake River Region, Southeastern Washington. *Northwestern Anthropological Research Notes* 4(1):1-29

Long, A., and B. Rippeteau
1974   Testing Contemporaneity and Averaging Radiocarbon Dates. *American Antiquity* 39:205-15.

Ludowdoicz, D.
1983   Assemblage Variation Associated with Southwestern Interior Plateau Microblade Technology. M.A. thesis in anthropology, University of British Columbia. Vancouver.

Luebbers, R.
1978   Excavations: Stratigraphy and Artifacts. Pp. 11-66 in Studies in Bella Bella Prehistory. J. Hester and S. Nelson eds. *Simon Fraser University Department of Archaeology Publication* 5. Burnaby.

Luternauer, J.L., J.J. Clague, I.W. Conway, J.V. Barrie, B. Blaise, and R.W. Mathewes
1989   Late Pleistocene Terrestrial Deposits on the Continental Shelf of Western Canada: Evidence for Rapid Sea-level Change at the End of the Last Glaciation. *Geology* 17:357-60.

MacDonald, G.F.
1969   Preliminary Culture Sequence from the Coast Tsimshian Area, British Columbia. *Northwest Anthropological Research Notes* 3:240- 54.

1971   A Review of Research on Paleo-Indian in Eastern North America, 1960-1970. *Arctic Anthropology* 8(2):32-41.

1979   Kitwanga Fort National Historic Site, Skeena River, British Columbia: Historical Research and Analysis of Structural Remains. National Museum of Man. Ottawa.

1983   Prehistoric Art of the Northern Northwest Coast. Pp. 99-120 in Indian Art Traditions of the Northwest Coast. R.L. Carlson ed. Archaeology Press, Simon Fraser University. Burnaby.

MacDonald, G.F., and R. Inglis
1981   An Overview of the North Coast Prehistory Project. *BC Studies* 48:37-63.

MacDonald, G.M.
1987   Postglacial Development of the Subalpine-Boreal Transition Forest of Western Canada. *Journal of Ecology* 75:303-20.

Mack, R.N., N.W. Rutter, V. Bryant Jr., and S. Valastro
1978a Reexamination of Postglacial Vegetation History in North Idaho, Hager Pond, Bonner County. *Quaternary Research* 10:141-55.

1978b Late Quaternary Pollen Record from Big Meadow, Pend Oreille County, Washington. *Ecology* 59(5):956-65.

Mack, R.N., N.W. Rutter, and S. Valastro
1978   Quaternary Record from the Sanpoil River Valley, Washington. *Canadian Journal of Botany* 56:1642-50.

Mackie, A., and B. Wilson
1994   Archaeological Inventory of Gwaii Haanas, 1993. Report on file, Parks Canada. Calgary.

MacNeish, R.S.
1955   Two Archaeological Sites on Great Bear Lake, Northwest Territories, Canada. *Annual report of the National Museum of Canada for the fiscal year 1953-54.* Department of Northern Affairs and National Resources. Ottawa.

Magne, M.
1979   Early Prehistoric Cultures of the Interior Plateau of British Columbia: An Examination of the Evidence for Cultural Change and Continuity. Unpublished manuscript.

Magne, M., and R.G. Matson
1982   Identification of "Salish" and "Athabascan" Side-notched Projectile Points from the Interior Plateau of British Columbia. Pp. 57-79 in Approaches to Algonquin Archaeology. M. Hanna and B. Kooyman eds. University of Calgary Archaeological Association. Calgary.

Mann, D.H.
1986   Wisconsin and Holocene Glaciation of Southeast Alaska. Pp. 237-65 in Glaciation in Alaska: The Geological Record. T.D. Hamilton, K.M. Reed, and R.M. Thorson eds. Alaska Geological Society. Anchorage.

Mathewes, R.W.
1984   Paleobotanical Evidence for Climatic Change in Southern British Columbia During Late-glacial and Holocene Time. Pp. 397-422 in Climatic Change in Canada 5. C.R. Harington ed. *Syllogeus* 55.

1989   Paleobotany of the Queen Charlotte Islands. Pp. 75-90 in The Outer Shores. G. Scudder and N. Gessler eds. Queen Charlotte Museum Press. Skidegate.

Mathewes, R.W., C.E. Borden, and C.E. Rouse
1972   New Radiocarbon Dates from the Yale Area of the Lower Fraser River Canyon, British Columbia. *Canadian Journal of Earth Sciences* 9(8):1055-7.

Mathewes R.W., and L. Heusser
1981   A 12,000-Year Palynological Record of Temperature and Precipitation Trends in Southwestern British Columbia *Canadian Journal of Botany* 59:707-10.

Mathewes, R.W., and M. King
1989   Holocene Vegetation, Climate, and Lake Level Changes in the Interior Douglas-fir Biogeoclimatic Zone, British Columbia. *Canadian Journal of Earth Sciences* 26:1811-25.

Mathewes, R.W., and C.E. Rouse
1975   Palynology and Paleoecology of Postglacial Sediments from the Lower Fraser River Canyon of British Columbia. *Canadian Journal of Earth Sciences* 12:745-56.

Mathews, W.H.
1978   Quaternary Stratigraphy and Geomorphology of Charlie Lake (94A) Map Area, British Columbia. *Geological Survey of Canada Paper* 76-20.

1979   Late Quaternary Environmental History Affecting Human History of the Pacific Northwest. *Canadian Journal of Archaeology* 3:145-56.

1980   Retreat of the Last Ice Sheets in Northeastern British Columbia. *Geological Survey of Canada Bulletin* 331.

Mathews, W.H., J.G. Fyles, and H. Nasmith
1970   Postglacial Crustal Movement in Southwestern British Columbia and Adjacent Washington State. *Canadian Journal of Earth Sciences* 7:690-702.

Matson, R.G.
1976   Prehistoric Adaptations at the Glenrose Cannery Site (DgRr 6) Fraser Delta, BC. *Canada. National Museum of Man. Mercury Series. Archaeological Survey Paper* 52. Ottawa.

1981   Prehistoric Subsistence Patterns in the Fraser Delta: The Evidence from the Glenrose Cannery Site. Pp. 124-35 in Fragments of the Past: British Columbia Archaeology in the 1970s. K.R. Fladmark ed. *BC Studies* 48.

1983   Intensification and the Development of Cultural Complexity: The Northwest Coast Versus the Northeast Coast. Pp. 125-48 in The Evolution of Maritime Cultures on the Northeast and Northwest Coasts of America. R.J. Nash ed. *Simon Fraser University, Department of Archaeology Publication* 11. Burnaby.

McIlwraith, T.F.
1948   The Bella Coola Indians. Vol. 1. University of Toronto Press. Toronto.

McKendry, J.
1983   Archaeological Skeletal Remains found near Clinton, BC Report on file, Library, Ministry of Tourism and Ministry Responsible for Culture. Victoria.

McMillan, A.D.
1975   Preliminary Report on Archaeological Survey in the Alberni Valley and Upper Alberni Inlet. Unpublished report, Heritage Conservation Branch. Victoria.

McMillan, A.D., and D.E. St. Claire
1982   Alberni Prehistory: Archaeological and Ethnographic Investigations on Western Vancouver Island. Theytus Books. Penticton.

Mehringer Jr., P.J.
1988   Weapons Cache of Ancient Americans. *National Geographic* 174:500-3.

Mehringer Jr., P.J., J.C. Sheppard and F. Foit Jr.
1984   The Age of Glacier Peak Tephra in West-Central Montana. *Quaternary Research* 21:36-41.

Mehringer Jr., P.J., and F. Foit Jr.
1990   Volcanic Ash Dating of the Clovis Cache at East Wenatchee, Washington. *National Geographic Research* 6(4):495-503.

Midden, The
1992   Residential Subdivision – Then and Now. *The Midden* 24:4-9. Archaeological Society of British Columbia. Vancouver.

Mierendorf, R.R.
1984   Landforms, Sediments, and Archaeological Deposits along Libby Reservoir. Pp. 107-36 in Environment, Archaeology, and Land Use Patterns in the Middle Kootenai River Valley. A. Thoms ed. *Washington State University Center for Northwest Anthropology, Cultural Resources Investigations of Libby Reservoir, Lincoln County, Northwest Montana Project Report* 2.

Millar, J.H.V.
1968   The Archaeology of Fisherman Lake, Northwest Territories. Ph.D. dissertation in archaeology, University of Calgary. Calgary.

Miller, M.M., and J.H. Anderson
1974   Out-of-phase Holocene Climatic Trends in the Maritime and Continental Sectors of the Alaska-Canada Boundary Range. Pp. 197-223 in *National Geographic Society Research Reports*, 1967 Projects.

Mitchell, D.H.
1965   Preliminary Excavations at a Cobble Tool Site (DjRi 7) in the Fraser Canyon, British Columbia. *Anthropology Papers, National Museum of Canada* 10. Ottawa.

1970   Archaeological Investigations on the Chilcotin Plateau, 1968. *Syesis* 3:45-65.

1988   Changing Patterns of Resource Use in the Prehistory of Queen Charlotte Strait, British Columbia. Pp. 245-90 in Prehistoric Economies of the Pacific Northwest Coast. B.L. Isaac ed. *Research in Economic Anthropology, Supplement 3*. JAI Press. Greenwich, Connecticut.

Mitchell, D.H., R. Murray, and C. Carlson
1981   The Duke Point Archaeological Project: A Preliminary Report on Fieldwork and Analysis. Pp. 21-52 in *Annual Research Report of the Heritage Conservation Branch* 1. B.O. Simonsen, R. Kenny, J. McMurdo, and P. Rafferty eds. Heritage Conservation Branch, Victoria.

Mobley, C.M.
1988   Holocene Sea Levels in Southeast
        Alaska: Preliminary Results. *Arctic*
        41:261-6.

1991   The Campus Site: A Prehistoric Camp at
        Fairbanks, Alaska. University of Alaska
        Press. Fairbanks.

Mochanov, Iu. A.
1977   Drevneishie Etapy Zaseleniia
        Chelovekom Severo-Vostochnoi Azii
        (The Most Ancient Stages of Human
        Settlement in Northeastern Asia).
        Izdatel'stvo "Nauka." Novosibirsk.

1978   Stratigraphy and Absolute Chronology of
        the Paleolithic of Northeast Asia, Ac-
        cording to the Work of 1963-1973. Pp.
        54-66 in Early Man in America: From A
        Circum-Pacific Perspective. A.L. Bryan
        ed. *University of Alberta Department of
        Anthropology Occasional Papers* 1.
        Edmonton.

Mochanov, Yu. A., and S.A. Fedoseeva
1984   Main Periods in the Ancient History of
        North-East Asia. Pp. 669-93 in Beringia
        in the Cenozoic Era (Reports of the All
        Union Symposium "The Bering Land
        Bridge and its Role in the History of
        Holarctic Floras and Faunas in the Late
        Cenozoic," Khabarovsk, May 10-
        15,1973). V.L. Kontrimavichus ed.
        Translated from the 1976 Russian
        edition and published by the Amerind
        Publishing Co. Pvt. Ltd. New Delhi for
        the U.S. Department of Interior and the
        National Science Foundation.

Molnia, B.F.
1986   Glacial History of the Northeastern Gulf
        of Alaska: A Synthesis. Pp. 219-36 in
        Glaciation in Alaska: The Geological
        Record. T.D. Hamilton, K.M. Reed, and
        R.M. Thorson eds. Alaska Geological
        Society. Anchorage.

Moody, U.
1978   Microstratigraphy, Paleoecology, and
        Tephrachronology of the Lind Coulee
        Site, central Washington. Ph.D. disserta-
        tion in anthropology, Washington State
        University. Pullman.

Morlan, R.E.
1970   Wedge-shaped Core Technology in
        Northern North America. *Arctic Anthro-
        pology* 7(2):17-37.

Moss, M.
1984   Analysis of the Vertebrate Assemblage.
        Pp. 126-50 in The Hidden Falls Site,
        Baranoff Island, Alaska. S.D. Davis ed.
        Manuscript on file Chatham Area Office,
        Tongass National Forest, USDA Forest
        Service. Sitka.

Moss, M., and J. Erlandson
1992   Forts, Refuge Rocks, and Defensive
        Sites: The Antiquity of Warfare along
        the North Pacific Coast of North
        America. *Arctic Anthropology* 29(2):73-
        90.

Movius, H.L.
1949   The Lower Paleolithic Cultures of South-
        ern and Eastern Asia. *Transaction of the
        American Philosophical Society,* N.S. 38
        (4):329-420.

Mullineaux, R.R., J.H. Hyde, and M. Rubin
1975   Widespread Late Glacial and Postglacial
        Tephra Deposits from Mount St. Helens
        Volcano, Washington. *Journal of Re-
        search, U.S. Geological Survey* 3(3):329-
        35.

Mullineaux, R.R., R.E. Wilcox, W.F. Ebaugh, R.
        Fryxell, and M. Rubin
1978   Age of the Last Major Scabland Flood of
        the Columbia Plateau in Eastern Wash-
        ington. *Quaternary Research* 120:171-80.

Murray, J.S.
1981   Prehistoric Skeletons from Blue Jackets
        Creek (FlUa4), Queen Charlotte Islands,
        British Columbia. Pp. 127-75 in Contri-
        butions to Physical Anthropology, 1978-
        1980. J.S. Cybulski, ed. *Canada. Na-
        tional Museum of Man. Mercury Series.
        Archaeological Survey Papers* 106.
        Ottawa.

Murray, R.A.

1982   Analysis of Artifacts from Four Duke Point Area Sites, Near Nanaimo, BC: An Example of Cultural Continuity in the Southern Gulf of Georgia Region. *Canada. National Museum of Man. Mercury Series. Archaeological Survey Paper* 113. Ottawa.

Musil, R.R.

1988   Functional Efficiency and Technological Change: A Hafting Tradition Model for Prehistoric North America. Pp. 373-88 in Early Human Occupation in Far Western North America: The Clovis-Archaic Interface. J.A. Willig, C.M. Aikens, and J.L. Fagan eds. *Nevada State Museum Anthropological Papers* 21. Carson City.

Owen, L.R.

1988   Blade and Microblade Technology. *BAR International Series* 441. Oxford.

Peacock, W.

1976   Cluster Analysis and Multi-Dimensional Scaling of Cultural Components at Glenrose. Pp. 214-30 in Prehistoric Adaptations at the Glenrose Cannery Site (DgRr 6) Fraser Delta, BC. R.G. Matson ed. *Canada. National Museum of Man. Mercury Series. Archaeological Survey Paper* 52. Ottawa.

Pettipas, L.F.

1980   The Little Gem Complex. *Saskatchewan Archaeology* 1:3-81.

Pokotylo, D.

1978   Lithic Technology and Settlement Patterns in Upper Hat Creek Valley, British Columbia. Ph.D dissertation, University of British Columbia. Vancouver.

Powers, R., and J. Hoffecker

1989   Late Pleistocene Settlement in the Nenana Valley, Central Alaska. *American Antiquity* 54(2):263-87.

Pratt, H.

1988   An Examination of Old Cordilleran Chipped Stone Tools at Milliken and Glenrose. Paper prepared for Professor Pokotylo. Laboratory of Archaeology, University of British Columbia. Vancouver.

Pyszczyk, H.

1991   A Wedge-shaped Microblade Core, Fort Vermilion, Alberta. Pp. 199-203 in Archaeology in Alberta 1988 and 1989. M. Magne ed. *Archaeological Survey Provincial Museum of Alberta Occasional Paper* 33. Edmonton.

Rains, G., D. Kvill, and J. Shaw

1990   Evidence and Some Implications of Coalescent Cordilleran and Laurentide Glacier Systems in Western Alberta. Pp. 1-15 in *Essays in Honour of William C. Wonders.* P.J. Smith and L.E. Jackson eds.

Reasoner, M.A., and N.W. Rutter

1988   Late Quaternary History of the Lake O'Hara region, British Columbia: An Evaluation of Sedimentation Rates and Bulk Amino Acid Ratios in Lacustrine Records. *Canadian Journal of Earth Sciences* 25(7):1037-48.

Reeves, B.O.K.

1971   On the Coalescence of the Laurentide and Cordilleran Ice Sheets in the Western Interior of North America with Particular Reference to the Alberta Area. Pp. 205-28 in Aboriginal Man and Environments on the Plateau of Northwest America. A H. Stryd and R.H. Smith eds. Calgary Archaeological Association, Department of Archaeology, University of Calgary. Calgary.

1975   Archaeological Investigations at the Lake Minnewanka Site (EhPu-1). Unpublished manuscript on file, Archaeological Research Services, Canadian Parks Service. Calgary.

1976   The 1975 Archaeological Investigations at the Lake Lake Minnewanka Site (EhPu 1). Unpublished manuscript on file, Archaeological Research Services, Canadian Parks Service, Calgary.

Rice, D.G.
1972   The Windust Phase in Lower Snake River Region Prehistory. *Washington State University Laboratory of Anthropology, Report of Investigations* 50. Pullman.

Richards, T.H.
1978   Excavations at EeRl 171. Report on file, Resource Management Branch. Victoria.

Richards, T.H., and M.K. Rousseau
1987   Late Prehistoric Cultural Horizons on the Canadian Plateau. *Simon Fraser University Department of Archaeology Publication* 16. Burnaby.

Richmond, G.M., R. Fryxell, G.E. Neff, and P.L. Weis
1965   The Cordilleran Ice Sheet of the Northern Rocky Mountains and Related Quaternary History of the Columbia Plateau. Pp. 231-42 in The Quaternary of the United States: A Review Volume of the VII Congress of the International Association for Quaternary Research. H.E. Wright Jr. and G. Frey eds. Princeton University Press.

Roberts, A., J.H. McAndrews, V.K. Prest, J.S. Vincent
1987   The Fluted Point People, 9500-8200 BC. Plate 2 in Historical Atlas of Canada, Vol 1. R.C. Harris ed. University of Toronto Press. Toronto.

Roberts, L.
1982   Southeastern Archaeology in Light of the Irish Creek Site. Paper presented at the 9th Alaska Anthropological Conference. Fairbanks.

Rohner, R.P.
1967   The People of Guilford: A Contemporary Kwakiutl Village. *National Museum of Canada Bulletin* 225, *Anthropological Series* 83. Ottawa.

Rousseau, M.K.
1991   Landels: An 8500-year-old Deer Hunting Camp. *The Midden* 23(4):6-9.

1993   Early Prehistoric Occupation of South Central British Columbia: A Review of Evidence and Recommendations. Pp. 140-83 in Changing Times: British Columbia Archaeology in the 1980s. K. Fladmark, ed. *BC Studies* 99.

Rousseau, M.K., and R. Gargett
1987   Prehistoric Resource Use on Cornwall Hills Summit. *The Midden* 19(5):6-9.

Rousseau, M.K., and T.H. Richards
1988   The Oregon Jack Creek Site (EdRi 6): A Lehman Phase Site in the Thompson River Valley, British Columbia. *Canadian Journal of Archaeology* 12:39-64.

Rousseau, M.K., R. Muir, D. Alexander, J. Breffit, S. Woods, K. Berry, and T. Van Gaalen
1991a   Results of the 1989 Archaeological Investigations Conducted in the Oregon Jack Creek Locality, Thompson River Region, South-Central British Columbia. Report on file, Ministry Library, Ministry of Tourism and Ministry Responsible for Culture. Victoria.

Rousseau, M.K., R. Muir, and D. Alexander
1991b   The 1990 Archaeological Investigations Conducted at the Fraser Bay Site (EfQt 1), Shuswap Lake, South-Central BC. Report on file, Ministry Library, Ministry of Tourism and Ministry Responsible for Culture. Victoria.

Ryder, J.
1978   Geomorphology and Late Quaternary History of the Lillooet Area. Pp. 56-67 in Reports of the Lillooet Archaeological Project 1. Introduction and Setting. A.H. Stryd and S. Lawhead eds. Canada. *National Museum of Man. Mercury Series. Archaeological Survey Paper* 73. Ottawa.

1981   Biophysical Resources of the East Kootenay Area: Terrain. *British Columbia Ministry of the Environment, APD Bulletin* 7.

Sanger, D.
1964   Excavations at Nesikep Creek (EdRk 4), A Stratified Site near Lillooet, British Columbia: Preliminary Report. *Contributions to Anthropology 1961-1962, Part 1, National Museum of Canada Bulletin* 193:130-61. Ottawa.

1966   Excavations in the Lochnore-Nesikep Locality, British Columbia: Interim Report. *National Museum of Canada Anthropological Papers* 12. Ottawa.

1967   Prehistory of the Pacific Northwest Plateau as Seen from the Interior of British Columbia. *American Antiquity* 32(2):186-97.

1968a   Prepared Core and Blade Traditions in the Pacific Northwest. *Arctic Anthropology* 5(1):92-120.

1968b   The High River Microblade Industry, Alberta. *Plains Anthropologist* 13:41.

1969   Cultural Traditions in the Interior of British Columbia. *Syesis* 2:189-200.

1970   The Archaeology of the Lochnore Nesikep Locality, British Columbia. *Syesis* 3, Supp. 1.

Schalk, R.F.
1977   The Structure of Anadromous Fish Resource. Pp. 207-49 in For Theory Building in Archaeology. L.R. Binford ed. Academic Press. New York.

Scott, W.E., W.D. McCoy, R.R. Shroba, and M. Rubin
1983   Reinterpretation of the Exposed Record of the Last Two Cycles of Lake Bonneville, Western United States. *Quaternary Research* 20:261-85.

Severs, P.
1974   Archaeological Investigations at Blue Jackets Creek, (FlUa 4), Queen Charlotte Islands, British Columbia, 1973. *Canadian Archaeological Association Bulletin* 6:163-205.

Sheppard, J.C., P.E. Wigard, C.E. Gustafson, and M. Rubin
1987   A Re-evaluation of the Marmes Rockshelter Radiocarbon Chronology. *American Antiquity* 52:118-25.

Smith, J.
1971   The Ice Mountain Microblade and Core Industry, Cassiar District, Northern British Columbia. *Arctic and Alpine Research* 3:199-213.

1974   The Northeast Asian-Northwest American Microblade Tradition (NANAMT). *Journal of Field Archaeology* 1:347-64.

Sokal, R.R., and F.J. Rohlf
1969   Biometry. Freeman. San Francisco.

Souch, C.
1989   New Radiocarbon Dates for Early Deglaciation from the Southeastern Coast Mountains of British Columbia. *Canadian Journal of Earth Sciences* 26:2169-71.

Souther, J.G., and A.M. Jessop
1991   Dyke Swarms in the Queen Charlotte Islands, British Columbia, and Implications for Hydrocarbon Exploration. Pp. 465-87 in Evolution and Hydrocarbon Potential of the Queen Charlotte Basin, British Columbia. *Geological Survey of Canada Paper* 90-10.

Southon, J.R., D.E. Nelson, and J.S. Vogel
1990   A Record of Past Ocean-atmosphere Radiocarbon Differences from the Northeast Pacific. *Paleoceanography* 5:197-206.

Spurling, B.E.
1980   The Site C Heritage Resource Inventory and Assessment Final Report: Substantive Results. Report on file with Heritage Conservation Branch. Victoria.

Stein, J.K. ed.
1992   Deciphering a Shell Midden. Academic Press. New York.

Stevenson, M.
1981   Peace Point: A Stratified Prehistoric Campsite Complex in Wood Buffalo National Park, Alberta. *Research Bulletin* 158, Parks Canada. Ottawa.

Stewart, T.G., and J. England
1983   Holocene Sea-Ice Variations and Paleoenvironmental Change, Northernmost Ellesmere Island, N.W.T., Canada. *Arctic and Alpine Research* 15(1):1-17.

Stijelja M., and T. Williams
1986   An Analysis of the Skeletal Remains of EiRm 7. Student paper submitted to Dr. M. Skinner for Archaeology 373, Department of Archaeology, Simon Fraser University. Burnaby.

Stoker, S.W.
1976   Ecological Conditions and Marine Mammal Distributions of Beringia during the Late Wisconsin Submergence. Pp. 54-114 in Bering Land Bridge Cultural Resource Study, Final Report. E.J. Dixon Jr. ed. Report submitted to Bureau of Land Management, Outer Continental Shelf Office by the University of Alaska Museum.

Storck, P.L.
1982   Palaeo-Indian Settlement Patterns Associated with the Strandline of Glacial Lake Algonquin in Southcentral Ontario. *Canadian Journal of Archaeology* 6:1-32.

Stryd, A.H.
1972   Housepit Archaeology at Lillooet, British Columbia: The 1970 Field Season. *BC Studies* 14:17-46.

1973   The Later Prehistory of the Lillooet Area, British Columbia. Ph.D. dissertation in archaeology, University of Calgary. Calgary.

1980   Review of the Recent Activities Undertaken by the Lillooet Archaeological Project. *The Midden* 12(2):5-20.

Stryd, A.H., and L.V. Hills
1972   An Archaeological Site Survey of the Lillooet-Big Bar Area, British Columbia. *Syesis* 5:191-209.

Stuiver, M., and B. Becker
1993   High-Precision Decadal Calibration of the Radiocarbon Time Scale, AD 1950-6000 BC. *Radiocarbon* 35(1):35-65.

Stuiver, M., N. Kromer, B. Becker, and C.W. Ferguson
1986   Radiocarbon Age Calibration back to 13,300 years BP and the 14C Age Matching of the German Oak and the U.S. Bristlecone Pine Chronologies. *Radiocarbon* 28(2B):969-79.

Stuiver, M., and P.J. Reimer
1987   User's Guide to the Programs CALIB and DISPLAY 2.1. Quaternary Isotope Laboratory, Quaternary Research Center, AK-60, University of Washington, Seattle, WA 98195.

1993   Extended 14C database and revised Calib 3.014C age calibration program. *Radiocarbon* 835:215-30.

Suttles, W.
1955   Katzie Ethnographic Notes. *Anthropology in British Columbia. Memoir 2.* Victoria.

1987   Northwest Coast Linguistic History – A View from the Coast. Pp. 265-81 in Coast Salish Essays. W. Suttles ed. Talonbooks. Vancouver.

Suttles, W. ed.
1990   Handbook of North Americanm Indians, 7, Northwest Coast. Smithsonian. Washington.

Suttles, W., and W.W. Elmendorf
1963   Linguistic Evidence for Salish Prehistory. Pp. 40-52 of the *Proceedings of the 1962 Annual Spring Meeting of the American Ethnological Society: Symposium on Language and Culture.*

Swanson, E.H., Jr.
1964   Geochronology of the DjRi 3 Site, British Columbia, 1959. *Tebiwa* 7(2):42-52.

Swanston, D.N.
1984   Reconnaissance Investigation of the Surficial Geology of the Area around the Lower Falls of Irish Creek, Kupreanof Island. Ms. on File, Forest Sciences Laboratory, U.S. Department of Agriculture. Juneau.

Swanton, J.R.
1905   Contributions to the Ethnology of the Haida. *Memoir of the American Museum of Natural History* No. 5, part 1. New York.

Swonnell, D.
1971   Surficial Geology of the South Yale Site, BC. Report on file, Thurber Consultants Ltd. Victoria.

Szathmary, E.J.E.
1981   Genetic Markers in Siberian and Northern North American Populations. *Yearbook of Physical Anthropology* 24:37-74.

1994   Modelling Ancient Population Relationships from Modern Population Genetics. Pp. 117-30 in Method and Theory for Investigating the Peopling of the Americas. R. Bonnichsen and D. Steele eds. Center for the Study of the First Americans, Oregon State University. Corvallis.

Thompson, L.C., and M.D. Kinkaide
1990   Languages. Pp. 30-51 in Handbook of North American Indians, 7, Northwest Coast. W. Suttles ed. Smithsonian Institution. Washington.

Thompson, R.S. and J. Mead
1982   Late Quaternary Environments and Biogeography in the Great Basin. *Quaternary Research* 17:39-55.

Turner, II, C.G.
1992   New World Origins: New Research from the Americas and the Soviet Union. Pp. 7-48 in Ice Age Hunters of the Rockies. D. Stanford and J. Day eds. Denver Museum of Natural History and University Press of Colorado. Boulder.

1994   Relating Eurasian and Native North American Populations through Morphology. Pp. 131-40 in Method and Theory for Investigating the Peopling of the Americas R. Bonnichsen and D. Steele eds. Center for the Study of the First Americans, Oregon State University, Cornvallis.

Valley, D.R.
1979   An Analysis of a Tool Type: Peripherally Flaked Cobbles. *Northwest Anthropological Research Notes* 13(1):51-90.

Valpeter, A.P.
1983   Ancient Shorelines on the Shelf and Coast of the USSR North East and Far East Marginal Seas. *XI Congress, International Union for Quaternary Research, Abstracts* 3:269. Moscow.

Vance, R.E.
1987   Meteorological Records of Historic Droughts as Climatic Analogues for the Mid-Holocene in Alberta. Pp. 17-32 in Man and the Mid-Holocene Climatic Optimum. N.A. McKinnon and G.S.L. Stuart eds. Proceedings of the Seventeenth Annual Conference of the Archeological Association of the University of Calgary.

Vasil'evskii, R.S.

1973   Dreunie Kurtury Tikhookeanskogo Severa (Ancient Cultures of the North Pacific Ocean). Izdatel'stvo "Nauka." Sibirskoe Otdelenie, Novosibirsk.

1976   The Pacific Microlithic Traditions and Their Central-Asian Roots. Pp. 131-53 in Le Paléolithique Inférieur et Moyen en Inde, en Asie Centrale, en Chine et dans Le Sud-Est Asiatique. A.K. Ghosh ed. Colloquium 7, IX Congrès, Union International des Sciences Préhistoriques et Protohistoriques. Nice.

1984   The Role of Beringia in the Colonization of the Aleutian Islands. Pp. 661-68 in Beringia in the Cenozoic Era (Reports of the All Union Symposium "The Bering Land Bridge and its Role in the History of Holarctic Floras and Faunas in the Late Cenozoic," Khabarovsk, May 10-15, 1973). V.L. Kontrimavichus ed. Translated from the 1976 Russian edition and published by the Amerind Published Co. Pvt. Ltd. New Delhi for the U.S. Department of Interior and the National Science Foundation.

Vigne, J.-D., and M.C. Marinval-Vigne

1983   Mèthode pour la mise en évidence de la consommation du petit gibier. Pp. 239-42 in Animals and Archaeology 1, Hunters and Their Prey. J. Clutton-Brock and C. Grigson eds. *British Archaeological Reports International Series* 163.

von Krogh, G.H.

1975   The Hope Archaeological Project 1974: Final Report on Site Survey in the Hope Yale Area and Archaeological Survey Work at DiRj 16, DiRi 24, and DiRi 49. Report on file, Heritage Conservation Branch. Victoria.

Warner, B.G., J.J. Clague, and R.W. Mathewes

1984   Geology and Paleoecology of a Mid-Wisconsin Peat from the Queen Charlotte Islands, British Columbia, Canada. *Quaternary Research* 24:173-86.

Warner, B.G., R.W. Mathewes, and J.J. Clague

1982   Ice-free Conditions on the Queen Charlotte Islands, British Columbia, at the Height of Late Wisconsin Glaciation. *Science* 218:675-7.

Warren, C.N.

1967   The San Dieguito Complex: A Review and Hypothesis. *American Antiquity* 32:168-87.

Warren, C., and A.J. Ranere

1968   Outside Danger Cave: A View of Early Man in the Great Basin. Pp. 6-18 in Early Man in Western North America. C. Irwin-Williams ed. *Eastern New Mexico Contributions in Anthropology,* Part IV. Portales.

Watson, G.D.

1976a   Soil Texture Classification by Particle Size Determination: Report on Computer Programming. Unpublished manuscript.

1976b   Soil Texture Classification by Particle Size Determination Hydrometer Method: Report on Equipment Calibration. Unpublished manuscript.

Wendland, W.M., and R.A. Bryson

1974   Dating Climatic Episodes of the Holocene. *Quaternary Research* 4:9-24.

West, F.H.

1967   The Donnelly Ridge Site and the Definition of an Early Core and Blade Complex in Central Alaska. *American Antiquity* 32(3):360-82.

1981   The Archaeology of Beringia. Columbia University Press. New York.

White, J.M.

1987   Late Pleistocene and Recent Environments of the Bow Valley, Banff National Park. Manuscript on file, Archaeological Research Services, Canadian Parks Service. Calgary.

White, J.M., R.W. Mathewes, and W.H. Mathews
1985 Late Pleistocene Chronology and Environments of the "Ice-Free Corridor" of Northwestern Alberta. *Quaternary Research* 24:173-86.

Willey, G.R.
1966 An Introduction to American Archaeology, Vol. 1, North and Middle America. Prentice-Hall. Englewood Cliffs.

Willey, G.R., and P. Phillips
1958 Method and Theory in American Archaeology. University of Chicago Press.

Willig, J.A., and C.M. Aikens
1988 The Clovis-Archaic Interface in Far Western North America. Pp. 1-40 in Early Human Occupation in Far Western North America: The Clovis-Archaic Interface. J.A. Willig, C.M. Aikens, and J.L. Fagan eds. *Nevada State Museum Anthropological Papers* 21. Carson City.

Wilmeth, R.
1978 Canadian Archaeological Radiocarbon Dates. *Canada. National Museum of Man. Mercury Series. Archaeological Survey Paper* 77. Ottawa.

Wilson, I.R.
1986a Heritage Resource Inventory and Impact Assessment Proposed Sikanni Pipeline, Northeastern BC. Report in the library of the Ministry of Tourism and the Ministry Responsible for Culture. Victoria.

1986b Pink Mountain Site (HhRr 1) Archaeological Assessment and Monitoring of an Early Man Site in Northeastern BC. Report in the library of the Ministry of Tourism and the Ministry Responsible for Culture. Victoria.

1989 The Pink Mountain Site (HhRr 1): An Early Prehistoric Campsite in Northeastern BC. *Canadian Journal of Archaeology* 13:51-67.

1991 Excavations at EdQx 41 and 42, and Site Evaluation at EdQx 43 Monte Creek, M.C. Permit 1990-140. I.R. Wilson Consultants Ltd. Report on file in the library of the Ministry of Tourism and the Ministry Responsible for Culture. Victoria.

Wilson, I.R., B. Smart, N. Heap, J. Warner, T. Ryals, S. Woods, and S. MacNab.
1992 Excavations at Baker Site, EdQx 43, Monte Creek, Permit 91-107. I.R. Wilson Consultants Ltd. Report on file in the library of the Ministry of Tourism and the Ministry Responsible for Culture. Victoria.

Wilson, I.R., and R.L. Carlson
1987 Heritage Resource Inventory in the Vicinity of Pink Mountain, Northeastern BC. Report on Permit 1987-30, Heritage Conservation Branch. Victoria.

Wormington H.M.
1964 Ancient Man in North America. *Denver Museum of Natural History Popular Series* 4. Denver.

Wormington, H.M., and R.A. Forbis
1965 An Introduction to the Archaeology of Alberta, Canada. *Denver Museum of Natural History Proceedings* 11. Denver.

Wright, M.J.
1980 The Coquitlam Area Mountain Study: An Assessment of Heritage Values. Report submitted to the Environment and Land Use Secretatiat, Provincial Government, British Columbia. Victoria.

Wright, M.J., and J.H. Williams
1982 Coquitlam Lake Reservoir: Culture History and Artifact Description. *The Midden* 14(1):2-9; 14(2):8-11.

Yesner, D.R.

1994   Subsistence Diversity, Faunal Extinction, and Hunter-Gatherer Foraging Strategies in Late Pleistocene/Early Holocene Beringia: Evidence from the Broken Mammoth Site, Big Delta. Paper presented at the 45th Arctic Science Conference. Anchorage.

Young, R.R.

1993   The Late Wisconsinan Laurentide Ice Sheet and Its Relationship to a Theoretical "Ice-free Corridor." Pp. A-113 in *Geological Association of Canada Meetings Abstracts*.

Zacharias, S.K., and Wanagun (R.S. Wilson)

1992   1991 Archaeological Resource Inventory of Southeastern Moresby Island within the Gwaii Haanas/South Moresby National Park Reserve. Report on file, Parks Canada. Calgary.

INDEX